AKHENATEN AND THE ORIGINS OF MONOTHEISM

Akhenaten and the Origins of Monotheism

James K. Hoffmeier

OXFORD
UNIVERSITY PRESS

OXFORD
UNIVERSITY PRESS

Oxford University Press is a department of the University of Oxford.
It furthers the University's objective of excellence in research, scholarship,
and education by publishing worldwide.

Oxford New York
Auckland Cape Town Dar es Salaam Hong Kong Karachi
Kuala Lumpur Madrid Melbourne Mexico City Nairobi
New Delhi Shanghai Taipei Toronto

With offices in
Argentina Austria Brazil Chile Czech Republic France Greece
Guatemala Hungary Italy Japan Poland Portugal Singapore
South Korea Switzerland Thailand Turkey Ukraine Vietnam

Published in the United States of America by
Oxford University Press
198 Madison Avenue, New York, NY 10016

Library of Congress Cataloging-in-Publication Data
Hoffmeier, James Karl, 1951–
Akhenaten and the origins of monotheism / James K. Hoffmeier.
p. cm.
Includes bibliographical references and index.
ISBN 978–0–19–979208–5 (hardcover : alk. paper) — ISBN 978–0–19–979214–6 (ebook) —
ISBN 978–0–19–021769–3 (online content) 1. Egypt—Religion. 2. Sun worship—Egypt. 3. Monotheism.
4. Akhenaton, King of Egypt—Religion. I. Title.
BL2443.H635 2015
299'.31—dc23
2014021568

5 7 9 8 6 4

Printed in the United States of America on acid-free paper

Dedicated to
Donald B. Redford,
my professor and friend
on the occasion of his eightieth birthday

Contents

Preface ix
Abbreviations xiii
Map of Egypt xv

1. *When the Sun Ruled Egypt* 1

2. *Far Frontiers: Sky and Sun Together* 32

3. *The Dawn of the Amarna Period* 62

4. *The Domain of Aten: The Temples of Aten at Karnak* 91

5. *Finding Aten and Founding Akhet-Aten* 136

6. *Aten Alone* 165

7. *Is Atenism Monotheism?* 193

8. *The Hymns to Aten: A Monotheistic Manifesto* 211

9. *The Influence of Atenism in Egypt and the Bible?* 238

BIBLIOGRAPHY 267
NAME INDEX 289
GENERAL INDEX 291

Preface

NO FIGURE FROM ancient Egyptian history has stimulated more interest and literature than Akhenaten, the 14th century B.C. pharaoh. Students of Egyptology, history, and religion, be they amateurs or academics, are equally fascinated by this intriguing ruler because of his bizarre appearance in statues and reliefs, as well as those of his family. The art of this period amazes the art historian with its naturalism and realism. The cuneiform tablets discovered in 1887 at Tell el-Amarna in Middle Egypt, known as the Amarna Letters, provide an unparalleled glimpse into dealings between Egypt and world potentates and local petty rulers of Anatolia, Mesopotamia, Canaan, and Syria. Then, too, there are all the perplexing issues surrounding his reign: moving his capital from Thebes to Amarna, his name change, and the uncertainty of the royal succession. Did Queen Nefertiti reign with him or succeed him? How was king "Tut" related to Akhenaten? Akhenaten's unique brand of solar worship evokes vigorous discussions. Was he a henotheist, monotheist, or merely focused on a novel ancestor cult, as has recently been proposed? Was he so preoccupied with his devotion to his sun-god, Aten, that he allowed Egypt's empire in western Asia to implode?

With so many mysteries surrounding Akhenaten and his relatively short 17-year reign, nearly every question raised here has been addressed and various interpretations argued over the decades. Indeed, the body of literature on Akhenaten and the so-called Amarna period is immense, with many excellent articles and books available by eminent scholars like Donald Redford, Cyril Aldred, Nicholas Reeves,

Jan Assmann, Erik Hornung, and Barry Kemp. With so much good literature on Akhenaten and his era, why would I even attempt to write another book on Akhenaten? A brief biographical note is in order. I grew up in Egypt. In fact, a small village in Middle Egypt was home. It was located on the western side of the Nile, not far from Tell el-Amarna, where Akhenaten established his capital (Akhet-Aten) around 1347 B.C. As a youth I was able to stroll the streets and explore the ruins and tombs of Akhet-Aten. Within 5 miles (8 km) of my childhood home in the village of Nazlet Herz was the ancient city of Hermopolis (in Arabic, Ashmunein). Its necropolis in the nearby desert was the location of one of Akhet-Aten's 14 boundary inscriptions. Many times my family visited this site, even having picnics near the strange depiction of Akhenaten, Nefertiti, and their daughters adoring the sun-disc that stood atop the stela.

These early experiences no doubt influenced my decision to study Near Eastern archaeology as my undergraduate major at Wheaton College (IL). Graduate studies took me to the University of Toronto, where one of my principal teachers was Dr. Donald Redford, professor of Egyptology, a distinguished scholar and one of the leading experts on Akhenaten. He was also the director of the Akhenaten Temple Project that was engaged in piecing together photographs of thousands of inscribed blocks that revealed amazing decorated scenes from Akhenaten's Theban temples. After the king's death they were violently destroyed and dismantled, and the blocks were dispersed and reused elsewhere. Through this painstaking work, Redford broke new ground on the early years of Akhenaten's developing religion, which is frequently called "Atenism."

In early 1975, Professor Redford began excavations east of Karnak temple in Luxor, Egypt, thought to be the area where Akhenaten's long-lost temples were located. During the summer season that year, I had the privilege of working with the project, and again in 1977. Subsequently, Dr. Redford invited me to study the assembled chariot scenes from the Theban temples for publication in *Akhenaten Temple Project*, Volume 2. Being able to work with the Akhenaten Temple Project furthered my interest in this king's religious revolution.

In 1992, when I was considering engaging in field work in Egypt, Dr. Redford, who by then was investigating Tell Kedua in North Sinai, wrote to me and encouraged me to come work in Sinai. There was some urgency to excavate endangered sites east of the Suez Canal before they were destroyed due to the As-Salam irrigation project. Following this suggestion, I spent short seasons in 1994, 1995, and 1998 investigating possible sites to dig. At the urging of Dr. Mohamed Abd el-Maksoud of the Supreme Council for Antiquities (now the Ministry of Culture for Antiquities), I visited a threatened site that had already experienced significant damage from the irrigation project; a drainage canal already crossed the east end of the tell, roads were being laid, and pipelines dug. It was Tell el-Borg. During the initial survey of the site in 1999, my team discovered scores of New Kingdom period potsherds on the surface, including a painted "Amarna blue" sherd that immediately caught my attention, since this type of decoration was so well known from Amarna period pottery. Could it be that this site flourished during the Amarna era? Subsequent excavations revealed two New Kingdom period frontier forts. During the first season's work, we uncovered some reused talatat blocks—the very type of building blocks developed by Akhenaten's architects for the Aten Temples at Karnak! Had there been an Aten temple that was demolished at the site or somewhere nearby in North Sinai? In the nearly decade of work at Tell el-Borg, it became clear that throughout the Amarna era this site was occupied, and we also found evidence of Akhenaten's iconoclasm against Amun (see Chapter 6).

In the light of my experiences in Egypt as a youth, along with my training with the Akhenaten Temple Project, combined with this new evidence from an unlikely location on Egypt's eastern frontier (or just outside Egypt proper) about Akhenaten and his religious program, there are good reasons to write a new book on Akhenaten.

Aware of the vast body of literature on every subject related to Akhenaten, a narrowly focused study seemed prudent. Because many issues about his religion remain unsettled, and there are some new data, this seemed like the route to take.

Often archaeologists and historians approach matters of religion with a jaundiced eye. I have tried to avoid this tendency by using my training at the Centre for Religious Studies at the University of Toronto, where I received my PhD. I benefited greatly from a course on religious studies methodologies from the late Professor Willard Oxtoby. He introduced me to the phenomenological approach to the study of religion, a method I have found to be fruitful in my study of ancient religions. This approach, which will be described in Chapter 5, has been used in the current study to offer some new insights into some of Akhenaten's inscriptions. This book inevitably touches on historical, art historical, political, and other areas of research, which could blossom into major studies. But this is avoided in favor of concentrating on Akhenaten's religion and the origins of monotheism.

Since the early 20th century, scholars have posited that there was some possible connection between Akhenaten and ancient Israelite religion, Moses and monotheism. These important issues will only be touched upon briefly at the end of Chapter 8 and in Chapter 9. The main thrust of this book is to try to tease out the motivation for Akhenaten's religious reforms and the quick transition to what will be argued was a monotheistic faith. The sources used will be the remains of the Aten temples, the iconography, and contemporary inscriptions. What prompted the unexpected oppression of Egypt's state god, Amun (or Amun-Re), at the height of his power and the attendant elevation of Aten to position of sole god or God?

In this regard, Donald Redford's work over the years has been essential and laid a solid foundation for my work. As my teacher he was always cheerful and friendly, ready to answer questions, discuss problems, and entertain theories. So in this book I have some new (provocative?) theories for him (and others) to ponder, and I dedicate this volume to my teacher on his eightieth birthday in appreciation for his friendship and encouragement over the years.

While on Sabbatical during the Fall of 2010, I was able to spend several days studying the Amarna collection at the Neues Museum in Berlin. The research conducted there laid the groundwork for the writing that followed. A follow-up visit to Berlin in March 2014 permitted some final study of various texts and reliefs. Then I also visited the Louvre in Paris where I was able to examine a number of important sculptures and reliefs. These visits were extremely valuable to my research and provided the opportunity to photograph many objects, some of which serve as illustrations in this volume.

The majority of the research and writing for this book took place during a Sabbatical I was awarded during the Fall of 2013. I am grateful to my dean, Dr. Tite Tienou, for this time off. I also want to acknowledge the helpful conversations and e-mail exchanges about the Amarna period with Arielle Kozloff over the past two years. I want to acknowledge the help provided by Edwin (Ted) Brock, who sent me a copy of his unpublished report on the drain/sewage project in East Karnak that exposed materials from Akhenaten's temple. I am very grateful to Dr. Foy Scalf, Archivist and Librarian at the Oriental Institute, for invaluable assistance with references and library material. Thanks are owed to William Hupper who created the bibliography for the book from the footnotes used in each chapter.

When I was writing Chapter 5, I thought that it offered a bit of a paradigm shift in how I understood Akhenaten's religious evolution. The data and the phenomenological readings of key texts actually resulted in a change in my working hypothesis about the motivation for Atenism. Aware of the potential breakthrough, I asked four respected Egyptologists to give me their feedback. I was delighted to receive helpful comments and positive responses from Kenneth Kitchen, Ellen Morris, Boyo Ockinga, and Richard Wilkinson, who were most encouraging. While the feedback was appreciated and helpful, I am obviously responsible for the ideas advanced here.

I am also grateful to Cynthia Read and her colleagues at Oxford University Press, New York, for assisting with this, my third book with OUP. Unless otherwise specified, quotations of Egyptian texts are my own translation, and when the Bible is cited, it is from the English Standard Version unless specified.

It is my hope that the ideas proposed here will stimulate discussion and advance our understanding of Akhenaten, his religion, and the origins of monotheism.

Abbreviations

ABD	*Anchor Bible Dictionary*, 5 Vols. (New York: Doubleday, 1992)
AJSLL	*American Journal of Semitic Languages and Literature*
ASAE	*Annales du Service des Antiquités de l'Égypte*
ATP	Akhenaten Temple Project
BASOR	*Bulletin of the American Schools of Oriental Research*
BES	*Bulletin of the Egyptian Seminar*
BIFAO	*Bulletin de l'Institut Français d'Archéologie Orientale* (Cairo)
BSEG	*Bulletin de la Société d'Égyptolgie, Genève*
CANE	*Civilizations of the Ancient Near East* I–IV (ed. J. Sasson; New York: Scribner, 1995)
CASAE	*Cahier Annales du Service des Antiquités de l'Égypte*
Cd'É	*Chronique d'Égypte*
COS	*Context of Scripture* I–III (W. W. Hallo & K. L. Younger; Leiden: Brill, 1997, 2000, 2003)
CT	Coffin Texts
GM	*Göttinger Miszellen*
JAMA	*Journal of the American Medical Association*
JEOL	*Jaarbericht ex Oriente Lux*
JETS	*Journal of the Evangelical Theological Society*
KB	Ludwig Koehler and Walter Baumgartner, *Lexicon in Veteris Testamenti Libros* (Leiden: Brill, 1985)

OEAE *Oxford Encyclopedia of Ancient Egypt*, 3 Vols. (ed. Donald Redford; New York: 2001).

PT Pyramid Texts

NIV New International Version of the Bible

SÄK *Studien zur Altägyptischen Kulture*

Urk. IV Kurt Sethe, *Urkunden der 18. Dynastie*, 4 Vols. (Berlin: Akademie-Verlag, 1961)

Urk. IV Wolfgang Helck, *Urkunden der 18. Dynastie: Historische Inschriften Thutmosis' III. und Amenophis' III* (Berlin: Akademie-Verlag, 1955)

Wb. Adolf Erman and Hermann Grapow, *Wörterbuch der ägyptischen Sprache*, 5 Vols. (Leipzig: J. C. Hinrichs'sche, 1926–1931)

Map of Egypt
(created by A. D. Riddle)

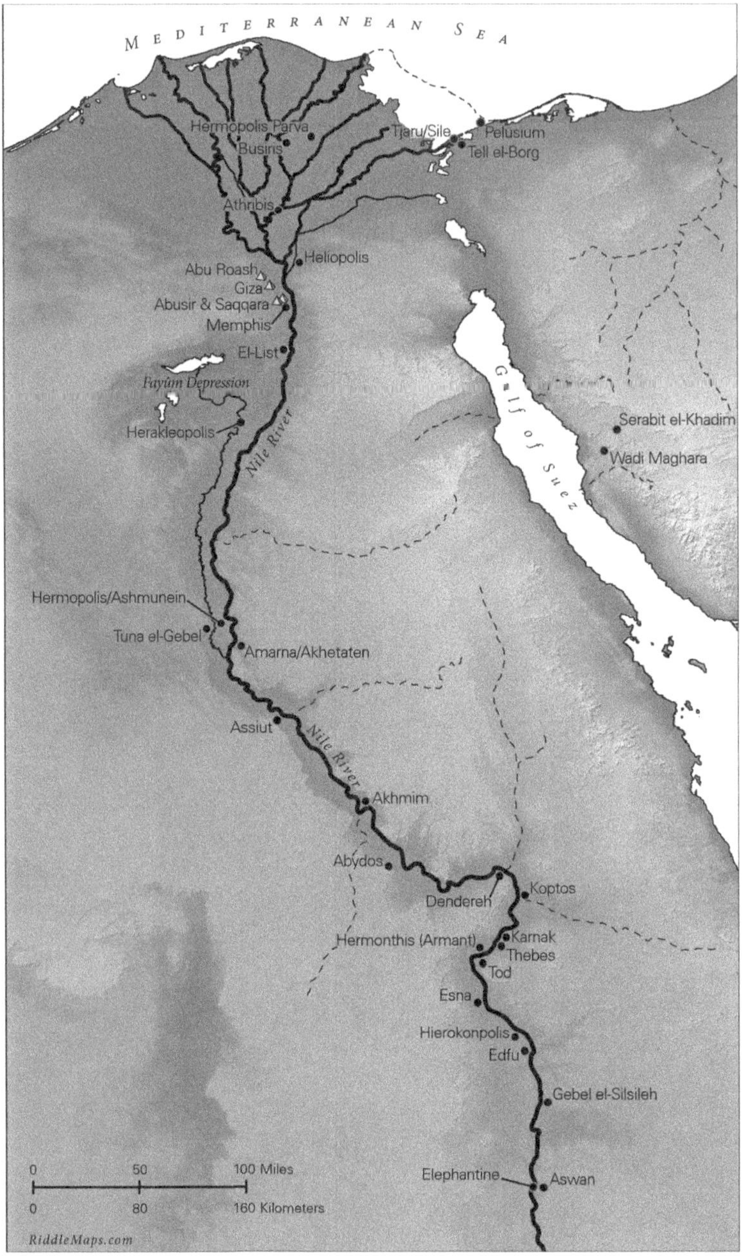
Mediterranean Sea
Hermopolis Parva
Busiris
Tjaru/Sile
Pelusium
Tell el-Borg
Athribis
Heliopolis
Abu Roash
Giza
Abusir & Saqqara
Memphis
El-Lisht
Fayûm Depression
Herakleopolis
Nile River
Gulf of Suez
Serabit el-Khadim
Wadi Maghara
Hermopolis/Ashmunein
Tuna el-Gebel
Amarna/Akhetaten
Assiut
Nile River
Akhmim
Abydos
Dendereh
Koptos
Hermonthis (Armant)
Karnak
Thebes
Tod
Esna
Hierokonpolis
Edfu
Gebel el-Silsileh
Elephantine
Aswan
0 50 100 Miles
0 80 160 Kilometers
RiddleMaps.com

Hail, O Re, in your beauty, your splendor,
On your thrones, in your radiance!
PYRAMID TEXT, 406

Chapter 1

When the Sun Ruled Egypt

THE DISCOVERY OF the Amarna letters in 1887 opened the door to a new, and largely obscure, period of Egyptian history now known as the Amarna period. The curiosity created by the diplomatic correspondence from Western Asia and Mesopotamia to Amenhotep III and Akhenaten during the mid-14th century B.C. led Sir Flinders Petrie to begin excavating the site of el-Amarna, or Akhet-Aten. Of special interest to early Egyptologists, and still the focus of considerable attention today, was Akhenaten's religious revolution. Not only has Akhenaten's religion been the focus of Egyptologists and historians of religion, but it has attracted the curiosity of academics in other fields, including Sigmund Freud[1] and C. S. Lewis.[2]

In various reliefs and in the decorated rock cut tombs of the high-ranking royal officials in middle Egypt, King Akhenaten and his famous Queen Nefertiti, sometimes along with their daughters, are shown in attitudes of worship and adoration of the sun-disc, that is, the Aten (Eg. *itn*), while in other instances they are seated in their living quarters or riding in chariots throughout the city. Regardless of the type of scene, the rays of the sun-disc cascade downward surrounding the royal family, with human hands extending to the devotees, sometimes with the sign for life (☥) being offered to the royals (Figure 1.1 a–b). Such scenes are found in different contexts

[1] Sigmund Freud, *Moses and Monotheism* (New York: Alfred A. Knof, 1939).
[2] C. S. Lewis, *Reflections on the Psalms* (New York: Harvest/Harcourt, 1986; reprint of 1958 edition), 85–87.

(a)

(b)

FIGURE 1.1 a. Akhenaten and Nefertiti and daughters under the sun and its rays (Neues Museum Berlin). Photo James K. Hoffmeier. b. Royal family worshiping Aten (Tuna el-Gebel Stela). Photo Charles S. Hoffmeier.

throughout the city of Akhet-Aten, even on the large boundary stelae that encircled the greater city, marking it as the Holy See of the Aten.[3]

Within the tombs of some of Akhenaten's loyal officials are found the words of hymns devoted to the Aten, including the so-called Great Hymn to the Aten that not only elevated this deity to a place of supremacy, but, as will be argued below, affirm the king's monotheistic religion (see Chapters 7 and 8). Along with this doctrine went the inevitable program of persecution of the Theban deity Amun by closing his (and other) temples and obliterating his name and image.[4] How does one explain this unusual behavior in conservative Egypt, where deities that had been worshiped and honored for 1,500 years suddenly fell into disfavor and were abandoned and even efforts to execrate their memories, especially Amun's, were undertaken mercilessly? Polytheism, by its very nature, is inclusive. Deities are not typically excluded. More than seven centuries after Akhenaten's day, Jeremiah the prophet of Judah castigates his audience in Jerusalem for abandoning their God YHWH for pagan deities (Jer. 2:5–8), a practice that was rare indeed, if not unparalleled in the ancient Near East. It was so extraordinary that the prophet was appalled: "For cross to the coasts of Cyprus and see, or send to Kedar and examine with care; see if there has been such a thing. Has a nation changed its gods, even though they are no gods?" (Jer. 2:10–11). The answer to this rhetorical question was "no"! Clearly something radical took place in Egypt during Akhenaten's reign that was unprecedented.

Scholars have offered different assessments of Akhenaten's extraordinary action. James Henry Breasted, early in the 20th century, described Akhenaten as engaged in a "revolutionary movement"[5] that came about because the king had "immersed himself heart and soul in the thought of the time, and the philosophizing theology of the priests"[6] at the expense of maintaining the great empire that his predecessors had won for Egypt. For John Wilson, Akhenaten's universalistic religion was a logical development out of Egypt's imperialism in the 15th century B.C. in which the power and scope of once local deities expanded with Egypt, thus giving birth to this revolutionary expression.[7]

Cyril Aldred, one of the late 20th-century premier specialists in the Amarna Period, described Akhenaten as having "single-minded zealotry" and depicted the king and his wife as "religious fanatics."[8] The director of the Akhenaten Temple

---

[3] William Murnane & Charles Van Siclen, *The Boundary Stelae of Akhenaten* (London/New York: Kegan Paul International, 1993).

[4] Donald Redford, *Akhenaten: The Heretic King* (Princeton, NJ: Princeton University Press, 1984), 175–176. Jacobus van Dijk, "The Amarna Period and the Late New Kingdom," in *The Oxford History of Ancient Egypt* (ed. Ian Shaw; Oxford: Oxford University Press, 2003), 269–270.

[5] James Henry Breasted, *A History of Egypt* (London: Hodder & Stoughton, 1921; 2nd edition), 367.

[6] Breasted, *A History of Egypt*, 356.

[7] John Wilson, *The Culture of Ancient Egypt* (Chicago: University of Chicago Press, 1951), 206–209.

[8] Cyril Aldred, *Akhenaten King of Egypt* (London: Thames & Hudson, 1988), 7.

Project for more than 40 years, Donald Redford, has called Akhenaten "the heretic king,"[9] and one who "consigned to the rubbish heap far more than he created."[10] More charitably, David Silverman has recently stated that Akhenaten "was a man of distinctive nature, character, and personality."[11]

Egyptologists who have seriously studied the half-century prior to Akhenaten's reign have rightly observed that there was a steep rise in solar religion during the first half of the 14th century B.C.; however, the word *ítn* was not new to this period. Rather, it can be traced back to the Old Kingdom.[12] One early attestation of Aten is in the 12th Dynasty Story of Sinuhe, when the death of Amenemhet I is announced: the king "went up to the sky, being united with the sun-disc (*ítn*), the god's (i.e., the king) person being joined with the one who created him."[13] Then there are more than a dozen occurrences in the Coffin Texts,[14] which largely date to the 12th Dynasty, although some go back to the First Intermediate Period. The Aten-disc especially grew in importance during the reigns of Akhenaten's father, Amenhotep III (1390–1353 B.C.) and Thutmose IV (1400–1390 B.C.).[15] Raymond Johnson has advanced the view that Amenhotep III was actually deified in his final years, and that identifying himself with "the sun god Ra-Horakhty must have been a major influence on his son Amenhotep IV/Akhenaten"; he "was referred to as 'the Dazzling Aten.'"[16] Based on this, Johnson suggests that Akhenaten's Aten cult was in reality the celebration of his deified father. In his words, they "were one and the same god."[17] (This view will be discussed further in Chapter 3.)

It is the contention of the present investigation that in order to understand fully the foundations of Atenism and some of the factors that motivated Akhenaten's unusual religious activities, one has to go back nearly 1,500 years before his day to the early dynasties of Egyptian history, especially to the Old Kingdom (ca. 2700–2200 B.C.), when the sun ruled Egypt.

---

9 Actually this is the subtitle of his excellent book, *Akhenaten: The Heretic King* (Princeton, NJ: Princeton University Press, 1984).

10 Donald B. Redford, "The Sun-Disc in Akhenaten's Program: Its Worship and Antecedents, I," *JARCE* 13 (1976): 47.

11 David Silverman, "Divinity and Deities in Ancient Egypt," in *Religion in Ancient Egypt* (ed. B. E. Shafer; Ithaca, NY: Cornell University Press, 1991), 75.

12 Redford, "The Sun-Disc in Akhenaten's Program," 47.

13 Translation the author's, based on A. M. Blackman, *The Story of Sinuhe*, Bibliotheca Aegyptiaca II (Brussels: Édition de la Fondation Égyptologique Reine Élisabeth, 1932), 3.

14 Rami van Der Molen, *A Hieroglyphic Dictionary of Egyptian Coffin Texts* (Leiden: Brill, 2000), 59.

15 Erik Hornung, *Akhenaten and the Religion of Light* (Ithaca, NY: Cornell University Press, 1995), 20–22. Stephen Quirke, *The Cult of Ra: Sun-Worship in Ancient Egypt* (London: Thames & Hudson, 2001), 147–151. The most significant study is that of Lawrence Berman, "Overview of Amenhotep III and His Reign," in *Amenhotep III: Perspectives on His Reign* (eds. D. O'Connor & E. Cline; Ann Arbor: University of Michigan Press, 1998), 1–26.

16 Raymond Johnson, "Monuments and Monumental Art under Amenhotep III: Evolution and Meaning," in *Amenhotep III: Perspectives on His Reign*, 89–90.

17 Johnson, "Monuments and Monumental Art under Amenhotep III: Evolution and Meaning," 91.

THE SUN-GOD AT THE DAWN OF EGYPTIAN HISTORY

The piercing blue sky and dazzling sun are the two most striking and inescapable forces of nature in the land of Egypt. So it is little wonder that the sun's dominance over the land has a corresponding ascendency in the religion and politics of Egypt from earliest times. More than 60 years ago, Henri Frankfort, the Dutch specialist in Near Eastern cultures and religions, held that "polytheism is sustained by man's experience of a universe alive from end to end. Powers confront man wherever he moves. . . ."[18] The blazing sun was such a power in Egypt, and this is probably why solar religion in various forms was supreme for the three millennia of the Pharaonic era. It is not surprising, as the historian of religion Mircea Eliade framed it, that "the religion of Egypt was, more than any other, dominated by sun-worship."[19] Eliade argued that the chief reason for embracing the sacred is that humans "become aware of the sacred because it manifests itself, shows itself, as something wholly different from the profane."[20] No doubt the early Egyptians saw the omnipresence of the sun during daytime as a potent presence through which the deity revealed itself. As a consequence of these factors, Egyptologists would agree with Richard Wilkinson, who concludes that "the sun god Re was arguably Egypt's most important deity."[21] This was certainly true during the Old Kingdom, as Rosalie David observes: "until the end of the Old Kingdom, no cult rivaled that of Reʿ in power and importance."[22]

The picture is not so clear in the late pre and early dynastic periods (ca. 3200–2700 B.C.). The fact that there are several different names of solar-deities documented in the Old Kingdom suggests that the names may have originated in different parts of Egypt and that some were fused together in the course of time to represent different facets of the sun. Atum, for instance is the name the patron deity of On (Eg. *iwnw*), אֹן (*ʾōn*) of the Hebrew Bible, and Heliopolis (city of the sun) to the Greeks, where his principal cult center flourished over the centuries.[23] The name Atum is often coupled with the more generic word Re or Ra (*rʿ*)[24] (Figure 1.2). Re is the standard term for the sun and also means "day."[25]

---

[18] Henri Frankfort, *Ancient Egyptian Religion* (New York: Columbia University Press, 1948), 4.

[19] Mircea Eliade, *Patterns in Comparative Religion* (Clinton, MA.: Meridian, 1963), 128.

[20] Mircea Eliade, *The Sacred and Profane* (New York: Harcourt, Brace & World, 1959), 11.

[21] Richard Wilkinson, *The Complete Gods and Goddesses of Ancient Egypt* (London: Thames & Hudson, 2003), 205.

[22] A. Rosalie David, *The Ancient Egyptian: Religious Beliefs and Practices* (London: Routeledge & Kegan Paul, 1982), 29.

[23] A. H. Gardiner, *Ancient Egyptian Onomastica* II (London: Oxford University Press, 1947), 144*–145*.

[24] Karol Mysliwiec, "Atum," in *OEAE* 1, 158–159.

[25] *Wb* 2, 401–402.

FIGURE 1.2 Atum (Deir el-Bahri Temple of Hatshepsut). Photo James K. Hoffmeier.

Khepri, or Kheperer, is another name for the sun god,[26] and that word means "come into being" and "exist," and as a noun means "form."[27] Often depicted as a scarab or dung beetle, this solar deity pushes the sun-disc across the sky, just as the beetle pushes the dung ball across the ground. In that ball were the eggs of the beetle. When they hatched, the tiny baby beetles emerged, seemingly in a spontaneous manner to the ancient Egyptians. "This mystery," Stephen Quirke writes, "could be expressed as an act of spontaneous self-creation, for which the Egyptians used the word *kheper*."[28]

A final manifestation of the sun god is found in the Re-Harakhty (Figure 1.3). This is a composite name meaning "Re [is] Horus of the Horizon," which Maya Müller suggests "should be understood as a surname describing the character of the god," or that Horus is the son of Re.[29] The name "Horus" derives from the Egyptian term *ḥr* meaning "the distant one" who was portrayed as a falcon that represented the sky in which hawks soar.[30] Horus is certainly one of the earliest deities whose iconography is known from the beginnings of kingship and was associated with the ruler throughout Egyptian history (Figure 1.4). The Horus-falcon is depicted on the famous Narmer Palette, and it appears on standards in the Scorpion Macehead and the Battle Field palette; on the Tjehenu or Cities palette fragment the falcon is shown hacking up an enemy city with a hoe.[31]

---

[26] Wilkinson, *The Complete Gods and Goddesses of Ancient Egypt*, 230.

[27] *CDME* 188–189.

[28] Quirke, *The Cult of Ra*, 25–26.

[29] Maya Müller, "Re and Re-Harakhty," *OEAE* 3, 123.

[30] Edmund Meltzer, "Horus," *OEAE* 2, 119.

[31] Jeffrey Spencer, *Early Egypt: The Rise of Civilisation in the Nile Valley* (Norman: University of Oklahoma Press, 1993), 52–54, 56.

FIGURE 1.3 Re-Harakhty (Louvre Stela). Photo James K. Hoffmeier.

The solar deities are brought together in a number of texts as early as the Pyramid Texts (PT). "I shine in the East like Re," says PT Spell 467, and then continues, "I travel in the West like Khoperer, I live on what Horus Lord of the sky lives on by the decree of Horus Lord of the sky" (PT§ 888).[32] Similarly, PT Spell 606: "O King, they (the gods of the Ennead) make you live and resemble the seasons of Harakhti when they made his name." ... "They will bring you into being like Re' in this his name of Khoperer; you will draw near to them like Re' in his name of Re'; you will turn aside from their faces like Re' in his name of Atum" (PT §1693–1695).[33] The former passage suggests that Re was associated with the rising sun in the east, whereas Khopri was identified with the afternoon sun.

From Dynasty 1 onward, one of the royal names by which the king was known was the Horus name, reflecting the mythic view that the king was the son of Re, that is the incarnation of Horus. The square box or *serekh*, representing the palace façade in

[32] R. O. Faulkner, *The Ancient Egyptian Pyramid Texts* (Oxford: Clarendon Press, 1969), 156.

[33] Faulkner, *The Ancient Egyptian Pyramid Texts*, 250–251.

FIGURE 1.4 Horus (Kom Ombo Temple). Photo James K. Hoffmeier.

which the king dwelt, would include the name of Horus king, and above the *serekh* Horus stood (Figure 1.5).

The view that the king in his capacity as Horus was the son of Re or Atum (or Re-Atum) is found in the Old Kingdom PTs. These texts, though first found on the interior of the Pyramid of Unas at Saqqara (ca. 2350 B.C.), are widely believed to have originated toward the end of the 4th Dynasty (2550–2500 B.C.), with some spells possibly going back to pre-dynastic times.[34] The PTs report that when the deceased king was transported to the realm of the gods, he was introduced to them as follows:

> O Re-Atum, this King comes to you . . . your son comes to you . . . (PT §158)
>
> O Re-Atum, your son comes to you, the King comes to you . . . for he is the son of your body forever (PT §160).[35]
>
> Like his father Atum who begot him (*ms sw*). He begot (*ms*) the king (PT §395).[36]

---

[34] James Allen, *The Ancient Egyptian Pyramid Texts* (Atlanta: Society of Biblical Literature, 2005), 4.

[35] R. O. Faulkner, *The Ancient Egyptian Pyramid Texts* (Oxford: Clarendon Press, 1969), 45; Jaromír Málek, "The Old Kingdom (c. 2686–2160 B.C.)," in *The Oxford History of Ancient Egypt* (ed. Ian Shaw; Oxford: Oxford University Press, 200), 102.

[36] Faulkner, *The Ancient Egyptian Pyramid Texts*, 80.

FIGURE 1.5 Serekh of Hor-Aha. Photo James K. Hoffmeier.

> The King conceived for Re, he is born for Re; the King is your seed, O Re, you being potent in this your name of "Horus at the head of the spirits . . ." (PT §1508).[37]

As early as Dynasty 2 (ca. 2820 B.C.), kings began to use "Re" in their names. Neb(i)-re, the first ruler to incorporate Re's name means "(my) lord is Re." Hermann Kees considered the appearance of "Re" in this royal name as marking the beginnings of Heliopolitan religious influence.[38] Other kings followed Nebre's lead, namely, Nefer-ka-Re, a name which occurs again in Dynasty 3.[39] Starting in the 4th Dynasty with king Redjedef (ca. 2550 B.C.), and his immediate successors Khafre and Menkaure, the inclusion of "Re" became a regular feature of the throne name or prenomen. It was Redjedef who first introduced the epithet *sꜣ rꜥ* or "son of Re," perhaps legitimizing his claim to the throne.[40] From the 5th Dynasty kings, the title "Son of Re" was permanently enshrined in the royal titulary.[41] The king of Egypt, then, was the son of Re and the living Horus. This long cherished ideology of kingship is reflected dramatically in texts (e.g., Pyramid Texts), iconography, and architecture of the Old Kingdom.

---

[37] Faulkner, *The Ancient Egyptian Pyramid Texts*, 231.

[38] Hermann Kees, *Ancient Egypt: A Geographical History of the Nile* (Chicago: University of Chicago Press, 1961), 154.

[39] J. von Beckerath, *Handbuch der Ägyptischen Königsnamen* (Mainz: Philipp von Zabern, 1999), 42–43, 45, 49.

[40] Ellen Morris, "The Pharaoh and Pharaonic Office," in *A Companion to Ancient Egypt* I (ed. A. B. Lloyd; Oxford: Wiley-Blackwell, 2010), 204.

[41] von Beckerath, *Handbuch der Ägyptischen Königsnamen*, 25–26.

SOLAR DEITIES IN OLD KINGDOM TEXTS

Some texts that identify the king as the son of Re in the PTs have been introduced already. This corpus offers much more on solar theology. Most significant is the dogma that Atum was the original god, the creator of subsequent deities. Solar cosmogony holds that Atum/Khopri is "self-created" (*ḫpr ḏs.f*—lit. "created or formed himself") (PT §1587).[42] One spell announces: "the King was fashioned by his father Atum before the sky existed, before earth existed, before men existed, before the gods were born . . ." (PT §1466).[43] Atum's mode of creation is described as follows:

> Atum is he who (once) came into being [*ḫpr*], who masturbated in On.
> He took his phallus in his grasp that he might create orgasm by means of it,
> And so were born the twins Shu and Tefnet (PT §1248).[44]

In a different version of the origin of these same deities, PT Utterance 600 records:

> Atum-Beetle (Khepri)! You became high, as the hill; you rose as the benben in the Benben enclosure in Heliopolis (On). You sneezed Shu and spat Tefnut (PT §1652).[45]

Thus, after he created himself, he began to create gods, personifications of nature. Both passages locate the beginnings of creation at On, that is, Heliopolis, and significant too is the inclusion of "the benben in the Benben enclosure in Heliopolis (On)." The *bnbn* stone is the cultic symbol sacred to the temple of Atum in Heliopolis, and its shape is that of the pyramidion (𓉴) or a truncated obelisk (𓉶).[46] The conventional thinking is that the word *bnbn* derives from the word *wbn*,[47] which means "to shine"[48] and applies to the sun.

The pyramid shape likely represents the primeval mound of creation.[49] Two different words are associated with this mound or hill, *ḫ*ʿ, determined by the 𓈍 sign, though it can serve as an ideogram or logogram, depicting a hill with the sun rising

[42] Faulkner, *The Ancient Egyptian Pyramid Texts*, 238.
[43] Faulkner, *The Ancient Egyptian Pyramid Texts*, 226.
[44] Faulkner, *The Ancient Egyptian Pyramid Texts*, 198.
[45] Allen, *The Ancient Egyptian Pyramid Texts*, 269.
[46] *Wb* 1, 457.
[47] Hermann Kees, *Der Götterglaube im alten Ägypten* (Berlin: Akademie-Verlag, 1956), 217. Quirke, *The Cult of Ra*, 27. Elena Tolmatcheva, "A Reconsideration of the Benu-bird in Egyptian Cosmology," in *Egyptology at the Dawn of the Twenty-first Century: Proceedings of the Eighth International Congress of Egyptologist, Cairo 2000*, Vol. 2 (ed. Zahi Hawass; Cairo: American University Press, 2003), 522.
[48] *Wb* 1, 292–293.
[49] Miroslav Verner, "Pyramid," in *OEAE* 3, 87. Tolmatcheva, "A Reconsideration of the Benu-bird in Egyptian Cosmology," 523.

behind it.[50] The verb *ḫꜥi* means "rise and shine."[51] The second word for mound is *ỉꜣt* and is written with a different mound sign, namely, ⌓,[52] a term that has wide application in the Coffin Texts,[53] the next generation of funerary texts that developed from the PTs in the 1st Intermediate Period and Middle Kingdom.

In the solar theology of the PTs, the mound first emerged from the primeval waters of Nun.[54] This is why the resurrected king re-enacts the sun's primal interaction with the emerging mound of earth: "I have cleansed myself upon the earth-hill (*ḫꜥ*) whereon Reʿ cleansed himself" the king announces in PT Spell 333 (PT §542).[55] Commenting on "the hill" in Spell 600 quoted above, James Allen explains that this "refers to the first mound of earth that appeared from the universal waters at the creation (i.e. Nun)."[56] Not only was the benben of Heliopolis the cult symbol, the name of the temple of the Re/Atum was *Ḥwt Bnbn*, "The Mansion or Temple of the Benben," the name by which it would be called throughout history.[57] *Ḥwt bnbn* was still the name of this temple in the 3rd Intermediate Period. The Kushite king Piankhy visited Heliopolis around 725 B.C., and we are informed that he "proceeded to the High Sands in On, making a great offering on the High Sands of On in the presence of Re when he rises (*wbn.f*) . . . He went up the great stairway to see Re in *ḥwt bnbn*, . . . breaking the bolt (of the shrine) and opening the doors (of the shrine), seeing his father Re in holy *ḥwt bnbn*."[58] Not only is *ḥwt bnbn* mentioned several times, but twice the "High Sands of On" are mentioned, and on it Piankhy made a great sacrifice. This may be the actual mound on which the temple precinct was built that was meant to represent the primeval hill.[59] Petrie may actually have discovered traces of this feature during his excavations at Heliopolis in 1911–1912. He described the structure "a great enclosure of earth, sand, and bricks, square in form with rounded corner," although he thought that it was a fortification.[60] More than 75 years ago, Herbert Ricke proposed that this elevated feature at Heliopolis

---

[50] Alan H. Gardiner, *Egyptian Grammar* (London: Oxford University Press, 1957), 889 n 27.

[51] *Wb* 3, 239–240.

[52] Gardiner, *Egyptian Grammar*, 489 n 31.

[53] van Der Molen, *A Hieroglyphic Dictionary of Egyptian Coffin Texts*, 11–12.

[54] Henri Frankfort, *Kingship and the Gods* (Chicago: University of Chicago Press, 1948), 151–152.

[55] Faulkner, *The Ancient Egyptian Pyramid Texts*, 107.

[56] The name occurs in PT Spell 600 quoted here, and rendered by Allen (*Ancient Egyptian Pyramid Texts*, 305, n. 48) as "the Benben enclosure in Heliopolis."

[57] Faulkner (*The Ancient Egyptian Pyramid Texts*, 246) translated this line as "you rose up as the *bnbn*-stone in the Mansion of the 'Phoenix in On'." He took *bnw* to refer to the Phoenix bird associated with the solar shrine in Heliopolis. See also Tolmatcheva, "A Reconsideration of the Benu-bird in Egyptian Cosmology," 522–526.

[58] Translation my own, based on the transcription of Nicolas Grimal, *La Stèle Triomphale de Pi(ankh)y au Musée du Caire* (Cairo: IFAO, 1981), 36*–37*.

[59] Kees, *Ancient Egypt*, 155. Quirke, *The Cult of Ra*, 85–88.

[60] W. M. F. Petrie, *Heliopolis, Kafr Ammar, and Shurafa* (London: Bernard Quaritch, 1915), 3.

was in fact a foundation platform for a temple.[61] Egyptologists ever since tend to agree with Ricke's thesis.[62]

Similar sand mounds have been discovered at other sites, including one at Hierakonpolis in Upper Egypt from early Dynastic times. There Petrie uncovered a similar stone revetment wall that "ran around in a curved or almost circular form," within which earth was packed that served as the foundation of the temple.[63] At Medamud (near Thebes) a brick enclosure wall was found that surrounded a mound approximately 1.75 meters high.[64] This feature, too, is likely a replica of the primeval mound that had a temple on it. The architectural use of this mythic archetype was extended to other temples.[65] In fact, as I pointed out 30 years ago, "the Holy of Holies where the cult object was placed was called *st ḏsrt nt sp tpy*, the holy place of creation (lit. the first occurrence),"[66] and the holy of holies of temples was usually the highest point within a temple complex.

As a result of his creative powers, other deities were created; of special significance are the Heliopolitan deities over which Atum was preeminent. This group of nine is frequent called the Heliopolitan, or Great Ennead, consisting of Shu and Tefnut (already encountered in PT §§1248 and 1652), Geb, Nut, Isis, Seth, Nephthys, Thoth, and Horus.[67] Hence Atum is called "father of the gods" (§§1521 and 1546). Spell 601 puts it this way: "O you Great Ennead which is in On . . . the name of Atum . . . presides over the Great Ennead. . . ." (§§1660–1661).[68]

The textual evidence reviewed here demonstrates the prominent position occupied by the creator, in his various manifestations, who was known by different names. As the creator of the forces of nature that were personified in the primeval gods, Re/Atum was supreme. Moreover, as the mound at On emerged from the Abyss or Nun and the sun shone on it, the spot was forever marked as sacred, and the pyramid-shaped *bnbn*-stone was placed in the most holy area of that temple. This solar theology then moved beyond Heliopolis and was central to Egyptian kingship, and Atum's lofty position was reflected in many spheres of culture, foremost of which are the architecture and iconography of that period.

---

61 Herbert Ricke, "Der 'Hohe Sand' in Heliopolis," *ZÄS* 71 (1935): 107–111.

62 Quirke, *The Cult of Ra*, 95.

63 J. E. Quibell & W. M. F. Petrie, *Hierakonpolis* I (London: Bernard Quaritch, 1900), 6.

64 Alexander Badawy, *A History of Egyptian Architecture* I (Cairo: Misr Studio, 1954), 115.

65 Frankfort, *Kingship and the Gods*, 151–152. Ragnhild Finnestad, *The Image of the World and Symbol of the Creator* (Wiesbanden: Harrasowitz, 1985), 21–23.

66 James K. Hoffmeier, *"Sacred" in the Vocabulary of Ancient Egypt* (Orbis Biblicus et Orientalis 59; Freiburg: Universitätsverlag, 1985), 173.

67 They are listed in Spell 219 and 600. Horus is not included in Spell 600, making eight deities, plus Atum the leader, making nine.

68 Faulkner, *The Ancient Egyptian Pyramid Texts*, 247–248.

ARCHITECTURE AND SOLAR RELIGION IN THE OLD KINGDOM

The Pyramid

The Old Kingdom pyramids are perhaps the most impressive architectural structures from ancient Egypt that have associations with solar religion. Regarding the Step Pyramid of Djoser at Saqqara, the first pyramid, Florence Friedman opines: "Djoser's complex is located on the highest ground of the Saqqara plateau, suggesting a desire to incorporate into his funerary monument the regenerative notion of the primeval hill, a mythological form manifested in the pyramid."[69] Most of the architecture in the Djoser Pyramid complex has to do with the performing of the Sed-festival for the renewal of the resurrected king's vitality;[70] however, there is a frieze showing carved uraei or cobras rearing up and facing the rising sun on the inner courtyard wall in the southwest corner (Figure 1.6).[71] The uraeus (i.e., the cobra associated with the sun), according to one PT, "came forth from Re'" (PT §1092), and another passage adds: "this King is the falcon which came forth [from Re'] and the uraeus which came from the eye of Re'" (PT §2206).[72] So clearly the uraei inside the Djoser complex have solar associations.

FIGURE 1.6 Uraei at Saqqara with Step Pyramid of Djoser in background. Photo James K. Hoffmeier.

[69] Florence Friedman, "Notions of Cosmos in the Step Pyramid Complex," *Studies in Honor of William Kelly Simpson* (ed. Peter der Manuelian; Boston: Museum of Fine Arts, 1996), 338.

[70] Jean-Philippe Lauer, *Saqqara: The Royal Cemetary of Memphis* (New York: Charles Scribner's Sons, 1976), 90–136. W. Stevenson Smith, *The Art and Architecture of Ancient Egypt* (Baltimore, MD: Penguin Books, 1965), 30–38.

[71] Lauer, *Saqqara*, 94.

[72] Faulkner, *The Ancient Egyptian Pyramid Texts*, 181, 307.

In the 4th Dynasty the step pyramid of the previous century evolved into the true pyramid so that it looked architecturally like the *bnbn*-stone of Heliopolis. From this century-long epoch come the pyramids of Sneferu and Khufu, which represent the greatest achievement in pyramid building. Interestingly, the names of these pyramids show their connection to solar theology. The northern pyramid at Dahshur is called "Shining (*ḫ*ʿ) Pyramid," while the Bent Pyramid is called "The Southern Shining (*ḫ*ʿ) Pyramid."[73] The Great Pyramid of Khufu is "The Pyramid which is in the Place of Sunrise and Sunset" (*ȝḫt mr*).[74]

That the pyramid shape replicates the *bnbn*-stone, the sacred symbol of Heliopolis, was already mentioned above. But what is behind the pyramid shape? Unfortunately, we have no textual evidence to answer this question. Hence we can only speculate. If one looks at the sun when partially obscured by clouds, the sun's rays break through at angles in the form of a pyramid (Figure 1.7). The solar iconography of the Old and Middle Kingdoms (see next section) never depicts the sun's rays. In fact, not until the Amarna period are the sun's rays included, and they are ubiquitous in Akhenaten's Aten iconography. Viewed in two dimensions, the triangular shape is obvious. It may be, then, that the sun's rays that are visible in a cloudy sky provide the inspiration for the shape of the *bnbn*-stone and therefore the pyramid.

FIGURE 1.7 Sun rays (Sinai, Egypt). Photo James K. Hoffmeier.

[73] John Baines & Jaromír Málek, *Atlas of Ancient Egypt* (New York: Facts on File, 1980), 141.

[74] Baines & Málek, *Atlas of Ancient Egypt*, 140.

The funerary temples in 4th Dynasty pyramid complexes, both the valley or lower temple and the funerary or upper temple face east. The causeway that connects the two structures served as the route the mummified king took to move from the eastmost temple to the western temple and the pyramid for burial.[75] This design may indicate the movement of the sun from birth and renewal in the east to setting and death in the west. This east-west orientation represents a shift from the plan of 3rd Dynasty funerary complexes, like that of Djoser, which is north-south. Rainer Stadelemann observes that the new layout of the 4th Dynasty complexes "were oriented east-west in accordance with the course of the sun" and that "this new alignment from east to west in the form of a strict sequence of valley temple, causeway, pyramid temple and pyramid tomb is most perfectly established at Giza."[76]

The Obelisk

Another solar architectural or cultic image was the obelisk, a tall square pillar that tapers toward the top that has a pyramidion or *bnbn* as the top (Figure 1.8). Given

FIGURE 1.8 Obelisks at Karnak Temple, including the broken one of Hatshepsut laying on its side. Photo James K. Hoffmeier.

---

[75] Dieter Arnold and others have rejected the early notion that the Valley Temple was the place of embalming, but he does acknowledge that the closed and roofed causeway was designed to ensure to the ritual purity of the connection between the lower and upper temples (see *Temples of Ancient Egypt* [ed. Byron Shafer; Ithaca, NY: Cornell University Press, 1997], 55). Further on the place of embalmment of the king in Old Kingdom pyramid complexes, see James K. Hoffmeier "Possible Origins of the Tent of Purification," *Studien zur Altägyptischen Kultur* IX (1981): 167–177.

[76] Rainer Stadelmann, "The Development of the Pyramid Temple in the Fourth Dynasty," in *The Temple in Ancient Egypt* (ed. S. Quirke; London: British Museum, 1997), 2.

this shape, it is obvious, as Labib Habachi observed, that "obelisks were considered by the ancient Egyptians to be sacred to the sun god." PT §1178 refers to "the two obelisks of Reʿ which are on earth."[77] Interestingly, some of the earliest obelisks from the Old Kingdom have been discovered at Heliopolis, giving rise to the idea that a tall slender obelisk or a more truncated variety was the *bnbn*-stone.[78] It has been suggested by David Jeffreys that if one were perched on the elevated temple at On, there was a line of site between it and the pyramids on the western side of the Nile, north of Abu Sir to south of Abu Roash.[79] In turn, from those sites, the obelisk or *bnbn*-image of Heliopolis would have been visible from the pyramids in the west. This intriguing proposal strengthens the view that it was the sun-cult in On that inspired the construction of the pyramids and later sun-temples (see below).

Obelisks continued in popularity throughout Pharaonic Egypt, and were typically erected in pairs at the front of temples. Hatshepsut's impressive monoliths and the granite bases on which they stood contain informative texts[80] (Figure 1.9). On the obelisk itself, we learn that it was covered with high quality electrum (*bꜣk m ḏʿm ʿꜣ wrt*[81] = lit. "made of very great electrum"), a gold-silver alloy. The site of these nearly 98 foot (29.5 m) high and 323 ton,[82] electrum-encased monoliths gleaming in the sun must have been stunning indeed to behold. This point is not missed in the inscription on the obelisks: *sḥḏ.n.<sn> tꜣ.wy mỉ ỉtn*[83]—"(they) brighten the land like Aten." The base inscription offers additional salient information: *mꜣꜣ.tw m gs.wy*[84] *ỉtrw, bʿḥ.n stwt.sn tꜣ.wy, wbn ỉtn ỉmywt ny mỉ ḫʿʿ.f m ꜣḫt n(y)t pt*[85]—"One sees (them) on both sides of the river, their rays flood the two lands (i.e., Egypt) when Aten rises between them, like when he appears in the horizon of heaven!" This verse is loaded with solar language (*wbn* and *ḫʿỉ* were introduced above). The writing of *gs.wy*, "two sides," is an odd writing, here rendered as "both sides." Normally this would be written with 𓐝, but the dual pillar (𓊽𓊽) is used, reminiscent of the word for Heliopolis, *ỉwnw* meaning "pillars."[86] The word *bʿḥ* which means "flood" and applies to the Nile's inundation,[87] is

[77] Faulkner, *Ancient Egyptian Pyramid Texts*, 190.

[78] Quirke, *The Cult of Ra*, 84–85, 88.

[79] Jeffreys, "The Topography of Heliopolis and Memphis: Some Cognitive Aspects," *Stationen. Beiträge zur Kulturegeschichte Ägyptens, Rainer Stadelmann gewidment* (Mainz-am-Rein: P. von Zabern, 1998), 63–71.

[80] *Urk*. IV, 356–369.

[81] *Urk*. IV, 357. 6.

[82] Measurements from Dieter Arnold, *Building in Egypt: Pharaonic Stone Masonry* (New York/Oxford: Oxford University Press, 1991), 60.

[83] *Urk*. IV, 357. 7.

[84] This is an odd writing of *gs.wy*, "two sides." Two pillars (𓊽𓊽), which should read *ỉwn.wy*, two pillars. This writing is not attested as a variant of *gs.wy* in *Wb* 5.196–197.

[85] *Urk*. IV, 362.13–16.

[86] Gardiner, *Grammar*, 495 (sign N 28).

[87] *Wb* 1, 448.

FIGURE 1.9 Hatshepsut's standing obelisk (Karnak Temple). Photo James K. Hoffmeier.

normally written with 𓈗. But here the word indicator is 𓅠. This sign shows a heron on a perch, which is a variation of the standing heron 𓅟. The heron is the *bnw*-bird of Heliopolitan solar mythology, which is considered to be the precursor of the Phoenix bird of later Greek mythology.[88] The orthography of the word on Hatshepsut's obelisks is written just with 𓅠. With regard to the writing on the Hatshepsut obelisk, one wonders if this represents a playful writing on the *bnw* > *bnbn* (and *wbn*, "to shine" or "rise") and the obelisk itself.[89] Heliopolis is mentioned in line 1 of the base

[88] Quirke, *The Cult of Ra*, 27–29.

[89] The connection between these terms has been discussed by John Baines, "*Bnbn*: Mythological and Linguistic Notes," *Orientalia* 39 (1970): 389–404.

inscription, and Southern Heliopolis, an epithet for Thebes in the New Kingdom, is found in line 4.[90]

So this obelisk text strikingly connects the monoliths to solar theology and Heliopolis. The obelisk, then, can be traced back to the Old Kingdom, and is one of the most enduring solar images from ancient Egypt. How early its precursor, the *bnbn*-stone, became the cult symbol at the temple of Atum in Heliopolis is not known. It surely goes back to before the unification of Egypt at the end of the fourth millennium.

SOLAR ELEMENTS IN OLD KINGDOM ICONOGRAPHY

The Sphinx

Another iconic image of ancient Egypt is the sphinx, and it too has solar connections, that textually can be traced back to the Old Kingdom (Figure 1.10). PT§ 1178 mentions the "two sphinxes of Reʿ which are in the sky."[91] The great sphinx of Giza that stands 64 feet (20 m) high and 235 feet (73.5 m) long is, to the best of our knowledge, the first sphinx, although Stadlemann thinks that there may have been "a prototype, perhaps in Heliopolis, the city of the sun god; later texts mention a great Sphinx of Heliopolis" which possibly goes back to Djoser or Sneferu.[92] Indeed, statues of sphinxes from the reign of Ramesses III have been discovered in recent decades at Tell el-Hisn (Heliopolis).[93]

The Giza sphinx wears a *nemes* or cloth crown, seen as early as the Dynasty 2 illustration of king Den on an ivory label.[94] The *nemes* crown, apparently without a uraeus, is found on the *serdab*[95] statue of Djoser from Saqqara (now in the Cairo Museum). From the 4th Dynasty onward the *nemes* crown becomes one of the standard royal symbols on statues of pharaohs, with the uraeus regularly affixed over the center of the brow of the king.[96]

There are no surviving 4th Dynasty inscriptions that explain the purpose or function of the sphinx. Even the "sphinx temple" situated in front the colossal image at

---

[90] *Urk.* IV. 361.9, 16.

[91] Faulkner, *Ancient Egyptian Pyramid Texts*, 190.

[92] Rainer Stadelmann, "Sphinx," *OEAE* 3: 309–310.

[93] Abdel Aziz Saleh, *Excavations at Heliopolis: Ancient Egyptian Ounu*, Vol. II (Cairo: Cairo University, 1983), pl. XLIV–XLV.

[94] Spencer, *Early Egypt*, 87

[95] *Serdab* is an Arabic word applied to the small, enclosed chamber on the north side of the step pyramid which contained this statue.

[96] A notable example in 4th Dynasty where the *nemes* is worn without the uraeus is the dyad of Menkaure and his queen in the Museum of Fine Arts, Boston.

FIGURE 1.10 The Great Sphinx (Giza). Photo James K. Hoffmeier.

Giza is completely anepigraphic; however, Ricke thought that it was a type of sun temple.[97] In the 18th Dynasty, Amenhotep II (1427–1400 B.C.) built a chapel near the sphinx dedicated to Horemakht (*Ḥr m 3ḫt*, Harmachis being the Greek form), which means "Horus in the Horizon." Horus, as noted previously, was associated with the horizon,[98] and in the New Kingdom the divine name for the sphinx further shows the connection to Horus. The focal point of Amenhotep II's sphinx temple is a large stela that contains reports from his days as a prince when he came from nearby Memphis to the Giza necropolis on chariot (Figure 1.11).[99] The Sphinx Stela describes the moment he became king: "the uraeus took its place on his brow; the image of Re (*tỉt rʿ*) was established on its post."[100] Additionally, we learn from the inscription that he would "stop at the resting place of Harmakhis. He would spend time there leading them (his chariot horses) around and observing the excellence of the resting-place of Kings Khufu and Khafra, the justified."[101] The reference to the "resting place of Harmakhis" (*ḫnw n ḥr m 3ḫt*) seems to be referring to the long abandoned Temple of the Sphinx, which must have been largely encroached by sand.

[97] Herbert Ricke & Siegfried Schott, *Der Harmachistempel des Chefren in Giseh* (Wiesbaden: Harrasowitz, 1970), 32–39.

[98] Wilkinson, *The Complete Gods and Goddesses of Ancient Egypt*, 201.

[99] For the text, see *Urk.* IV, 1276–1286. For translation, see Miriam Lichtheim, *Ancient Egyptian Literature* II (Berkeley: University of California Press, 1976), 39–43.

[100] Lichtheim, *Ancient Egyptian Literature* II, 42.

[101] Lichtheim, *Ancient Egyptian Literature* II, 42.

FIGURE 1.11 Sphinx Stela Amenhotep II (Giza). Photo James K. Hoffmeier.

More significant is the stela inscribed by Amenhotep II's son, Thutmose IV (1400–1390 B.C.), which stands between the forelegs of the sphinx (Figure 1.12). In it Prince Thutmose, like his father, recalls his visit to the sphinx after hunting wild game in the area and taking target practice with his bow.[102] Prince Thutmose recalls taking his siesta in the shadow of "the image of the very great Khepri." In a dream, the sphinx spoke to him, introducing himself: "I am your father Hor-em-akht / Khepri / Atum."[103] The sphinx predicts that this prince would become king, which may explain why as king he twice describes himself in the stela as "the son of Atum (*s3 itm*)"[104] and "excellent heir of Khepri."[105]

---

[102] For the text, see *Urk*. IV, 1539–1544. For translation, see Barbara Cumming, *Egyptian Historical Records of the Later Eighteenth Dynasty* (Westminster: Aris & Phillips, 1984), 247–251.

[103] *Urk*. IV, 1542.17.

[104] *Urk*. IV, 1540.7, 19.

[105] *Urk*. IV, 1540.7.

FIGURE 1.12 Sphinx Stela of Thutmose IV (Giza). Photo James K. Hoffmeier.

These two 18th Dynasty stelae clearly associate the sphinx with his various solar forms. Moreover, the link between the pharaoh and Atum as the son of Re is firmly re-established, showing the continuity of the tradition that goes back a thousand years earlier.

The Sun-Disc

Reliefs of the king in action with vulture, falcon, or the sun-disc hovering overhead to represent the presence and protection of the deity are a staple of New Kingdom royal art. In some cases, a combination of these deities occurs. Seti I at Karnak, for example, is portrayed with a double uraei sun-disc along with the vulture goddess, Nekhbet, while another scene depicts all three together (Figure 1.13).[106] For the first

[106] Epigraphic Survey, *The Battle Reliefs of Seti I* (Chicago: Oriental Institute, 1986), pl. 3, 5.

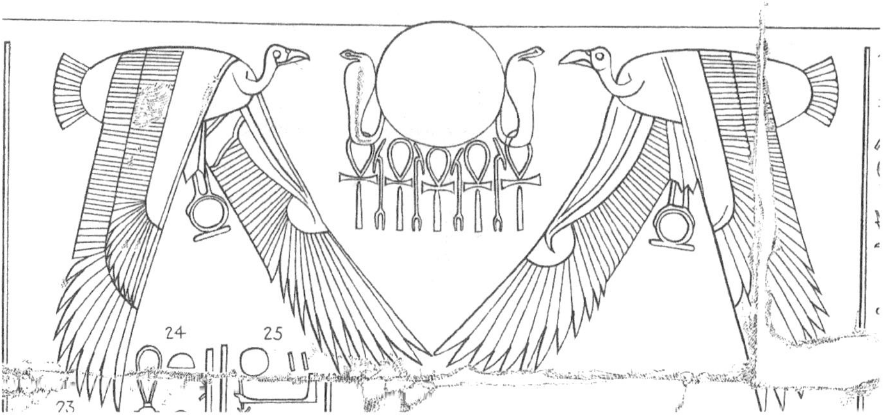

FIGURE 1.13 Sun-disc with uraei from Seti I relief (Karnak Temple). Epigraphic Survey, *The Wars of Sety* I (Chicago: The Oriental Institute, 1986), pl. 35.

six dynasties there are only a limited number of reliefs depicting kings in action where protective deities might have been shown. For example, no such reliefs have been recorded or survived from the 4th Dynasty pyramid complexes.

The motif of a winged deity floating over the king is found as early as the Narmer mace-head, where a vulture occupies this position.[107] The vulture goddess Nekhbet was patron of Hierokonpolis where the mace-head was discovered. The 3rd Dynasty king Sekhemkhet is portrayed smiting the heads of a desert-dweller at Maghara in Sinai,[108] but no protective deity is included. On the carved panels of Djoser beneath his pyramid, however, the king is shown engaged in various ritual acts (none is militaristic). In each case the protective deity Horus hovers overhead.[109] A decorated panel of Sneferu at Maghara shows the king smiting an enemy, but no protective deity is portrayed; rather there is an elongated cartouche containing the royal titulary, less the Horus name, which stands opposite Sneferu.[110]

Also at Maghara there is a carved panel of Khnum-Khufu,[111] "smiting tribesmen" (*sḳr ỉwntyw*), with the Horus falcon shown flying overhead.[112] The area where the talons would have been included is partially damaged, although a circular object is apparent. This could either be the top loop of the *ꜥnḫ*-sign or the *šnw*-sign (a

[107] Walter B. Emery, *Archaic Egypt* (Baltimore: Penguin, 1961), 46.

[108] A. H. Gardiner, T. E. Peet, & J. Černý, *The Inscriptions of Sinai* I (London: Egypt Exploration Society, 1952), Pl. I.

[109] Florence Friedman, "The Underground Relief Panels of King Djoser at the Step Pyramid Complex," *JARCE* 32 (1995): 1–42.

[110] Gardiner, Peet, & J. Černý, *The Inscriptions of Sinai* I, II.

[111] Khnum-Khufu is the full name of Khufu, the builder of the great pyramid at Giza.

[112] Gardiner, Peet, & J. Černý, *The Inscriptions of Sinai* I, pl. II, III. A photograph is included in A. H. Gardiner, T. E. Peet, & J. Černý, *The Inscriptions of Sinai* II (London: Egypt Exploration Society, 1955), pl. I.

circular cartouche). Both symbols are shown on the different depictions of Horus in the Djoser panels introduced above. The celebrated statue of Khafre with the falcon behind his head is how this protective motif was incorporated into a sculpture (Figure 1.14). It appears that during Dynasties 1 though 4, the practice of illustrating winged deities over the king in action was not consistently included, and examples with the sun-disc are unknown.

Beginning in the 5th Dynasty, the sun-disc starts to appear with some regularity in reliefs showing the king in action. A block discovered by J. E. Quibell at Saqqara, possibly from Sahure's funerary complex at Abusir, shows the king standing between two deities, but directly over his head is a large sun-disc, on either side of which a vulture flutters[113] (Figure 1.15). On the left, Nekhbet holds a *šnw*, while in her mirror image on the right side, she holds an *ʿnḫ*-sign. The fusion of wings and sun-disc is found with regularity from the 6th Dynasty onward.[114] It appears based on the limited evidence available at present that the inclusion of the iconic sun-disc in the sky over the pharaoh has its roots in the expansion of solar religion in the 24th century B.C.

FIGURE 1.14 Statue of Khafre with Horus (Cairo Museum). Photo James K. Hoffmeier.

[113] J. E Quibell, *Excavations at Saqqara (1908–9, 1909–10): The Monastery of Apa Jeremias* (Cairo: IFAO, 1912), pl. 89.

[114] For examples, see Gardiner, Peet, & Černý, *The Inscriptions of Sinai* I, pl. VI, VIII.

FIGURE 1.15 Sun-disc over Sahure (Saqqara). J. E Quibell, *Excavations at Saqqara (1908–9, 1909–10): The Monastery of Apa Jeremias* (Cairo: IFAO, 1912), pl. 89.

In a detailed scene of Ni-user-re at Maghara, he is "smiting Bedouin of all foreign lands" (*sḳr mnṯyw ḫꜣswt nb(w)t*),[115] and a victim raises his hand begging for mercy as the king is about to bludgeon him. The top of the scene is framed with a sun-disc with a uraeus on each side and a pair of wings extends from the disc. Above the winged sun-disc is a row of stars to complete the picture.

From the 5th Dynasty onward, the sun-disc or winged variety is depicted with regularity in the art, but it is worth noting that the central image of Akhenaten's religion seems to have had its artistic origin in the very period when the sun-god attained his zenith of power, and this is the golden age that Akhenaten seems to be emulating.

SUN TEMPLES

The impressive 4th Dynasty pyramids, especially those of Sneferu, Khufu, and Khafre, mark the pinnacle of pyramid building. Miroslav Verner, who for decades has directed the Czech Archaeological Mission at Abusir, is surely correct when he opines that "the pyramids of Giza became the symbol of the power of the state and authority of the pharaoh at its height."[116] The third pyramid of the Giza pyramids, that of Menkaure, was not even half the size of those of Khufu and Khafre.[117] Despite the plan to encase this pyramid with red granite from Aswan, which would have enhanced its prestige, the decline of pyramid building had begun. Menkaure's son and successor, Shepseskaf (the last ruler of the 4th Dynasty), was not even buried

[115] Gardiner, Peet, & J. Černý, *The Inscriptions of Sinai* I, pl. VIII.

[116] Verner, "Pyramid," 89. Labib Habachi, *Tell Basta* (Cario: CASAE, 1957), figs. 2–3 and pl. 2–3.

[117] For a helpful chart comparing all the statistics of the pyramids, see Mark Lehner, *The Complete Pyramids* (London: Thames & Hudson, 1997), 16–17.

in a pyramid. Rather he was interred in a large stone *mastaba*,[118] 327 feet (99.6 m) long, 244 feet (74.4 m) wide, and 59 feet (18 m) high.[119] As if to avoid comparison between his burial monument and those of his fathers at Giza, Shepseskaf located his large stone mastaba around 12 miles (19 k) to the south, between Dahshur and south Saqqara.

The 5th Dynasty saw an embarrassing diminution of the size and quality of the pyramids, which seems to parallel a loss of prestige of the kingly office. The first king of the 5th Dynasty is Userkaf, whose pedigree remains uncertain. Scholars differ on the political rationale for the story in Papyrus Westcar that offers a prophecy regarding the origins of this royal family. The tales within the papyrus are set in the 4th Dynasty court of Sneferu and Khufu, but are written in Middle Kingdom style. Since this is the only surviving witness to the tales, and the papyrus dates to the 17th–16th century B.C., it is difficult to know when the story about the birth of the kings originated.[120] It may be that the apologetic value of the stories regarding the origin of the 5th Dynasty requires that the tales go back to that period, otherwise there is no legitimizing value to the story.[121]

Prince Hardedef, the tale recounts, brings the magician Djedi to entertain his father, King Khufu, who asks the sage, "it was also said that you know the number of the secret chambers in the sanctuary of Thoth," to which Djedi announces, "I do not know their number, O king, my lord. But I know the place where it is."[122] He then explained that the information is contained in a stone chest in a building named

---

[118] *Mastaba* is an Arabic word meaning "bench." The shape of the mud brick single-story royal burials of the first two dynasties is similar to the mud or mud brick benches commonly located in front of adobe homes in rural Egypt.

[119] Lehner, *The Complete Pyramids*, 139.

[120] W. K. Simpson, R. O. Faulkner, & E. F. Wente, *The Literature of Ancient Egypt* (New Haven, CT: Yale University Press, 1973), 15.

[121] Amenemhet I, the founder of the 12th Dynasty, mastered the use of literature to legitimize his new dynasty (e.g., Story of Sinuhe, Wisdom of Amenemhet, Prophecy of Neferti). Could it be that Papyrus Westcar came into its present form in the Middle Kingdom, based on oral versions of the stories that were in circulation from the 24th century B.C. onward? On the literary and oral dimensions of folktales, see Susan T. Hollis, "Tales of Magic and Wonder from Ancient Egypt," in *CANE*, 2255–2264. For studies on early 12th Dynasty apologetic literature, see A. de Buck, "La Litterérature et la politique sous la douzième dynastie," in *Symbolae ad jus et historian antiquitatis pertinentes Juli Christiano van Overn dedicatae* (eds. M. David, B. A. van Gronigen, & E.M. Neijers; Leiden: Brill, 1946), 1–28. E. Otto, "Weltanschauliche und politische Tendenzscriften," in *Handbuch der Orientalistik*, 1 Bd.: Aegptologie, 2. Abschnitt: Literatur (Leiden: Brill, 1952), 111–119. G. Posener, *Littérature et politique dans l'Egypte de la XIIe dynastie* (Paris: Champion, 1956). R. J. Williams, "Literature as a Medium of Political Propaganda in Ancient Egypt," in *Seed of Wisdom: Essays in Honour of T. J. Meek* (ed. S. McCullough; Toronto: University of Toronto Press, 1964), 14–30.

[122] Lichtheim, *Ancient Egyptian Literature* I, 219. All quotes in this paragraph are taken from Lichtheim's translation.

"Inventory in On," apparently in the temple complex in Heliopolis. Khufu orders Djedi to get it for him, but he declines, indicating "the eldest of the three children who are in the womb of Ruddedet . . . will bring it to you." "Who is this Ruddedet" the king asked. The answer: "she is the wife of a priest of Re, lord of Sakhbu, who is pregnant with three children of Re, lord of Sakhbu. He has said concerning them that they will assume this beneficent office in this whole land, and the eldest of the them will be high priest in On." News of kings who would reign that were not his offspring was troubling to the monarch. Djedi offered some consolation by informing Khufu that his son and grandson would rule prior to the first of these three kings.

The divinely conceived babies are born in the next episode. As the birth pangs set in, Ruddedet is attended in her delivery by goddesses associated with birthing, Isis, Nephthys, Meskhenet, and Heket, and Khnum the creator of humans.[123] The names of the three baby boys were announced as they were delivered: Userkaf, Sahure, and Kaki (i.e., Neferirkare), the first three kings of Dynasty 5. Historically, the dynastic link between the 4th and 5th Dynasty appears to be via Khentkawes,[124] whose *mastaba*-like tomb at Giza is located between the causeways of Khafre and Menkaure. There are those who think she was Menkaure's queen,[125] while others suggest she was his daughter.[126] Khentkawes, then, appears to be the mother of the 5th Dynasty, and the legend preserved in Papyrus Westcar considers Re to be their father. This latter point seems to be critical to royal ideology that the king was indeed the son of Re, and should erase any question about the legitimacy of Userkaf and his successors.

There is no evidence that Userkaf served as priest of Re,[127] unless the Westcar "prophecy" has something else in mind. While he built his small and now dilapidated pyramid just outside the northeastern corner of the Djoser pyramid complex at Saqqara (Figure 1.16), most significant is the fact that he was the first pharaoh to build a sun temple. That sun temple may be the first major royal building of the 5th Dynasty.[128] In fact, the first six kings of Dynasty 5 appear to have constructed such structures that shared many features in common with the pyramid complex,

---

[123] Lichtheim, *Ancient Egyptian Literature* I, 220.

[124] A. H. Gardiner, *Egypt of the Pharaohs* (Oxford: Oxford University Press, 1961), 83–84. Michel Baud, "The Old Kingdom," in *A Companion to Ancient Egypt* I (ed. A. B. Lloyd; Oxford: Wiley-Blackwell, 2010), 66.

[125] Málek, "The Old Kingdom," 91.

[126] Miroslav Verner, *Abusir: Realm of Osiris* (Cairo: American University Press, 2002), 55.

[127] Verner (*Abusir: Realm of Osiris*, 71) allows for the possibility that Userkaf was a Heliopolitan priest.

[128] Jarmír Krejcí, "Appearance of the Abu Sir Pyramid Necropolis during the Old Kingdom," in *Egyptology at the Dawn of the Twenty-first Century: Proceedings of the Eighth International Congress of Egyptologist, Cairo 2000*, Vol. 1 (ed. Zahi Hawass; Cairo: American University Press, 2003), 281.

FIGURE 1.16 Pyramid of Userkaf (Saqqara). Photo James K. Hoffmeier.

namely, valley temple, causeway, upper temple, and, in place of the pyramid, a large truncated obelisk or *bnbn*-stone (Figure 1.17). It is widely believed that the sun cult of Heliopolis served as the model for these sun temples. W. Stevenson Smith described the focal point of the temple as "an imitation of the Benben stone" of the Re temple at Heliopolis.[129] More recently, Nicholas Grimal offers the same observation that the 5th Dynasty sun temples were "doubtless modeled on the original sun temple at Heliopolis."[130] Could it be that Userkaf's identification as the priest of Re in the divine birth story in Papyrus Westcar was intended to reflect Userkaf's role in erecting the first sun temple?

Despite the fragmentary remains of the temples of Userkaf and Niuserre, the certainty that a truncated obelisk was the focal point of these temples was based on the hieroglyphic signs used when writing the names of these temples (e.g., 𓉶 & △). In 1974 a stunning discovery was made while clearing the mastaba of Ptahshepses at Abusir: a pink granite pyramidion, the top part of which was inset, apparently for a sheet of glistening metal (Verner suggests copper).[131] It did not originate in

---

[129] W. Steveson Smith, "The Old Kingdom in Egypt," in *Cambridge Ancient History*, Vol. 1, part 2 (eds. I. E. S. Edwards, C. J. Gadd, & N. G. L. Hammond; Cambridge: The University Press, 1971), 180.

[130] Nicholas Grimal, *A History of Ancient Egypt* (Oxford: Blackwells, 1992), 124.

[131] M. Verner, "Discovery of an Obelisk at Abusir," *Revue d'Egyptologie* 28 (1976): 111–118; Verner, *Abusir*, 83–85.

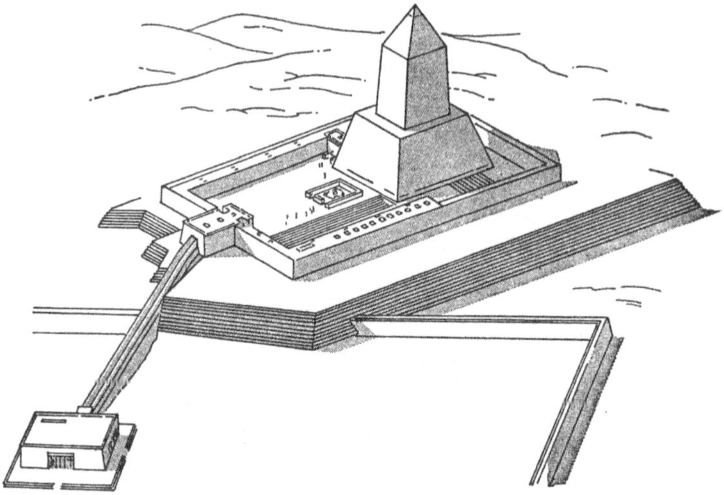

FIGURE 1.17 Reconstruction of Sun Temple of Niuserre (Abu Ghurab). Adapted from W. Stevenson Smith, *The Art and Architecture of Ancient Egypt* (Baltimore, MD: Penguin, 1958), 74.

this tomb, and may have been a part of Sahure's sun temple complex, which Verner thinks was never fully completed.[132]

Unfortunately, only the scant remains of two have been identified, those of Userkaf (just north of the Abusir pyramids) and Niuserre at Abu Ghurab, slightly north of Abusir. Those of the next four monarchs have not been discovered or did not survive. Their names are known from various inscriptions, as well as the titles of priests and officials who were attached to these sanctuaries. Enough survived of the sun temples of Userkaf and Niuserre to establish the architectural plan, and extant ruins and reliefs reveal something of the activities in these sanctuaries. The names of the six temples unambiguously reveal the connection to Re:

1. Userkaf: *Nḫn Rʿ*—"Re's Stronghold"
2. Niuserre: *Sḫt-Rʿ*—"Delight of Re"
3. Neferfre: *St ib Rʿ*—"Re's offering table"
4. Sahure: *Ḥtp Rʿ*—"Field of Re"
5. Neferirkare: *šsp ib Rʿ*—"Place of Re's Pleasure"
6. Menkauhor: *3ḫt Rʿ*—"Horizon of Re."[133]

[132] Verner, *Abusir*, 84.

[133] Verner, *Abusir*, 71–84; Jaromír Krejcí & Dušan Magdolen, "Research into Fifth Dynasty Sun Temples – Past, Present and Future," *The Old Kingdom Art and Archaeology: Proceedings of the Conference Held in Prague, May 31–June 4, 2004* (ed. M. Bárta; Prague: Academy of Sciences of the Czech Republic), 186.

Why these temples were constructed, why at this time and this time only they were made, and why so close to the funerary complexes of the respective kings are probing questions that remain the subject of scholarly investigation, thought, and speculation. The fact that the size of the sun temples rivaled the actual pyramid complexes surely contributed to the diminished size and quality of the pyramids of this era.

Excavations in the sun temple complexes have revealed that an altar was located in front of the obelisk feature. The altar in the Niuserre's temple is circular, possibly to represent the round shape of the sun, and was the main feature of a large open court (Figure 1.17).[134] Adjacent to the open court were "slaughter houses" and in the Niuserre's complex, large travertine (Egyptian alabaster) blocks with circular basins cut into them were discovered.[135] A rim around the basins contains nodules protruding from it and encircling it. It is unclear whether these nodules were meant to represent the sun's rays or not, but it is believed that the basins were used in connection with animal sacrifices. The altar, sacrificial basins, and a slaughter house all adjacent to the benben-obelisk, in combination with the names of the temples, leave no doubt that these structures have been rightly called sun temples where cultic activity took place in the name of Re.

Why they were constructed only during the 5th Dynasty remains a probing question. Why the practice ended later in the 5th Dynasty might easily be attributable to the weakening economy and the reduced power of the kingship. Thus the demands of maintaining the great temples of Egypt and building one's pyramid complex were all the late Old Kingdom pharaohs could handle.

Why the sun temples should emerge at this time is harder to answer. There are those who see a rise in solar religion in the 4th Dynasty (as witnessed by the royals' names, i.e., Radjedef, Khafre, Menkaure), making sun temples merely the culmination of a movement that had begun in the previous century.[136] Jaromír Málek considers the sun-temple phenomenon to be "the outcome of a gradual rise in importance of the sun-god."[137] A different and intriguing suggestion for the reason for the sun temples, made by Jeffreys, is that their placement north of Abusir (where most of the most 5th Dynasty rulers were buried) was so that a line of sight could be established between the Abu Ghurab sun temple and its prototype that inspired them in Heliopolis.[138] From Giza, one could see Heliopolis, and vice versa. This connection

---

[134] Verner, *Abusir*, 78.

[135] Conveniently depicted in Verner, *Abusir*, 76.

[136] Smith, "The Old Kingdom in Egypt," 179–180. Quirke, while recognizing the Sun Temples represent a "radical addition to his (Userkaf's) cult architecture," thinks it is wrong to believe that the 5th Dynasty kings were "more sun-fixated that the 4th Dynasty" (*The Cult of Ra*, 127).

[137] Málek, "The Old Kingdom (c. 2686–2160 B.C.)," 99.

[138] David Jeffreys, "The Topography of Heliopolis and Memphis: Some Cognitive Aspects," 63–71. Followed by Quirke, *The Cult of Ra*, 88–90.

was lost when Userkaf chose Saqqara for his burial site. The same was true of the Abusir necropolis. According to Jeffreys' explanation, if one takes into account the ancient landscape (without the obstructions caused by subsequent construction), the royal tombs north of the Niuserre sun temple at Abu Ghurab were in view of the Mansion of the Benben in Heliopolis, and so the visual link was re-established.

It may well be that Niuserre's sun temple was built at its location with the view to Heliopolis in mind. This explanation, however, does not account for the placement of the first sun temple, that of Userkaf, in northern Abusir. It is about 1500 feet (500 m) south of Abu Ghurab, and apparently just out of sight of the Re temple in On, and the location of the remaining 5th Dynasty solar cult centers are unknown.

Alternatively, other scholars see the 5th Dynasty sun temples as representing shifts and developments in solar theology or religious practice. Dieter Arnold has recently acknowledged that during the 4th Dynasty solar elements were significant, "but beginning with the Fifth dynasty that tendency had become so dominant that solar cult installations needed independent structures separated from the funerary cult complexes."[139] Arnold's interpretation of the data seems quite compelling. The position taken here, then, is that a simple developmental process in religion and architecture cannot explain why the solar cult became so dominant that it resulted in six sun temples being built in a period of about a century.

More than 60 years ago, John Wilson considered the emergence of a more powerful solar cult and priesthood in 24th century B.C. as reaction against "the political absolutism of the king" that had prevailed in the 4th Dynasty.[140] He considered the shrinking pyramid and the building of the sun temples as evidence for "the rebellion of Re against the pharaoh."[141] Put another way, the son of Re (as the massive size of the 4th Dynasty pyramids demonstrate) had superseded Re himself. It is certainly true, in support of Wilson's proposal, that the power of the pharaoh would never achieve the heights it had enjoyed in the previous era, and by the 6th Dynasty royal authority had waned considerably, power had been decentralized from the royal family, and provincial governors assumed greater authority.[142]

The name of Userkaf's solar edifice may offer a further hint that a radical development had occurred. *Nḫn Rʿ*—"Re's Stronghold" is a surprisingly militaristic name for a temple. The word *nḫn* echoes the name of Nekhen, the Upper Egyptian capital

---

139 Dieter Arnold, "Royals Cult Complexes of the Old and Middle Kingdoms," in *Temples of Ancient Egypt* (ed. B. Shafer; Ithaca, NY: Cornell University Press, 1997), 61–63,

140 John Wilson, *The Culture of Egypt* (Chicago: University of Chicago Press, 1951), 87.

141 Loc. cit.

142 Barry Kemp, "Old Kingdom, Middle Kingdom and Second Intermediate Period, c. 2686-1552," in *Ancient Egypt a Social History* (eds. B. Trigger, B. Kemp, D. O'Connor, & A. Lloyd; Cambridge: Cambridge University Press, 1983), 107–112.

and stronghold from which came the early pharaohs who forcefully united Egypt. Hence, Verner wonders if the choice of this name for the first sun temple "give(s) symbolic expression to the final victory in the struggle to assert the cult of Re and the invincibility of the stronghold of the new faith?"[143]

Wilson and Verner's views, though somewhat different, agree that religio-political factors were involved in the appearance of sun temples at this time that represent a new and different expression of solar worship. Fragmentary reliefs from Niuserre's Abu Ghurab complex depict the king conducting the Sed-festival,[144] the renewal of kingship, which was celebrated in life and in the afterlife (hence the Sed court in the Djoser pyramid complex). When this factor is considered, along with the placement of sun temples on the west side of the Nile in the necropolis region, it has led to the credible theory that just as the pyramid complexes were designed to assist the king in his renewal and ascension to the heavenly realm, the solar shrines functioned to do the same for the sun as it died in the west.[145]

CONCLUDING OBSERVATIONS

The sources reviewed above, be they textual (e.g., PTs, personal names, royal titles), architectural (e.g., temple at On, pyramids, obelisks, *bnbn*-stones, sun temples), or iconographic (e.g., the sphinx, uraei, sun-disc) leave no doubt that solar theology played an increasingly powerful role in the religion and royalty in the 4th Dynasty, reaching its apex in the 5th Dynasty. In fact Málek has observed that in the 24th century B.C. Re had achieved a status approximating "a state god."[146]

It is the contention of this study that the 5th Dynasty represents the golden age of Egyptian history when the sun ruled Egypt, and it is this era that Akhenaten, a thousand years later, sought to revive, and then transform into a genuine monotheistic religion.

---

143 Verner, *Abusir*, 71.

144 Mathias Rochholz, "Sedfest, Sonnenheiligtum und Pyramidbezirk. Zur Deutung der Grabanlagen der Könige der 5. und 6. Dynastie," in *Agyptsiche Tempel—Struktur, Funktion und Program* (eds. R. Gundlach & M. Rochholz; Mainz: Hamburg Ägyptishe Beitrage, 1994), 255–280.

145 Rainer Stadelmann, *Die ägyptischen Pyramiden* (Mainz: Harrassowitz, 1991), 164. Rochholz, "Sedfest, Sonnenheiligtum und Pyramidbezirk," 255–280.

146 Málek, "The Old Kingdom," 99.

Chapter 2

Far Frontiers

Sky and Sun Together

THE COLLAPSE

THE PROTRACTED REIGN of Pepi II toward the end of the 6th Dynasty (2350–2190 B.C.) in many ways marked the end of the Old Kingdom. The king reigned for at least 90 years, according to the Turin canon of kings; 99 years is the figure preserved in Manetho![1] During his final decades he was surely decrepit and feeble, which seems to parallel the downward spiral of the power and prestige of the kingly office and Egypt itself. A number of factors doubtless contributed to the demise of the great Old Kingdom that had become moribund. A weakened king and the emergence of powerful regional officials made Egypt politically vulnerable to fragmentation. Then, too, there is growing scientific evidence that low Niles and drought may have further contributed to bad economic times.[2] These

---

[1] Manetho allots 99 years, a figure that agrees with the Ramesside era Turin Canon, which has 90 + years; see A. H. Gardiner, *Egypt of the Pharaohs* (Oxford: Oxford University Press, 1961), 436.

[2] J.-D. Stanley et al., "Short Contribution: Nile Flow Failure at the End of the Old Kingdom, Egypt: Strontium Isopotic and Petrologic Evidence," *Geo-Archaeology: An International Journal* 18, no. 3 (2003): 395–402. Michel Baud, "The Old Kingdom," in *A Companion to Ancient Egypt* I (ed. A. B. Lloyd; Oxford: Wiley-Blackwell, 2010), 78–80. M. Bárta & A. Bezdek, "Beetles and the Decline of the Old Kingdom: Climate Change in Ancient Egypt," in *Proceedings of the Conference Held in Prague (June 11–14, 2007)* (Prague: Charles University, 2008), 215–224. Karin Sowada, "Evidence for Late Third Millennium Weather Events from a Sixth Dynasty Tomb at Saqqara," *Studia Quaternaria*, vol. 30, no. 2 (2013): 69–74. Miroslav Bárta, "In Mud Forgotten: Old Kingdom Paleolecological Evidence from Abusir," *Studia Quaternaria*, vol. 30, no. 2 (2013): 75–82.

causes brought Egypt to what is commonly known as the First Intermediate Period (2160–2106 B.C.). The fragmentation that had begun in the 5th and 6th Dynasties fully bloomed into periods of civil strife, with multiple pharaohs claiming rival thrones. The breakdown in central authority and the attendant cultural decay after Pepi II's reign resulted in the dearth of firsthand written sources during this period, and major architectural activities ground to a halt. As a consequence of a hiatus in data, we are often in the dark about what transpired, and one has to look to later sources that may reflect on this period, even if that information is stereotypical and exaggerated. Literature from the early 12th Dynasty (1960–1940 B.C.), such as the Prophecy of Neferti, seems to have this tumultuous period in mind when gloomy pictures are portrayed of the recent past:

> The land is shrunk—its rulers are many, it is bare—its taxes are great; the grain is low—the measure is large, it is measured to overflowing. Re will withdraw from mankind, though he will rise at his hour, one will not know when noon has come.[3]

Reference to the sun not shining properly may have a metaphorical meaning that relates to the proper function of the land as envisioned by the creator god Re, who established *m3ʿt* (justice, order, and the Egyptian way!). The king, who was the son of Re, was ordained to ensure that *m3ʿt* prevailed, and the anti-*m3ʿt* forces, *isft* and *grg*, were kept at bay.[4]

The last line before Neferti's prophecy turns from the crisis caused by the chaos in Egypt to the messianic hope that would reverse Egypt's plight: "Gone from the earth is the nome[5] of On, the birthplace of every god."[6] This statement seems to acknowledge a breakdown in the proper cultic practice at Heliopolis, which in turn may account for the cosmic and social disorder. The tendency in ancient Egypt was to blame domestic and cosmic failures on the ignoring of or not giving proper care

---

[3] Miriam Lichtheim, *Ancient Egyptian Literature* I (Berkeley: University of California Press, 1975), 142–143. For the text, see Wolfgang Helck, *Die Prophezeiung des* Nfr.tj (Wiesbaden: Harrassowitz, 1970).

[4] On kingship in Egypt, see Henri Frankfort, *Kingship and the Gods* (Chicago: University of Chicago Press, 1948), 15–214. Marie-Ange Bonhême & Annie Forgeau, *Pharaon: Les secrets du pouvoir* (Paris: Armand Colin, 1988). Numerous essays in D. O'Connor & D. Silverman, eds., *Ancient Egyptian Kingship* (Leiden: Brill, 1995). J. K. Hoffmeier, "The King as God's Son in Egypt and Israel," in *Papers Presented in Memory of Ronald J. Williams, JSSEA* 24 (1994): 28–38. P. J. Fransden, "Aspects of Kingship in Ancient Egypt," in *Religion and Power: Divine Kingship in the Ancient World and Beyond* (ed. Nicole Brisch; Chicago: The Oriental Institute, 2008), 47–73.

[5] The term used for Egyptian governing provinces.

[6] Lichtheim, *Ancient Egyptian Literature* I, 143.

to various cults.[7] "Then a king will come from the South, Ameny, the justified, by name," Neferti foretells, and "he will take the white crown, he will wear the red crown."[8] Ameny is a diminutive form of the name Amenemhet, which means "Amun is foremost" or "preeminent." By virtue of wearing the white and red crowns, he will be king of Upper and Lower Egypt; the prophecy continues to claim that he will set things right in Egypt, and will take on Egypt's foreign enemies, Asiatics and Libyans, and build border defenses to protect against foreign infiltration (a serious problem that began toward the end of the Old Kingdom). When this happens, Neferti concludes, "then Order (*m3ʿt*) will return to its seat, while Chaos (*ỉsft*) is driven away."[9] As it turns out, it was anticipating Amenemhet I, the founder of the 12th Dynasty, who would bring about this reversal (even though Egypt had already been reunited several decades earlier in the 11th Dynasty!).

The Admonitions of Ipuwer contains similar themes, including complaints that there were problems with the flow of the Nile and farming, birth rates were down, the distant lands of Byblos and Crete were no longer reached by ships to bring luxury items back to Egypt, and the social order was completely reversed.[10] "What the pyramid hid is empty" Ipuwer claims,[11] suggesting that during the previous intermediate period the royal tombs were looted. He continues: "See now, the land is deprived of kingship . . . [Stolen] is the crown of Re, who pacifies the Two Lands."[12]

---

[7] During the reign of Ahmose, there was a terrific and devastating storm that some connect to the eruption of Santorini and the tidal wave that struck Egypt. This happened because "the gods were vexed, they were angry" (Donald Redford, "Textual Sources for the Hyksos Period," in *The Hyksos: New Historical and Archaeological Perspectives* [ed. E. D. Oren; Philadelphia: University Museum, 1997], 16). In response, Ahmose began a program of restoring temples that had decayed. Another example is found during Hatshepsut's reign. She restored the temple of Hathor at Cusae in Middle Egypt; she describes it as having fallen into ruin. She restored and staffed other temples, too, and seems to associate this neglect due to the presence of the Asiatic Hyksos (A. H. Gardiner, "Davies Copy of The Great Speos Artemidos Inscription," *JEA* 32 [1946]: 43–56). For a more recent translation, see Redford, "Textual Sources for the Hyksos Period," 16–18.

[8] Ibid., 16–18.

[9] Ibid., 16–18.

[10] The dating of the Admonitions is debated. Gardiner thought it was a Middle Kingdom text that reflected on the turmoil of the 1st Intermediate Period (A. H. Gardiner, *The Admonitions of an Egyptian Sage* (Leipzig: J. C. Hinrichs, 1909). Some now think it comes from the 2nd Intermediate Period (J. Van Seters, "A Date for the 'Admonitions' in the Second Intermediate Period," *JEA* 50 [1964]: 13–23). Lichtheim holds that this document does not reflect historical realities, but is a highly exaggerated "composition on the theme 'order versus chaos,'" (Lichtheim, *Ancient Egyptian Literature* I, 150). In my view, there may be hyperbole used here, but these do derive from bitter memories of the past dark ages, and are not inconsistent with data that emerge from archaeological sources and contemporary texts. Some would agree that these literary texts contain at least "kernels of historical truth" (Harco Willems, "The First Intermediate Period and the Middle Kingdom," in *A Companion of Ancient Egypt*, Vol. 1 (ed. A. B. Lloyd; Oxford: Wiley-Blackwell, 2010), 83).

Translations of the Admonitions, see Lichtheim, *Ancient Egyptian Literature* I, 150–163; R. O. Faulkner, "The Admonitions of an Egyptian Sage," in *The Literature of Ancient Egypt* (ed. W. K. Simpson; New Haven, CT: Yale University Press, 1973), 210–219.

[11] Lichtheim, *Ancient Egyptian Literature* I, 156.

[12] Ibid., 156.

These literary compositions seem to be supported by some texts of the period in question, such as the biography of Ankhtifi, a powerful governor of the nome south of Thebes, centered at Edfu.[13] He claims to have militarily unified the nomes to his north, Thebes and Coptos, and thought of himself as a mini-ruler, but he did not have the audacity to call himself king. He does, however, claim that Horus brought him to his position. He also boasts that

> I gave bread to the hungry and clothing to the naked; I anointed those who had not cosmetic oil; I gave sandals to the barefooted, I gave a wife to him who had no wife, I took care of the towns of Hefat and Hor-mer in every [situation of crisis, when] the sky was clouded and the earth [was parched (?) and when everybody died] of hunger... The whole country has become like locusts going upstream and downstream (in search of food); but never did I allow anybody in need to go from his nome to another one.[14]

There is some reason to question the military successes of Ankhtifi and the extent of his power, but it is going too far in the minimalist direction to dismiss such claims as "literary topoi," as some recent scholars claim.[15] The fact that boasting and hyperbole occur does not mean that the general picture offered in this biography is fiction. Low Niles and consequent famine and hunger were realities of ancient riverine cultures, and Egypt was no exception. One concurs with Stephan Seidlmayer that "there can be no doubt that these texts indeed relate to fact," he reasons, because more sober reports from the same period agree with Ankhtifi's claims.[16]

Eventually two power centers emerged from the fragmented and decentralized Egypt. In the north there was Herakleopolis (located south of Memphis); its rival in the south was Thebes. Dynasties 9 and 10, often known as the Herakleopolitan period, are remembered for producing some classical literature, such as the Eloquent Peasant and the Instruction for Merikare, and in the funerary arena, the Coffin Texts began to be produced in both areas of Egypt.

In Merikare, the future king is offered insights and advice from his father Meryibre-Khety I (ca. 2150 B.C.) about being an effective ruler. In lines 69–74, the king makes a startling admission of wrongdoing. Candid confession by a pharaoh would not be expected during the Old, Middle, or New Kingdoms.

---

[13] J. Vandier, *Mo'alla: La tombe d'Anktifi et la tombe de Sebekhotep* (Cairo: Bibliothèque d'étude 18, 1950).

[14] Stephan Seidlmayer, "The First Intermediate Period (c. 2160–2055)," in *The Oxford History of Ancient Egypt* (ed. Ian Shaw; Oxford: Oxford University Press, 2000), 118–119.

[15] Willems, "The First Intermediate Period and the Middle Kingdom," 83.

[16] Seidlmayer, "The First Intermediate Period," 119.

> Troops will fight troops as the ancestors foretold; Egypt fought in the graveyard, destroying tombs in vengeful destruction. As I did it, so it happened, as is done to one who strays from god's path. Do not deal evilly (*bin*) with the Southland . . . I attacked This (the Abydos nome) to its southern border. I engulfed it like a flood; King Meryibre, justified, had done it.[17]

After 45 lines of discussing other matters, he returns to this incident:

> Lo, a shameful deed occurred in my time: the nome of This was ravaged; though it happened through my doing, I learned it after it was done. There was retribution for what I had done, for it is evil to destroy, useless to restore what one has damaged, to rebuild what one has demolished.[18]

These passages bear witness to military action between the Herakleopolitans and the Theban domain. Apparently this particular battle occurred in a sacred burial area of Abydos that caused significant damage. Meryibre, uncharacteristically for a pharaoh, takes the blame, even though he was not directly involved, nor had he commanded his troops to desecrate the long revered necropolis that went back to the end of the 4th millennium B.C. There is also acknowledgment that fitting divine retribution was leveled against him: perhaps a stinging military defeat in subsequent battles?

Some scholars question the use of wisdom literature for historical reconstruction. Gun Björkman, in particular, rejected relying on King Meryibre's claims and suggested that "it might be, more or less, a product of his imagination."[19] This explanation is excessively skeptical. What makes Meryibre's confessions credible is that Egyptian kings rarely admit wrongdoing, and there is no political advantage for this monarch to make such an admission. The reality is that pharaohs typically do not report on failures, or they turn them propagandistically into successes! No such thing happens in this wisdom text. Furthermore, wisdom texts typically do not contain historical information,[20] so one should consider the king's *mea culpa* and the calamity that resulted from the debacle at Abydos as instrumental to his instruction. Consequently, one ought to consider the descriptions of fighting in Abydos as reflecting the struggle between north and south in the 1st Intermediate Period.

---

17 Lichtheim, *Ancient Egyptian Literature* I, 102.

18 Lichtheim, *Ancient Egyptian Literature* I, 105.

19 Gun Björkman, "Egyptology an Historical Method," *Orientalia Suecana* 13 (1964): 11.

20 An exception to this general practice is the Instruction of Amenemhet, where the king mentions some of his acts, including details surrounding his assassination, see R. O. Faulkner, "The Teaching of Ammenemes I to His Son Sesostris," in *The Literature of Ancient Egypt* (New Haven, CT: Yale University Press), 193–197.

THE RISE OF THEBES

Ancient Waset, dubbed "Thebes" by the Greeks in later times, has been described as a "third-rate provincial town"[21] that grew in size and political importance during the 1st Intermediate Period. The 11th Dynasty Theban ruler Intef II (2090–2041 B.C.) is the first to reclaim the old regal titles, such as Son of Re and King of Upper and Lower Egypt,[22] and there is textual evidence to suggest that he built some sort of temple called "the abode of Amun" in Karnak.[23] He pushed Theban control north to include Abydos (the Thinite Nome). Tjetji, his treasurer, refers to his sovereign's control of the land from Elephantine (Egypt's southern frontier town) to Abydos in the north.[24] Clearly, the sacred city of Abydos was a site whose control was desired for historical, religious, and political reasons by both the south and the north. Meryibre's allusions to the fighting at Abydos are a testimony to that desire.

Historians generally agree that under the reign of the later 11th Dynasty Theban king Montuhotep II, Egypt was reunited politically after a period of war, thus ending the 1st Intermediate Period and ushering in the Middle Kingdom. He altered his Horus name twice. The third, *sm3 t3.wy* (Uniter of the Two Lands), which was assumed in his 37th regnal year, signaled the final unity of Upper and Lower Egypt.[25] Two more kings followed, also named Montuhotep, that marked the end of the 11th Dynasty. The fact that the last four rulers of this family bore the name Montuhotep indicates that the influence of Montu, previously a little-known Theban deity, had begun to grow. Representations of Montu regularly portray him in human form with a falcon head, on top of which was a sun-disc (Figure 2.1). The cult of Montu in Thebes may go back to the Old Kingdom,[26] evidently predating the emergence of Amun.

There are strong connections between Montu and the solar religion of Heliopolis (Eg. On).[27] In fact, the Egyptian name of his cult center at Armant (from Greek Hermonthis), just south of Thebes, is *iwn(w)-mntw*, "On of Montu," and among its titles are "Armant of On,"[28] and "On of Upper Egypt."[29]

During the New Kingdom (ca. 1550–1100 B.C.), Montu became virtually a god of war. He is often shown in martial contexts, such as guiding Thutmose IV, who fires

---

[21] Seidlmayer, "The First Intermediate Period (c. 2160–2055)," 123.

[22] Gardiner, *Egypt of the Pharaohs*, 119. Jürgen von Beckerath, *Handbuch der ägyptishen Königsnamen* (Mainz: Philipp von Zabern, 1999), 77.

[23] Nicholas Grimal, *A History of Egypt* (Oxford: Blackwell, 1992), 298.

[24] Lichtheim, *Ancient Egyptian Literature* I, 91.

[25] Grimal, *A History of Egypt*, 155–157. Gardiner, *Egypt of the Pharaohs*, 119.

[26] Grimal, *A History of Egypt*, 298.

[27] Edward Werner, "Montu," in *OEAE* II, 435–436.

[28] Ibid., 435–436. A. H. Gardiner, *Ancient Egyptian Onomastica* II (London: Oxford University Press, 1947), *23.

[29] Ibid., 24*.

FIGURE 2.1 Montu of Thebes (Karnak Temple). Photo James K. Hoffmeier.

his bow while driving his chariot;[30] on a ivory bracelet in Berlin, Montu stands before Thutmose IV as he smites his foes. The Sphinx Stela describes the militaristic Amenhotep II (Figure 1.11), as having "the might of Montu in his limbs" . . . "he was acquainted with the works of Montu" . . . and "his majesty appeared on his chariot like Montu in his strength."[31] In all, Montu's name occurs six times on that stela.

Montu, then, enjoyed a rapid rise in power in Thebes with the 11th Dynasty rulers, but was soon eclipsed in the 12th Dynasty, when a new royal family followed who instigated the ascendancy of another Theban deity, namely, Amun. Although Montu's prominence waned, in later times he continued to play an important role in military matters, as already noted.

---

30 Howard Carter & Percy Newberry, *The Tomb of Thoutmôsis IV* (London: Archibald Constable, 1904), pl. X.

31 *Urk.* IV, 1278.14, 1279.11, 1280.18.

AMUN LORD OF THE TWO LANDS

Amun's origin remains shrouded in mystery, which seems fitting since his name *ỉmn* means "the hidden one" or "the secret one."[32] When written as a verb or adjective, *ỉmn* uses the classifier of a squatting man hiding under a shelter, but this sign is not used in writing the deity's name.[33] In the Book of the Dead (Spell 165), dating from New Kingdom times, Amun is presented as "the eldest of the gods (of) the east of the sky, Amon, thou hidden of aspect, mysterious of form" . . . "thy name is Hidden One."[34] It is apparent that Amun's very name communicates something about him. When depicted in relief or as a statue, Amun is invariably shown as a man, often as a bluc figure that likely represented the air in the sky. His flat crown has a pair of tall plumes standing on it (Figure 2.2).

FIGURE 2.2 Ramesses II before Amun-Re (Karnak Temple). Photo James K. Hoffmeier.

[32] V. A. Tobin, "Amun and Amun-Re," *OEAE* 1, 82.

[33] *Wb* 1, 83–84.

[34] T. G. Allen, *The Book of the Dead or Going Forth by Day* (Chicago: University of Chicago Press, 1974), 161.

The Ramesside Period artisan Nebre details in a hymn how he had experienced Amun's wrath due to his wrongdoing. After Nebre's contrition, however, he experienced divine forgiveness and restoration, which he described as "[h]is breath come back to us in mercy, Amun returns upon his breeze."[35] Though pietistic, Nebre's confession reveals that he encountered the deity in a tangible way through a pleasant breeze illustrating his invisible nature that could still be experienced by humans.

There is a dearth of information about Amun in the Old Kingdom. He is only named twice in the Pyramid Texts (PTs), and these occurrences tell us little about this deity. In Spell 301, Amun and his consort Amunet are listed among other deities who receive bread offerings (PT §446c).[36] In Spell 579, the king is called the "son of Geb (who is) upon the throne of Amun" (PT §1540). The title "throne of Amun" seems to anticipate the title that originated in the Middle Kingdom, that is, "lord of the thrones of the two lands."[37] The Coffin Texts from the 1st Intermediate Period and Middle Kingdom mention Amun by name only once (CT VII, 470), which is unexpected since it is during this period that Amun begins to emerge as a major player in Egyptian religion. He is thought to be associated with the Eight-Chaos or Primeval Deities: Nun (primeval sea), Hehu (boundlessness), Keku (darkness), and Amun (air), and their female counterparts,[38] but he is not specifically named as one of the Eight-Chaos gods in the CTs. Subsequent New Kingdom theological interpretation connects Amun and the Eight-Chaos gods. The Leiden Hymns to Amun, for example, offer the following explanation:

> The Eight Great Gods were your first incarnation to complete this world, while you were one alone. Your body was hidden among the oldest primordial beings, for you had concealed yourself as Amun from the face of the gods.[39]

The point is that Amun was somehow mysteriously "hidden" and "concealed" among primeval gods. These eight deities are associated with the town of Khenemu (meaning "eight") in Middle Egypt, whose name survives in the Arabic name of the village, Ashmunein. It seems either that Amun was present but obscured (in keeping with his name) in the CTs, or, more likely, that later theological reflection used the ambiguity to place him among the primeval deities.

---

[35] Lichtheim, *Ancient Egyptian Literature* I, 107.

[36] R. O. Faulkner, *The Ancient Egyptian Pyramid Texts* (Oxford: Clarendon Press, 1969), 90.

[37] *Wb* 2, 322.10.

[38] Kurt Sethe, *Amun und die acht Urgotten von Hermopolis* (Berlin: Abhandlungen der Preussischen Academie der Wissenschaften, 1929). Siegfried Morenz, *Egyptian Religion* (Ithaca, NY: Cornell University Press, 1973), 175. James K. Hoffmeier, "Genesis 1 & 2 and Egyptian Cosmology," *JANES* 15 (1983): 42–44.

[39] John Foster, *Hymns, Prayers, and Songs: An Anthology of Ancient Egyptian Lyric Poetry* (Atlanta: Scholars Press, 1995), 74.

One reason for the limited role played by Amun in the CTs is that they were largely a continuity of the PTs' (with some new materials added) tradition, whose focus is largely funerary in nature. And, as noted above, Amun is an inconsequential character in the PTs, probably because he lacked mortuary connections. Another factor in the dearth of references to Amun in the CTs (despite the fact that their development coincides with Amun's emergence as a major player) is that approximately 70 percent of the coffins in de Buck's seven volumes of CTs come from central Egypt, while only about 10.7 percent originate in Thebes.[40] The new spells in the CTs, such as the Book of Two Ways, are found almost exclusively in coffins from el-Bersheh in Middle Egypt. Consequently, it is not surprising that the CTs offer little information about the ascendancy of Amun.

The best indicator of Amun's rise to prominence is that suddenly, with the founder of the 12th Dynasty, the name of Amun is incorporated into his birth name, Amenemhet. Amenemhet means "Amen/Amun is foremost." Four kings of the 12th Dynasty embraced this name. Clearly, the choice of this name was a religio-political affirmation, and with it, Amun vaulted to great heights in the 12th Dynasty. Furthermore, Amun's growing status is demonstrated by the fact that more than 30 personal theophoric names have been documented in the Middle Kingdom that employ the name of Amun, which are borne by non-royal individuals.[41]

The background of Amenemhet I (1963–1934 B.C.) and why he embraced and elevated Amun are not known, although Grimal is certainly on the right track when he thinks that the name gives testimony to his religio-political agenda: "his own name (i.e. Amenemhet), served to announce a political programme that was to combine the primacy of Amun with return to Heliopolitan theology"[42] (more on this in the following sections). It is widely believed that he was the vizier named "Amenemhet" who led quarrying expeditions on behalf of Montuhotep IV, the final monarch of Dynasty 11.[43] The king seemingly died without an heir, opening the way for Amenemhet to step into the vacancy and take power.

The literature from this period offers no explanation about why Amenemhet I was so interested in the deity behind his name. Since Amenemhet was his name

---

[40] That is, 16 out of 149 sources in de Buck's seven volumes are from Thebes. For a study of the regional developments and regional variants, see James K. Hoffmeier, "Are There Regionally Based Theological Differences in the Coffin Texts," in *The World of the Coffin Texts: Proceedings of the Symposium Held on the Occasion of the 100th Birthday of Adriaan de Buck, Leiden, December 17–19, 1992* (ed. Harco Willems; Leiden: Nederlands Instituut voor het Nabije Oosten: 1996), 45–54.

[41] Hermann Ranke, *Die Ägyptischen Personennamen* I (Glückstadt: J. J. Augustin, 1935), 26–32.

[42] Grimal, *A History of Ancient Egypt*, 159.

[43] Detlef Franke, "Amenemhet I," *OEAE* 1, 68. Grimal, *A History of Ancient Egypt*, 158–159. Gae Callender, "The Middle Kingdom Renaissance (c. 2055–1650 B.C.)," in *Oxford History of Ancient Egypt* (ed. Ian Shaw; Oxford: Oxford University Press, 2000), 144–145.

when he was an official, it was obviously given at birth, indicating that Amun's influence was already growing in the Thebaid toward the end of the 11th Dynasty.

Inscriptions left by vizier Amenemhet from the Wadi Hammamat mentioned the above report on the miracles (*biꜣ*) that took place during the expedition. Gae Callender has made the cogent observation that they "appear to signal that he was the one for whom miracles were performed."[44] The inscriptions left by Vizier Amenemhet near the site of the theophanies were recorded "for his father Min, lord of the highlands," and "Min of Coptos."[45] Min was credited with the miracles, one of which was a rainstorm (a rare phenomenon in the Red Sea Desert!) that provided much needed water for the expedition force of 3,000.[46]

Min's original cult center was in Coptos, north of Thebes, and can be traced back to pre-dynastic times.[47] This ithyphallic fertility god in the Middle Kingdom became closely associated with Amun. Richard Wilkinson has observed that "the Amun-Min association had direct political overtones, however, and from Middle Kingdom times the coronations and jubilee festivals of the pharaoh seem to have incorporated rituals of Min aimed at promoting the potency of the king."[48]

The White Chapel of Senusert I (1943–1898 B.C.), one of the oldest surviving edifices at Karnak, contains vitally important textual and iconographic data on the religious developments of the early 12th Dynasty (Figure 2.3). The iconography of Amun-Re varies considerably in this elegantly carved chapel.[49] First he is presented in the traditional manner as man and, like the king, wearing a kilt with a bull's tail that hangs down from the belt on his back side. In each case, two tall plumes adorn his head, but in some instances they stand on a flat-base crown that looks like the red crown (less the tall rear portion) (Figure 2.4).[50] In other cases, the feathers are secured to the head by a band or fillet[51] (Figure 2.5). In both cases, a ribbon flows down from the back of the diadem.

A second form is that in which Amun-Re is presented with the iconographic features of Min. Min is normally portrayed as a man standing, mummy-formed (like

---

[44] Callender, "The Middle Kingdom Renaissance (c. 2055–1650 B.C.)," 146.

[45] Adriaan de Buck, *Egyptian Reading Book* (Leiden: Nederlands Instituut voor het Nabjje Oosten, 1970), 74.11, 75.5.

[46] The figure of 3,000 is found in de Buck, *Egyptian Reading Book*, 75.9.

[47] Eugene Romanosky, "Min," in *OEAE* 2, 413–415.

[48] Richard Wilkinson, *The Complete Gods and Goddesses of Ancient Egypt* (London: Thames & Hudson, 2003), 155. On the Sed-festival connections, see Hermann Kees, "Die Weisse Kapelle Sesostris I. in Karnak und das *sed*-fest," *MDAIK* 16 (1958): 194ff.

[49] Pierre Lacau & Henri Chevrier, *Une Chapelle de Sésostris Ier à Karnak* (Cairo: IFAO, 1956), idem. *Une Chapelle de Sésostris Ier a Karnak, Planches* (Cairo: IFA, 1969).

[50] Lacau & Chevrier, *Une Chapelle de Sésostris Ier à Karnak, Planches*, e.g., pl. 12, scenes 1 & 2; 14, scenes 5 & 6; 16 scene 10.

[51] For examples, see ibid., pl. 16, scene 9; 17 scene 12; 24 scene 25.

FIGURE 2.3 White Chapel of Senusert I (Karnak Temple). Photo James K. Hoffmeier.

Osiris), with erect phallus (his most characteristic attribute), and standing with feet together perched on a shoebox-sized stand.[52] In scenes where Min is depicted, a patch of growing lettuce often stands behind him and/or a worshiper extends his arm with a head of lettuce to the deity, which further demonstrates that lettuce is associated with Min (Figure 2.6).[53] In the White Chapel, however, the Min-like deity is always identified as Amun-Re or Amun, while Min's name does not occur, neither as Amun-Min.[54] Indeed, the majority of depictions of Amun/Amun-Re on the White Chapel are in the ithyphallic form, and there are more than a dozen examples where lettuce is shown, either growing behind the standing deity or in the hand of the presenter.[55] Then, too, there are several instances in the White Chapel where the Min-like figures bear the name *ỉmn kȝ mwt.f*, "Amun Bull of his mother."[56] This epithet, which begins at this time, is associated with the fertility aspect of Amun,[57] and thus would be similar to Min. Evidently, the White Chapel celebrates the fusion

[52] Wilkinson, *The Complete Gods and Goddesses of Ancient Egypt*, 115–116.

[53] Ludwig Keimer, "Die Pflanze des Gottes Min," *ZÄS* 59 (1924): 140–143.

[54] For examples, see ibid., pl. 17, scenes 12 & 13; 18 scenes 13 & 14; 20 scenes 17 & 18; 21 scene 20. With the writing only of Amun, see pl. 32 scene 12'; 40, scenes 28'.

[55] Lacau & Chevrier, *Une Chapelle de Sésostris Ier a Karnak, Planches*, pl. 20, scenes 17; 21 scene 19 & 20; 22 scene 21; 23 scenes 23 & 24; 26 scenes 29 & 30; 29 scenes 5' & 6'; 35 scene 17'; 36 scene 19'; 38 scene 26'.

[56] Ibid., pl. 20 scene 18; 21 scene 19; 32 scene 14'.

[57] Wilkinson, *The Complete Gods and Goddesses of Ancient Egypt*, 93.

FIGURE 2.4 Senusert I and Amun (White Chapel Karnak Temple). Photo James K. Hoffmeier.

FIGURE 2.5 Ithyphallic form of Amun (White Chapel Karnak Temple). Photo James K. Hoffmeier.

FIGURE 2.6 Amun-Re as Min with lettuce plants (White Chapel Karnak Temple). Photo Willeke Wendrich.

of Min and Amun-Re in Thebes.[58] The conjoining of Amun and Re had apparently already taken place during the reign of Amenemhet I. Unfortunately, no Theban temple of Amenemhet that might have celebrated that union exists or has survived.

Senusert I did build another limestone chapel at Karnak that was also dedicated to Amun-Re. To judge from the extant blocks present in the open air museum at Karnak, Amun-Re appears in his traditional form (Figure 2.7).[59] Here there is no trace of the ithyphallic form.

---

[58] Further on the politics and art of Senusert I, see now David Lorand, *Arts et Politique sous Sesostris Ier: Littérature, sculpture et architecture dan leur contexte historique* (Turnhout: Brepols, 2012).

[59] Blocks from this chapel are on display in the open-air museum at Karnak Temple, which the author was able to examine in March 2013.

FIGURE 2.7 Amun-Re in another limestone chapel (Karnak Temple). Photo James K. Hoffmeier.

Could it be that even though Amun was not a major player in the 11th Dynasty, he was launched to the place of supremacy as Amenemhet's influence grew? Accepting Callender's theory that the revelations of Min in the eastern desert were for Amenemhet's benefit (i.e., to create some legitimacy for the non-royal successor), it might be suggested that they were subsequently interpreted as manifestations of Amun. This may explain the unexpected association between Min of Coptos and Amun of Thebes, and why the iconography of the White Chapel of Senusert I at Karnak treats them as one and the same. This fusion may have been facilitated because the two names, Amun and Min, are homophonous: *ỉmn* and *mn(w)*.

It is noteworthy that Senusert I also built a temple at Heliopolis. All that remains of this temple to the sun-god is a lone obelisk, which Labib Habachi observed "is the oldest surviving obelisk."[60] The second obelisk of the pair has not survived, although

[60] Labib Habachi, *The Obelisks of Egypt* (Cairo: American University Press, 1984), 47.

it appears to have been standing as recently as the 4th century A.D. since a Christian writer refers to idols of Heliopolis and reports that "there are two great columns which excite admiration."[61] The fact that the 12th Dynasty rulers built at Heliopolis, thereby honoring Re/Atum, shows that the emergence of Amun of Thebes did not obscure the old sun-god of On; rather there was a coalescence of the two.

THE ORIGINS OF AMUN-RE

At some point early in the 12th Dynasty, one of the most enduring mergers occurred, that of Amun of Thebes and Re of Heliopolis. It is conceivable that this religious union was motivated by political considerations. After the political breach and hostilities between the north and the south during the preceding intermediate period, and the mysterious circumstances under which Amenemhet seized the throne, gestures and policies to promote the unity of the nation were sorely needed. The politically savvy Amenemhet recognized this need and took several steps to unite the land. His initial Horus name was "Calming or Pacifying the Heart of the Two Lands"—*sḥtp ỉb t3.wy*, while his prenomen was "Calming or Pacifying the Heart of Re"—*sḥtp ỉb r*.[62] In his seventh year, the Horus name was changed to *wḥm mswt*,[63] literally meaning "repeating births" or "Renaissance Era." This name suggests that Egypt had embarked on a new epoch,[64] which may coincide with the next measure he took.

Amenemhet I also established a new capital just south of Memphis, the Old Kingdom capital. According to the tradition preserved in the Memphite Theology, or Shabaka Stone, Memphis became the capital of a unified Egypt after the clash between Horus and Seth (symbolic of the wars between Upper and Lower Egypt that resulted in the beginning of Dynastic Egypt and rule by one pharaoh). In the Memphite Theology the epithet "Balance of the Two Lands" (*mḫ3t t3.wy*) is used for Memphis.[65] The pertinent lines recall that Horus and Seth were "pacified and unified"—*ḥtpw sm3w* (line 15c).[66] Memphis therefore was located at the balancing point of the two regions that had been at war. Apparently an awareness of this mytho-historical tradition is the reason Amenemhet I chose the site of his capital, just south of Memphis, and named it Amenemhet *ỉṯ-t3.wy*, "Amenemhet Seizer of

---

[61] Habachi, *The Obelisks of Egypt*, 47–48.

[62] Von Beckerath, *Handbuch der ägyptishen Königsnamen*, 82–83.

[63] Willems, "The First Intermediate Period and the Middle Kingdom," 90.

[64] At the coronation of a new king, the Horus name (and other titles) were adopted and were intended to reflect the new king's political aspirations.

[65] The dating of the Memphite Theology remains a subject of academic debate. Shabaka (716–702 B.C.) claims to have copied an ancient and tattered document on the stone so as to preserve it. Proposals range from the Old Kingdom and down to the New Kingdom.

[66] For the text of the Shabaka Stone, see J. H. Breasted, "The Philosophy of a Memphite Priest," *ZÄS* 39 (1901): pl. I, II.

the Two Lands." The choice of the name "Seizer of the Two Lands" hints that this union required some military action.[67]

There was also a strategic advantage of having the capital close to the Delta in order to control the north more effectively. The move north may have coincided with his decision to build his pyramid complex near his capital, a move that likely occurred early in his reign.[68] With this new city, apparently, the new era begins.

The third initiative made by Amenemhet I (and introduced above), and the most enduring, was the theological (and political) fusion of Amun of Thebes with Re of Heliopolis. The latter, as we noted in the previous chapter, was the god of the Egyptian state during the Old Kingdom. With the decline of the Old Kingdom, it has been suggested by Eberhard Otto that "the sun-god Ra . . . had become 'old' in the mythological parlance of the period."[69] The union of Amun and Re was a way of revitalizing Re with the new upstart Amun. Amun-Re possibly means "Amun who is Re."[70] The logic of this combination also proved to be a powerful way of uniting the emerging power of Thebes of the south with Re and his traditional powerful cult center at Heliopolis, which was situated in northern Egypt.

When exactly this union occurred is uncertain. The White Chapel of Senusert I provides iconographic and textual evidence that Amun-Re was already a singular deity. This edifice was built for the celebration of the Sed-festival of that king in conjunction with his thirtieth year (ca. 1913 B.C.). Architectural remains and stelae for the reign of Amenemhet I are limited indeed, and his capital (Itj-tawy), is yet to be located and excavated. Consequently there are little data available during Amenemhet I's reign to inform us about the circumstances and timing of the fusing of Amun and Re. One might speculate that such an action might have occurred in connection with the establishment of Itj-tawy as the new capital. Just as it became the new balance of the two lands, Amun-Re would now be "lord of the two lands."

AMUN-RE IN THE 18TH DYNASTY

After the interlude when foreign kings dominated Egypt between the Middle and New Kingdom, that is, the Hyksos period, Amun-Re quickly returned to his supreme position with the return of Theban kings to power. In fact, during the 18th Dynasty Amun-Re is viewed as the imperial god of Egypt.

Hatshepsut (1479–1457 B.C.) looked back on the days when foreign pastoralists roamed the land and the Hyksos (*ʿ3mw*—"Asiatics") reigned (ca. 1650–1540 B.C.),

---

[67] Gae Calender, "The Middle Kingdom Renaissance (c. 2055–1650 BC)," 146–147.

[68] So suggests Willems, "The First Intermediate Period and the Middle Kingdom," 90.

[69] Eberhard Otto, *Egyptian Art and the Cults of Osiris and Amon* (London: Thames & Hudson, 1968), 81.

[70] Otto, *Egyptian Art and the Cults of Osiris and Amon*, 81.

and said that "they ruled without Re, nor did he act by divine decree right down to my majesty('s time)!"[71] Naturally she is arguing that the Hyksos rulers were illegitimate as part of her apologetic to help legitimize herself. The charge that the Hyksos kings "ruled without Re" is no doubt true from an Egyptian point of view, but a review of the surviving names of Hyksos rulers shows that the name of Re was a part of the titulary.[72] Of the Hyksos kings whose names are recorded in contemporary sources, we find them written in hieroglyphs and within cartouches. Even when the pre-nomen is of Semitic origin, the nomens are Egyptian. For example, Khayan's throne name is *nṯr nfr swsr.n rʿ* = "The Good God Whom Re Has Strengthened"; Apophis I's nomen is *ʿ3 ḳni.n rʿ* = "Great Is the Bravery of Re"; Apophis (II?) includes in his name *nb ḫpš rʿ* = "Lord of a Powerful Arm Is Re"; Sheshi adds the name *m3ʿ ib rʿ* = "True Is the Heart of Re"; and Yacob-har calls himself *s3 rʿ mry wsr rʿ* = "Son of Re, Beloved Is the Strength of Re."[73] These names, and the use of the epithet "Son of Re," make it clear that even these foreign rulers recognized that kingship in Egypt did require the sun-god's support. Interestingly, Amun's name is absent in the royal names of the Hyksos kings.

The Theban rulers during the 2nd Intermediate Period continued to employ the Pharaonic titles Re, and occasionally Re is incorporated into royal names in the 17th Dynasty, while Amun's name is not found. Some examples are *nbw ḫrpw Rʿ* = Golden is Form of Re," *sḫm-Rʿ šd t3.wy* = "The Power of Re Rescues the Two Lands," and *snḫt.n Rʿ* = "The One Whom Re Made Victorious."[74]

As we approach the dawn of the New Kingdom, the name Re seems to enjoy regular use,[75] climaxing with Ahmose, who is of the Theban 17th Dynasty family, but is considered to be the founder of the 18th Dynasty and the New Kingdom. The name of Re is used in every royal name, and four monarchs of this dynasty were named Amenhotep ("Amun is satisfied"),[76] including Akhenaten.[77]

Information about Amun/Amun-Re's status during the 2nd Intermediate Period in the Theban region is negligible, in part because of the perpetual reuse of earlier temple blocks in later edifices at Karnak, combined with the fact that building activity on a grand scale during this period was limited indeed. Kamose's Karnak stela was actually carved on the backside of a pillar from a sanctuary of Senusert I (not the White Chapel).[78]

---

[71] Redford, "Textual Sources for the Hyksos Period," 17.

[72] The names of the earliest Hyksos kings, e.g., Salitis, Neon/Bnon, and Apachns/Pachnan are only known from Manetho in Greek.

[73] Beckerath, *Handbuch der ägyptishen Königsnamen*, 114–117.

[74] Ibid., 124–131.

[75] Ibid., 128–131.

[76] Ibid., 132–147.

[77] Ibid., 143.

[78] Gun Björkman, *Kings at Karnak: A Study of the Treatment of the Monuments of Royal Predecessors in the Early New Kingdom* (Upsala: Acta Universitatis Upsaliensis, 1971), 56.

On this stela and the Carnarvon Tablet, Kamose uses one of the timeless epithets for Amun-Re, "Lord of the Throne of the Two Lands."[79] At the end of his second stela, Kamose commands his chief officer User-neshi to record his military achievements on a stela at Karnak Temple in Thebes.[80] Evidently, Amun-Re's cult continued to flourish during the time between the two kingdom periods.

Amun-Re's return to prominence, if it was ever lost during the 2nd Intermediate Period, can be seen at the outset of the 18th Dynasty on a stela of King Ahmose discovered at Karnak Temple. The king calls himself "the beloved bodily son of Amun-Re" (*ỉmn-rꜥ sꜣ n ẖt.f mry.f*).[81] In line 6 of the stela, the king is described as "well loved like Amun" (*mrw.ty mỉ ỉmn*).[82] Later in the text, the divine protection of the king is put this way: "The holiness of Re is hovering over him, Amun being his protection."[83] Re and Amun are used in this text in synonymous parallelism, thereby equating the two deities.

While there are no standing buildings or inscribed blocks at Karnak from Ahmose's quarter-century reign, there is some textual evidence to suggest that the founder of the 18th Dynasty did build at Karnak. In year 22, Ahmose reopened the fine limestone quarry at Tura (Maâsara), just south of Cairo, and left an inscription indicating that he had reopened the quarry to obtain stone for building a temple for Ptah at Memphis, and for "Amun in Karnak" (*ỉmn m ỉpt sw*[*t*]).[84] The abovementioned Karnak stela ends with a list of donations of gold, silver, lapis lazuli, and turquoise "for his father Amun-Re."[85] It seems, then, that in addition to setting up a stela at Karnak, Ahmose also made offerings, and either renovated or expanded a temple, or constructed a chapel *de novo*.[86]

From the early 18th Dynasty, Paheri, mayor of Nekhen (south of Thebes), begins his lengthy tomb inscriptions with an offering formula of "Amun, Lord of the thrones of the Two Lands."[87] Later in the inscription he speaks of life in the beyond (which looks remarkably like life on earth!):

> You will look upon Re in the horizon of the sky (*ꜣḫt n(y)t pt*),
> You will glimpse Amun when he shines (*wbn.f*).[88]

---

[79] Frank T. Miosi, *A Reading Book of Second Intermediate Period Texts* (Toronto: Benben Publications, 1981), 35.9.

[80] Miosi, *A Reading Book of Second Intermediate Period Texts*, 52.14.

[81] *Urk.* IV, 14.8.

[82] *Urk.* IV, 15.15.

[83] *Urk.* IV, 18.15–16. For a discussion of this passage, see James K. Hoffmeier, *"Sacred" in the Vocabulary of Ancient Egypt* (*Orbis Biblicus et Orientalis* 59; Freiburg, Switzerland: Universitätsverlag, 1985), 165–167.

[84] *Urk.* IV, 25.10.

[85] *Urk.* IV, 22.3–23.9.

[86] Björkman, *Kings at Karnak,* 56 believes that a *ḥwt nt ḥḥ m rnpwt* was a chapel for royal statues.

[87] *Urk.* IV, 111.7.

[88] *Urk.* IV, 117.6–8.

The same parallelism found in the royal stela of the Ahmose is used here in a non-royal passage. Furthermore, Amun's solar attributes are made clear by the use of *wbn*, a standard term associated with the sun-god (see the previous chapter on *wbn*, and Chapter 5). The occurrence of Amun and Re in Paheri's tomb illustrates that the influence of Amun-Re went beyond royal circles.

Amun-Re's status grew in intensity over the following centuries. The burgeoning of Karnak Temple, destined to become the largest sanctuary complex anywhere in Egypt by the time of Ramesses II (ca. 1279–1213 B.C.), is a testimony to the power and influence of this deity. Nearly every king of the 18th Dynasty felt obliged to add to the complex in some manner to honor the patron of Thebes.

Amenhotep I (ca. 1525–1504 B.C.) erected a simple but elegant travertine (Egyptian alabaster) shrine to house the bark of Amun, the cult object of Amun-Re at Karnak (Figure 2.8). Inscribed on the shrine is a dedication to "Amun Lord of the Thrones of the Two Lands." Additionally, Amenhotep I built a limestone copy of the Senusert I shrine and some small chapels.[89]

The next ruler, Thutmose I (ca. 1504–1492 B.C.), was also active at Karnak, building the IVth and Vth Pylons and a pillared hall between them.[90] Significantly, Thutmose I set up a pair of granite obelisks, although only one stands today (Figure 2.9).[91] As noted in the previous chapter, the obelisk is a classic icon of solar theology. These granite monuments were 63.4 feet (19.5 m) high and weigh 143 tons.[92] On the obelisk, Thutmose I proclaims that "he made (it) as his monument for his father Amun-Re chief of the Two Lands, having set up two great obelisks at the double gates of the temple, the pyramidion (*bnb<n>t*) being (made) of electrum."[93] The significance of Thutmose I's obelisk project is that these were the first ones erected in Thebes, and this represents a transfer of the Heliopolitan Benben symbol to the realm of Amun, thereby further consolidating the fusion of the hidden one Amun and the sun-god Atum/Re.

Thutmose II's (ca. 1492–1479 B.C.) reign is not well documented and, as Betsy Bryan recently observed, "the nearly ephemeral nature of Thutmose II's rule is underlined by the paucity of his monuments generally, and their absence in the north of Egypt."[94] Despite this dearth of building activities, Thutmose II did build an impressive monumental gateway that must originally have stood in the axis of his predecessors pylons, but it was dismantled and incorporated into the 3rd Pylon by

---

[89] Björkman, *Kings at Karnak,* 58.

[90] Ibid., 61.

[91] Habachi, *The Obelisks of Egypt*, 57–61.

[92] Ibid., 116.

[93] *Urk.* IV, 93.5–7. Egyptian *ḏ3m* is "electrum," a gold-silver alloy.

[94] Betsy Bryan, "The 18th Dynasty before the Amarna Period (c. 1550-1352 B.C.)," in *The Oxford History of Ancient Egypt*, 226.

.FIGURE 2.8 Alabaster (travertine) shrine of Amenhotep I (Karnak Temple). Photo James K. Hoffmeier.

Amenhotep III. Its precise original location is not known, but it seems that it was removed for the erection of Hatsheptsut's obelisks.[95]

Just recently, in north Sinai a temple at Tell Hebua II (ancient Tjaru/Sile) was uncovered that can now be attributed to Thutmose II, based on at least four inscribed blocks containing his cartouche.[96] One inscribed panel depicts "Montu Lord of Thebes" presenting "life" to Thutmose II, while a second one shows the king being received by

---

[95] Björkman, *Kings at Karnak*, 64.

[96] M. Abd el-Maksoud & D. Valbelle, "Tell Héboua: Sur le décor et lépigraphie des elements architectoniques découverts au cours des campagnes 2008–2009 dans la zone centrale du *Khétem* de Tjarou," *Revue d'Égyptologie* 62 (2001): 2–3, 5–6, pl. 1, 3, II, V.

FIGURE 2.9 Obelisk of Thutmose I (Karnak Temple). Photo Stephen Moshier.

"Hathor Lady of (heaven)."[97] No one would have guessed that this king, whose imprint in Egypt is meager, would leave a substantial temple in Egypt's frontier town.

Thutmose II conducted a military campaign to Nubia to put down a revolt. He attributed his success to "his father Amun who loves him."[98] The connection between the military expansion of Egypt during the 15th century B.C. and Amun-Re only grows stronger with the reign of Thutmose III. In fact, expeditions and consequent victories were "ordained" (*wḏ*) by Amun-Re. On the 7th Pylon at Karnak, it reports of Thutmose III that "his majesty went to Retenu (Canaan) in order to subdue northern foreign lands as his first victorious campaign (*wḏyt.f tpt n(y)t nḫt*) according to that which Amun-Re, Lord of the Thrones of the Two Lands, ordained

[97] Ibid., pl. 1, 3.
[98] *Urk.* IV, 141.7.

(*wḏ*)."[99] On a stela at the fortress Buhen in Nubia, the king speaks in the first person, declaring: "I proceeded from the house of my father, the king of the gods who ordained (*wḏ*) victory for me."[100] Going from the house of Amun-Re implies that the pharaoh received his marching orders from an oracle at the Karnak.

Not only were military victories ordained by Amun-Re from Karnak, but so was the imperial expansion of Egypt's borders through conquest. In connection with the Megiddo campaign in the Annals of Thutmose III at Karnak, we are told that this campaign was "to expand the borders of Egypt according to what his [brave] and victorious father [Amun-re] ordained (*wḏ*) that he conquer."[101] And it was Amun-Re who supported the king with miracles (*bỉ3*),[102] as the Gebel Barkal stela reports.[103] A shooting star discomfited the enemy, leading to it being completely routed. This victory was summed up with the king celebrating what "my lord [Amun-Re lord of the thrones of the Two Lands] who ordained (*wḏ*) the victories."[104] These victories brought tremendous wealth to Amun-Re and his priesthood at Karnak, which in turn helped to finance the construction of massive temples, pylons, statues, and obelisks.

Devotion to Amun accelerates considerably with the dual reigns of Hatshepsut and Thutmose III. Due to the succession dilemma after Thutmose II's death that led to Hatshepsut's 21-year reign, she prudently undertook an aggressive propaganda campaign to show that she was Amun-Re's elect ruler and to demonstrate her regal bloodline.[105] At Deir el-Bahri, a scene shows her mother, Ahmes, approaching Amun, who impregnates her. In the next scene, Ahmes is shown to be pregnant, followed by the birthing scene. From this perspective, Hatshepsut can truly call Amun-Re her father, and she his daughter. On her magnificent obelisks at Karnak, it is said:

> The daughter of Amen-Re, his beloved, his only one who was fashioned by the powers of On; who holds the Two Lands like her maker; whom he created so as to wear his diadems; who has forms like Khepri, who rises like Harakhti; pure egg, splendid seed, whom the Two Magicians nursed; whom Amun himself made appear upon the throne of Southern On.[106]

---

[99] *Urk.* IV, 184.4–7.

[100] Ricard Caminos, *The New-Kingdom Temples of Buhen* (London: Egypt Exploration Society, 1974), pl. 62, line 11. For the translation by Caminos of the entire stela see 49–50.

[101] *Urk.* IV 648.15–649.1. Note Amun-Re's name was erased by Atenist iconoclasm.

[102] On miracles or wonders occurring on behalf of Egyptian warring kings, see J. F. Borghouts, "Divine Intervention in Ancient Egypt and Its Manifestation (*b3w*)," in *Gleanings from Deir el-Medinah* (eds. R. J. Demarée & J. J. Janssen; Leiden: Netherlands Institute for Near Eastern Studies, 1982), 1–70. James K. Hoffmeier, "Understanding Hebrew and Egyptian Military Texts: A Contextual Approach," in *COS* III, xxxixxxvii.

[103] *Urk.* IV. 1238–1239. See the author's translation in *COS* II, 14–18.

[104] *Urk.* IV. 1239.5–6.

[105] Bryan, "The 18th Dynasty before the Amarna Period," 228–229.

[106] Lichtheim, *Ancient Egyptian Literature* II, 26.

On the top of the obelisk, the coronation of Hatshepsut is depicted, with the queen herself kneeling in front of the enthroned Amun-Re who places the blue or *ḫprš* crown on her head (Figure 2.10).

The enormous monoliths were 96 feet (29.56 m) tall, weighed 323 tons,[107] and were established for "her father Amun, Lord of the Thrones of the Two Lands" and overlaid "with extremely fine electrum" (*m ḏʿm ʿ3 wrt*) (see Figure 1.9 in Chapter 1). In addition to the two great granite obelisks, she built and completed projects associated with her two predecessors. One structure shows Thutmose II and Hathsepsut together, on the

FIGURE 2.10 Pyramidion of Hatshepsut's obelisk (Karnak Temple). Photo James K. Hoffmeier.

[107] Habachi, *The Obelisks of Egypt*, 60.

same scale, worshiping Amun-Re.[108] She is also shown as queen, standing alone, burning incense to Amun-Re, while in another scene Thutmose II pours libations; in a third portrayal the royal couple, along with their daughter Neferure, make offerings together.[109]

Hatshepsut built and decorated chambers ancillary to the central holy of holies of the temple,[110] and she built the unique "Chapelle Rouge," made of red quartzite and granodiorite foundations and doorways (Figure 2.11a–b),[111] that was constructed early

(a)

(b)

FIGURE 2.11 a. Chapelle Rouge of Hatshepsut (Karnak Temple). Photo James K. Hoffmeier. b. Hatshepsut before the bark of Amun-Re. Photo James K. Hoffmeier.

[108] Luc Gabolde, *Monumments décoré en bas relief aux noms de Thoutmosis II et Hatschepsout à Karnak* (Cairo: IFAO, 2005).

[109] Ibid., pl. 1–3.

[110] Björkman, *Kings at Karnak*, Fig. 2.

[111] Ibid., 78–84.

in her reign when co-regent with Thutmose III. Here, too Amun-Re is the recipient of this beautiful temple and the offerings depicted on the scenes that fill the shrine.

The greatest expansion of Amun-Re's sanctuary occurred during Thutmose III's sole reign. Not only did he encase the holy of holies with granite and carve it with reliefs showing the bark of Amun in procession, but also Thutmose III had the distinctive square lotus-form columns set up before the central shrine, in front of which he built the 6th Pylon.[112] Also on the wall that surrounds the north side of the central shrine, his famous annals were carved, along with images of his gifts to Amun-Re. Included in this collection is a pair of obelisks (Figure 2.12), one of which was probably the Latern

FIGURE 2.12 Relief showing pair of Thutmose III's obelisks (Karnak Temple). Photo James K. Hoffmeier.

[112] Ibid., 73–76.

obelisk now in Rome.[113] It was made for "Amun-Re Lord of the Thrones of the Two Lands."[114] He also "erected a pair of great, benbens of electrum" for "his father Re-Harakhty" at Heliopolis, although they have not survived.[115] But his greatest building project was the Akh-menu temple, constructed east of (or behind) the holy of holies.

Thutmose III's sole reign began in 1456 B.C. with word that an insurrection was brewing in the Levant with the ouster of the Egyptian garrison that had been in Megiddo, a rebellion instigated by the Prince of Kadesh.[116] As noted previously, Thutmose III attributed this victorious campaign to the will of his father Amun, and his Poetical Stela contains a speech by Amun-Re acknowledging that it was he who gave victory to Thutmose III over enemies from Nubia to Mesopotamia, and Libya to the Levant.[117] While on those distant campaigns, stelae were commissioned and erected to commemorate the king's victories and to acknowledge that Amun-Re made it possible. None of the stelae set up in western Asia have survived,[118] but in Nubia the famous Gebel Barkal Stela of Thutmose III was discovered at the temple of Amun-Re at Napata. Here Thutmose III established a new Egyptian southern border, and built a fort and a temple to Amun-Re.[119] The stela hails the king as "Lord of every foreign land" (*nb n ḫ3swt nb(w)t*). Thutmose's divine patron, Amun-Re, who had given Egypt domination over other nations, ascends to virtual universal status. This is why it can be said that not only did Amun-Re ordain victories and give Thutmose III the kingship of Egypt, but also "that which the sun-disc (*ỉtn*) encircles is in my grasp!"[120] This universal idea of the world being that which the sun-disc encircles, however, is also found at the very beginning of the 18th Dynasty. Ahmose is declared ruler of Egypt (*ḥq3 m t3 mrỉ*)[121] and "he ruled that which the sun-disc encircles."[122] To Hatshepsut, Amun announced: "I will give to you all lands, all foreign

[113] Habachi, *The Obelisks of Egypt*, 112–114.

[114] Ibid., 113, Fig. 27.

[115] *Urk.* IV, 590.13–14.

[116] The annals of Thutmose III begins with a report of the circumstances that gave rise to his first campaigns. See *Urk* IV. 647–648, and William Murnane, "A Rhetorical History? The Beginning of Thutmose III's First Campaign in Western Asia," *JARCE* 26 (1989): 183–189.

[117] *Urk.* IV, 610–619. Translation in Lichtheim, *Ancient Egyptian Literature* II, 35–39.

[118] Thutmose III claims in the Annals to have set up a stela in Naharin, i.e., Mesopotamia (*Urk.* IV. 698). Echoing this claim, the Armant Stela reports that he erected a stela on the east side of Euphrates (Urk. IV 1246.1–2). Also on the same stela, he declares to have set on up a "stela there (in Nubia), just as he had down in the farthest reaches of [Asia]" (Urk. IV, 1246.4–6.). The Gebel Barkal Stela repeats the claim of a Mesopotamian stela (*Urk.* IV, 1232.11–12). On royal Ramesside stelae in the Levant see Alan Millard, "Ramesses Was Here... And Others, Too!" in *Ramesside Studies in Honour of K. A. Kitchen* (eds. M. Collier & Steven Snape; Bolton: Rutherford Press, 2011), 305–312.

[119] Timothy Kendall, "Napata," in *OEAE* II, 492–493.

[120] *Urk.* IV. 1234.1–4.

[121] *Urk.* IV. 16.4.

[122] *Urk.* IV. 16.7.

lands which the sun-disc (*itn*) which is in heaven encircles."[123] Concerning Thutmose III's son and successor, Amenhotep II (ca. 1427–1400 B.C.), Amun is to make him "rule that which Aten encircles."[124]

The ideology of the universally ruling pharaoh required a universal deity, and Amun-Re, the fusion of sky and sun, was well suited to this role. One of the epithets applied to Amun-Re is "Lord of heaven or the sky" (*nb pt*).[125] This expression clearly has universal implications. In excavations at Tell el-Borg in north Sinai that the writer directed between 1999 and 2008, we uncovered doorjambs of a structure of Amenhotep II, which contained the epithet "Amun-Re lord of heaven."[126] Additionally, two other blocks mention Nut the great sky goddess, and another block refers to the Semitic goddess Anat as "lady of heaven" (*nbt pt*). To this we must recall the important of role of Horus, the sky god, to the eastern frontier.[127] Because of the several occurrences of sky deities and epithets at the outer edge of Egypt's eastern frontier, it was suggested that the appeal to sky deities "was intended to project the imperial ideology that Egypt's hegemony extended beyond her territory, just as the sky represented by Horus, Amun-Ra, Nut and 'Anat transcended Egypt's borders."[128]

Thutmose III's successors, Amenhotep II and Thutmose IV (ca. 1400–1390 B.C.), were active militarily in the Levant and Nubia,[129] but they made no major additions to Karnak. The former decorated some walls and columns left by his father, and he commissioned the construction of a travertine bark shrine, which now stands in the open-air museum at Karnak. It is dedicated to "Amun Re Lord of heaven" (Figure 2.13a–b). Thutmose IV made a nearly identical travertine shrine and an impressive limestone double-pillared court that stood in front of Thutmose I's 4th Pylon.[130] This structure was subsequently removed and the blocks reused. It is now partially reconstructed and likewise stands in the open-air museum. The king is shown in the embrace of Amun-Re, who is called "king of the gods."[131]

By the time we reach Amenhotep III's lengthy 38-year reign (ca. 1390–1352 B.C.), Egypt was able to experience the blessings of a large empire combined with peace.

---

[123] *Urk.* IV. 253.7–8.

[124] *Urk.* IV. 1293.5.

[125] For occurrences, see *Urk.* IV. 154.8, 336.10, 340.14, 619.17, 620.4.

[126] James K. Hoffmeier & Ronald D. Bull, "New Inscriptions Mentioning Tjaru from Tell el-Borg, North Sinai," *RdÉ* 56 (2005): 79–86 & pl. XII–XV; James K. Hoffmeier, "Deities of the Eastern Frontier," in *Scribe of Justice: Egyptological Studies in Honour of Shafik Allam* (eds. Z. A. Hawass, Kh. A. Daoud, & R. B. Hussein; Cairo: Supplement aux Annales du Service des Antiquites de l'Egypte, Cahier 42, 2011), 197–216.

[127] Hoffmeier, "Deities of the Eastern Frontier," 197–199.

[128] Ibid., 206.

[129] For Amenhotep II, see the Sphinx, Amada, Memphis, Karnak, and Elephatine Stela of Amenhotep II (see *Urk.* IV, 1287–1316) and for Thutmose IV, see Sphinx and Konosso Stela (see *Urk.* IV, 1539–1552).

[130] Björkman, *Kings at Karnak*, 101.

[131] This text is written below the cornice shown on Figure 2.13a.

(a) (b)

FIGURE 2.13 a. Pillared hall of Thutmose IV (Karnak Temple). Photo James K. Hoffmeier b. Thutmose IV before Amun-Re. Photo James K. Hoffmeier.

Gardiner described this era as the "zenith of its magnificence."[132] More recently, Lawrence Berman sums up the achievements of this prolific builder: "No king of Egypt left more monuments, more tangible proofs of his greatness, than Amenhotep III, except Ramses II."[133] Amenhotep III's major building projects are reviewed on a stela from his mortuary temple, which was subsequently appropriated by Merneptah at the end of the 13th century on which he inscribed his own text on the backside. Today, because of Merneptah's recording of the so-called "The Israel Stela" on the reverse side of the stela,[134] the original inscription of Amenhotep III is often overlooked. In addition to his massive mortuary temple at Kom el-Hettan in western Thebes, which is currently being investigated by Hourig Sourouzian,[135] the stela mentions his construction of Luxor temple "for his father Amun, Lord of the Thrones of the Two Lands."[136] It reports on "another monument that his majesty made for

[132] Gardiner, *Egypt of the Pharaohs*, 205.

[133] Lawrence M. Berman, "Overview of Amenhotep II and His Reign," in *Amenhotep III: Perspectives on His Reign* (eds. David O'Connor & Eric Cline; Ann Arbor: University of Michigan, 2001), 1. For a review of the full scope of Amenhotep III's building program throughout Egypt and Nubia, see W. Raymond Johnson, "Monuments and Monumental Art under Amenhotep III: Evolution and Meaning," in *Amenhotep III: Perspectives on His Reign*, 63–94.

[134] W.M.F Petrie, *Six Temples at Thebes, 1896* (London: Bernard Quaritch, 1897), pl. XI–XII (Amenhotep III stela) & pl. XIII–XIV (Merneptah/Israel stela).

[135] For a recent report, see, Hourig Sourouzian, "Investigating the Mortuary Temple of Amenhotep III," *Egyptian Archaeology* 39 (2011): 29–32.

[136] Petrie, *Six Temples at Thebes*, pl. 12, line 10.

his father Amun was making for him a viewing place as a divine offering"[137] within which was a "great temple" (*ḥwt ꜥ3t*). The exact location of this edifice, which apparently was surrounded by gardens, is uncertain, although it may have been along the route between Karnak and Luxor temples.[138] The king also recalls making a new bark for Amun-Re, the 3rd Pylon at Karnak, and another sanctuary for Amun-Re at Karnak.[139]

In the foregoing section we sketched out the enormous influence of Amun-Re over the 18th Dynasty royal family, as evidenced by the impressive architectural structures built in his honor at Thebes and in particular at Karnak Temple. Cyril Aldred is surely on target to call Thebes "the holy city of Amun, the king of the Gods."[140] The massive temples, pylons, and towering obelisks were only made possible through the booty, taxes, and tribute[141] that the pharaohs obtained through their military campaigns ordained by Amun-Re. As we reach the middle of the 14th century B.C., Amun-Re enjoyed unrivaled power, a firm grip on Egypt and its far-flung vassal states and colonized territories. Given this religious and political *status quo*, which had been ensconced for two centuries, how could Amenhotep IV/Akhenaten (ca. 1353–1336 B.C.) bring about such radical changes in such a short period of time?

---

[137] Translation of Miriam Lichtheim, *Ancient Egyptian Literature* II, 45.

[138] Johnson, "Monuments and Monumental Art under Amenhotep III," 68.

[139] Petrie, *Six Temples at Thebes*, pl. 12, lines 10–26.

[140] Cyril Aldred, *Akhenaten King of Egypt* (London: Thames & Hudson, 1988), 70.

[141] On taxes and tribute, *b3k* and *inw*, see Edward Bleiberg, *The Official Gift in Ancient Egypt* (Norman: University of Oklahoma, 1996).

Worshiping before Amun when he shines as Horakhty . . .
Hail to you Aten of daytime who creates everything
who makes them live!
STELA OF SUTY & HOR

Chapter 3

The Dawn of the Amarna Period

AMENHOTEP IV

THE AGING AMENHOTEP III died in his thirty-eighth year and was succeeded by Amenhotep IV,[1] who adopted the throne name Neferkheperure waen-Re,[2] which means "beautiful[3] are the forms of Re, the unique one of Re." He was not the heir apparent. An older son of Amenhotep III named Thutmose died in his youth. He is known from a relief in Berlin, where he stands behind his father making an offering (Figure 3.1). Notably, he is wearing the princely side-lock and the leopard skin of a Sem-priest. He is also shown in a small mummiform statue (also in the Berlin museum), lying on a funeral bier with the *ba*-bird laying over him with extended wings (Figure 3.2). Here, too, his side-lock is visible, a testimony to youth when he died.

Prince Thutmose was engaged in activities in the north as priest of Ptah in Memphis. He is depicted with his father on a relief at the Apis Bull burial complex (i.e.,

---

[1] William J. Murnane, "On the Accession Date of Akhenaten," in *Studies in Honor of George R. Hughes* (eds. J. Johnson & E. Wente; SAOC 39, 1977), 163–167.

[2] Jürgen von Beckerath, *Handbuch der ägyptishen Königsnamen* (Mainz: Philipp von Zabern, 1999), 143.

[3] While *nfr* often has an aesthetic meaning, in many cases *nfr* appears to have a far more dynamic nuance. V. A. Donohue thought "rejuvenation" might be appropriate in funerary contexts ("*Pr nfr*," *JEA* 64 [1978]: 143–148). Jan Assmann makes a good case for understanding *nfr* in the Amarna age as "*parousia*," that is, "the physical presence of the divinity," because *nfr* is closely connected to *stwt* or the rays by which the Aten manifests himself (*Egyptian Solar Religion in the New Kingdom: Re, Amun and the Crisis of Polytheism* [London: Kegan Paul International, 1995], 74).

FIGURE 3.1 Prince Thutmose (Berlin Museum). Photo James K. Hoffmeier.

FIGURE 3.2 Prince Thutmose as Ba-statue (Berlin Museum). Photo James K. Hoffmeier.

Serapeum), which suggests that he may have played a significant role in the establishment of the Apis cult and Serapeum.[4] His fullest title is found on a cat sarcophagus that describes him as "Crown Prince, Overseer of the Priests of Upper and Lower Egypt, High Priest of Ptah in Memphis and Sem-priest (of Ptah)."[5] When and under what

---

[4] Nicholas Reeves, *Akhenaten: Egypt's False Prophet* (London: Thames & Hudson, 2001), 61.

[5] Aidan Dodson, "Crown Prince Djhutmose and the Royal Sons of the Eighteenth Dynasty," *JEA* 76 (1990): 88.

circumstances this prince died is not known, but his untimely death left the throne to his younger and only brother, Amenhotep. From what little is known of Prince Thutmose, no special interest in solar cults (i.e., Re, Atum, Re-Harakhty or Aten) is apparent.

As for Amenhotep III's younger son and namesake, little is known of his early years leading up to his accession. It is thought that with the untimely death of his elder brother Thutmose, he fell heir to his office as high priest of Ptah,[6] but evidence is lacking. As a young prince he probably spent time at the palatial harem of Mi-wer in the Fayum and would have been educated, like his father before him, in the *k3p* or royal nursery.[7] He probably would have spent time in the royal palace at nearby Memphis, home to pharaohs since Thutmose I built it when he moved the capital from Thebes. From this royal residence princes Amenhotep II and Thutmose IV rode their chariots to the Giza plateau to behold the pyramids and sphinx.[8] Memphis was within easy reach of Heliopolis and, as noted previously (Chapter 1), from the elevated desert plateau just to its south (Abu Sir area), the sanctuary of Heliopolis and its Benben Stone were likely visible.

This proximity has given rise to the notion that prince Amenhotep would have come in contact with the solar religion of On. It was suggested long ago by Ludwig Borchardt that Amenhotep IV's uncle, Anen (brother of Queen Tiye), in his capacity as High Priest of Re at Heliopolis, may have played a prominent role in shaping Amenhotep IV's solar theology.[9]

In year 29 of Amenhotep III, the king relocated to Thebes to reside in his new palace that had been built to celebrate his first *ḥb sd* (the Sed) or jubilee festival in his thirtieth year.[10] The purpose of the Sed-festival was to renew and revitalize the kingship after 30 years.[11] There is no reason to think that the young prince was left in Memphis (and close to Heliopolis) during this period, which would have coincided with his more formative years, when he would be influenced by solar theology.[12] Indeed, a jar

---

[6] Cyril Aldred, *Akhenaten King of Egypt* (London: Thames & Hudson, 1988), 259.

[7] Arielle Kozloff, *Amenhotep III: Egypt's Radiant Pharaoh* (Cambridge/New York: Cambridge University Press, 2012), 25–31. Further on the *k3p*, see Erika Feucht, "The *Ḫrdw n k3p* Reconsidered," in *Pharaonic Egypt: The Bible and Christianity* (ed. S. Israelit-Groll; Jerusalem: Magnes Press, 1985), 41–44, and Betsy Bryan, *The Reign of Thutmose IV* (Baltimore, MD: The Johns Hopkins University Press, 1991), 261. Investigations at this Fayum harem just recently began; see Ian Shaw, "The Gurob Harem Palace Project, Spring 2012," *JEA* 98 (2012): 43–54.

[8] See discussion of the relevant texts in Chapter 1.

[9] Ludwig, Borchardt, "Ein Onkel Amenophis' IV. Als Hoherpriester von Heliopolis," *ZÄS* 44 (1907): 97–98. But see Hermann Kees, "Ein Onkel Amenophis' IV. Hoherpriester von Heliopolis," *ZÄS* 53 (1917): 81–83.

[10] Lawrence Berman, "An Overview of Amenhotep III and His Reign," in *Amenhotep III: Perspectives on His Reign* (eds. David O'Connor & Eric H. Cline; Ann Arbor: University of Michigan Press, 1998), 15.

[11] Anthony Spalinger, "Festivals," in *OEAE* 1, 522.

[12] I concur with those who believe there was no co-regency between Amenhotep III and Amenhotep IV, or minimally, a very short one. More on this in the following chapters.

sealing from Amenhotep III's Malkata palace in western Thebes, that probably dates to year 28 or 29, reads "the house of the re[al] king's son [i.e., prince], Amenhotep."[13] William C. Hayes believed that this prince is none other than the future Akhenaten, and that he was called the "real" prince so as to avoid confusion with Amenhotep the Viceroy of Kush (i.e., the king's son of Kush).[14] Donald Redford rightly observes that it is "unnecessary" to theorize direct contact between Amenhotep IV and Heliopolis because "the sun god and this theology so permeated the Egyptian cultus that it would have been hard to insulate a young prince from solar influence wherever he might be brought up."[15] Given Anen's family connection to Akhmim, just north of Thebes, one might be inclined to think that his priestly connections to the solar cult of On could occur within the Theban realm,[16] and this is consistent with Anen's priestly title as *sm iwnw rsy*, "Sem priest of Southern Heliopolis."[17]

The actual Egyptian name of Hermonthis (the Greek name, which survives into Arabic as Armant), the original cult center of Montu,[18] was *Iwni* or *Iwnw*, that is, On (Heliopolis), the very name of the center of solar worship in the Delta.[19] Subsequently known as *iwnw šm3w*, "Upper Egyptian Heliopolis," the epithet was also applied to Thebes.[20] Amenhotep IV actually incorporated this epithet in his Golden Horus name "Uplifted of Diadems in Southern Heliopolis" (*wṯs ḫ3w m iwnw šm3w*)."[21] So it is evident that from the 12th Dynasty onward (see Chapter 2) that Atum/Re played an influential role in Thebes in general and Karnak Temple in particular. Consequently, Amenhotep IV's penchant for solar theology may well have developed in Thebes itself.

Images of prince Amenhotep are limited or nonexistent, which is quite consistent with 18th Dynasty practice for royal scenes.[22] Alternatively Redford suggests that his absence may have been an intentional one "because of a congenital ailment which made him hideous to behold."[23] The odd appearance of Amenhotep IV in reliefs and statuary have triggered endless debate about whether the traits portrayed were

---

[13] William C. Hayes, "Inscriptions from the Palace of Amenhotep III," *JNES* 10 (1951): 159, 272 fig. 27 KK.

[14] Ibid., 159.

[15] Donald B. Redford, *Akhenaten the Heretic King* (Princeton, NJ: Princeton University Press, 1984), 59.

[16] Ibid., 59.

[17] Kees, "Ein Onkel Amenophis' IV. Hoherpriester von Heliopolis," 81.

[18] See discussion in Chapter 2.

[19] Alan H. Gardiner, *Ancient Egyptian Onomastica* II (Oxford: Oxford University Press, 1947), 22*.

[20] Edward K. Warner, "Armant," *OEAE* 1, 126. Gardiner, *Ancient Egyptian Onomastica* II, 24*.

[21] von Beckerath, *Handbuch der ägyptishen Königsnamen*, 143.

[22] David Silverman, Josef Wegner, and Jenifer Wegner, *Akhenaten and Tutankhamun: Revolution and Restoration* (Philadelphia: University Pennsylvania Museum, 2006), 15. Although as we noted, Prince Thutmose is shown with his father, Amenhotep III in the Berlin fragment and the Serapeum relief.

[23] Redford, *Akhenaten the Heretic King*, 57–58.

purely artistic exaggerations or reflected the authentic physiology of the king (more on this below). Regardless, the earliest representations of Amenhotep IV as king show him to be quite normal.

At Karnak Temple on the remains of the 3rd Pylon, constructed by Amenhotep III, but decorated by Amenhotep IV who appears in the classic pose of the warrior king smiting his enemies (Figure 3.3).[24] The king's limbs are very muscular, but his head is missing, and there was an attempt to chip out his image. His name was successfully erased. This image is surely one of the earliest surviving of the future Akhenaten.

Another early portrayal of Amenhotep IV is found in tomb number 55 in the Theban necropolis, belonging to Ramose.[25] He was vizier in the latter years of Amenhotep III and into the reign of his successor. This tomb shows the dramatic differences between the elegant raised relief style of Amenhotep III's artists and the sunken

FIGURE 3.3 Pylon showing Amenhotep IV (Karnak Temple). Photo James K. Hoffmeier.

[24] R. Saad, "Les travaux d'Aménophis au IIIe pylône du temple d'Amon-Re à Karnak," *Kêmi* 20 (1970): 187–193.

[25] Norman de Garis Davies, *The Tomb of the Vizier Ramose* (London: EES, 1941), pl. XXIX.

relief of the early "Amarna" style. On one wall Amenhotep IV is shown enthroned, apparently as the newly crowned king, in the artistic canons of his father. Some suggest that this presentation points to the beginning of his co-regency (Figure 3.4).[26] There is nothing, however, in the adjoining inscription or the scene itself to support this theory.

A second early portrayal of the new king occurs in the tomb of Kheruef (Theban Tomb no. 192), a high official who figured prominently in the celebrations of Amenhotep III's jubilee festivals (*ḥb sd*). The young king here looks very normal. There is another scene in which Amenhotep IV stands before his parents and pours a libation (Figure 3.5).[27] This scene was intentionally defaced, with Amenhotep IV's

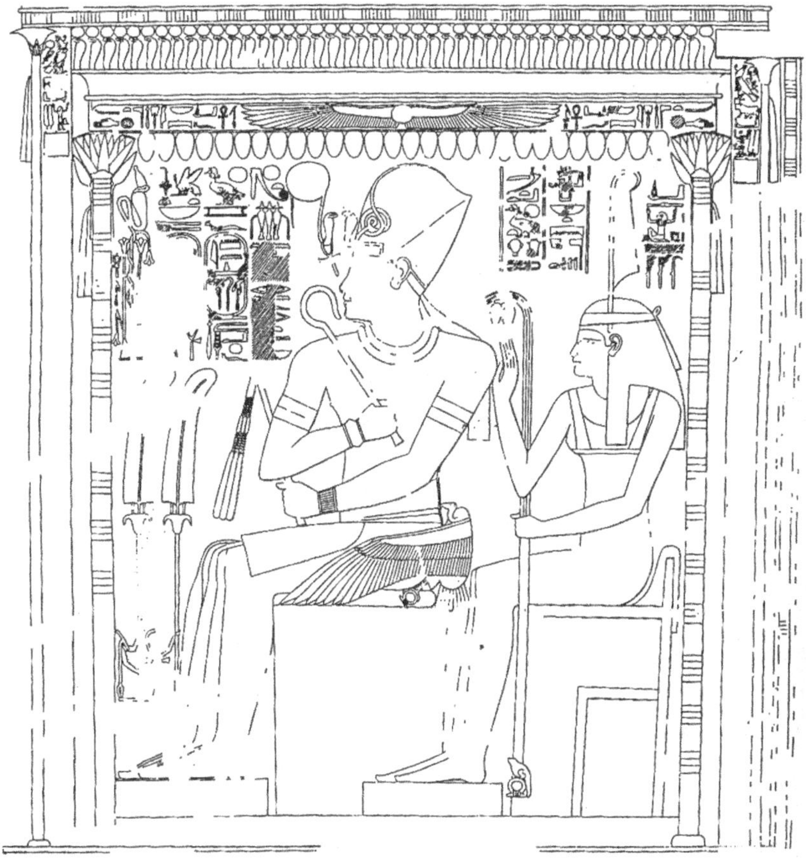

FIGURE 3.4 Early depiction of Amenhotep IV (Tomb of Ramose). Norman de Garis Davies, *The Tomb of the Vizier Ramose* (London: EES, 1941), pl. xxix.

[26] Reeves, *Akhenaten: Egypt's False Prophet*, 98, who also offers a drawing of the enthronement scene from Ramose's tomb.

[27] Epigraphic Survey, *The Tomb of Kheruef, Theban Tomb no. 192* (Chicago: Oriental Institute, 1980), pl. 11, 12.

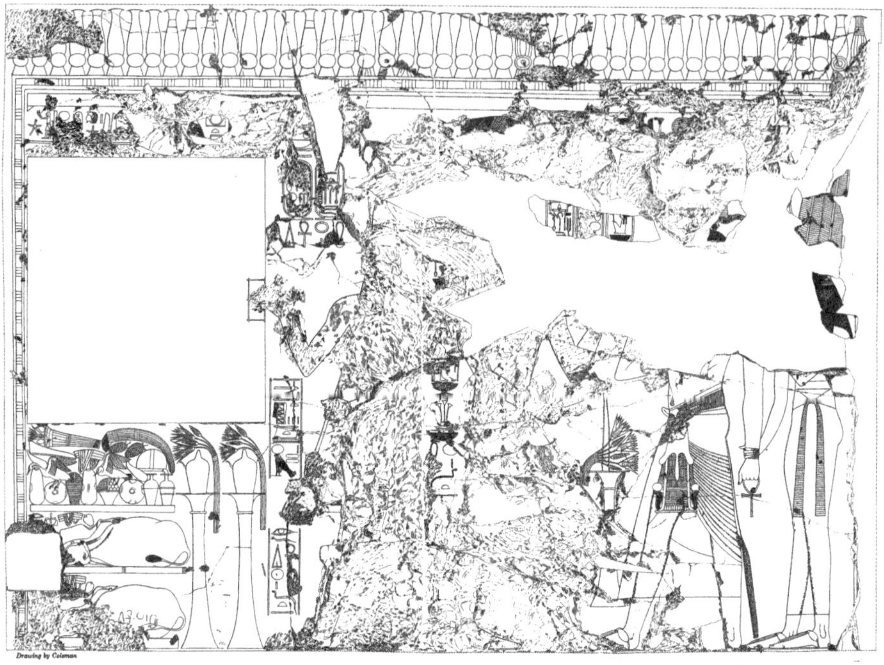

FIGURE 3.5 Amenhotep IV (Tomb of Kheruef). Epigraphic Survey, *The Tomb of Kheruef, Theban Tomb no. 192* (Chicago: Oriental Institute, 1980), pl. 11, 12.

figure nearly entirely erased; his cartouche is barely discernible. Amenhotep IV in the same panel is then shown facing the opposite direction, making an offering to Re-Harakhty.

Some think that the juxtaposition of Amenhotep IV and King Amenhotep III in Kheruef's tomb is evidence for a co-regency between the two, a theory that will be further examined below. The problem is that the scene is so badly mutilated that one cannot tell whether or not the senior Amenhotep is *m3ʿ ḫrw* (i.e., deceased). Pouring libations for one's deceased parents is a traditional motif in Egyptian funerary art. One might not expect, however, that Amenhotep IV would offer to his deceased parents when his mother, Tiye, was still alive, as she lived some years beyond the demise of her husband.[28] Redford dismisses this scene as evidence for a co-regency, believing that Amenhotep III was deceased, arguing rather that "the scene merely expresses Akhenaten's piety towards the memory of his father."[29] The reality is that the scene is too fragmentary to draw any firm conclusions about what it portrays.

---

[28] Kozloff, *Amenhotep III*, 240–241. Aldred, *Akhenaten King of Egypt*, 193–194.

[29] Donald Redford, *History and Chronology of the Eighteenth Dynasty of Egypt: Seven Studies* (Toronto: University of Toronto, 1967), 116.

A possible indication that Amenhotep III had already died when these scenes in Kheruef's tombs was decorated is that Tiye is shown on the door lintel standing behind her son, rattling a sistrum as he offers to "Re-Harakhty, the great god, lord of heaven" (Figure 3.6). On the left side of this scene, she also stands as he burns incense before "Atum Lord of Heliopolis."[30] Her presence with her son, and the absence of Amenhotep III, suggests that he was sole ruler and a new, young king.

Perhaps the most compelling critique of using Kheruef's tomb as evidence for the co-regency was penned recently by Peter Dorman.[31] He points to the "incompatibilities" between Amenhotep IV's presentation of himself in the raised reliefs in the tomb with sunken reliefs of the monarch in the Aten temples at Karnak because they should be contemporaneous in the co-regency theory. Furthermore, he notes the obvious problems with Re-Harakhty's portrayal in Kheruef's tomb, which lacks the name Aten, and the sun-disc with its rays is not used in the raised reliefs in the tomb.

The figure of the new king Amenhotep IV portrayed in the tombs of Ramose and Kheruef, furthermore, show no physical abnormalities, and typically follow the traditional canons of art. However, the tomb of Kheruef and that of his contemporary Parenefer (Theban Tomb 188) also have walls decorated in the early "Amarna style." The transition from the orthodox style of Amenhotep III's day to the Amarna style took a few years, but the change is quite abrupt in these two tombs. The early "Amarna-style" scene in Ramose's tomb has Amenhotep IV and his wife Nefertiti basking under the full-orbed sun-disc with the rays of Aten streaming down over

FIGURE 3.6 Amenhotep IV making offerings to Atum and Re-Harakhty (Tomb of Kheruef). Epigraphic Survey, *The Tomb of Kheruef, Theban Tomb*, pl. 9.

[30] Epigraphic Survey, *The Tomb of Kheruef*, pl. 8–9.

[31] Peter Dorman, "The Long Coregency Revisited: Architectural and Iconographic Conundra in the Tomb of Kheruef," in *Causing His Name to Live: Studies in Egyptian Epigraphy and History in Memory of William J. Murnane* (eds. P. J. Brand & L. Cooper; Leiden and Boston: Brill, 2009).

FIGURE 3.7 Akhenaten and Nefertiti with early depiction Aten-disc (Tomb of Ramose). Davies, *The Tomb of the Vizier Ramose*, xxxiii a.

the royal couple (Figure 3.7).[32] Regrettably, the entire scene below the sun-disc in Parennefer's tomb is completely obliterated.[33] Since the sun-disc is situated at the center of the baldachin, or canopy, it is likely that the monarch was seated within it and under the sun.

The evidence provided in these tombs, unfortunately, does not really illustrate any transitional steps in the art that might reveal Amenhotep IV's theological transformation.

THE EARLIEST STAGES OF AKHENATEN'S RELIGION

Returning to the lintel scene of Amenhotep IV in the tomb of Kheruef, we see some very early religious iconography. As mentioned in the previous section, the recipients

---

[32] Davies, *The Tomb of the Vizier Ramose*, XXXIIIa.

[33] For Parennefer, see N. de Garis Davies, "Akhenaten at Thebes," *JEA* 9 (1923): pl. XXIII & XXIV no. 1. For a recent study of this tomb, including some important restoration work, see Susan Redford, "Theban Tomb No. 188 (The Tomb of Parennefer): A Case Study of Tomb Reuse in the Theban Necropolis," 2 Vols. (Ph.D. diss., Pennsylvania State University, 2007).

of the king's offerings are Re-Harakhty (left side) and the goddess Ma'at, who stands behind him, and Atum (right side) and the goddess Hathor, who likewise stands behind the sun-god. Dividing the panel is the sun-disc with a pair of uraeus-cobras with ☥-signs around their necks (Figure 3.6). The label *bḥdt* occurs on either side of the sun, which associates the disc with Horus of Edfu.[34] Below the hovering sun is the symbol of the royal *ka* with the cartouche of the king's name taken at coronation, Neferkheperure Waen-Re. In his seminal study of the royal *ka*, Lanny Bell has shown how important the king's *ka* was to royal ideology, observing that "the representation of this *ka* is indeed proof of his divine origins and sufficient evidence he was predestined to rule."[35] The royal *ka* was instrumental in the divinity of the king. The transformation of the king occurs "when his human form is overtaken by this immortal element," which Bell maintains "happens at the climax of the coronation ceremony."[36] The presence of the royal *ka* emblem indicates that Amenhotep IV was king, and in the absence of his father further demonstrates that he was no mere coregent, but sole ruler.

Further discussion of male deities in this scene is required. They are both solar in nature and are seated on thrones. Atum of Heliopolis appears as a king, wearing the double crown of Upper and Lower Egypt. Re-Harakhty, on the other hand, is presented with the falcon head and a large sun-disc with a uraeus on his head.[37] The presence of the two goddesses, and the mention of Amun-Re and other deities in the hymns and texts within the tomb, show that the exclusion of other deities had not begun. Charles Nims, the principal epigrapher of Kheruef's tomb, confirms that "nothing in the inscriptions indicates the new religious emphasis that appeared very early in the reign of Amenhotep IV."[38] That said, one detects a predisposition for the solar deities since Atum and Re-Harakhty, who were prominently displayed, are recipients of the king's worship. These deities would continue to be central to Amenhotep IV's reform program. The long history of solar theology in northern Egypt and its subsequent assimilation in Thebes have been discussed in the two previous chapters. Karol Mysliwiec, however, has argued that Atum actually becomes Aten, and that this development began during Hatshepsut's reign when she enhanced the role of Atum in Thebes that climaxed with the Amarna Period.[39]

---

[34] Alan Gardiner, "Horus the Beḥdetite," *JEA 30* (1942): 23–36. Richard Wilkinson, *The Complete Gods and Goddesses of Ancient Egypt* (London: Thames & Hudson, 2003), 202.

[35] Lanny Bell, "Luxor Temple and the Cult of the Royals *Ka*," *JNES* 44 (1985): 258.

[36] Ibid., 258.

[37] Epigraphic Survey, *The Tomb of Kheruef*, pl. 9.

[38] Ibid., 12.

[39] Karol Mysliwiec, "Amon, Atum and Aton: The Evolution of Heliopolitan Influences in Thebes," in *L'Egyptologie en 1979: Axes prioritiaires de recherches*, Vol. II (ed. J. Leclant; Paris: Éditions du centre national de la recherché scientifique, 1982), 285–289.

Re-Harakhty is again the recipient of Amenhotep IV's offering in a second scene in Kheruef's tomb[40] and it is his name that will be incorporated into the early form of the name of the Aten, namely *rꜥ ḥr-ꜣḫty ḥꜥy m ꜣḫt m rn.f m šw nty m ỉtn*—"Re-Harakhty who rejoices in his horizon in his name of light which is in the disc (Aten)."[41]

The antipathy that developed later toward Amun in Amenhotep IV's reign had not yet officially taken hold when work began at the sandstone quarry of Gebel es-Silsileh, located approximately halfway between Aswan in the south and Edfu in the north. This quarry had been periodically worked since the days of Hatshepsut and Thutmose III down to the reign of Amenhotep III, based on inscriptions found in the small chapels cut into the eastern face of the escarpment.[42] Amenhotep IV also exploited this quarry to obtain building blocks for his temples in the Theban area. Accompanying the inscription marking the beginning of work was an image of Amun.[43] The undated inscription includes Amun-Re's words offering the traditional blessing of "life, stability and dominion" for Amenhotep IV. The presence of the image and words of Amun-Re at this early period, even while obtaining material for an Aten temple, demonstrates that a period of "coexistence," to use Murnane's expression,[44] prevailed for the first two or three years of Amenhotep IV's period.

The Gebel es-Silsileh inscription reveals several significant developments. First, Amun is still present, his image and his speech, but a few years later this very same image was hacked out, and, ironically, Amenhotep IV's name was subsequently removed by his own zealots. Second, the king is called "the high priest (*ḥm nṯr tpy*) of Harakhty[45] who rejoices in the horizon in his name of light which is in the disc

---

[40] Epigraphic Survey, *The Tomb of Kheruef*, pl. 12.

[41] Aldred, *Akhenaten King of Egypt*, 19, fig. 3 shows the two names side by side.

[42] Ricardo Caminos & T. G. H. James, *Gebel es-Silsilah* I (London: EES, 1963), 11. Examination of the quarries by Rosemarie and Dietrich Klemm (*Stones and Quarries in Ancient Egypt* [London: British Museum, 2008], 180–201) suggest, based on the typed of chisel marks, that there may have been quarrying activity during the Middle Kingdom, though no inscriptions from this period have survived. James Harrell, a geologist and expert in quarrying and mining in Egypt, has also examined the area that the Klemms identified as worked in the Middle Kingdom and he concurs with their suggestion (Verbal communication from Harrell via email, June 18, 2013).

[43] Georges Legrain, "Les Stèles d'Aménôthès IV à Zernik et à Gebel Silseleh," *ASAE* 3 (1902): 259–266. This text is also transcribed in Maj Sandman, *Texts from the Time of Akhenaten* (Brussels: Queen Elizabeth Foundation of Egyptology, 1938), 143–144, §CXXXVII. Translation and discussion in William Murnane, *Texts from the Amarna Period in Egypt* (Atlanta: Scholars Press, 1995), 30–31.

[44] William Murnane, "Observations on Pre-Amarna Theology during the Earliest Reign of Amenhotep IV," in *Gold of Praise: Studies on Ancient Egypt in Honor of Edward F. Wente* (eds. Emily Teeter & John Larsen; Chicago: Oriental Institute, 1999), 303.

[45] The usual sun-disc over the head of the falcon is missing in Legrain's edition, but present later in the text (l. 5), cf. Legrain, "Les Stèles d'Aménôthès IV à Zernik et à Gebel Silseleh," 263. Sandman, *Texts from the Time of Akhenaten*, 144, line 4.

(Aten)." This priestly title was dropped within a few years,[46] but it is worth noting that Amenhotep IV regarded himself as the chief cleric of the new developing cult and it suggests that he likely had a direct hand in establishing it. Third, and perhaps most significant, we see one of the earliest writings of the lengthy and explanatory, sometimes called the "didactic," name of the Aten. A careful examination of the two occurrences of the name of Aten in this inscription reveals that they are not written identically. In line 1 of the stela, it reads *ḥr ȝḫty ḥ*ʿ*y m ȝḫt m rn.f m šw nty m itn*—whereas in line 5 has *r*ʿ *ḥr ȝḫty m rn.f m šw nty m itn*. In the first writing, the sun-disc over the falcon (*ḥr*) is missing. The writing in line 5 omits the clause *ḥ*ʿ*y m ȝḫt*—"who rejoices in the horizon." These variations in the name of the new deity in the same text suggest that at this very early date in Amenhotep IV's reign, the name was either in flux or so new that the scribes who carved it were not completely familiar with it. It seems improbable, though, that a mere scribal error can explain such an egregious mistake on the same text by a royal scribe. Conspicuous by its absence is any iconographic representation of Amenhotep IV's deity. Perhaps that earliest stage of Aten's iconography was still being developed.

Fourth, the purpose of the quarrying expedition is disclosed. It was to obtain stone "in order to make the great benben (*pȝ bnbn* ʿ*ȝt*) of (or for) 'Re-Harakhty in his name of light which is in the disc (Aten) in Karnak.'"[47] It is evident that plans called for building a temple of some sort for this new, developing deity in Karnak Temple. While this was in Amun's domain, there is no evidence to suggest that any existing Amun or Amun-Re structure was removed or usurped for this building effort, and for that matter, even the great Aten temples were erected on largely virgin ground. Whether this quarrying was just to obtain a "great benben," that is, an obelisk of some sort for the new cult, or whether this was the name of a temple is uncertain.

One of the temples within the Aten complex in east Karnak that was built in the first five years of Amenhotep IV's reign was called *ḥwt bnbn* ("Mansion of the Benben").[48] It is no mere coincidence that the first structure the new king built had the obvious connection to the solar religion of Heliopolis. Rather, in keeping with the general thesis of this study, there is an intentional revival of solar religion that had dominated the religion and royal ideology of the 4th and 5th Dynasties.

Probably the earliest structure erected at Karnak by Amenhotep IV was indeed made of Gebel es-Silsileh sandstone. One of these blocks, which was brought to Berlin in 1845, shows Re-Harakhty facing left with the same iconographic features

---

[46] Other early examples of the title of *ḥm nṯr tpy* are found on a block from the 10th Pylon at Karnak (Donald Redford, "A Royal Speech from the Blocks of the 10th Pylon," *BES* 3 [1981]: 89).

[47] Legrain, "Les Stèles d'Aménôthès IV à Zernik et à Gebel Silseleh," 263.

[48] Donald Redford, "Studies on Akhenaten at Thebes, II: A Report on the Work of the Akhenaten Temple Project of the University Museum, The University of Pennsylvania, for the Year 1973–4," *JARCE* 12 (1975): 9–14.

seen in Kheruef's tomb (Figure 3.8).[49] Surrounding the falcon's sun-disc is the name "[Re-H]arakhty who rejoices in the horizon [in] his name [of l]ight [which is in] the disc (Aten)." Behind the deity is a vertical band inscribed with typical royal titles and a cartouche with the king's nomen, Neferkheperure. To the right of the vertical text, the king faces right, while the *bḥdt* sun-disc, with multiple ☥-signs extend from the orb; two hang from the necks of uraei (Figure 3.8).

Additional blocks from this edifice have been identified that came from the contents of the 10th Pylon, which had been constructed out of blocks from dismantled Aten temples, likely by Horemheb.[50] In fact, Jean-Luc Chappaz has matched another block to this Berlin block, and has studied other inscribed pieces from the same structure, which he believes was the first temple built by Amenhotep IV, and was dedicated to Re-Harakhty "who rejoices in the horizon in his name of light which is in the disc (Aten)."[51] Indeed, as of the early 1980s, Chappaz had identified 24 examples of the writing of this form of the name that were not enclosed in a cartouche. Another indicator that these blocks pre-date the well-known main Aten temples (see next chapter) is that the sizes of the blocks vary and are typically larger than the standard *talatat* block (52 × 26 × 24 cm) used consistently in the temples located in East Karnak, as well as at Amarna and elsewhere.[52] Comparatively, these blocks have a maximal length ranging between 110 and 145 cm.[53] Queen Nefertiti,

FIGURE 3.8 Berlin Block. Photo James K. Hoffmeier.

[49] Aldred, *Akhenaten King of Egypt*, pl. 27.

[50] Redford, *Akhenaten the Heretic King*, 65. Jean-Luc Chappaz, "Le Premier édifice d'Amenophis IV à Karnak," *BSEG* 8 (1983): 13–45.

[51] Chappaz, "Le Premier édifice d'Amenophis IV à Karnak," 17–45.

[52] By "east Karnak" I mean the area outside the east-most temenos wall at Karnak, where the Akhenaten Temple Project worked beginning in 1975. For the standard *talatat* size, see Redford, *Akhenaten the Heretic King*, 65.

whose name and image are ubiquitous in the later Theban temples, is surprisingly absent in these earliest blocks,[54] as she was in the tomb of Kheruef (except in the early "Amarna- style" reliefs). The king continues to be presented in the pre-Amarna style, and many illustrations of Amenhotep IV were hacked out prior to the dismantling of the building.[55]

There is evidence for another inscribed block from the earliest temple(s) at Karnak that is somewhat elusive. The whereabouts of the block itself is presently unknown and all that remains is a copy made by Émile Prisse d'Avennes in the mid-19th century, which was subsequently studied by Baudouin van de Walle in 1980[56] and most recently by Orly Goldwasser.[57] This scene preserves five lines of vertical texts; between lines 3 and 4 (from the left) is the figure of the bearded god Shu with the *šw* feather (𓆄) on his head (Figure 3.9). On the far right is a female figure with the tall-feather crown that represents Tefnut.[58] The text in the first column contains part of the early didactic name of Aten, "Harakhty who rejoices <in> the horizon." The rest of the name is missing, but the written section does have some anomalies. First, the top of the register line appears to be the sky-sign (𓇯), which is a fitting way to start the didactic name, followed by *ḥr ꜣḫty* (Harakhty) without the sun-disc. This variant writing was also found on the Gebel el-Silseleh inscription discussed above. Absent, too, is the preposition *m* (𓐝) before *ꜣḫt* "horizon." One might suggest

FIGURE 3.9 Relief showing Shu and Tefnut from early in Amenhotep IV's reign (Karnak Temple). 19th century drawing by E. Prisse d'Avennes reprinted in B. van de Walle, "Survivances mythologiques dans les coiffers royales de l'epoque atonienne," *Cd'É* 55 (1980), fig. 1: redrawn by Johsua Olsen.

---

53 Chappaz, "Le Premier édifice d'Amenophis IV à Karnak," 16.

54 Ibid., 24.

55 Ibid., 24–28, 36.

56 Baudouin van de Walle, "Survivances mythologiques dans les coiffers royales de l'epoque atonienne," *Cd'É* 55 (1980): 23–36, fig. 1.

57 Orly Goldwasser, "The Essence of Amarna Monotheism," in *In.t ḏr.w—Festschrift für Friedrich Junge* (eds. Gerald Moers et al.; Göttingen 2006: Seminar für Ägyptologie und Koptologie), 269, Fig. 1.

58 On equating Tefnut's iconography with Nefertiti, see Lise Manniche, *The Akhenaten Colossi of Karnak* (Cairo: American University Press, 2010), 93–94.

that these textual variants, similar to the one at Gebel el-Silsileh, illustrate that at this very early stage of the development of Atenism the didactic name was still in flux and the standard orthography had not been set. "Shu son of Re" occurs in the second line, while in the third "Shu father of the gods" is written. The name Nun, the primeval waters, is found in the fourth line, and in the fifth is "the tall plumed, Horus the strong-armed" (*ṯmꜣ-ꜥ*). Assuming that this 19th-century transcription is accurate, we find the names of several primeval deities, and it appears that at this very early stage, Amenhotep IV and his priests were not disinclined to thinking in polytheistic terms.

Among the Re-Harakhty temple blocks from the 10th Pylon are two extremely informative inscriptions regarding the early phase of the new theology. In the one, Amenhotep IV is identified possibly as the high priest of "Re-Harakhty who rejoices in the horizon in his name of light which is in the disc (Aten)."[59] The second block, though containing many lacunae, contains a "royal sitting" address that Redford maintains was a genre where the king typically announces a new temple building program.[60] There is no doubt that this deity was more than just a new expression of the old Re-Harakhty. He required an entirely new cult center.

Moreover, the reliefs and texts from the earliest temple of Amenhotep IV, possibly from the first or second year of his reign,[61] indicate that in "Re-Harakhty who rejoices in the horizon in his name of light which is in the disc (Aten)" we have a name that was not attested prior to this time. This deity, however, was fundamentally rooted in traditional solar theology. Many questions are raised by this development. What or who is the Aten? What is behind this didactic name? And what is the cause or causes that led to this development?

ATEN BEFORE ATENISM

Aten did not burst on the scene with the reign of Amenhotep IV in the mid-14th century B.C. with no pre-history. Although it is approaching 40 years since it was written, Redford's article, "The Sun-disc in Akhenaten's Program: Its Worship and Antecedents, I,"[62] remains the authoritative study on the origin of the Aten and the

---

[59] Donald Redford, "A Royal Speech from the Blocks of the 10th Pylon," *BES* 3 (1981): 87–102.

[60] Ibid., 97.

[61] Redford thinks that some gateway blocks decorated with the falcon and the large sun-disc (likely part of the first temple) date to the first year (Redford, *Akhenaten the Heretic King*, 64).

[62] Donald Redford, "The Sun-disc in Akhenaten's Program: Its Worship and Antecedents, I," *JARCE* 13 (1976): 47–61.

development of its iconography. He traces the word *i͗tn* back to the 5th Dynasty, where it was associated with the funerary cult, although little can be said about it.[63]

Not until the Coffin Texts (ca. 2200–1800 B.C.), however, are there a sufficient number of occurrences of *i͗tn* that offer more details about the Aten. In fact, Aten occurs more than 15 times, with the basic meaning being "sun" or "disc of sun," normally written as *i͗tn* + ⊙ sign as the classifier.[64] In one text, *i͗tn* + ⊙ is written as a variant for Re, which is what is used in other witnesses to Spell 105.[65] Aten also is equated with the solar bark that ferries the sun across the sky.[66] All six writings[67] of this line in Spell 47 consistently use the ⊙-sign, while one version (B1Y) includes the seated god determinative (𓀭). The correlation with the solar bark is found in Spell 1033: "Prepare a path for me into the bow of his (Re's) bark; brightness is in his disc (*i͗tn*) and power is in his shape (*b3*)."[68]

The element of sailing and Aten's association with the cosmic egg come together in Spell 335, pt. II: "O Re who are in your egg, rising in your disc (*i͗tn*) and shining in your horizon, swimming in your firmament, having no equal among the gods, sailing over the Supports of Shu, giving the winds with the breath of your mouth, illumining the Two Lands with your sunshine . . ."[69] The parallelism between the Aten and the egg prompts Redford to conclude that "it might suggest a connection between the Disc and pre-existent substance from which Re emerges."[70]

Goldwasser has further studied the connection between the *i͗tn* and the egg in Coffin Text Spell 335. In one instance the word egg (*swḥt*) is classified with the sign for "gold" (CT IV 292b-c [BgC[a]]), while in the next clause (*wbn m i͗tn.f*—"shines" or "arises in his *i͗tn*") the word *wbn* is determined with the egg sign, just like the word *swḥt* in the preceding clause. This collocation demonstrates to Goldwasser that the Aten equals the golden egg. Just as the egg hatches life, so does the Aten! She agrees with Redford on the idea of "pre-existent substance," and adds: "It seems that in the conceptual realm represented in the Coffin Texts, the *'Itn* not yet fully realized as a 'god,' might have been interpreted as an 'Ur'-substance—the Divine 'Golden Egg,' out of which emerged the familiar, pictorially defined image of the sun-god."[71]

---

[63] Ibid. 47–48.

[64] Rami van der Molen, *A Hieroglyphic Dictionary of Egyptian Coffin Texts* (Leiden: Brill, 2000), 59.

[65] Adriaan de Buck, *The Egyptian Coffin Texts* (Chicago: University of Chicago Press, 1935–1962), II, 112 (compare S2c and S1C).

[66] ibid., 209a–c.

[67] There are seven witness of Spell 47. The text of B13C is lost at this point.

[68] R. O. Faulkner, *The Ancient Egyptian Coffin Texts* III (Warminster: Aris & Phillips, 1978), 129.

[69] R. O. Faulkner, *The Ancient Egyptian Coffin Texts* I (Warminster: Aris & Phillips, 1973), 261.

[70] Redford, "The Sun-disc in Akhenaten's Program," 48.

[71] Orly Goldwasser, "*'Itn*—the 'Golden Egg' (CT IV 292b-c [B9C[a]])," in *Essays on Ancient Egypt in Honour of Hermann te Velde* (ed. J. Van Dijk; Gronigen: Styx Publications, 1997), 83.

According to the views of Redford and Goldwasser, then, latent in Aten as early as the Coffin Texts, 500–600 years before the beginning of the Aten revolution, was the philosophical and theological basis for the developments of the 14th century B.C. Redford further observes, based on statements like "Re who is in his Disc," "the Lord of the Disc," and "Re and his Disc," that Re and the disc are separate entities.[72] In essence the disc is a "potent symbol" and thus, Redford observes, "one might formulate a rule that, in Egyptian religion, deities are distinct from merely potent hierophanies by the complete subordination of the latter to the former as non-personalized agents through whom the gods work."[73] This is an important concept for understanding that in later Atenism the visible disc is the vehicle through which the Aten's power was revealed.

From the 12th Dynasty (ca. 1934 B.C.), there is the announcement of the death of Amenemhet I in the Story of Sinuhe: "the god arose to his horizon (*ꜣḫt.f*),[74] the King of Upper and Lower Egypt, Sehetepibre flew up to heaven, uniting with the sun-disc (*ỉtn*), the god's [i.e. the king] body merging with his maker."[75] Later in the story, Sinuhe lauds Senusert I, Amenemhet I's successor, saying, "fear of you is repeated in lands and foreign lands, you having subdued what the sun disc encircles (*šnnt ỉtn*)."[76] This same expression is applied to Senusert III (ca. 1862–1843 B.C.): "to him belongs that which the sun-disc encircles daily."[77] One can reasonably conclude from these limited 12th Dynasty occurrences of Aten that this universal solar image already was associated with the king's conquests and the territories he controls, a concept that will only grow in the New Kingdom. Indeed, Redford affirms that "by the 18th Dynasty" it had "become firmly established as indicating Pharaoh's worldwide dominion."[78]

Multiple names of solar deities are actually associated with king Ahmose (1550–1525 B.C.), founder of the New Kingdom. On a stela from Karnak Temple we read:[79]

He is gazed upon like Re when he rises	= *dgg.tw.f mỉ rꜥ wbn.f*
Like the shining of Aten,	= *mỉ psdw ỉtn*
Like rising Khepri at the	= *mỉ ḫꜥỉ ḫprỉ m*
sight of his rays on high	*ỉrr stwt.f m ḥrw*
Like Atum in the eastern sky	= *mỉ ỉtm m ỉꜣbt pt*

72 Redford, "The Sun-disc in Akhenaten's Program," 48.

73 Ibid.

74 Here *ꜣḫt* could also mean tomb, see R. O. Faulkner, *A Concise Dictionary of Middle Egyptian* (Oxford: Oxford University Press, 1962), 5, *ꜣḫt* meaning b.

75 Translation based on the critical edition in A. M. Blackman, *Middle Egyptian Stories. Bibliotheca Aegyptiaca*, Vol. 2. (Brussels: Fondation Égyptologique Reine Elisabeth, 1932), 3 (R 6–8).

76 Blackman, *Middle Egyptian Stories*, 33 (B 212–213).

77 Redford, "The Sun-disc in Akhenaten's Program," 48.

78 Ibid.

79 *Urk*. IV, 19.6–9.

For our interest, the various names show the multiplicity of forms or manifestations of the sun-god. The expression "He ruled that which the Aten has encircled" (*ḥqꜣ.n.f šnwt.n ỉtn*), an expansion of the 12th Dynasty expression, is also applied to Ahmose in this stela.[80]

The Stela from Tombos Island in the 3rd Cataract records that Thutmose I (1504–1492 B.C.) became king "in order to rule that which the Aten encircled."[81] Such statements continue, but with Thutmose IV (1400–1390 B.C.) there is an increased intensification of associating the king himself with the sun-god.[82] The Sphinx Stela is perhaps the best witness to this development, according to Betsy Bryan[83] (see Chapter 1 and further below). Furthermore, from this period, the trusted scribe and high official Tjaneny describes witnessing the king in the palace: "entering before his lord (in) the sanctity of the palace, gazing at the Aten [in his horizo]n from moment to moment."[84] The connection between the Aten and the king is unmistakable here.

Under Amenhotep III, occurrences of Aten proliferate. The familiar epithet that the king was "to rule that which Aten encircles (or encircled)" is found with some regularity.[85] On an dedicatory inscription of Amenhotep III for Montu at Karnak, the king is spoken of as the one "whom [~~Amun~~][86] put on his throne to rule that which Aten encircles and the throne of Geb, the office of Atum and the kingship of Re-Khepri."[87] Even though this text appears on a monument of his father, Amenhotep IV's zealots hacked out the name of Amun, but the names of other deities were unmolested, especially solar related gods (more on Atenist iconoclasm in Chapter 7).

A further connection between Aten and kingship is reflected in the statement: "the kingship of Re in heaven is for you; your lifetime is like Aten within it."[88] Then, too, in a version of Amenhotep III's Golden Horus name, he is called "Good god, Re's likeness, who brightens (*sḥḏ*) the Two Lands like (Re-Har)akhty,[89] lord of rays (*stwt*) in sight like Aten in whom the ladies rejoice (*ḥꜥꜥw*)."[90]

---

[80] *Urk.* IV, 16.7.

[81] *Urk.* IV 82.13.

[82] Lawrence Berman, "Overview of Amenhotep III and His Reign," in *Amenhotep III: Perspectives on His Reign* (eds. D. O'Connor & E. Cline; Ann Arbor: University of Michigan Press, 1998), 3.

[83] Betsy Bryan, *The Reign of Thutmose IV* (Baltimore, MD: John Hopkins University Press, 1991), 149.

[84] *Urk.* IV, 1016.6–8.

[85] E.g., *Urk.* IV, 1667.7, 1696.20, 1702.15.

[86] This is an example of Atenist iconoclasm of Amun's name; see Chapter 7.

[87] *Urk.* IV, 1667.7–8.

[88] *Urk.* IV, 1664.18–19.

[89] What is written is *ꜣḫty*, "those who are of the horizon." Helck renders this as "horizon dwellers," and considers this to be an abbreviation of Re-Harakhty (Wolfgang Helck, *Egyptian Historical Records of the Later Eighteenth Dynasty*, fascicle. IV, trans. Benedict Davies [Warminster: Aris & Phillips, 1992], 10, 34).

[90] *Urk.* IV, 1670.7–8.

The massive scale of Amenhotep III's mortuary temple and its gleaming quality are described as: "their heights arise to the sky, their rays (*stwt*) are in sight like Aten when he shines (*wbn*) in the morning."[91] A scarab records the god Khepri saying of the king, "you are the lord of that which the Aten brightens (*sḥḏ ỉtn*)."[92] On a stela from Amenhotep III's mortuary complex the word *ṯḥn*, meaning "lighten," "glitter," "flashing," and "shining,"[93] is linked to *ỉtn*. The passage hails the new cedar Amun bark made by the king that was decked in gold and silver.[94] When the new resplendent bark sails south to celebrate the Opet Festival at Luxor Temple, "its prow[95] makes radiant (*sthn*) the primeval waters (*nnw*) like rising[96] Aten in the sky."[97] Interestingly, in this text, it is Amun's cult symbol that is radiant or dazzling like the Aten. It is worth noting that Amun's dominant place in Egyptian religion at this time was in no way diminished by the increased importance of Aten, and texts cited here show that Amun can be likened to Aten. There is certainly no foreshadowing of the persecution of Amun that would follow in the third quarter of the 14th century B.C.

Another important epithet that gains popularity during this period is when the element *ṯḥn* ("radiant" or "dazzling") is used as an attribute of the Aten to form the expression "Dazzling Aten" (*ỉtn ṯḥn*). The epithet is variously applied, including to the king himself. On his year 11 scarab, the king sails on his royal yacht called "Dazzling Aten" (*itn ṯḥn*).[98] A regiment of the army was called *s3w n* (*nb m3ʿt rʿ*) *ỉtn tḥn*[99]—"the regiment of Nebmaatre[100] the Dazzling Aten," based on the title on a statue of the standard bearer Kamose.

Mention was made at the outset of this chapter that Amenhotep III built a large and sprawling palace complex south of Medinet Habu in western Thebes, known as Malkata today. There his three jubilees were celebrated in regnal years 30, 34, and 37, according to the dates on wine jar labels from Malkata.[101] A number of the wine

---

[91] *Urk*. IV, 1648, 17–18.

[92] *Urk*. IV, 1754.6.

[93] *Wb*. 5, 392.

[94] *Urk*. IV, 1652.10–18.

[95] Written in the plural form, *ḥ3wt*.

[96] I take *ḫʿʿ* to be an imperfective active participle that stresses repetition and continuity; see Alan Gardiner, *Egyptian Grammar* (London: Oxford University Press, 1969), §365.

[97] *Urk*. IV, 1653.14–15.

[98] A. de Buck, *Egyptian Readingbook: Exercise and Middle Egyptian Texts* (Leiden: Netherlands Institute for Near Eastern Studies, 1970), 67.10.

[99] *Urk*. IV, 1923.12, 18.

[100] The nomen or throne name of Amenhotep III.

[101] William C. Hayes, "Inscriptions from the Palace of Amenhotep III," *JNES* 10, no. 1 (1951): 37–37. Kheruef, who played an important role in the king's *sd* festivals, depicts events from the year 30 and year 37, but not year 34 for some reason; see Epigraphic Survey, *The Tomb of Kheruef*, plates 34, 36, 38, 39, and 40.

dockets mention the "House (*pr*) of Nebmaatre, the Dazzling Aten,"[102] suggesting that this was the name of the Malkata Palace, or a section of it. The name of this palace is found in the titles of the royal scribe Nefersekheru, who was the "steward (*ỉmy-r pr*) of 'the House of Nebmaatre, the Dazzling Aten.'"[103] Then, too, canopic jars of royal ladies associated with Amenhotep III refer to "the House of Dazzling Aten the Great" and "the city (*nỉwt*) of Aten."[104] Hayes, who more than 60 years ago studied the various jar inscriptions and ostraca in great detail, suggested that "the House of Dazzling Aten" was the earlier name of the palace, which seems to have been subsequently replaced by "House of Rejoicing" (*pr ḥʿʿ*).[105]

These epithets show that the "Dazzling Aten" applied to Amenhotep III, which is supported by direct application of this epithet in royal inscriptions to the king himself. On a statue from Amenhotep III's mortuary temple at Kom el-Ḥettan, of which the Colossi of Memnon are the most visible remnant, the Golden Horus name of the king includes *nṯr nfr tỉt rʿ tḥn ḥr ḫʿʿ mỉ ỉtn ḥr nṯry*—"the good god, image of Re of dazzling face who arises like Aten, the divine falcon."[106]

This brief review demonstrates that the sun-disc or Aten had a long history before the "Amarna Revolution" and that during the century prior to Amenhotep IV's reign, the sun-disc especially grew in prominence. Amenhotep III's reign saw an upsurge in uses of the word *ỉtn*, and a broader array of usages occur, even equating Aten with the king himself. There is not a hint of the exclusivism that will pervade the last decade of Amenhotep IV's reign. The religious ecumenicity of the period of Amenhotep III is nowhere better seen than in the hymns on the stela of the architect brothers, Suty and Hor, which show a happy coexistence between Theban (Amun) with solar Heliopolitan theologies, even as Aten's position was on the ascendency:[107]

> Worshiping before Amun when he shines (*wbn*) as Horakhty
> by the supervisor of works of Amun, Suti (and
> by) the supervisor of works of Amun, Hor.
> They say: 'Hail to you beautiful Re of everyday, who shines (*wbn*)
> daily without ceasing!
> Your rays (*stwt*) are seen[108] (though) one may not know it . . .[109]

---

[102] Hayes, "Inscriptions form the Palace of Amenhotep III," nos. 21, 54, 104, 108, 143, 174, figs. 17–21.

[103] *Urk.* IV, 1881.18, 1882.6, 16.

[104] Georges Legrain, "Fragments du Canopes," *ASAE* 4 (1903): 138–147.

[105] William C. Hayes, "Inscriptions form the Palace of Amenhotep III," *JNES* 10, no. 3 (1951): 178–179.

[106] *Urk.* IV 1761.6–7.

[107] The reigning king, Amenhotep III's name does occur on this stela (*Urk.* IV, 1946.12).

[108] *M-ḥr* literally means "in the face," and idiomatically means "sight" (Faulkner, *Concise Dictionary of Middle Egyptian*, 174).

[109] *Urk.* IV, 1943.12–19.

Hail to you Aten of daytime who creates everything who makes them live!
Great falcon of many colored feathers,
Scarab beetle (*ḫprr*) who alone raised himself up,[110]
Who created himself without being born . . .[111]
Khepri whose birth is distinguished,
The one who raised his beauty in the belly of Nut,
Who brightens the Two Lands with Aten,
The Primeval one of the Two Lands who alone made (*ir*) himself . . .
Who shines in the sky having come into existence (*ḫpr*).[112]

With these hymns one gets the impression that the solar creative powers of Harakhty, Re, and Khepri are linked closely to Amun, even as Aten's role as mysterious creator begins to make its appearance, a central doctrine of Amarna theology evident in the Aten hymns found at Amarna. Finally, the Suty and Hor hymns reveal the connection between (Re)-Harakhty, Aten, and the falcon, all of which come together in the earliest expression of Atenism, namely in the didactic name and in the iconography of Re-Harakhty as falcon with large sun-disc.

THE EARLY NAME OF ATEN

Earlier in this chapter, the first representations of Amenhotep IV were introduced in which he is depicted worshiping solar deities, notably "Re-Harakhty, the great god, lord of heaven."[113] A short time later, a year or two at the most, this solar deity's name is incorporated into what is commonly known as Aten's didactic or dogmatic name: *rꜥ ḥr ꜣḫty ḥꜥy m ꜣḫt m rn.f m šw nty m itn*—"Re-Harakhty who rejoices in his horizon in his name of light which is in the disc (Aten)" and is found on blocks from the first edifice that the king built at Karnak.[114] This long and descriptive name, Hornung points out, seems to be a creedal statement more than a name, per se.[115]

Why Re-Harakhty? This solar deity actually represents a fusion of Re, the sun, "Horus of the horizon" or "Horus in the two horizons," that is, where the sun rises and sets. As early as the Pyramid Texts of the Old Kingdom, Nut the sky goddess gives the resurrected king "the two horizons that he may have power in them as Ḥarakhti" (PT §4).[116]

110 Literally "who raised himself by himself."
111 *Urk*. IV, 1945.2–6.
112 *Urk*. IV, 1945.2–6, 18–19—1946.3, 12.
113 Epigraphic Survey, *The Tomb of Kheruef*, pl. 8–9.
114 Chappaz, "Le Premier édifice d'Amenophis IV à Karnak," 13–45.
115 Erik Hornung, *Akhenaten and the Religion of Light*, trans. D. Lorton (Ithaca, NY: Cornell University Press, 1999), 34.
116 R. O. Faulkner, *The Ancient Egyptian Pyramid Texts* (Oxford: Oxford University Press, 1969), 1.

Harakhty plays a role in ferrying the king across the sky to the sun-god: "That Ḥarakhti may cross on them to Re' . . . that I may cross on them to Ḥarakhti and to Re'" (PT §337).[117] The close association between Re and Ḥarakhti is seen throughout the Pyramid Texts (cf. §§855–856; 932–933; 1103; 1449), and they actually merge in one instance in Spell 488 (§1049) as Re-Harakhty: "May you (the king) cross the firmament by the waterway of Re'-Ḥarakhti."[118]

Re-Harakhy's presence in the Pyramid Texts and associations with Re suggest that he had Heliopolitan connections and that by New Kingdom times he was associated with the midday sun, that is, when the sun was at its peak of brightness and power.[119] Consequently he enjoys a prominent role in the 18th Dynasty, both in private solar hymns,[120] and in the royal arena.

Hatshepsut, for example, records that "she made (it) as her monument for her father Re-Harakhty" at Deir el-Bahri.[121] Thutmose III erected a pair of obelisks in Heliopolis "for his father Re-Harakhty,"[122] which have been identified as the obelisks now in London and New York.[123] There is textual evidence that he also built an enclosure wall around the Re-Harakhty temple complex at Heliopolis.[124] Limited inscriptional records suggests to Bryan that Thutmose IV was also active at Heliopolis, likely emulating his grandfather's building program.[125] It must be recalled (see Chapter 1) that it was Haremakhet-Khepri-Atum who spoke in a dream to Thutmose IV in the Giza Sphinx Stela and foretold that he, though not the crown prince, would nevertheless rule,[126] and the Sphinx/Haremakhet is the recipient of King Thutmose IV's offering at the top of the stela (Figure 3.10). He also engaged in some restoration and protective measures for the Sphinx and its temple, a sure sign of his devotion to Haremakhet.[127]

Bryan believes that Haremakhet was a regional deity, but that there was a "gradual assimilation of Horemakht to Horakhty" during the reign of Amenhotep II.[128] Given

---

117 Ibid., 72. Similar to this spell, see Spell 265 (§342), where Ḥarakhti occurs four times, and Spell 265 (§351), where his name occurs three times.

118 Ibid., 174.

119 H. M. Stewart, "Traditional Egyptian Sun Hymns of the New Kingdom," *Bulletin of the Institute of Archaeology* 6 (1966), 34.

120 For examples, see Jan Assmann, *Egyptian Solar Religion in the New Kingdom* (London: Kegan Paul International, 1995), 13, 15, 20, 21, 31.

121 *Urk.* IV, 295.14.

122 *Urk.* IV, 590.12–14.

123 Labib Habachi, *The Obelisks of Egypt* (Cairo: American University Press, 1984), 165–167.

124 Bryan, *The Reign of Thutmose IV*, 143.

125 Ibid., 143–144.

126 *Urk.* IV, 1542.17–1543.1.

127 Bryan, *The Reign of Thutmose IV*, 150–155.

128 Ibid., 155.

FIGURE 3.10 Sphinx Stela of Thutmose IV (Giza). Photo James K. Hoffmeier.

that the two names are so close in meaning, "Horus in the horizon" versus "Horus of the two horizons," and since Giza and Heliopolis were so close to each other (about 8 mi/13 km), where Re-Harakhty had long been championed, one wonders if the two are not one and the same solar deity and that the two names are simply variant writings. Regardless, it is clear that under Thutmose III and IV there was increased interest in the old Heliopolitan solar deity and Re-Harakhty.

It was left to Amenhotep IV himself to associate Re-Harakhty and the sun-disc. There is no rationale in contemporary texts for the fusion of these solar images or deities. As noted previously, the earliest reliefs of Amenhotep IV show him making offerings to "Re-Harakhy, the Great God, Lord of Heaven" (Figure 3.6), an epithet found elsewhere in this early period.[129] The falcon-headed deity is seated on a throne

[129] E.g., the tomb of Parennefer: Davies, "Akhenaten at Thebes," pl. 23. While largely damaged, the large sun-disc on the Re-Harakhty is partially preserved.

while extending the *w3s*-staff to the king and holding an ☥-sign is his left hand. The disc on the falcon's head is quite large and has a uraeus hanging from the front. It is essentially this iconography that Amenhotep IV adopted into his earliest portrayals of the new deity.

The explanation of *m rn.f m šw nty m ỉtn*—"in his name of *šw* which is in the Aten" is in order. The word "shu" has been intentionally left untranslated here. Shu/*šw* has more than one meaning. First and foremost, Shu is a primeval god who is known in the Pyramid Texts as the atmospheric air who holds up the heavens (cf. CT Spell 335, quoted in previous section).[130] Second, it means "light" and "sun light."[131] Third, *šw* means "dry," which clearly is not intended in the Aten's name[132] as it does not fit the solar dimension of the name. It has been shown that Amenhotep IV, for mythological reasons, was closely associated with the god Shu early in his religious odyssey.[133] Some of the colossal statues of Amenhotep IV discovered in east Karnak had the king wearing a *nemes*-crown with long feather extensions that are associated with the iconography of Shu.[134] The didactic name of Aten was changed after year 9, and the word *šw* was removed,[135] suggesting that the primeval god Shu lurked behind the name, or, possibly, if the meaning was "light," the removal of *šw* was necessary to avoid any confusion with Shu once Atenism was demythologized.[136] The depiction of Shu in the aforementioned drawing of Prisse d'Avennes (Figure 3.9) illustrates that at the earliest stage of Atenism, Shu was shown as the deity in anthropomorphic form. In the writing of the didactic name, *šw* was consistently written without any classifier (sign) for a divinity.

The second possibility, that *šw* means light, may make the best sense. Jan Assman, Erik Hornung, and other prominent Egyptologists consider Atenism to be ultimately a religion of light.[137] Likewise, Redford believes that this name or epithet "identifies him with the light which is in the sun-disc."[138] It is hard not to agree with the view that the light that emanates from the sun (disc) is the focus of Atenism.

---

[130] *Wb.* 4, 429. Wilkinson, *The Complete Gods and Goddesses of Ancient Egypt,* 129–130.

[131] *Wb.* 4, 430.

[132] *Wb.* 4, 429.

[133] Redford, *Akhenaten The Heretic King,* 102–103. More recently, see Eugene Cruz-Uribe, "Atum, Shu and the Gods during the Amarna Period," *JSSEA* 25 (1995): 17–18. He also offers a review of the scholars who have called attention to this connection.

[134] E.g., Cairo Museum catalogue numbers, JE 98894, JE 49528, and JE 99065; see Manniche, *The Akhenaten Colossi of Karnak,* 21, 36–40.

[135] Redford, *Akhenaten The Heretic King,* 186.

[136] Redford sees "no mythology" associated with Aten and whatever early traces there were likely were residual from long-standing tradition (Redford, "The Sun-disc in Akhenaten's Program," 47).

[137] Jan Assmann, "Akhanyati's Theology of Light and Time," *Proceedings of the Israel Academy of Sciences and Humanities* VII, no. 4 (Jerusalem: Israel Academy of Sciences and Humanities, 1992), 143–176. Hornung, *Akhenaten and the Religion of Light,* 54–55.

[138] Redford, *Akhenaten The Heretic King,* 173.

FIGURE 3.11 Early didactic name of Aten in cartouches (Berlin Museum). Photo James K. Hoffmeier.

Hornung's translation of the name, "Re-Harakhty, who rejoices in the horizon in his name Shu, who is Aten," suggests that he thought the primeval god Shu was understood in the name, but, at first glance, this does not appear to comport well with his "religion of light" as central to Atenism. For Hornung, however, Shu is not only the "space between earth and sky," but also "the light that fills that space."[139] Here we have the connection between the cosmic atmosphere and light, and it might be that this understanding of *šw* was intended, with the emphasis being on light that emanates from Re-Harakhty-Aten. In any event, the element *šw* subsequently had to be expunged altogether, even though the clear meaning of *šw* had become "light," lest there be confusion between the light of space and the primeval deity, Shu.

By the end of regnal year 3 of Amenhotep IV, the didactic name was divided into two parts and placed within two vertical cartouches, a move that signals that Aten

[139] Erik Hornung, *Conceptions of God in Ancient Egypt: The One and the Many*, trans. John Baines (Ithaca, NY: Cornell University Press, 1982), 283.

was king (Figure 3.11).[140] This dual cartouche became ubiquitous in the next, or "intermediate," stage of the development of the Aten, possibly in year 3, Redford suggests.[141]

AMENHOTEP III'S DEIFICATION

The "Dazzling Aten" was an epithet that apparently originated with Amenhotep III. In fact, numerous scholars now believe that this title was applied to the king around the time of his first jubilee (i.e., "Nebmaatre is the Dazzling Aten"), and that on this occasion Amenhotep III was deified, his son Amenhotep IV became co-regent and that the new Aten cult was directly tied to the divinized Amenhotep III.[142] In essence Amenhotep IV's Aten cult was in fact "an exclusively royal cult founded solely for the veneration and perpetuation of the deified king as the sun-disc (the living embodiment of all ancestral kings) by the royal family and the court," claims Raymond Johnson.[143] While Johnson has developed and articulated this intriguing and provocative theory,[144] aspects of this reconstruction, especially the deification of Amenhotep III and his connection to the sun, as well as the co-regency with Amenhotep IV, go back to earlier in the 20th century.

In 1905–1906, James Henry Breasted and a team from the Oriental Institute (Chicago) surveyed and recorded monuments extensively in Nubia. At Soleb, between the 2nd and 3rd Cataracts, he reported on the temple built by Amenhotep III and completed by Amenhotep IV and described it as "the most important monument in the Sudan, and one of the two greatest architectural works surviving in the Nile valley."[145] While the temple was dedicated to Amun-Re, the Sed-festival of Amenhotep III figured prominently in its decoration program, including a scene showing Amenhotep IV worshiping his deified father, Amenhotep III.[146] Based on these

[140] Redford, "The Sun-disc in Akhenaten's Program," 55. Edwards, *Akhenaten King of Egypt*, 18–19.

[141] Redford, "The Sun-disc in Akhenaten's Program," 54–55.

[142] W. Raymond Johnson, "The Deified Amenhotep III as the Living Re-Horakhty: Stylistic and Iconographic Considerations," in *VI Congresso Internazional di Egittologia Atti* (eds. Gian Zaccone & Tomaso di Netro; Turin: 1993), 231–236. For a more recent and expanded presentation of his views, see W. Raymond Johnson, "Amenhotep III Amarna: Some New Considerations," *JEA* 82 (1996): 65–82. Kozloff, *Amenhotep III: Egypt's Radiant Pharaoh*, 182–184, 252–253. Reeves, *Akhenaten: Egypt's False Prophet*, 100–101. David Silverman, Josef Wegner, Jennifer Wegner, *Akhenaten, Tutanhkamun: Revolution and Restoration* (Philadelphia: University of Pennsylvania Museum, 2006), 29–31. Silverman et al., however, do not hold to the co-regency aspect of the theory (p. 13).

[143] Johnson, "The Deified Amenhotep III as the Living Re-Horakhty," 23.

[144] For more recent and expanded presentation of his views, see W. Raymond Johnson, "Amenhotep III Amarna: Some New Considerations," *JEA* 82 (1996), 65–82.

[145] James Henry Breasted, "Second Preliminary Report of the Egyptian Expedition," *AJSLL* 25 no. 1 (1908): 84.

[146] Breasted, "Second Preliminary Report of the Egyptian Expedition," 87–88.

scenes, Breasted concluded that these scenes and texts represented a continuity of traditional solar religion that was to connect "the cult of his father."[147]

Cyril Aldred was firmly committed to the co-regency of the two Amenhoteps, and that they had overlapping Sed-festivals, but he did not seem to correlate Amenhotep III's divination as the transformative aspect of the first jubilee.[148] Further, he believed in a long co-regency beginning in Amenhotep III's twenty-eighth year, with the senior partner dying in his son's eleventh regnal year.[149] He continued to hold to a protracted co-regency—meaning that Akhenaten had built his sprawling temple complex at Karnak and an entire city at Amarna while Amenhotep III continued to rule from Thebes.[150]

Because the focus of the present study is on the religion of Akhenaten, the political history and questions about co-regency are not our concern per se. Since Johnson ties Amenhotep III's first jubilee with his divination and marking the beginning of Amenhotep IV's co-regency, however, we cannot completely ignore the issue. Redford has offered perhaps the most systematic dismantling of the co-regency theory.[151] Other historians concur, including William Murnane, who have thoroughly reviewed the evidence advanced in favor of a co-regency, and have found it wanting.[152] These considerations led Kenneth Kitchen to recently conclude that "the formerly-accepted co-regency of Amenophis III and Akhenaten remains unproven so far," but he allows the possibility that if there was one, it lasted "a few months only."[153]

A short, few-month-long, co-regency is plausible given Amenhotep III's long reign (38 years) and declining health and vitality in his final years. His second and third Sed-festivals (three in seven years!) may further have been attempts to revitalize the ailing and decrepit monarch. It may well be that Amenhotep III's divinized status can be attributed to a transformation that occurred during the Sed-festival, as Johnson avers:

> innovations in his titulary, dramatic changes in the style and iconography of his subsequent statue and monument decoration, and the simultaneous

---

[147] Ibid., 89.

[148] Cyril Aldred, "The Beginning of the El-'Amarnah Period," *JEA* 45 (1949): 31–32.

[149] Ibid., 32.

[150] Aldred, *Akhenaten King of Egypt*, 169–182.

[151] See his comments earlier in the chapter regarding the tomb of Kheruef. For his full discussion, see Redford, *History and Chronology of the Eighteenth Dynasty of Egypt*, 88–169.

[152] William J. Murnane, *Ancient Egyptian Co-Regencies* (Chicago: The Oriental Institute, 1977), 123–168.

[153] Kenneth A. Kitchen, "Regnal and Genealogical Data of Ancient Egypt (Absolute Chronology I): The Historical Chronology of Ancient Egypt, A Current Assessment," in *The Synchronisation of Civlisations in the Eastern Mediterranean in the Second Millennium B.C.* (ed. M. Bietak; Vienna: Österreichischen Akademie der Winnenschaften, 2000), 44.

> appearance of votive sculpture of Amenhotep III in a multitude of divine forms indicate that his living deification was a consequence of his expanded jubilee rites . . . Amenhotep III was officially considered to be a living manifestation of the creator god Re, particularly in his manifestation as the sun's disc, Aten, and hence was a living embodiment of all the gods of Egypt . . . [154]

The next step in Johnson's innovative theory is less convincing. In essence, he argues that the deified Amenhotep III, that is "Nebmaatre is the Dazzling Aten," is behind the Aten cult of Amenhotep IV.[155] Put another way, the Aten cult was developed by Amenhotep IV for the devotion of his father. Again, in Johnson's own words, "Akhenaten's new solar cult was not only rooted in the deification programme of his father, but was probably the culmination of that deification programme. Amenhotep III' deification and worship as the sun's disc supplies a theological rationale for the joint rule of the two kings."[156]

This conclusion demonstrates how Johnson's theory builds on three essential points, namely, the jubilee(s), the co-regency, and the emergent Aten cult. This three-legged stool, however, teeters if the co-regency leg is eliminated, and completely topples over if the Aten cult is not the worship of the deified Amenhotep III. It seems fitting to return to the observation made by Breasted when he offered his thoughts on the depictions of Amenhotep IV presenting offerings to his father, thereby laying the groundwork for Johnson's more expansive theory. While favoring the idea that the Soleb evidence suggests that "in continuing his (father's) cult it is conceivable that Ikhnaton's theory simply regarded him (Amenhotep III) as identical with the sun-god," he also cautioned that "Ikhnaton might respect his father's figure without adopting or continuing his father's cult."[157]

The interpretation of the data followed here is that indeed Amenhotep III was associated with the sun (as earlier monarchs were), and was deified and revered by his son, but that this is not a new phenomenon. Bryan has suggested that a similar pattern on a lesser scale occurred between Thutmose IV and his father Amenhotep II, who also was associated with the sun and who had a cult center beside the Sphinx, the very manifestation of "Horemakhet-Khepri, Re-Atum."[158] It is one thing to say that Amenhotep III and the Aten were associated, but it is quite another to believe that Amenhotep IV's devotion to his father's cult was the *raison d'être* of

154 Johnson, "Amenhotep III Amarna: Some New Considerations," 68.

155 Johnson, "The Deified Amenhotep III as the Living Re-Horakhty," 23. Johnson, "Amenhotep III Amarna: Some New Considerations," 80–82.

156 Johnson, "Amenhotep III Amarna: Some New Considerations," 82.

157 Breasted, "Second Preliminary Report of the Egyptian Expedition," 88.

158 Bryan, *The Reign of Thutmose IV*, 155.

Atenism. That simply goes beyond the evidence. The developing Aten cult, in particular within Amun-Re's domain at Karnak where a massive temple complex was built before the move to Amarna, it will be argued, shows no special connection to Amenhotep III. To pursue this argument and to understand the next stages of the fledgling religious reforms, we must investigate the Theban Aten temples of East Karnak.

His majesty gave orders . . . to carry out all the work projects . . .
quarrying sandstone in order to make a great benben (stone) for
"Re-Harakhty in his name of light which is in the disc (Aten)" in Karnak
GEBEL ES-SELSILEH Inscription from Akhenaten's first year

Chapter 4

The Domain of Aten

The Temples of Aten at Karnak

THE SEARCH FOR ATEN'S TEMPLES

FOR OVER FIVE hundred years, Thebes was the realm of the god Amun/Amun-Re, whose temple complex at Karnak during the 16th and 15th centuries grew impressively, with each monarch seemingly trying to surpass his predecessors' building efforts. Tall obelisks, towering pylon gateways, a sacred lake, statues, and temples were constructed, and texts and various images were carved for the glory of Amun (see Chapter 2). So it must have been unsettling to the powerful Amun priesthood when Amenhotep IV began building temples and chapels to "Re-Harakhty who rejoices in his horizon in his name of light which is in the disc (Aten)."

None of these temples had survived because of the backlash against Atenism, its apostasy, and the war on traditional orthodoxy. Horemheb (ca. 1323–1295 B.C.), the Amarna period general who served as the last king of the 18th Dynasty, demolished the Aten edifices and reused some of the blocks in the construction of the 10th Pylon at Karnak, while other blocks were later reused by Ramesses II (1279–1213 B.C.) in his construction of the 2nd and 9th Pylons, and at nearby Luxor Temple.[1]

[1] Donald Redford, "Studies of Akhenaten at Thebes I, A Report on the Work of the Akhenaten Temple Project of the University Museum, University Pennsylvania," *JARCE* 10 (1973): 77–94. Donald Redford, "Studies of Akhenaten at Thebes II, A Report on the Work of the Akhenaten Temple Project of the University Museum, The University Pennsylvania for the Year 1973–4," *JARCE* 12 (1973): 9–14. Ray W. Smith & Donald Redford, *The Akhenaten Temple Project*, Vol. 1 (Warminster: Aris and Phillips, 1976). Donald Redford, *The Akhenaten Temple Project*, Vol. 2 (Toronto: Akhenaten Temple Project/University of Toronto Press, 1988).

It appeared that the effort to eradicate the memory of the Aten heresy and its principal advocate, Amenhotep IV (Akhenaten), by removing his temples had succeeded. This eradication extended to other areas as well. For example, the offering king list in Seti I's Abydos temple excludes the names of Akhenaten and his successors (i.e., Smenekhkare, Aakheperure [?], Ay, Tutankhamun), with Horemheb's name placed immediately after that of Amenhotep III.[2] Over the centuries, however, these pylons began to collapse, revealing the core material to contain inscribed Aten temple blocks. Among the first recovered inscribed blocks were those from the earliest shrine built by Amenhotep IV for the falcon-headed Re-Harakhty-Aten discussed in the previous chapter (Figure 3.8).

Another celebrated inscribed block came into the collection of Major R. G. Gayer-Anderson early in the 20th century and was published in 1918 by Francis Ll. Griffith and now is in the collection of the Fitzwilliam Museum in Cambridge (Figure 4.1).[3] It shows Amenhotep IV, adorned in the traditional Sed garment and engaged in rites associated with the royal jubilee. That this theme was depicted so early in the king's reign, rather than at the traditional 30-year mark, is quite unexpected. The didactic name of the Aten is written within a pair of cartouches on this block. The inscription identifies the location of the celebration of the Sed-festival in "Southern Heliopolis," *ḥry-ib ḥ'y m 3ḫt itn*—"which is within 'rejoicing in Akhet-Aten.'"[4] The appearance of the name Akhet-Aten might incline one to think that this block came from Amarna. The block, however, was obtained by the major in

FIGURE 4.1 Akhenaten celebrating Heb Sed-festival on the Gayer-Anderson block (Fitzwilliam Museum, Cambridge). Photo James K. Hoffmeier.

[2] Translation available in James K. Hoffmeier, "Abydos List," in *COS* I, 69–70.

[3] Francis Ll. Griffith, "The Jubilee of Akhenaten," *JEA* 5 (1918): 61–63.

[4] Ibid., 62. The text is included in Maj Sandman, *Texts from the Time of Akhenaten* (Brussels: Queen Elizabeth Foundation of Egyptology, 1938), 152 §CLX.

Cairo, and the reference to "Southern Heliopolis" makes it clear to William Murnane that it originated in Thebes.[5] A variant writing of this name was discovered on some granite altars at Karnak that contain the early form of the didactic name of Aten, who is said to be "residing in 'Rejoicing in Horizon of Aten' (*3ḫt n itn*) in Upper Egyptian Heliopolis, the great primeval (place) of the Disk (*itn*)."[6] The use of the indirect genitive (*n*) distinguishes this name from that of the new city of Aten at Amarna, *3ḫt itn*, always written with the direct genitive. Regarding Theban "Rejoicing in Horizon of Aten"—*ḥ'y m 3ḫt n itn*, Murnane concluded that the name does not simply refer to a particular building, "but with a larger territory that was the setting for the Atenist Theban temples."[7] This interpretation seems to imply that Amenhotep IV was not merely erecting chapels and temples to Aten, but was transforming the Theban realm into Aten's domain, presaging what would happen at Amarna a few years later.

Also surprising is the fact that this block was made of limestone, rather than sandstone, the building block of choice for the Aten temples at Karnak. Other limestone blocks associated with the Gayer-Anderson block were found in the 2nd Pylon.[8] Consequently, Murnane determined that these blocks came from an "independent temple" somewhere in the Karnak complex[9] that was different from the sandstone Aten temples, also known from inscribed blocks found at Karnak and other nearby sites.[10] At Luxor Temple during the 1890s, thousands of inscribed blocks, typically measuring 52 × 26 × 24 cm (52 cm being the length of the royal cubit and 26 cm half a royal cubit;[11] ca. 18 × 9 × 8 in), were found within the pylon built by Ramesses II. These uniquely sized building blocks were dubbed "talatat,"[12] for reasons that remain

---

[5] William Murnane, "Observations on Pre-Amarna Theology During the Earliest Reign of Amenhotep IV," in *Gold of Praise: Studies on Ancient Egypt in Honor of Edward F. Wente* (eds. E. Teeter & J. Larson; Chicago: Oriental Institute, 1999), 306.

[6] Murnane, "Observations on Pre-Amarna Theology during the Earliest Reign of Amenhotep IV," 305.

[7] Ibid., 306.

[8] M. Doresse, "Observations sur la publication des blocs des temples atoniens de Karnak: The Akhenaten Temple Project," *GM* 46 (1981): 67–68 n. 14. M. Doresse, "Les temples antoniens de la region thébaine," *Orientalia* 24 (1955): 121–125. Murnane concludes that the limestone blocks from the 2nd Pylon are associated with the same building as the Gayer-Anderson Sed-festival block (Murnane, "Observations on Pre-Amarna Theology during the Earliest Reign of Amenhotep IV," 306).

[9] Murnane, "Observations on Pre-Amarna Theology during the Earliest Reign of Amenhotep IV," 306.

[10] For a discussion of the discovery of the Aten Temple talatat, see Ray W. Smith, "Description of the Project," in *The Akhenaten Temple Project*, Vol. I, 1–5; Cyril Aldred, *Akhenaten King of Egypt* (London: Thames & Hudson, 1988), 69–85; Donald Redford, *Akhenaten: The Heretic King* (Princeton, NJ: Princeton University Press, 1984), 63–71.

[11] Pierre Grandet, "Weights and Measures," *OEAE* 3, 494.

[12] It has been suggested this term was derived from Islamic architecture; *talata* means 3 in Arabic. So a *talatat* would be a block three handbreadths long; see Nicholas Reeves, *Akhenaten: Egypt's False Prophet* (London: Thames and Hudson, 2001), 93.

unclear (though theories abound), and the term has been used ever since. The presence of these blocks at Luxor Temple led George Darressy to think that an Aten temple originally stood at Luxor.[13] It is now evident that they originated in Karnak and were recycled at Luxor.

The first clue as to the general location of the Aten temples came in the mid-1920s when a drainage canal was being dug east of the great enclosure wall of Karnak Temple. Due to the high mound or tell that occupied the area outside the eastern temple enclosure wall, the engineers decided to circle around the mound, as maps and aerial photographs reveal (Figure 4.2a).[14] Here the first of the bizarre colossal

(a)

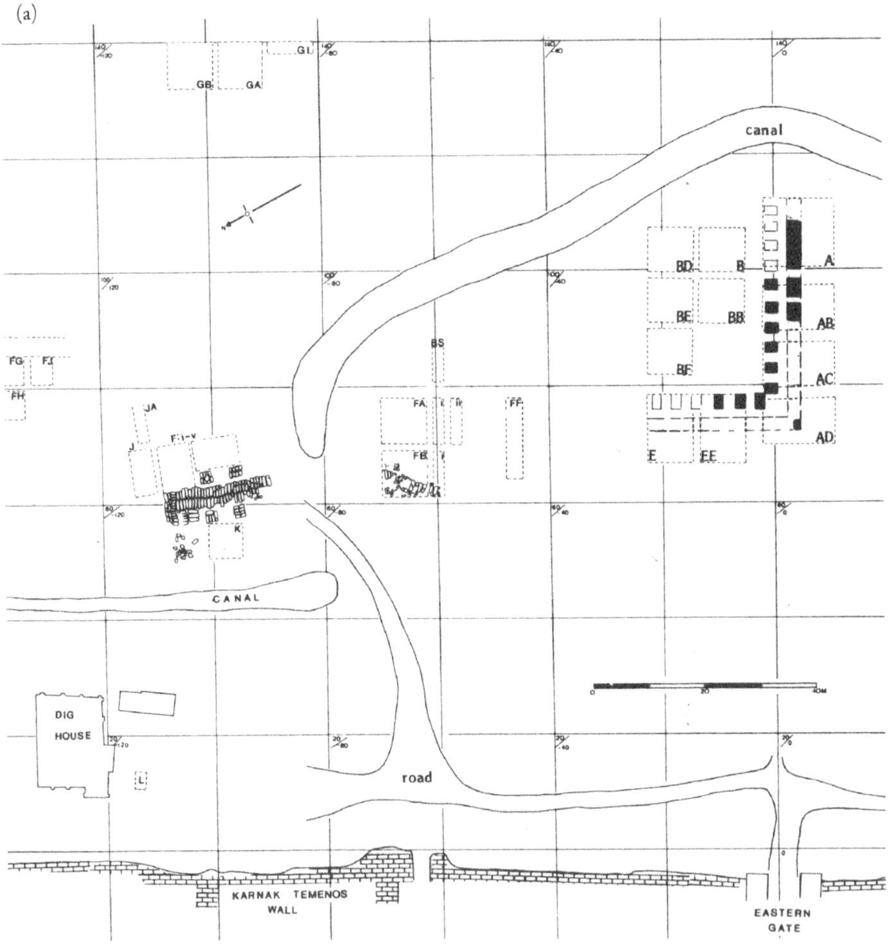

FIGURE 4.2 a. Akhenaten Temple Project excavation area (East Karnak). D. B. Redford, *Akhenaten: the Heretic King* (Princeton: Princeton University Press, 1984), 87. b. Part of Chevrier's area re-excavated in 1976–1977. Courtesy of Donald Redford.

[13] Georges Daressy, *Notice explicative des ruines du temple de Louxor* (Cairo: Impremerie Nationale, 1893), 3–4.

[14] The canal in recent years has been filled in, as the latest Google Earth images show.

(b)

FIGURE 4.2 b.

statues of Akhenaten was uncovered, initially by Maurice Pillet, but mostly by Henri Chevrier who took over Pillet's work (Figure 4.3).[15] The statues portray the king with a long narrow face and pointed jaw, with slender shoulders, but with hips like a woman, and one of the colassi appears to be androgynous (Figure. 4.4).

These unusual statues have inspired considerable interpretive debate over the years. Recently, Lise Manniche has produced a monograph with a wonderful summary of the debate, complete with drawings and pictures of all the statues and fragments in various states of preservation.[16] Many of the heads and torsos found intact (though severed at or around the waist) by Chevrier were found face down on the ground, the result of a deliberate act of defilement. Behind the statues were the foundations of rectangular pillars (1.80 × 2.00 m = 5 ft 10 in × 6 ft 6 in) made of roughly hewn stones (Figure 4.5). The piers, situated about

[15] Henri Chevrier, "Rapport sur les travaux de Karnak (mars-mai 1926)," *ASAE* 26 (1926): 119–125, & "Rapport sur les travaux de Karnak (novembre 1926-mai 1927)," *ASAE* 27 (1927): 133–149. Chevrier's plans are rather limited. For a more recent mapping of east Karnak, on which the 120 m. figure is based, see D. B. Redford, "Interim Report on the Excavations at East Karnak (1981–1982 seasons)," *JSSEA* 13, no. 4 (1983): 24, and Redford, *Akhenaten: The Heretic King*, 87.

[16] Lise Manniche, *The Akhenaten Colossi of Karnak* (New York/Cairo: American University Press, 2010).

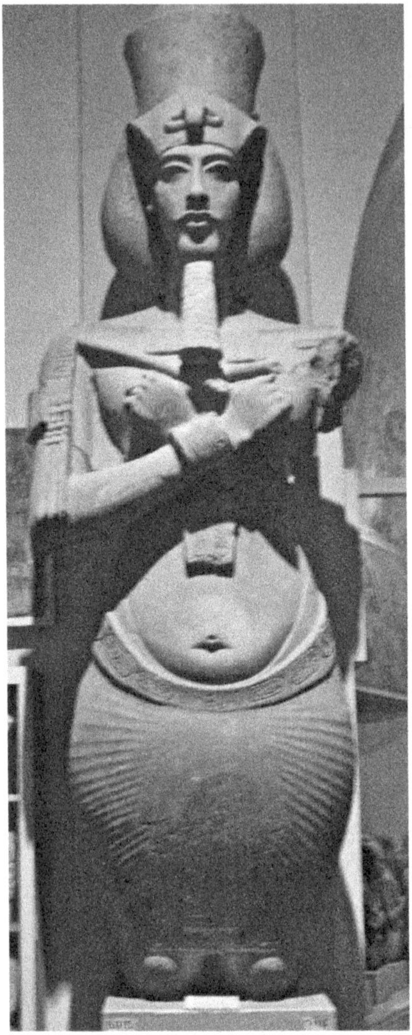

FIGURE 4.3 Colossus of Akhenaten from *Gm*(*t*) *p3 ỉtn* (Cairo Museum). Photo Edwin C. Brock.

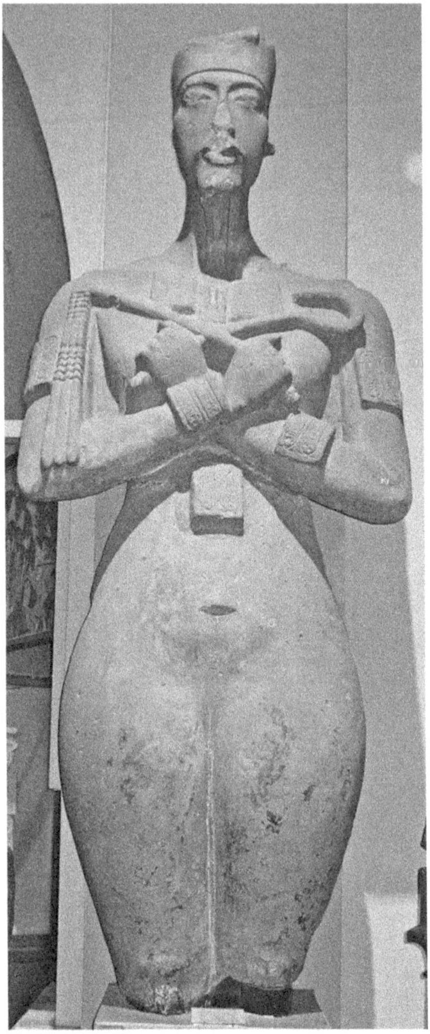

FIGURE 4.4 Androgynous colossus of Akhenaten from *Gm*(*t*) *p3 ỉtn* (Cairo Museum). Photo Edwin C. Brock.

2 meters (6 ft 6 in) apart, were covered with a veneer of fine sandstone that was decorated.[17] Against the piers the colossal statues originally stood. About 1.75 meters (5 ft 8 in) behind (south) the rectangular pillar, the foundation of a talatat wall was uncovered. The combination of the unique statues of Akhenaten and the talatat foundation wall demonstrated that this area was the location of at least one of the Aten temples.

[17] Redford, *Akhenaten: The Heretic King*, 105.

The excavations of 1926 and 1927 were limited to exposing two wide trenches, one running east to west from the point where the drainage ditch severed the Aten temple and the Akhenaten statues and west to just before the Nectanebo (eastern) Gate of the temenos wall, approximately 120 meters away (Figures 4.2a and 4.5).[18] The second trench turned north, following the foundations of the piers and the line of fragmentary statues. The French team's efforts subsequently turned to recovering more talatat from the 13th-century structures of Karnak and Luxor Temple. Medamud, 5 km (3 mi) north of Karnak, also yielded talatat blocks from Karnak.[19] By the 1940s, over 20,000 inscribed blocks had been recovered, and by 1965, that figure had swelled to 45,000.[20]

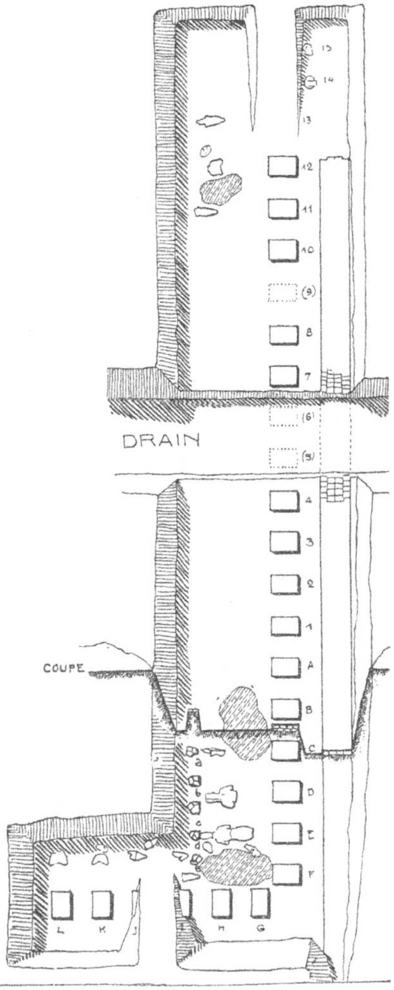

FIGURE 4.5 H. Chevrier's excavation plan (East Karnak). H. Chevrier, "Rapport sur les travaux de Karnak (mars-mai 1926)," *ASAE* 26 (1926): 123.

THE NAMES OF THE ATEN TEMPLES REVEALED

As early as the 1950s, the names of Theban Aten temples were already recognized from the abundance of inscribed talatat studied by Marianne Doresse.[21] More systematic efforts to study the burgeoning number of inscribed talatat became the focus of scholarly attention in the 1960s and 1970s. In fact, tens of thousands of decorated talatat were documented and photographed by the Akhenaten Temple Project (ATP) and the Centre Franco-Egyptien

[18] For Chevrier's plans, see *ASAE* 26, 123, and *ASAE* 27, 144. Chevrier's plans are also reproduced in Manniche, *The Akhenaten Colossi of Karnak*, 5, 8. Redford measures the drainage canal as being 124 m east of the Nectanebo gate, "Preliminary Report of the First Season of Excavation in East Karnak, 1975–76," *JARCE* 14 (1977): 9.

[19] Rémy Cottevielle-Giraudet, *Rapport sur les fouilles de Médamoud (1932): Les reliefs d'Aménemphis IV Akhenaten* (Cairo: Institut Français d'Archéologie Orientale, 1936).

[20] Redford, *Akhenaten: The Heretic King*, 67–68.

[21] Marianne Doresse, "Les Temples atoniens de la region thébain," *Orientalia* 24 (1955), 113–130.

d'Étude des Temples de Karnak.[22] The new data shed further light on the Aten temples.

The talatat, all made of Gebel el-Silseleh sandstone, indicate that there were at least four named temples, plus named shrines within a large complex called *pr-itn*, "House" or "Domain of Aten."[23] The names are as follows:

1. *Gmt p3 itn* has variant writings, including *Gm p3 itn.* It is this very temple that is named in the famous window of appearances scene in the tomb of Ramose (Fig. 3.4). As early as 1879, the scene of the Amarna pharaoh in the tomb of Ramose in western Thebes had drawn the attention of Villiers Stuart and subsequent Egyptologists.[24] The famous window of appearances scene, showing Amenhotep IV and Nefertiti in the sunken relief of the early Amarna style, stood out as strikingly different from the exquisite raised reliefs in the same tomb that date to the reign of Amenhotep III.[25] The epithet of the Aten that is centered over the royal couple is "the great living Aten who is in the Sed-festival, lord of heaven and earth who is in the midst of *Gm p3 itn* in the Domain of Aten."[26]

   The basic meaning of *Gm(t) p3 itn* is "the Aten is Found or Discovered,"[27] although there is some uncertainty about the grammar behind the name. Sayed Tawfik suggested that the "*t*" was the sign that *gmt* was the writing for the infinitive, which would mean "discovery of the Aten."[28] The fact that in many writings, the "*t*" is absent, makes the infinitive seem less likely, as the "*t*" is necessary for writing the infinitive of a third weak root, *gmi.*[29] In fact, of the 280 examples of the writing of *Gmt p3 itn* and *Gm p3 itn* amassed from the talatat by Edmund Meltzer, 186 occurrences are uncertain due to breaks and incomplete writings, while 53 are written with the "*t*" and 41 lack it.[30]

---

[22] See note 1 for Akhenaten Temple Project reports. For extended bibliography see the Centre's (CFEETK) website: http://www.cfeetk.cnrs.fr/. Also see Jean Lauffray, *Karnak d'Egypte Domaine du divin* (Paris: Éditions du Centre Nationale de la Recherch Scientifique, 1979), 144–192, and Lauffrey, *Karnak VI* (Cairo: CFEETK, 1980).

[23] Redford, "Studies of Akhenaten at Thebes II," 9; Redford, *Akhenaten: The Heretic King*, 70–78.

[24] Norman de Garis Davies, *The Tomb of the Vizier Ramose* (London: Egypt Exploration Society, 1941), 6.

[25] Ibid., pl. xxxiii.

[26] Ibid., pl. xxxiii.

[27] For *gmi*, see *Wb* V, 166.

[28] Sayed Tawfik, "Aten and the Names of His Temple(s) at Thebes," in *The Akhenaten Temple Project*, Vol. I, 61.

[29] Alan Gardiner, *Egyptian Grammar* (London: Oxford University Press, 1969), § 299.

[30] Edmund Meltzer, "Glossary of Amenophis IV-Akhenaten's Karnak Talatat," in *The Akhenaten Temple Project* Volume 2, 110.

Jocelyn Gohary thinks that the inclusion or omission of *t* was not arbitrary and might signal that its inclusion was the sign of the feminine and an indication that this particular part of the temple may have been "reserved for Nefertiti."[31] This idea is not a particularly convincing explanation since the *Gm.t p3 itn/Gm p3 itn* temple's primary function was for celebration of the jubilee of the king.

Most scholars see the different writing as reflecting grammatical variations. Redford has transliterated the name of the temple as *Gm.t(w) p3 itn* [32] and *Gm.t p3 itn*.[33] The former indicates the *sḏm.t(w).f* or passive form, "The Aten is Found," whereas the latter could be understood to be the relative form,[34] and would mean "that which the Aten has found." The advantage of the passive is that it could explain the variant writings as *sḏm.t(w).f* or the *sḏm(w).f* passive form—"the Aten is found or has been found." Regardless of how one parses *Gm.t(w) p3 itn/Gm p3 itn*, the meaning seems clear; this cult center at Karnak was discovered by the sun-disc in the sense of a theophany or divine revelation or appearance. It is the contention of this study that the name of this temple is critical to explaining the crucial transition toward Atenism (and this will be discussed in detail in Chapter 5).

The scenes associated with the *Gm p3 itn* temple are overwhelmingly associated with Amenhotep IV's Sed-festival, in which the king and members of the royal family are portrayed in various processions associated with the king's renewal, and it stands to reason that the very purpose of *Gm p3 itn* was for the celebration of that event (Figure 4.6).[35] The reliefs further show that the sun-disc with extended sunrays had become the standard iconography of the Aten, while the falcon-headed Re-Harakhty was banished.[36] In the earliest appearance of the sun-disc on the head of Re-Harakhty, the uraeus is included on the right or left side of the disc, depending on which way the deity faces (Fig. 3.8). Similarly, when the *bḥdt* sun-disc appears in scenes (e.g., the

---

[31] Jocelyn Gohary, *Akhenaten's Sed-festival at Karnak* (London: Kegan Paul International, 1992), 34–35.

[32] Redford, "Studies of Akhenaten at Thebes II," 9.

[33] Redford, "Preliminary Report of the First Season of Excavation in East Karnak, 1975–76," 26.

[34] Ibid., 31–32, n 79.

[35] Redford ("Studies of Akhenaten at Thebes II," 10) comments that "a large portion of the talatat, all from *Gm.t(w)-p3-itn*, are concerned with the sed-festival." Donald Redford, "East Karnak and the Sed-festival of Akhenaten," in *Hommages Jean Leclant*, Vol. 2, (eds. C. Berger, G. Clerc, & N. Grimal; Cairo: IFAO, 1994), 485–492. Redford et al., "East Karnak Excavations, 1987–1989," See also Jocelyn Gohary, "Jubilee Scenes on Talatat," in *The Akhenaten Temple Project*, Volume 1, 64–67, and Gohary, *Akhenaten's Sed-festival at Karnak*.

[36] Donald Redford, "The Sun-Disc in Akhenaten's Program," *JARCE* 13 (1976): 54–55. There are only a few small illustrations of the Re-Harakhty shown as a man with a falcon head among the talatat, cf. Redford, *The Akhenaten Temple Project* Vol. 1, pl. 186, nos. 8, 9.

FIGURE 4.6 a. & b. Talatat blocks showing Akhenaten wearing the Sed garment (Louvre). Photo James K. Hoffmeier.

tomb of Kheruef and the Berlin block) from the beginning of Amenhotep IV's reign, the uraei appear typically on either side of the sun (Fig. 3.6). In the new representation of the sun-disc in the *Gm(t) pꜣ ỉtn* talatat, the cobra is placed at the bottom center of the orb and faces outward.[37] These dramatic changes in iconography seem to have occurred between regnal year 3 and 4, prompted by a philosophical and theological shift that occurred at the beginning of year 3.[38] Although his name remains in the early form of the didactic name, it is now written in two cartouches: (Re-Harakhty who rejoices in the horizon)| (in his name of light which is in the Aten)|.[39] This new writing seems to parallel the centuries-old practice of kings writing their names in a pair of cartouches.[40]

---

[37] E.g., *The Akhenaten Temple Project* 1, plates. 5, 6, 7, 8.

[38] Donald Redford, "Akhenaten: New Theories and Old Facts," *BASOR* 369 (2013): 19–20.

[39] For examples, see plates in *The Akhenaten Temple Project,* Vol. 1.

[40] Battiscombe Gunn, "Notes on the Aten and His Names," *JEA* 9 (1923): 168.

It is suggested that the earliest temple of the area was *pr ỉtn*, which was subsequently, in Redford's words, "transformed into the *Gm-p3 ỉtn*,"[41] at which point *pr ỉtn* becomes the name for the entire complex. The role of the Jubilee festival will be treated in more detail below.

2. The name of the second temple, *Ḥwt bnbn*, the "House or Temple of the Benben," was evidentally situated initially within *Gm(t)-p3 ỉtn* to judge from the full name of the sanctuary: *Ḥwt bnbn m Gm(t)-p3 ỉtn*,[42] that is, "The Temple of the Benben in *Gm(t)-p3 ỉtn*." Later, the preposition *m* is replaced by the compound preposition *ḥry-ib*, meaning "within."[43] The use first of *m* and then *ḥry-ỉb* suggests that *Ḥwt bnbn* was located within or somehow connected to the *Gm(t)-p3 ỉtn* precinct.

The significance of the name of this temple cannot be overstated, as *Ḥwt bnbn* was the name of the temple of Atum/Re of Heliopolis, whose sacred symbol—the *bnbn* stone or truncated obelisk—was its focal point (see Chapters 1 and 3). As argued previously, Atenism had close ties to the classic, Heliopolitan solar cult of the Old Kingdom. Writings of *Ḥwt bnbn* in the talatat of Thebes use an obelisk as the determinative rather than the expected pyramid or pyramidion.[44] Redford has suggested that the Gebel es-Silsileh inscription (introduced in the previous chapter) signaled the beginning of the quarrying work for this temple.[45] The famous Silsileh inscription specifies that the quarrying was "in order to make the great benben (*p3 bnbn ʿ3t*) of (or for) 'Re-Harakhty in his name of light which is in the disc (Aten) in Karnak.'"[46] In the previous chapter it was suggested that this text marked the very beginnings of Amenhotep IV's building program that pre-dated the *Gm(t) p3 itn* project, which was built with the standard talatat. The text is, unfortunately, silent on the name of the temple for which "the great *bnbn*" was destined.

Concerning the writing *p3 bnbn ʿ3t* in the Silsileh inscription, Georges Legrain, who recorded the text, was quite emphatic that the determinative was a pyramid (𓉴) and not an obelisk (𓉶), as is the case in Lepsius's earlier copy of the inscription.[47] The indicator used consistently for the writing of

---

[41] Ibid., 18.
[42] Tawfik, "Aten and the Names of His Temple(s) at Thebes," 61.
[43] Redford, "The Sun-Disc in Akhenaten's Program," 55.
[44] Tawfik, "Aten and the Names of His Temple(s) at Thebes," 61.
[45] Meltzer, "Glossary of Amenophis IV-Akhenaten's Karnak Talatat," Fig. 13, nos. 17, 18, 19, and possibly 20.
[46] Georges Legrain, "Les Stèles d'Aménôthès IV à Zernik et à Gebel Silseleh," *ASAE* 3 (1902): 259–266.
[47] Ibid., 264.

Ḥwt bnbn in Karnak talatat is the 𓉶 sign.[48] The use of the different signs between the quarry inscription and those describing the actual temple *Ḥwt bnbn* may suggest that two different cult objects were intended. Sayed Tawfik thought the *bnbn*-stone of the *Ḥwt bnbn* temple may well have been an obelisk based on the use of the 𓉶 sign.[49]

One appealing theory recently advanced by several scholars is that the great obelisk of Thutmose III (relocated and rededicated by Thutmose IV)[50] in the Amun-Re temple nearby might have in some way been the focal point of the *Ḥwt bnbn* temple.[51] This obelisk, now in Rome, was removed from Karnak in the 4th century A.D. on the orders of Constantine, the first Christian emperor. It finally was erected in the Circus Maximus in Rome by Constantinus, Constantine's son, somewhere between A.D. 340 and 357. Today it is known as the Lateran obelisk.[52] Standing just over 31.18 meters (105 ft) in height, this obelisk was to our knowledge the tallest erected at Karnak,[53] and thus would have been a stunning sight, visible from any point in the Karnak precinct. Its original location at Karnak, however, remains uncertain.

Paul Barguet uncovered what he believed was the foundation for the great obelisk, a base made of large blocks interlocked with butterfly clamps (Figure 4.7).[54] It is located east of the Akh-Menu Temple of Thutmose III, and is aligned with the central axis of the temple complex and lines up with the later Nectanebo gate to the east, which today leads to the east Karnak Aten temple complex. In the 13th century B.C. Ramesses II built a temple in such a way that the great obelisk was the focal point, and then in the early 7th century, Taharqa the Kushite king erected a pillared hall in front (west) of Ramesses II's edifice.[55] Given the fact that later monarchs regarded this obelisk as such a significant feature that temples were situated to highlight the great Thutmoside obelisk, it is not unreasonable to believe that Amenhotep IV would somehow orient the *Ḥwt bnbn* temple to optically focus on it, one of the great symbols of Heliopolitan solar religion.

[48] Sandman, *Texts from the Time of Akhenaten*, 144.4–10.

[49] Tawfik, "Aten and the Names of His Temple(s) at Thebes," 61.

[50] Labib Habachi, *The Obelisks of Egypt* (Cairo: American University Press, 1984), 112–114.

[51] R. Vergnieux and M. Gondran, *Aménophis IV et les pierres du soleil: Akhénaten retrouvè* (Paris: Arthaud, 1997), 86, 102. Barry Kemp, *The City of Akhenaten and Nefertiti: Amarna and Its People* (London: Thames Hudson, 2012), 82. Redford, "Akhenaten: New Theories and Old Facts," 22.

[52] Habachi, *The Obelisks of Egypt*, 115.

[53] The unfinished obelisk of the Aswan Quarry would have surpassed it.

[54] Paul Barguet, "L'Obélisque de Saint-Jean-de-Latran dan le temple de Ramsès à Karnak," *ASAE* 50 (1950): 269–280, and *Le Temple D'Amon-Re À Karnak, essai d'exégèse* (Cairo: IFAO, 1962), 241–242.

[55] Barguet, "L'Obélisque de Saint-Jean-de-Latran dan le temple de Ramsès à Karnak," 270, fig. 1.

FIGURE 4.7 Place of great obelisk foundation (Karnak Temple). Paul Barguet, "L'Obélisque de Saint-Jean-de-Latran dan le temple de Ramsès à Karnak," *ASAT* 50 (1950): 275.

If indeed the obelisk of Thutmose III/IV was the focal point of Amenhotep IV's *Ḥwt bnbn* temple located to its east, it begs the question: What became of the great sandstone benben quarried at Gebel el-Silsileh? Several options present themselves. First it was a part of an earlier, smaller shrine that was now superseded and abandoned by the new *Ḥwt bnbn* ediface. Alternatively, one wonders if the old cult object was incorporated in the new structure and aligned with or oriented toward the Thutmoside obelisk. This suggestion is shared by Barry Kemp, the present excavator of Tell el-Amarna, who describes the placement of the obelisk by Thutmose IV on the axis of Karnak Temple "where it formed the focus of attention for the approaching the temple from the east side . . ."[56] Then he suggests that the Silsileh Quarry

[56] Kemp, *The City of Akhenaten and Nefertiti*, 82.

inscription's reference to the great *bnbn*-stone "probably points to the building of a temple that gave greater attention to the existing obelisk."[57]

Suffice it to say, this sandstone obelisk has not been found, but fragments of an obelisk pyramidion of Akhenaten were found at Karnak by Legrain more than a century ago. Made of granite, the inscription was only partially preserved; one surface contains the cartouche of Akhenaten and ///// *m ꜣḫt-n-ỉtn m ỉwnw šmꜥw*—"///// in Akhet-en-Aten in Southern Heliopolis." Regrettably the name of the obelisk or the temple within which it stood is in the lacunae.[58] To judge from the dimensions of the fragmentary remains (.42 × .40 ×.40 m), it appears to have been a rather small obelisk.[59] No photograph of the object was included in the report, so it is uncertain whether the name of Akhenaten is original or secondary (i.e., as is the case on many of the talatat where Amenhotep is replaced by Akhenaten).

Like the name *Gm(t) pꜣ ỉtn,* which was used for a temple at Amarna, the name *Ḥwt bnbn* was also transferred to a temple at Amarna.[60] In fact, the largest temple uncovered at Amarna, known as the "Great Aten Temple," is called both *pr ỉtn* (House of the Aten) and *Ḥwt bnbn.*[61]

One surprising feature of this temple is that Nefertiti and her daughter Meritaten are shown exclusively as the celebrants in cultic activities.[62] The absence of Amenhotep IV is conspicuous in the scenes. Why the queen should be the one so closely connected to this temple inspired by Heliopolitan solar temples is a mystery. Furthermore, when the figures of the royal couple in the Theban talatat are totaled, Nefertiti is portrayed twice as often as Akhenaten, leading Redford to deduce, "it is hard to avoid the conclusion that this high profile which Nefertiti enjoyed during the first five years of the reign is evidence of her political importance."[63] Her importance earned her an extension to her name before year 5 with the addition of *nfr nfrw ỉtn* "Most beautiful one of Aten."[64] The name Nefer-neferu-aten Nefertiti was the name by which the queen would be known throughout the sojourn at Amarna.

---

57 Ibid., 82.

58 Georges Legrain, "Sur un Temple d'Aten à Hermonthis," *Recuil de Travaux Relatifs à la Philolgie et à L'Archeologie Égyptiennes et Assyriennes* 23 (1901): 62.

59 Ibid., 62.

60 *Ḥwt bnbn* frequently occurs in the private tombs at Amarna, Norman de Garis Davies, *The Rock Tombs of El-Amarna*, Vol. 1–6 (London: EEF, 1903–1908); cf. Vol. 1, pl. 30, 37; Vol. 2, pl. 9, 21; Vol. 4, pl. 33, 43; Vol. 6 pl. 14, 16, 25, 39.

61 Kemp, *The City of Akhenaten and Nefertiti*, 82.

62 Redford, "Studies on Akhenaten at Thebes, II," 9–10.

63 Redford, *Akhenaten: The Heretic King*, 79.

64 Redford, *The Akhenaten Temple Project*, 84, 5. Redford, *The Akhenaten Temple Project*, Fig. 12, nos. 20.

3. The name *Sḥ-n-ỉtn m Gm(t) pꜣ ỉtn*—“the booth of Aten in *Gm(t) pꜣ ỉtn*”—is a third name found in the Karnak talatat,[65] which is attested at least five times.[66] *Sḥ* is the word for “tent,” or “canopy” as the determinative  often used with the word suggests, or with  means “booth.” [67] When written as , *sḥ nṯr* means “god’s booth” and is often associated with Anubis and the funerary cult.[68] This shrine was obviously rather small, and like *Ḥwt bnbn,* was located within the massive *Gm(t)* p*ꜣ ỉtn*. Tawfik may be right to suggest that due to Akhenaten’s aversion to using the word “god” (*nṯr*) may explain why the name of this sacred structure was *Sḥ-n-ỉtn* instead of *sḥ nṯr*.[69] While little can be said about this shrine, in some instances, Queen Nefertiti is shown on talatat where the name of this shrine occurs.[70]
4. *Rwd mnw n ỉtn r nḥḥ*—“Enduring of Monuments for Aten forever”—is the name of a structure that was clearly a major temple that occurs 36 times at least in that talatat.[71] This temple appears to be independent of *Gm(t) pꜣ ỉtn* at Karnak, although when the name is found at Amarna it is “in” (*m*) *Gm(t)* p*ꜣ ỉtn*.[72]

Matched blocks from scenes from this temple show Amenhotep IV standing before offering tables stacked with loaves of bread and other food offerings.[73] In some instances, the king holds up vessels containing an undisclosed liquid offering as he looks straight on, not upward toward the sun-disc with its descending rays pouring down on the offering. Another tableau depicts rows, one register on top of the other, of offering stands atop of which bowl-like braziers are perched.[74] Seventy-nine of these braziers, approximately the same height as the male attendants who are fanning (the coals?), are present.[75] The king is not shown in the assembled blocks of this scene, although the royal chariots which brought the entourage to the temple are included.[76]

---

[65] Tawfik, “Aten and the Names of His Temple(s) at Thebes,” 61.

[66] Ibid., Meltzer, “Glossary of Amenophis IV-Akhenaten’s Karnak Talatat,” 106.

[67] *Wb* 3, 464–465. For a more detailed discussion, see James K. Hoffmeier, “The Possible Origins of the Tent of Purification in the Egyptian Funerary Cult,” *SAK* 9 (1981): 167–177.

[68] *Wb* 3, 465. Hoffmeier, “The Possible Origins of the Tent of Purification in the Egyptian Funerary Cult,” 173–174.

[69] Tawfik, “Aten and the Names of His Temple(s) at Thebes,” 61.

[70] Ibid., 61.

[71] Redford, *The Akhenaten Temple Project* 2, xiii.

[72] Tawfik, “Aten and the Names of His Temple(s) at Thebes,” 61.

[73] Redford, *The Akhenaten Temple Project* 2, pl. 29, 34.

[74] Ibid., pl. 6, 42, 43.

[75] Ibid., 3.

[76] Ibid., pl. 43.

Evidently the king had already departed the court with the braziers, and the depicted chariots represent the end of the royal train.

Numerous chariot scenes, showing Amenhotep IV and Nefertiti and other members of the royal court, are found in the *Rwd mnw* talatat that this writer studied in detail for *The Akhenaten Temple Project*, Volume 2.[77] The Theban Aten temple chariot scenes, like their later counterparts from the tombs of Amarna, present the king and queen moving between the palace and various temples to preside over ceremonies and offerings.

5. *Tnỉ mnw n ỉtn r nḥḥ*—"Exalted (or Lofty) are the monuments of the Aten forever"—is the final temple named in the talatat, for which there are nine attestations at Karnak and two at Medamud.[78] Most of the *Tni mnw* temple blocks were found in the 9th Pylon.[79] This sanctuary seems to have been a stand-alone structure that features scenes of domestic activities, including bread making and storing wine amphorae, and there are displays of the king engaged in cultic activities with the queen in a supportive role.[80]

The Centre Franco-Egyptien has assembled an impressive talatat scene that now occupies a wall in the Luxor Museum. The central theme has Amenhotep IV approaching the temple or shrine's entrance, and the Aten disc overhead shoots down its rays, which enfold the royal figure with its hands extending ☥ and 𓌀 signs.[81] The door of the shrine is opened by a priest, allowing the king to approach the offering table. One of the priests frequently shown with the king in these scenes bears the title *wr m3w*, the "Greatest of Seers,"[82] which is the title of the high priest of Heliopolis.[83] Here, too, is another vital link to the old solar religion.

In the adjacent scene, Amenhotep IV stands before an altar piled high with loaves of bread and prepared ducks, topped off with flaming bowls as the sun's rays reach down to the offering. A smaller panel to the left of this royal worship scene portrays the king and queen standing with hands upraised to the Aten.[84] A frieze across the top of the kiosk in which the king appears has a row of cobras with hands held up in a gesture of worship.

---

77 James K. Hoffmeier, "The Chariot Scenes," in *The Akhenaten Temple Project* 2, 35–45.

78 Tawfik, "Aten and the Names of His Temple(s) at Thebes," 62.

79 Lauffray, *Karnak d'Egypte Domaine du divin*, 175.

80 Redford, *Akhenaten: The Heretic King*, 71.

81 Lauffray, *Karnak d'Egypte Domaine du divin*, 188, fig. 155.

82 Redford, *The Akhenaten Temple Project* 2, 89, figs. 3:5, 6, 7, pl. 29.

83 M. Moursi, *Die Hohenpriester des Sonnengottes von der Frühzeit Ägyptens bis zum Ende des Neuen Reiches* (Munich: Münchner Ägyptologische Studien 26, 1972).

84 Lauffray, *Karnak d'Egypte Domaine du divin*, 188, fig. 155.

The adoring cobras are reminiscent of the east-facing uraei from the pyramid complex of Djoser at Saqqara (Figure 1.6). The vast majority of this scene shows the bustling activity in the nearby palace: food preparation, servants carrying water jars on yokes, cattle being attended, and the like.[85]

THE KARNAK PALACE

The young king lived initially at the Malkata Palace, where he had had his own royal apartment as a prince, and then would have moved into the main palace, where his father had resided in the final decade of his life. Seal impressions first mention "the house of the re[al] king's son [i.e., prince], Amenhotep."[86] Then, too, other seal impressions attest to the presence of Neferkheperure (Amenhotep IV) at the Malkata residence; like the impressions of Prince Amenhotep, the royal names were found in the "western villa."[87] Under his father the name for this palace had been known as The House of Rejoicing (*pr ḥꜥy*), but under Amenhotep IV, the name was expanded to The Mansion of Rejoicing in the Horizon (*pꜣ bḫn ḥꜥy m ꜣḫt*).[88] This may have remained the official residence of the royal family until the move to Amarna, but the Karnak talatat also reveal that there was another palace associated with the Aten temples.

Akhenaten Temple Project, Volume I, contains a study by Redford of these palace scenes.[89] The *Tni mnw* scenes mentioned above apparently depict the same palace. Due to the proximity of the palace scenes to the temples, it seems evident that the palace or palaces depicted in the talatat are not the same as the Malkata palace complex in western Thebes. One of the key features of this palace is the so-called window of appearance, where the king and other members of the royal family would pose and the king could reward officials or make pronouncements.[90] One such recipient of a reward of gold was the vizier Ramose, whose tomb largely reflects the elegant raised relief artistic style of Amenhotep III; but on the back wall of the tomb is a full-fledged early Amarna style scene in which the Aten shines its rays and beneficences on the royal couple as they stand in the window of appearances.[91] The didactic name of the Aten is written in a pair of cartouches, and the drama depicted is said to be "within *gm pꜣ itn* in the Domain of Aten." This window of appearances,

---

[85] Ibid, 186–187, fig. 153, 158, fig. 125.

[86] William C. Hayes, "Inscriptions from the Palace of Amenhotep III," *JNES* 10 (1951): 159, 272 fig. 27 KK.

[87] Ibid., 176 (fig. 33 S 124), 177; 235 (fig. 34. R 18–20).

[88] Ibid., 180.

[89] Redford, "The Palace of Akhenaten in the Karnak Talatat," in *The Akhenaten Temple Project*, Volume 1, 122–136.

[90] Ibid., 128–131.

[91] Aldred, *Akhenaten King of Egypt*, 91.

with adjacent pillared halls, then, ought to be located within the great Aten temple precinct, *Pr-itn*. The Ramose scene surely portrays the same palace scene as those in the Karnak talatat that are closely connected to the Aten temple complex.

The talatat scenes further show the procession of the chariots of the royal family between the temples and the palace, or the chariots are shown awaiting the return of the royal family and their entourage.[92] This motif is also a main staple of the reliefs in the private tombs of Amarna.[93] In some cases at Amarna, the chariots are parked, awaiting the members of the royal party.[94] The role played by chariots according to the artistic representations at Karnak and Amarna were essentially the same, namely transporting the king and royal family between the palace and the temple.

It has been observed that while the talatat scenes show ample domestic duties going on in the palace complex, what is plainly missing is any depiction of bedrooms. At Amarna, on the other hand, palace scenes do show sleeping chambers, by way of comparison.[95] This absence in the Karnak talatat leads Redford to suggest that the function of the palace shown in the Aten temple reliefs was ceremonial in nature, primarily used in connection with banqueting and domestic activities related to various ceremonies such as changing regalia during the Sed-festival. No architectural remains for this palace have been discovered thus far, but excavations in east Karnak have established the western sector of the *Gm(t) p3 itn* temple, which in turn offers a possible location for that structure (see discussion below and Figure 4.11).

REDISCOVERING THE ATEN TEMPLE PRECINCT

After a decade of studying the thousands of talatat scenes and seeking to match them on paper in order to reconstruct larger scenes, the ATP initiated excavations in east Karnak in 1975 with field seasons in April, August, and September, involving surveying and excavations. Under the direction of Donald Redford of the University of Toronto, work commenced in the very areas where Chevrier had worked 50 years earlier. This was a wise move as it allowed our team to see what the French had left behind, as well as to pick up where they left off. The author was privileged to work as photographer and a field supervisor that summer season, and again in 1977. Between 1975 and 1991, 17 campaigns were devoted to this area, including Kom el-Ahmar,

[92] Redford, *The Akhenaten Temple Project* I, pl. 50, 58; Redford, *The Akhenaten Temple Project* 2, pl. 17, 18, 19 20, 35, 37, 42, 43.

[93] Davies, *The Rock Tombs of El Amarna* Vol. 1, X, XVII, XIX; Idem., *The Rock Tombs of El Amarna* 3, pl. XXXII, XXXIIa.
Davies, *The Rock Tombs of El Amarna*, Vol. 4, pl. XX, XXII.

[94] Davies, *The Rock Tombs of El Amarna*, Vol. 1, pl. IV, IX, XXIV; Davies, *The Rock Tombs of El Amarna*, Vol. 4, pl. VIII, XII, XIV; Davies, *The Rock Tombs of El Amarna*, Vol. 6, pl. IV.

[95] Davies, *The Rock Tombs of El Amarna*, Vol. 3, XIII, XXIV, XXXIII.

a muddy hillock that was thought by an earlier generation of Egyptologists to be part of the Aten temple complex. Barguet, for example, thought that this feature might be the location of *Ḥwt bnbn*.[96] This feature instead turned out to be a mud brick constructed platform, perhaps used for offerings during the 3rd Intermediate Period (early 1st millennium B.C.), and therefore had nothing to do with the Aten temple complex.[97]

Chevrier had dug a long trench exposing the colossi of Amenhotep IV. The rectangular pillar foundations and the trace of a talatat wall[98] and his trench were still visible in places once the debris of the intervening years was removed (Figures 4.2a–b and 4.5). Decades of erosion and thistles posed an early challenge to reaching the levels he had exposed, and on either side of the trenches, Chevrier's workers dumped their excavation debris (Figure 4.8).[99] In addition to clearing the area where the 1920s excavations left off in the first season, five meters south of the east-west talatat wall the ATP excavators uncovered the lower levels of a mud brick enclosure wall that

FIGURE 4.8 Chevrier's excavation cut through the tell (East Karnak). Photo James K. Hoffmeier.

[96] Barguet, *Le Temple D'Amon-Rê à Karnak*, 8.

[97] Donald Redford, *The Akhenaten Temple Project Volume 3: The Excavations of Kom-el Ahmar and Environs* (Toronto: Akhenaten Temple Project/University of Toronto Press, 1994).

[98] Chevrier, "Rapport sur les travaux de Karnak (mars–mai 1926)," 119–125, and "Rapport sur les travaux de Karnak (novembre 1926–mai 1927)," 133–149.

[99] Donald Redford, "Preliminary Report of the First Season of Excavation in East Karnak 1975–76," *JARCE* 14 (1977): 9–32, see plate I for photographs. Redford, *Akhenaten: The Heretic King*, 86–101.

likely surrounded the temple complex.[100] Chevrier had not excavated far enough to the south to reach this wall, as his plan reveals (Figure 4.5). Additionally, new talatat blocks were discovered, including decorated ones whose motifs unmistakably connected them to the Sed-festival scenes already matched by the ATP. One block showed men with the long pole hoisted on their shoulders that bore the king's palanquin,[101] and another portrayed two attendants bowing in the direction of the monarch.[102] Several pieces have the didactic name of Aten in cartouches,[103] one of which was from a granite statue. A scant section of an inscription on one block mentions *Gm p3 ỉtn*.[104] As a consequence of these finds, it became clear that part of the decorative program of the east-west wall was the Sed-festival ceremonies and that the walls and colossi were part of the *Gm(t) p3 ỉtn* temple. With this piece of the puzzle in hand, Professor Redford could declare: "the problem was solved; we had found our temple!"[105] This news made it to the front pages of the *New York Times*. The headline on February 24, 1976, read, "Long-Sought Temple Is Uncovered in Egypt."[106]

Excavations continued, exposing not only domestic areas from the Second Intermediate Period, but also later remains from the 3rd Intermediate Period;[107] however, our concern here is with the Aten temple finds. In 1977 the southwestern corner of *Gm(t) p3 ỉtn* was uncovered, which includes a round, torus roll, which served as the outside corner (Figure 4.9).[108] While the north-south line of the temple had been exposed by Chevrier, the external corner had not been reached in the 1920s (Figure 4.5). Thanks to excavations in the 1980s, the incredible size of *Gm(t) p3 ỉtn* was fully realized. Following the line of the walls and colossal statues toward the north, the northwestern corner of the wall was revealed 220 meters from the southwest corner (Figure 4.2a).[109] The eastern extent of the walls of *Gm(t) p3 ỉtn* was not determined when the ATP concluded excavations in East Karnak in 1991, although by then the general plan and incredible size were established (Figure 4.10). Then,

---

[100] D. B. Redford, "Interim Report on the Excavations at East Karnak (1981–1982 seasons)," *JSSEA* 13, no. 4 (1983): 206, fig. 3.

[101] Redford, "Preliminary Report of the First Season of Excavation in East Karnak 1975–76," pl. VI, no. 4, and Redford, *Akhenaten: The Heretic King*, 94.

[102] Redford, "Preliminary Report of the First Season of Excavation in East Karnak 1975–76," pl. XIV, no.1.

[103] Ibid., pl. XI, no. 2, and XV, no. 4.

[104] Ibid., pl. XI, no. 3.

[105] Redford, *Akhenaten: The Heretic King*, 94.

[106] Henry Tanner, "Long-Sought Temple Is Uncovered in Egypt," *New York Times* (February 22, 1976).

[107] Redford, "Interim Report on the Excavations at East Karnak (1981–1982 seasons)," 203–223. Donald Redford, et al., "East Karnak Excavations, 1987–1989," *JARCE* 28 (1991), 75–106.

[108] Redford, *Akhenaten: The Heretic King*, 107, fig. 7.4 & 7.5.

[109] For the plan of the western side of the *Gm(t) p3 itn* temple, see Redford, "Interim Report on the Excavations at East Karnak (1981–1982 seasons)," 204 & 205; Redford, et al., "East Karnak Excavations, 1987–1989," *JARCE* 28 (1991): 76. Redford, "East Karnak and the Sed-festival of Akhenaten," 485–492.

FIGURE 4.9 Southwest corner of *Gm(t) p3 itn* exposed in 1977. Photo James K. Hoffmeier.

too, Redford's work along the northern wall proved to be fruitless because the destruction of this segment of the wall was found to be more complete than its counterpart to the south.[110] It was thought that the villages of Nag el-Fokhani and Nag el-Tawil on the east side encroached over the once sacred area, making it impossible to know the temple's eastern limits.

Fortuitously, the location of the eastern wall and therefore the footprint of the temple and its dimensions were determined in 2003 when trenching to install pipes for a sewage system took place in and around Nag el-Tawil. There new remains of *Gm(t) p3 itn* were uncovered. The sewage excavation project was already underway when archaeologist Edwin Brock, working in cooperation with the Supreme

[110] Redford et al., "East Karnak Excavations, 1987–1989," 89.

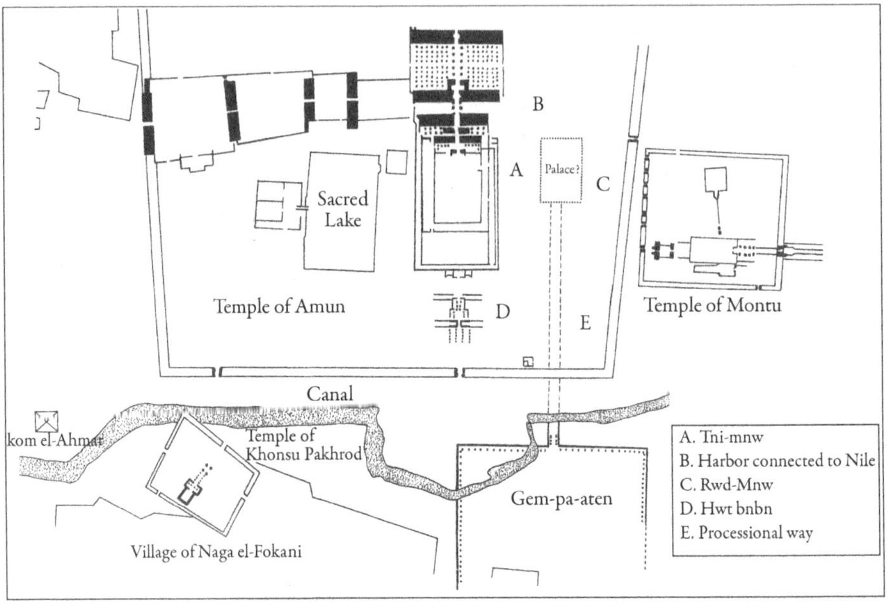

FIGURE 4.10 Donald Redford's plan of East Karnak and proposed locations of Aten temples. Donald Redford, "Akhenaten: New Theories and Old Facts," *BASOR* 369 (2013): 10.

Council for Antiquities (Egypt's antiquities department), began supervising the handling of archaeological finds when they were encountered. He also studied and documented the remains.[111] Furthermore, he was able to sink some probes and test trenches to follow leads. Included in the discoveries were three granite altars containing the cartouches of Akhenaten, Nefertiti, and the dual cartouches of the didactic name of the Aten.[112] A number of inscribed talatat blocks were encountered that displayed scenes connected to the Sed-festival, including bowing priests standing by a door to the temple and men carrying standards.[113] Parts from colossal statues—the same as those discovered by Chevrier—were found (i.e., a square-ended royal beard and three kneecaps).[114] Some of this material was discovered at a point approximately 160 meters east of the northwest corner discovered by Redford.

Brock's probes also laid bare lower sections (foundations?) of talatat walls, and he found four rectangular bases of crushed stone that served as the foundation of pillars (like those found earlier by Chevrier and then Redford along the south wall) against which the colossal statues stood.[115] By plotting coordinates from the newly

---

[111] Edwin Brock was kind enough to provide a copy of his report, along with images and a plan of the work. His report, "Archaeological Observations in East Karnak, 2002–2003," in press.

[112] Brock, "Archaeological Observations in East Karnak, 2002–2003," figs. 1, 2, 12, 13.

[113] Ibid., figs. 6, 8.

[114] Ibid., figs. 19, 20.

[115] Ibid., figs. 14, 15.

discovered data along with the two western corners unearthed by Redford and using surveying equipment, Brock concluded that the eastern wall, running between two adjacent villages, was located 220 meters (715 ft) east of the western wall. This means that *Gm(t) p3 ỉtn* was square in its configuration, ca. 220 × 220 meters (715 × 715 ft). If the size of the mud brick temenos wall were factored into the size of the temple (perhaps 2 m thick and 5 m behind the exterior of the talatat wall), it would have exceeded 500,002 meters (ca. 5,480,002 ft). Concerning this massive structure, Brock observes, "it would appear that this temple construction of Akhenaten was nearly equal in size to the contemporary temple of Amen at Karnak, constructed over the reigns of at least eight previous kings."[116]

Combining the new archaeological data with what was previously known from Chevrier's discoveries, along with the architectural features presented in the talatat scenes, a partial reconstruction of *Gm(t) p3 ỉtn* became feasible. In essence, this temple was a huge open court with a surrounding decorated talatat wall. A narrow roof spanned the 2 meters between the outside talatat wall and the square or rectangular pillared wall in front of which stood the colossal statues of Amenhotep IV. The pillars too were inscribed, but the main Sed-festival scenes were on the inside walls behind the statues (Figure 4.11).[117] Within the colonnaded court, open to the sun, scores of altars once were spaced throughout the open court, as the talatat scenes demonstrate, and perhaps smaller shrines or chapels were located within this massive open court.[118] A number of these have been found and were made of granite. While known from the early stage of the Aten temple, there was a large altar to Re-Harakhty that was approached by a ramp that may well have been within *Gm(t) p3 ỉtn*'s court.[119] The same type of altar, approached by a ramp or stairs, continued to be used at Amarna (Figure 4.12). A stepped altar similar to those depicted in Aten's temples stands at Karnak, although little can be said about its date of origin and the span of time it was used as it contains no inscriptions (Figure 4.13a–b).

The Aten temples, with their open courts, resemble earlier solar sanctuaries, such as the 5th Dynasty Sun Temples (Figure 1.7). Cultic activities were performed in the open space. The Aten cult, too, was practiced where there could be direct contact

---

[116] Ibid., 14.

[117] Redford, "Interim Report on the Excavations at East Karnak (1981–1982 seasons)," fig. 3. Redford, *Akhenaten: The Heretic King*, 103.

[118] A construction of the Jubilee Festival, including the massive open court area with scores, if not hundreds, of altars; see *Akhenaten: The Heretic King*, 118.

[119] For the talatat scene of the Re-Harakhty altar, see Redford, *The Akhenaten Temple Project* 1, pl. 78–80. That the altar was associated with the earliest phase of worship at Karnak; see Redford, "Akhenaten: New Theories and Old Facts," 17.

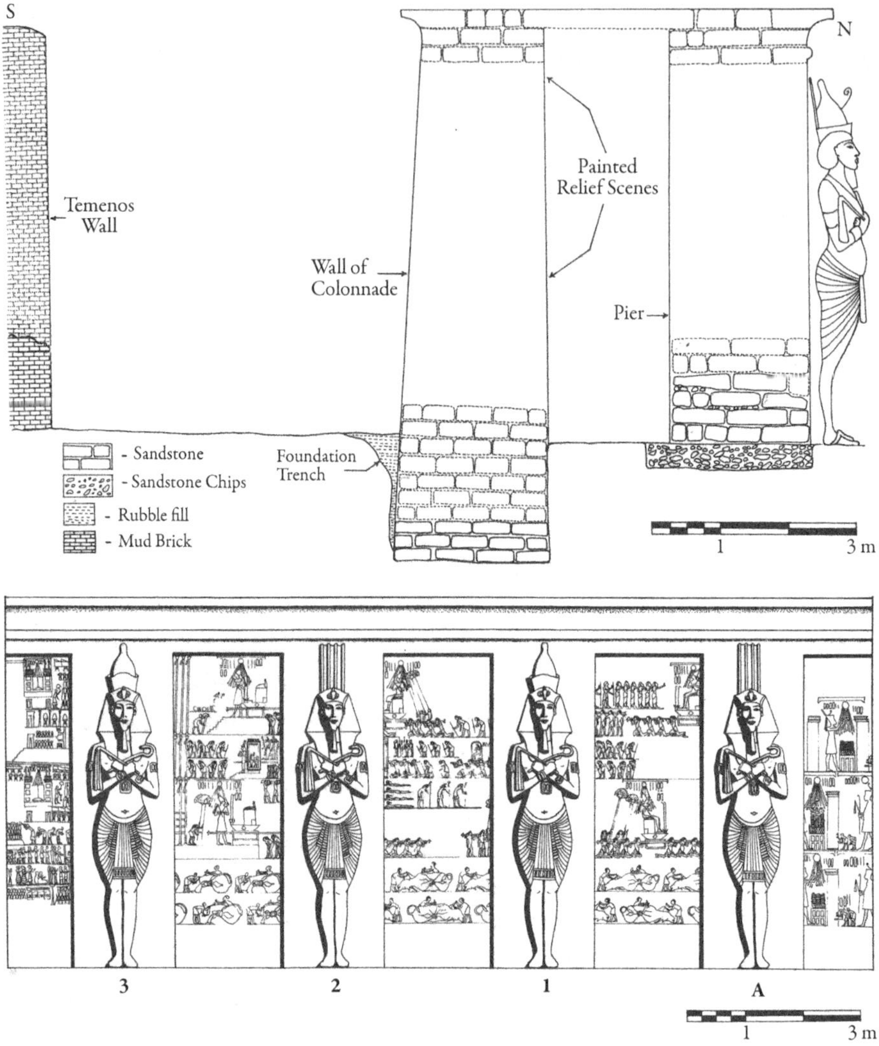

FIGURE 4.11 Donald Redford's reconstruction of interior of *Gm(t) p3 ỉtn*. Donald Redford, *Akhenaten: The Heretic King* (Princeton, NJ: Princeton University Press, 1984), 103.

with the sun, a sharp contrast with the dark and enclosed temples and shrines of other deities, most notably that of Amun at Karnak.

Another significant architectural discovery was made by the ATP in the western wall of *Gm(t) p3 ỉtn*. At the mid-point of the wall, it made a westward turn (Figure 4.10). The same pattern of decorated talatat wall, with rectangular pillars fronted by the colossal statues on both sides of a narrow avenue (4.15 m wide) continued west for 20 meters and then, after a hiatus caused by the canal that cut through this area in the 1920s, a segment of the wall was found approximately 60

FIGURE 4.12 Akhenaten standing on elevated altar. Norman de Garis Davies, *The Rock Tombs of Amarna* II (London: EEF, 1905), pl. XVIII.

meters to the west of the opening.[120] This narrow approach to the *Gm(t) p3 itn* precinct obviously led to an important edifice, possibly the ceremonial palace known from the talatat (see above). Redford believes that this palace was located between the Amun temple complex to the south and the Montu sanctuary to the north, approximately 150 meters north of the point where the avenue of colossi entered *Gm(t) p3 itn* (Figure 4.10).[121]

While the location and dimensions of *Gm(t) p3 itn* are now known, as well as the possible placement of the palace to its north, the positions of the other three temples remain uncertain. No archaeological evidence is presently available to determine their locations, although it is clear from the inscriptions and talatat reliefs that they were in area of Karnak, and likely in the vicinity of *Gm(t) p3 itn.*

[120] Redford, "Interim Report on the Excavations at East Karnak (1981–1982 Seasons)," 205 (fig. 2), 208–222. The later plan shows the west-most unit where the talatat wall was encountered, Redford et al., "East Karnak Excavations, 1987–1989," 76, fig. 1.

[121] Redford, "Akhenaten: New Theories and Old Facts," 22. For the theoretical placement of the palace on a plans, see 10, fig. 1.

FIGURE 4.13 a. Stepped altar, side view (Karnak temple). Photo James K. Hoffmeier. b. Stepped altar, front view (Karnak temple). Photo James K. Hoffmeier.

Robert Vergnieux and Michael Gondran have offered a theoretical reconstruction the *pr-itn* complex at Karnak in their 1997 book.[122] Working from the certain location of *Gm(t) p3 itn*, they place the early Ra-harakhty-Aten edifice, a single pylon, in alignment with the great Thutmoside obelisk at the rear of the Amun-Re

[122] Vergnieux & Gondran, *Aménophis IV et les Pierres du Soleil*, 194–195.

temple, and south of the Ra-Harakhty-Aten pylon, they locate *Ḥwt bnbn.*[123] As noted earlier in this chapter, a number of scholars, including Vergnieux and Gondran, have suggested a line-of-sight between the *bnbn*-stone of *Ḥwt bnbn* and the great obelisk a short distance to its west. They, however, incorrectly placed the entry avenue with the gate of *Gm(t) pꜣ ỉtn,* a third of the way from the southwest corner of the temple discovered by the ATP in 1977. This placement is likely based on Redford's early (1983) interpretation that an open area in the west wall was originally where a pylon had once stood, which he surmised had been thoroughly robbed of its masonry in the aftermath of Akhenaten's reign.[124] The subsequent discoveries of the walls and pillar bases turning 90 degrees to the west and the northwestern corner of *Gm(t) pꜣ ỉtn* made it clear that the walled boulevard was situated at the center of the western wall, and then proceeded to the west (Figure 4.10).[125]

Vergnieux and Gondran's reconstruction of the pillared avenue leads to no building of any sort. They do place the *Rwd mnw* temple west of *Gm(t) pꜣ itn,* with its outer wall aligning with the outer wall of the smaller *Rwd mnw.* Their model of the Karnak-Aten complex does not attempt to locate the palace seen so frequently in the talatat as being in the immediate vicinity of the temple precincts.

Surrounding the palace, Redford proposes the possible locations of the other temples (Figure 4.10). Based on the layout of the various temples *vis à vis* the palace, he suggests that other Aten temples were adjacent to it: *Tnỉ mnw* being to its south, *Rwd mnw* to its north, and *Ḥwt bnbn* being between *Tnỉ mnw* and the west side of *Gm(t) pꜣ ỉtn* (Figure 4.10).[126] The palace may have been an expansion of an earlier palace, which the talatat suggest was accessible by the Nile, prompting Redford to posit that a canal from the Nile led to a harbor and quay where boats could dock.[127] Archaeological data from within Karnak is presently lacking, but this hypothetical reconstruction is a tantalizingly plausible scenario.

THE JUBILEE FESTIVAL

The Sed-festival (*ḥb sd*) was traditionally celebrated in connection with a pharaoh's thirtieth anniversary of his kingship, and was intended to renew the king's potency to rule as the pharaoh aged.[128] This understanding is preserved in the Greek

---

123 Ibid., 194–195.

124 Redford, "Interim Report on the Excavations at East Karnak (1981–1982 Seasons)," 208–210.

125 Redford et al., "East Karnak Excavations, 1987–1989," 76; Redford, "Akhenaten: New Theories and Old Facts," 10, fig. 1.

126 Redford, "Akhenaten: New Theories and Old Facts," 10, fig. 1, 22–23.

127 Ibid., 23.

128 Henri Frankfort, *Kingship and the Gods* (Chicago: University of Chicago, 1948), 79.

text of the Rosetta Stone from the reign of Ptolemy V Epiphanes (196 B.C.), which renders the Egyptian expression as τριακονταετερις, that is, "marking 30 years."[129] As noted in the previous section, the *Gm(t) p3 itn* temple, the largest of those built by Amenhotep IV in Thebes, had as its primary function the celebration of the king's Sed-festival. References to the Heb Sed are not limited to *Gm(t) p3 itn*, however. Though not dated specifically among the inscribed remains from the Aten temples at Karnak, Akhenaten's first celebration must have occurred sometime between years 4 and 5, prior to the move to Amarna in year 6.[130] One reason for this dating is that the first three of Amenhotep IV and Nefertiti's daughters are depicted in the Sed scenes being carried on palanquins in procession (Figure 4.14).[131] It is reckoned that the third daughter, Ankesenpaaten, the future wife of Tutankhamun, was born around year 4, making her at best a toddler during the festivities.[132]

There is no disputing the early date of the Karnak Sed-festival, which raises the question, why? What motivated the premature move by more than two decades to renew the kingship? Amenhotep III had followed the tradition and had observed his first Jubilee on year 30, followed by two more in years 34 and 37 (see Chapter 3). As with everything related to Akhenaten, these questions have spawned lively deliberations ever since Griffith published the limestone Gayer Anderson block in 1918 that showed the king donning the Sed-garment and making offerings (Figure 4.1).[133]

FIGURE 4.14 Three daughters of Akhenaten at Heb Sed-festival in *Gm(t) p3 itn* temple. Donald B. Redford, "Preliminary of the First Season of Excavations in East Karnak, 1975–1976, *JARCE* 14 (1977): plate XIX.

[129] Griffith, "The Jubilee of Akhenaten," 61.

[130] Gohary, "Jubilee Scenes on Talatat," *Akhenaten Temple Project* 2, 64.

[131] Redford, *The Akhenaten Temple Project*, Vol. 1, pl. 41.

[132] Redford, *Akhenaten: The Heretic King*, 79–80.

[133] Griffith, "The Jubilee of Akhenaten," 61–63.

Why should a new and relatively young king need rejuvenating? There are anthropological data from east African tribes that conducted ceremonies to renew the leadership of their chief, an ancient practice that may ultimately stand behind the Egyptian Sed-festival.[134] In African tradition, the well-being of the chief or king was essential for the vitality and fertility of the land, which corresponded to that of its ruler. Henri Frankfort, in his classic study of Egyptian kingship, argued that the health and vitality of a king, rather than just advancing age, may also have been a factor in determining when and if the royal jubilee occurred.[135] He points to Thutmose IV, who reigned but a decade and yet held a jubilee, to illustrate that a 30-year reign was not a prerequisite to celebrating a Heb Sed.

Building on Frankfort's observations, Carleton Hodge offered an intriguing explanation for the early date of Amenhotep IV's Heb Sed.[136] He suggested that a crisis resulted before the king's succession due to the physical abnormalities of the prince, as reflected in the art and statuary discovered in Thebes and Amarna. Amenhotep IV, Hodge theorized, was deemed ceremonially impure and unqualified to serve as the royal priest and thus was rejected by the Amun priesthood as suitable to carry out a king's priestly role. Because the handwriting was on the wall, Amenhotep III associated his son with him through a co-regency.[137] When he succeeded, Amenhotep IV rejected Amun and his priesthood as payback. Then, within a few years, he entirely eliminated the human form to represent the deity, elevated the Aten, built temples, and established an alternative cult over which he would be the ultimate high priest. The Heb Sed was the vehicle for removing any uncertainties about the king's fitness to rule Egypt and ensure his and the land's fecundity and vitality.

This theory certainly has some merits and explains some theological developments and religious practices. However, it is based on two important assumptions that lack clear supporting evidence. First, the co-regency is by no means a certainty. Second, there is still no proof that Amenhotep IV was physically deformed; rather it may be suggested that the odd appearance of the king was symbolic (see below). Third, Hodge assumed that Levitical taboos in the Old Testament—citing Leviticus 21:17, "no man among your descendants for all time who has any physical defect shall come and present the food for his God"—were universal and would apply to Egyptian priests.[138] However, we lack evidence that in the New Kingdom physical deformities would disqualify a priest or king from serving in the cult. To be sure, cleanliness, shaved bodies, and possibly circumcision were required for Egyptian

[134] Frankfort, *Kingship and the Gods*, 33–34.

[135] Ibid., 166–167, no. 2.

[136] Carleton Hodge, "Akhenaten: A Reject," *Scripta Mediterranea* 2 (1981): 17–26.

[137] Ibid., 20.

[138] Ibid., 20.

priests,[139] but there is nothing to suggest that physical deformities were disqualifers for temple service. In fact, thanks to surviving New Kingdom royal mummies, it is known that some pharaohs did have physical deformities. Siptah (1194–1188 B.C.), for example, had a deformed (club) foot,[140] and recent analysis of Amenhotep III's and Tutankhamun's remains shows that they, too, were club-footed.[141] If Amenhotep IV's father and successor both had physical ailments, and they enjoyed complete access to temple service, it seems unlikely that he would have been rejected because of physical abnormalities, if indeed he had any. So while Hodge's theory is ingenious, it is highly problematic.

Those who maintain some sort of co-regency between Amenhotep III and IV tend to think, as Nicholas Reeves does, that "the timing of Amenophis IV's *sed* was influenced not by the regnal years of his own reign, but by those of his father."[142] Raymond Johnson, a strong advocate of the long co-regency and champion of the view that the Aten religion was the cult of the deified Amenhotep III, follows Aldred in thinking that Akhenaten's jubilee at Karnak (somewhere between 4 and 5) coincides with Amenhotep III's second Sed-festival in year 34.[143] This theory seems most untenable and will be critiqued in the following section. It seems like a desperate attempt to foster the father cult theory.

Then, too, there are those who believe that the first Sed-festival of Amenhotep IV was not his but Aten's.[144] It is salutary to note that there is the repeated epithet of Aten in the Gayer Anderson block and other Karnak talatat that read, "the very great living Aten who is in Sed-festival, lord of heaven and earth" (*ỉtn ꜥnḫ wr ỉmy ḥb sd nb pt tꜣ*).[145] Variations on this epithet are found at Amarna, where a second Jubilee apparently was celebrated. One of the epithets is "the very great living Aten, lord of Sed-festivals, lord of all that the Aten encircles, lord of heaven, lord of earth in Akhetaten (or in the horizon of the Domain of Aten)" (*ỉtn ꜥnḫ wr nb ḥb sd nb šnnt nb ỉtn nb pt nb tꜣ m pr ỉtn* [*m ꜣḫt ỉtn pr ỉtn*]).[146] In other words, the Aten was

---

139 Serge Sauneron, *The Priests of Ancient Egypt* (Ithaca, NY: Cornell University Press, 2000), 35–42.

140 J. E. Harris & Kent Weeks, *X-Raying the Pharaohs* (New York: Charles Scribner's Sons, 1973), 45.

141 Zahi Hawass et al. "Ancestry and Pathology in King Tutankhamun's Family," *Journal of the American Medical Association* 303, no. 7 (2010): 640, table 1.

142 Reeves, *Akhenaten: Egypt's False Prophet*, 96.

143 W. Raymond Johnson, "Monuments and Monumental Art under Amenhotep III: Evolution and Meaning," in *Amenhotep III: Perspectives on his Reign* (eds. David O'Connor & Eric H. Cline; Ann Arbor: University of Michigan Press, 1998), 90–93.

144 Jacobus van Dijk, "The Amarna Period and Later New Kingdom," *The Oxford History of Ancient Egypt* (ed. Ian Shaw; Oxford/New York: Oxford University Press, 2000), 268.

145 Redford, *The Akhenaten Temple Project*, Vol. 1, e.g., pl. 3, 5, 19, 20, 23, 31.

146 Davies, *The Rock Tombs of El Amarna*, Vol. 1, pl. VII, X, XI; Vol 4, e.g., pl. IV, VIII, IX, XI, XIII, XIV, XVI, XVII.

celebrating (constantly?) the Sed-festival, a point noted early on by Batiscombe Gunn, who thought that the later title "lord of Sed-festivals" began after the celebration of a second Jubilee observed at Amarna (Akhet-Aten).[147] Gohary cautions that beyond this epithet for the Aten, there is little evidence in the reliefs at Amarna that a Sed-festival was celebrated there, possibly because it was considered too closely connected with old traditions involving multiple deities.[148]

In the collection of the Louvre in Paris is a pre-talatat sized (1.30 × .60 m = 4 ft 3 in × 23 in) block from the 10th Pylon that shows Amenhotep IV burning incense to Aten (Figure 4.15a-b).[149] The two figures of the king, shown in the early and pre-Amarna style (i.e., not with the grotesque physique), are surrounded by the spindly arms (rays) of the sun, whose hands offer the expected 𓋹 and 𓌀 signs, but also two hands, on either side of the scene, offer the dual figures of the king the combination of signs for "millions of Heb Seds." At some later date, the name "Amenhotep" was erased and "Akhenaten" replaced it. Cyril Aldred believed that these data, the iconography and the epithets, show "that the jubilees of the Aten were closely connected with the jubilees of Pharaoh, or vice versa."[150] The implication of this scene is that it was the Aten who bestowed the Sed-festival on the king, and in turn the king celebrated the jubilee of the Aten. This interpretation of the data requires that Akhenaten also was the beneficiary of the Jubilee, not just the Aten.

(a) (b)

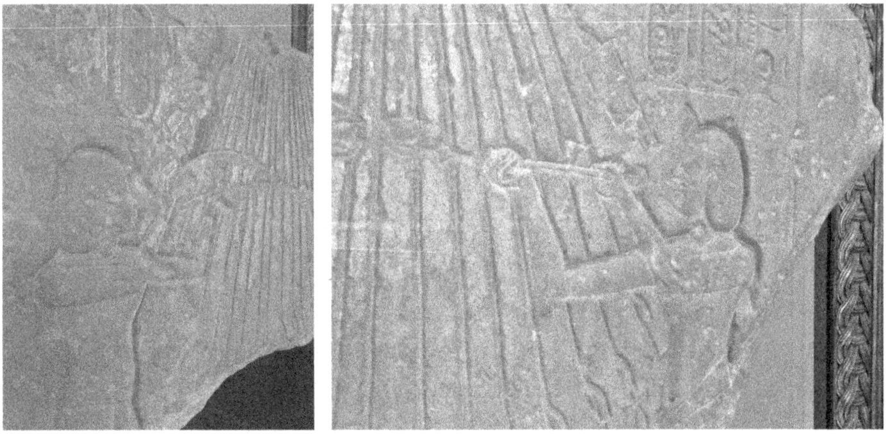

FIGURE 4.15 a. Louvre block with earlier relief of Akhenaten burning incense to Aten (left side). b. Louvre block with earlier relief of Akhenaten burning incense to Aten (right side). Photo James K. Hoffmeier.

---

[147] Gunn, "Notes on the Aten and His Names," 170–172.

[148] Gohary, *Akhenaten's Sed-festival at Karnak*, 33.

[149] Henri Asselbergs, "Ein merwürdiges Relief Amenophis' IV. im Louvre-Mueusm," *ZÄS* 58 (1923): 36–38.

[150] Cyril Aldred, "The Beginning of the El-'Amarna Period," *JEA* 45 (1959): 30.

Eric Uphill, on the other hand, noted that the Sed-festival traditions included the presence of other gods who were assembled as witnesses to the event; the jubilee scenes of Osorkon II (ca. 874–850 B.C.) at Bubastis bear this out.[151] In the case of Amenhotep IV's ceremonies, Aten alone was the attending deity.

The view favored here is that the Sed-festival of the Aten was not a celebration of the deified Amenhotep III, but a step in elevating the Aten to a new status. The appearances of the Aten in the talatat from the *Gm(t) p3 ỉtn*, *Tnỉ mnw*, *Ḥwt bnbn* and *Rwd mnw* temples are unanimous in writing the didactic name Aten in cartouches, namely (*rʿ ḥr 3ḫty ḥʿʿ m 3ḫt*)(*m rn.f šw nty m ỉtn*) = (Re-Harakhty who Rejoices in the Horizon)(in his name of light which is in the Aten). It will be recalled that this long descriptive name, when it appears written during the first year or two of Amenhotep IV's reign, lacked this regal marker. Placing the name of a deity within a cartouche before this time is rare in Egypt. When it does occur before this time and after, the deity is identified as king. In a Middle Kingdom stela, Osiris is called "king of Upper and Lower Egypt, Osiris the Justified"—.[152] In the Turin Canon of Kings from the 13th century B.C., and thus post-Amarna, the gods who ruled before historical kings, such as Seth, Horus, and Thoth, are called "Kings of Upper and Lower Egypt" and their names are placed within cartouches.[153]

Why was Aten's long explanatory name now written as signifying kingship? He obviously was king, the ultimate sovereign of the world. And like the pharaoh, there could only be one! The orthographic development of writing the didactic name in a cartouche signaled not only the elevation of the Aten, but also the diminution of Amun who had been known as "the king of the gods" (see Chapter 2). Now Aten was the king, and Akhenaten his son ruled on earth. Not only does he retain the epithet Son of Re (*s3 rʿ*), as kings had done regularly since the 5th Dynasty (see Chapter 1), he refers to himself as "your son" (*s3.k*) when addressing the Aten in the great hymn.[154] When the cartouches of the deity and king occur together on the same inscription in the Karnak talatat[155] and on texts from Amarna, too,[156] the king's name is consistently inscribed on a much smaller scale than that of the Aten.

Thus we conclude that the Sed-festival celebrated at Karnak between year 4 and 5 had the dual purpose of establishing the kingship of Aten as supreme, if not sole

[151] Eric Uphill, "The Sed-festivals of Akhenaton," *JNES* 22 (1963): 123.

[152] Kurt Sethe, *Aegyptische Lesestücke zum Gebrauch in akademischen Unterricht* (Leipzig: J. C. Hinriches'sche, 1928), 63.22. I am grateful to Edmund Meltzer for this reference.

[153] James K. Hoffmeier, "Turin Canon," in *COS* I, 71. Alan Gardiner, *The Royal Canon of Turin* (Oxford: Oxford University Press, 1959).

[154] Sandman, *Texts from the Time of Akhenaten*, 95.16.

[155] Redford, *The Akhenaten Temple Project*, Vol. 1, pl. 8, 31, 34, 35, 75; Redford, *The Akhenaten Temple Project*, Vol. 2, p. 26, 29, 35, 37.

[156] E.g., Davies, *The Rock Tombs of El Amarna*, Vol. 1, pl. VI, VII, X, XVII, XXII, XXVI, XXVII.

deity (noticeably absent is Amun-Re's title, King of the gods), and associating the earthly king with the Aten, a view also advanced by Erik Hornung, who saw the connection between the *ḥb sd* and the kingship of Aten.[157] This was not a co-regency with the glorified and deified Amenhotep III, but between Akhenaten and the Aten. It may well be that it was the on occasion of the Jubilee observed in the *Gm p3 ỉtn* complex that the new royal name, Akhenaten ("Useful" or "Beneficial to the Aten"), became official, and Amenhotep, his name from birth that honored the old patron of Karnak, was dropped. In many cases when the name Akhenaten is written, the earlier name was erased and replaced by the Atenist name.[158] Even among some of the earliest, pre-talatat Aten temple blocks, the name Akhenaten usurps his birth name Amenhotep.[159] This practice suggests that the talatat temples were nearing completion or were completed when the decision was made to change the king's name, and adjustments were made.

Redford reminds us that "a key act in the jubilee was the reenactment of the coronation."[160] At the coronation of the Pharaoh the full titulary of throne names were divinely proclaimed and written on leaves of the *ỉšd*-tree by Thoth and Seshet the goddess of writing. Amenhotep IV's coronation is recalled on a scarab with the lengthy title:

> Long live the Good God whose renown is great; possessor of the great name, whose titulary is holy; [possessor of] jubilee(s) like Tatenen[161] master of lifetime [like] Aten in heaven, established on the Ished-tree which is in Heliopolis—namely (?)[162] the King of Upper and Lower Egypt, NEFER-KHEPRURE-WAENRE . . .[163]

The location of the Ished-tree in Heliopolis once again stresses the king's inclination toward the old solar religion and its various traditions.

The re-enactment of the naming and coronation of the king is dramatically displayed in the Sed-festival scenes of Ramesses II and Ramesses III in their

---

157 Erik Hornung, *Akhenaten and the Religion of Light*, trans. D. Lorton (Ithaca, NY: Cornell University Press, 1999), 42.

158 Redford, *The Akhenaten Temple Project*, Vol. 1, pl. 90 n 8; Redford, *The Akhenaten Temple Project*, Vol. 2, fig. 15–19, pl. 35, 40.

159 Jean-Luc Chappaz, "Le Premier Edifice d'Amenophis IV a Karnak," *BSEG* 8 (1983): 21–25. Jean-Luc Chappaz, "Un Nouvel Assemblage de Talâtât: une paroi du *Rwḏ-mnw* d'Aton," *Cahiers de Karnak* VIII (1987) 81–121.

160 Redford, *Akhenaten: The Heretic King*, 126.

161 Tatenen, meaning "Arising earth or land" is the primeval earth that emerges at creation.

162 The text reads, *ḏd.f*, which literally means "he says." For the text for the scarab, see Sandman, *Texts from the Time of Akhenaten*, 148, CXLV.

163 William Murnane, *Texts from the Amarna Period in Egypt* (Atlanta: Scholars Press, 1995), 41.

respective funerary temples (Figure 4.16).[164] What better occasion than this festival for Akhenaten's name to be declared in anticipation of an ongoing kingship and the celebration of millions of Heb Seds? In the Sed scenes, along with others showing the coronation of a new monarch during the New Kingdom, Amun-Re was normally portrayed placing the crown on the royal head. A classic example of this scene is found on the pyramidion of Hatshepsut's obelisks at Karnak (Figure 2.10). This common motif is surprisingly absent from the numerous Sed-festival scenes of Akhenaten's Theban temples, unless the reliefs showing the Aten's rays that surround the head and crown of the king represent the placing of the symbols of kingship on his head. In some instances the hands at the extremity of the sun's rays enfold the crowns of Akhenaten and Nefertiti as if crowning the duo.[165]

We return to the question of the co-regency between Amenhotep III and IV and the Jubilee Festivals. According to the long co-regency theory promoted by Aldred, Reeves, Johnson, and others, Amenhotep III would have celebrated his first Sed in year 30, possibly Amenhotep IV's 2nd year, and then, Johnson concludes,

FIGURE 4.16 Coronation scene of Ramesses II at his Heb Sed (Ramesseum Temple). Photo James K. Hoffmeier.

[164] Epigraphic Survey, *Medinet Habu V, The Temple Proper*, pt. 1 (Chicago: University of Chicago, 1957), pl. 316, and *Medinet Habu VI, The Temple Proper*, pt. 2 (Chicago: University of Chicago, 1965), pl. 448, 460.

[165] Vergnieux & Gondran, *Aménophis IV et les Pierres du Soleil*, 73, 170–171, 178.

"Amenhotep IV changed his name to Akhenaten in his Year 5, which coincided with the celebration of Amenhotep III's second jubilee (also the jubilees of the Aten), and founded Akhetaten. . . ."[166] The amount of materiel, manpower, and administrative supervision to prepare and execute dual Sed-festivals, one at Malkata and the other at Karnak, at the same time (or even months apart), would have been staggering. Then, too, the incredible number and gigantic scale of Amenhotep III's building activities during his final decade were on an unprecedented scale and must be taken into account when considering a decade-long co-regency.[167] It defies credulity to believe that while father was completing his enormous temples in Nubia, Thebes, and elsewhere, celebrating jubilees at Malkata, at the same time Amenhotep IV would have been building his Aten temples at Karnak, which represent a major building program, and, on top of that, then he would have started to build his new city, Akhet-Aten.

The logistical considerations alone militate against the long co-regency theory. But there are other considerations as well. The *Gm(t) p3 itn* temple, whose reliefs focus on the Sed-festival themes, neither include the image of Amenhotep III nor his name,[168] nor is the epithet "Dazzling Aten"—supposedly the name of the deified king and the focus of Akhenaten's Aten cult—yet to be found in the tens of thousands of inscribed talatat from the Karnak Aten Temples. Indeed, there are a number of representations of the deified Amenhotep III at Amarna,[169] but even so, on those occasions he is not called the "Dazzling Aten."

We conclude, therefore, that Akhenaten's Sed-festival was focused on Akhenaten and the Aten, their relationship, and Aten's ascendency to status as king (as the new usage of the cartouches indicate). Further, it appears from the total absence of Amenhotep III in the Aten temple reliefs that he predeceased the decorating of the temples and the momentous Jubilee Festival of year 4 or 5.

THE COLOSSAL STATUES

When first encountered in 1925, the unusual colossal statues of Akhenaten sparked great interest and cause for speculation. In a sense they were only three-dimensional portrayals of the strange looking pharaoh known already from the reliefs at Amarna

---

166 Johnson, "Monuments and Monumental Art under Amenhotep III," 92.

167 Johnson is well aware of enormity of Amenhotep III's building endeavors, as he has ably documented them: Johnson, "Monuments and Monumental Art Under Amenhotep III," 64–80.

168 Gohary (*Akhenaten's Sed-festival at Karnak*, 33) has found only one block that has Amenhotep III's name on it, but it is in raised relief, unlike the sunk relief of the talatat. So clearly this piece was not used in the talatat temples.

169 Johnson, "Amenhotep III and Amarna: Some New Considerations," 72–80.

and others from various Theban contexts. Though no one colossus has survived completely intact, enough parts have been preserved and critical architectural information remains so that it can be established that the statues originally stood about 4 meters high (13 feet), were made from sandstone, and over 30 were documented in Manniche's recent study.[170] Her study includes fragments of statues that were found in excavations of the ATP[171] and in the East Karnak sewage project from 2003 documented by Brock.[172] Some of the statues found at East Karnak were representations of Nefertiti. Additional granite statue fragments of Akhenaten and a colossal statue base of Nefertiti (with her feet plus two sets of her daughters' feet) were found at the Mut Temple in south Karnak.[173] These likely originated in the *Pr ỉtn* complex, and possibly from *Gm(t) p3 ỉtn* since the inscription on one granite block mentions Aten being in "the sed-festival . . . in *Gm(t) p3 ỉtn*."[174]

Based on the number of pillar foundations against which the large statues stood, there may have been 30 statues on the west side and likely that many along the south wall, totaling 120 on all four sides. The piers continue on the avenue leading west from *Gm(t) p3 ỉtn*. There could have been dozens more. As for the northern wall, which was investigated by Redford in the 1980s, no traces of the sandstone colossi were found, although fragments of smaller quartzite statuary were found.[175]

A recent and intriguing suggestion is that these sandstone colossi were originally even larger ones carved initially for Amenhotep III, but relocated and recut for Akhenaten. Arielle Kozloff came to this conclusion after carefully examining the colossi in the Cairo and Luxor museums in 2008. She then suggests that they had been Osirian statues in the sun court of Luxor Temple.[176] One clue to the remodeling of these statues is that in some cases where the abdomen is preserved, a second, lower, larger, and wider navel is visible (Figure 4.3).[177] The smaller original navels were likely covered by plaster that has since fallen out. Kozloff also points to other signs of recarving.[178]

---

170 Manniche, *The Akhenaten Colossi of Karnak*, x.

171 Redford, "Interim Report on the Excavations at East Karnak (1981–1982 seasons)," 222.

172 Brock, "Archaeological Observations in East Karnak, 2002–2003," figs. 7–11.

173 Jacobus van Dijk, "A Colossal Statue Base of Nefertiti and Other Early Atenist Monuments from the Precinct of the Goddess Mut in Karnak," in *The Servant of Mut: Studies in Honor of Richard Fazinni* (ed. S. D'Auria; Leiden, Brill, 2008), 246–252.

174 Ibid., 248.

175 Redford, "East Karnak and the Sed-festival of Akhenaten," 487.

176 Arielle Kozloff, "Chips off Old Statues: Carving the Amenhotep IV Colassi of Karank," *KMT* 23, no. 3 (Fall 2012), 19–32; see also Kozloff, *Amenhotep III: Egypt's Radiant Pharaoh* (Cambridge/New York: Cambridge University Press, 2012), 242.

177 Rita Freed et al., *Pharaohs of the Sun: Akhenaten, Nefertiti, Tutankhamun* (Boston: Museum of Fine Arts, 1999), 19, fig. 4; Manniche, *The Akhenaten Colossi of Karnak*, 55, 76.

178 Kozloff, "Chips off Old Statues: Carving the Amenhotep IV Colassi of Karank," 21–25.

The regal emblems on the statues vary, although the king is consistently presented with wrists crossing the chest, holding the crook and flail of kingship in a pose associated with Osiris.[179] The connections between the renewal aspects of the Osiris cult and the Sed-festival have been recognized.[180] Considerable variation is seen in the range of crowns and combinations of diadems. Manniche has documented eight different combinations, but all display a uraeus over the brow.[181] The popular blue crown or *ḫprš* has not been found, however. The king wears the long square beard associated with a living king rather than the slender pointy beard that curls at the end, which typically Osiris and male deities wear. Where the king's names survived on the colossi, often on the belt, Neferkheperure and either Amenhotep (IV) or Akhenaten were inscribed.[182] In addition to the king's cartouches, the statues are covered with the double cartouche of the Aten, written on wrist and bicep bands, on the chest on either side of the beard and in the midsection below the crossed arms (Figures 4.3 and 4.4).[183] Saturating the king and queen's body with the cartouched didactic name of Aten is a regular feature of talatat scenes[184] and on the reliefs of the king and queen at Amarna (Figure 4.17).[185] The fact that images of the king are covered with the name of his god emphasizes the close relationship between the two.

Opinions vary on the interpretation of these great statues because they are so different from anything witnessed in the preceding 1,500 years of Egyptian history. Rita Freed is surely correct to say that these statues are "depicted in a manner that can only have been shocking to the ancient viewer accustomed to the traditional rendering of the human figure."[186] To add to the bizarre figures of the king with enlarged hips and thighs, narrow face with protruding chin and slanted eyes with heavy eyelids, one of the statues (now in the Cairo Museum [JE 55,938; Exhibition n. 6182]) lacks the belt and kilt, and appears to be nude.[187]

If the royal figure is indeed not clothed, the genitalia are not shown, making the image seem almost androgynous. It could be that a tight-fitting sheer garment was intended[188] or that a garment of some sort was originally attached.[189] Because this statue

---

179 Manniche, *The Akhenaten Colossi of Karnak*, 24, 29, 31, 32, 40, 42, 55, 56, 58, 60, 68, 69, 70, 71, 72, 73

180 Gohary, *Akhenaten's Sed-festival at Karnak*, 2.

181 Ibid., 23.

182 Ibid., 76, 82–83, 99.

183 Ibid., 55, 68, 69, 70, 72, 74, 75, 76, 78, 79.

184 Redford, *The Akhenaten Temple Project*, Vol. 1, pl. 9, 21, 29.

185 Davies, *The Rock Tombs of El Amarna*, Vol. VI, III, IV.

186 Freed, "Art in the Service of Religion and the State," in *Pharaohs of the Sun: Akhenaten, Nefertiti, Tutankhamun*, 112.

187 For good quality pictures, see Manniche, *The Akhenaten Colossi of Karnak*, 55, 56, 57. Reeves, *Akhenaten: Egypt's False Prophet*, 165.

188 Manniche, *The Akhenaten Colossi of Karnak*, 57.

189 Redford, *The Heretic King*, 104.

FIGURE 4.17 Talatat of Nefertiti covered with Aten's didactic name (Ashmolean Musem, Oxford). Photo James K. Hoffmeier.

does not have a belt, where the king's name is normally written on the other colossi, the identity of this royal figure is not known. One other indicator that a woman was the intended figure is that the beard, now missing, appears to have been added, to judge from the hole in the neck where it would have been attached. The other statues indicate that the beards were part of the original image.[190] Consequently, some scholars think that it represents Nefertiti,[191] although the art historian Gay Robins has argued that the so-called sexless colossus was actually "an early attempt to reproduce the two dimensional image (of the king) in three-dimensions. It may have been deemed unsuccessful and thus not repeated on other monuments."[192] If she is correct, the question remains of why this statue and the other representations of the king are so feminized. Robins, like others, posits that the dual traits could reflect that Aten the creator is one who creates without the aid of a female consort.[193]

A STATUE OF THE ATEN?

If the odd statue of an asexual figure was intended to represent that ability of Aten to reproduce without a consort, another recently published statue thought to represent

[190] Manniche, *The Akhenaten Colossi of Karnak*, 56–57.

[191] Reeves, *Akhenaten: Egypt's False Prophet*, 165–166.

[192] Gay Robins, "The Representation of Sexual Characteristics in Amarna Art," *JSSEA* 23 (1993): 38.

[193] Robins, "The Representation of Sexual Characteristics in Amarna Art," 37.

the Aten, on the other hand, seems to stress his male potency. Robert Bianchi in 1990 brought to light a unique and odd statue that remains in a private collection.[194] Its provenance is unknown, adding to the mystery of the statue and depriving scholarship of critical information about its origin. Bianchi was able to study the image and included a picture of it in his publication.[195] The lower portion of the image, from mid-thigh to the feet, is missing and now stands only 92.7 cm tall.[196] It originally was probably lifesize. Four features of the statue are conspicuous: (1) the sun-disc as the head (i.e., not a sun-disc on top of a human or animal head); (2) his left arm crosses the mid-section, with his hand holding a *ḫrp* or *sḫm* scepter; (3) the penis sheath garment worn by the male figure; and (4) the muscular chest. Bianchi focuses on the first three elements and suggests rather ingeniously that they be interpreted as a rebus: the disc = Aten, the penis sheath with its looped strap = *ꜥnḫ* (life), and the scepter being *sḫm* = image, which when read together would mean "living image of Aten.[197]

Assuming this reading is correct, and one must admit that it is highly speculative, Bianchi thinks that the statue could "very well represent an initial attempt to render the Aton as a typically composite deity before its transformation into the more canonical image of the sun-disc fronted by a single uraeus which became the icon of the Aton in Year 3 of Akhenaten."[198] On stylistic grounds, he suggests a possible date of late in Amenhotep III's reign.

Eugene Cruz-Uribe subsequently commented on Bianchi's interpretation of the image.[199] While he does not question the basic reading of the rebus, he added that the disc could also represent the moon since *ỉtn* has lunar applications as well. The nocturnal aspects of the disc, he reminds us, have Osirian connections.[200]

Hornung has addressed Bianchi's interpretation of the odd statue, and notes that there is no uraeus on the disc (contra Bianchi), and he argues that rather than being a representation of Aten, it is "an image of the traditional sun god."[201]

Bianchi's proposed understanding of the statue may be correct, and if his dating is right (i.e., the reign of Amenhotep III), then this image is of little import to Atenism as developed during Akhenaten's reign, especially if, as argued here, there was no co-regency between the two Amenhoteps. Had the image been discovered among those in the *Gm(t) pꜣ ỉtn* complex, this statue would require a lengthy discussion

---

194 Robert Bianchi, "New Light on the Aton," *GM* 114 (1990): 35–41.

195 Ibid., 45, fig. 1.

196 Ibid., 35 no. 2.

197 Ibid., 38–39.

198 Ibid., 39.

199 Eugene Cruz-Uribe, "Another Look at an Aton Statue," *GM* 126 (1992): 29–32.

200 Ibid., 29–31.

201 Hornung, *Akhenaten and the Religion of Light*, 78.

regarding the relationship between Akhenaten's theology and iconography. Lacking the find spot limits interpretive possibilities. It would be fair to say, however, even if Bianchi's rebus read is set aside, the statue certainly communicates the virility and strength of the sun-god, regardless of which aspect is in view. Moreover, this statue would represent a very different perspective on Aten from those displayed on the *Gm(t) pꜣ ỉtn* colossi, which are effeminate.

AKHENATEN'S PHYSICAL PRESENTATION: A GENETIC DISORDER?

A range of genetic disorders have been proposed and rejected over the years to explain Akhenaten's anomalous appearance in these colossi and on other representations of the king. Some suggestions are more plausible than others. The feminine features, especially breasts, have been attributed to adolescent gynecomastia, an endocrinological disorder that manifests itself before the onset of puberty in boys.[202] The study cited here actually points to the well-known statue of Tutankhamun standing on the back of the black leopard[203] as illustrative of "familial gynecomastia," a characteristic shared by other family members.

Fragile X Syndrome is another theory to account for the unusual features Akhenaten's images display. Some of the characteristics of Fragile X are "enlarged heads . . . young children may have large or protruding ears and later on may also have long faces . . . flat feet."[204] These features are certainly recognizable in representations of Akhenaten and his family.

One of the more recently suggested pathologies to explain Akhenaten's odd features is Marfan's Syndrome, thought to be the mutant gene that affected Abraham Lincoln.[205] Characteristics of Marfan's Syndrome include "tall stature, slender bones, long face, high palate . . . elongated extremities, arm span exceeds height, spinal anomalies are common: Kyphosis (exaggerated angulation of the neck & spine), scoliosis . . . deficiency and often localized distribution of subcutaneous fat, . . . flat feet, . . . visual impairment, myopia & Keratoconys (the cornea is cone-shaped causing blurred vision), enophthalmos (eyes appear slit-like because they are set back into the eye socket due to lack of retrobular fat behind the eye) . . . dolichocephy (abnormally elongated skull), prognathism (chin protrudes past forehead in profile)."[206]

---

202 C. Patrick Mahoney, "Adolescent Gynecomastia," *Current Issues in Pediatric and Adolescent Endocrinology* 37, no. 6 (1990): 1389–1404.

203 Ibid., 1399.

204 Deborah Barnes, "'Fragile X' Syndrome and Its Puzzling Genetics," *Science* 243 (1989): 171–172.

205 Alwyn Burridge, "Akhenaten: A New Perspective, Evidence of a Genetic Disorder in the Royal Family of the 18th Dynasty Egypt," *JSSEA* 23 (1993): 63–74.

206 Ibid., 66–67.

After reviewing these symptoms, Alwyn Burridge believes that Marfan's Syndrome best explains Akhenaten's appearance and that of other members of this immediate family.[207] She claims that some of these characteristics are apparent in the mummy of Amenhotep III, especially the enlarged head.[208] Nearly all the characteristics of Marfan's Syndrome listed here can be tied to Akhenaten's appearance in the statuary and reliefs at Karnak (and at Amarna, too, although there is some softening of the excessively grotesque facial features in this phase), making Burridge's proposal extremely attractive.

As enticing as the Marfan's Syndrome theory is, it seems that it can be no longer sustained in the light of an extensive study of royal mummies of Amenhotep III's family, including those of Queen Tiye, her parents Yuya and Tuya, Tutankhamun, and the mysterious male occupant of Tomb 55 in the Valley of the Kings. CT scans (in 2005) and DNA analysis (2007–2009) were performed by a large international team of experts in the fields of archaeology, medicine, pathology, and genetics, headed by Dr. Zahi Hawass, the former director of the Supreme Council for Antiquities (now known as Ministry of State for Antiquities). The results of this study were published in a scientific report in the *Journal of the American Medical Association* in 2010 and a more popular version appeared in *National Geographic*, also in 2010.[209]

The identity of the mummy found in Tomb 55 has been the subject of debate ever since the tomb was discovered by Theodore Davis in 1907.[210] There is no doubt that some of material in the tomb was made for Queen Tiye, and more recently it has been suggested, based on the careful reading of a cosmetic jar, that it belonged to Queen Kiya (a secondary wife of Akhenaten), which is why the reinterred mummy was initially thought to be that of a woman.[211] Subsequent investigation of the skeletal remains by mummy experts Elliot Smith and D. E. Derry recognized the individual to be that of a male.[212] Furthermore, the coffin was evidently originally designed for a woman, but was modified for a king by adding a uraeus. H. W. Fairman believed that the coffin had been created for Meritaten, Akhenaten and Nefertiti's eldest daughter, but was altered for Smenkhkare, her husband.[213] On the other hand,

---

[207] Ibid., 67.

[208] Ibid., 74 n 8. Further on the skull of Amenhotep III, see James E. Harris, "The Mummy of Amenhotep III," in *Gold of Praise: Studies on Ancient Egypt in Honor of Edward F. Wente* (eds. Emily Teeter & John Larsen; Chicago: University of Chicago, 1999), 163–174.

[209] Hawass et al. "Ancestry and Pathology in King Tutankhamun's Family," 638–647; Zahi Hawass, "King Tut's Family Secret," *National Geographic* 218, no. 3 (September 2010): 34–60.

[210] Theodore Davis, *The Tomb of Queen Tiyi* (London, Constable and Co., 1910).

[211] For a helpful review of the debate, see Aldred, *Akhenaten King of Egypt*, 195–236, including the identity of the male mummy.

[212] Ibid., 199–201. Reeves, *Akhenaten: Egypt's False Prophet*, 80–84.

[213] Herbert Fairman, "Once Again the So-Called Coffin of Akhenaten," *JEA* 47 (1961): 25–40.

after considerable debate many Egyptologists now think that the coffin was originally Kiya's, but was reworked for Akhenaten.

The mummy has been identified both as that of Smenkhkare (Akhenaten's ephemeral successor) and Akhenaten. The problem with assigning a name to the body in the mummy case is that the cartouches had been removed and the gold face of the mask was torn off.[214] The decorated gold bands that wrapped the mummified remains also had the cartouches ripped out. These bands were stolen in Cairo many years ago (along with the coffin lid), but recently ended up at the Museum of Egyptian Art in Munich (Staatlichen Sammlung Ägyptischer Kunst, München) after being privately owned.[215] It was subsequently returned to the Cairo Museum where it is now exhibited.

It seems likely that the royal male buried in Tomb 55 was Akhenaten rather than Smenkhkare because the former's name was found on some objects in the tomb, even if not on the coffin or mummy itself, while the latter's name is not found at all.[216] The names Akhenaten and/or Neferkheperure-waenre were found on objects belonging to Queens Tiye and Kiya.[217] Fortuitously, the cartouches of Akhenaten survived the desecration of the wooden shrine of Tiye (the gold foil having been removed in antiquity), although his figure was erased.[218] The later version of the didactic name of the Aten is also engraved on this panel, as it was on a fragment of gold foil that had decorated the mummy, and the double cartouche of the Aten was found on the uraeus on the mummy's brow.[219] Most significantly, two of the four magical mud bricks, which were protective amulets buried with the deceased, found in the tomb contain the name Neferkheperure-waenre.[220] These inscribed objects seem to tip the identification of the mummy in favor Akhenaten.

The recent DNA study concludes that the mummies of Amenhotep III, the male in KV 55 and Tutankhamun, "share the same paternal lineage,"[221] which seemingly clinches the link to Akhenaten. This study determined that there was no evidence of Marfan's Syndrome or many of the other genetic disorders previously proposed.[222] On the other hand, the CT scans revealed that Akhenaten suffered from a cleft palate and scoliosis (characteristics associated with Marfan's!).[223] The results of the

[214] Davis, *The Tomb of Queen Tiyi*, pl. xxx.

[215] Mark Rose, "Royal Coffin Controversy," *Archaeology* 53, no. 5 (September/October 2000), web version.

[216] Alan Gardiner, "The So-called Tomb of Queen Tiyi," *JEA* 43 (1957): 10–25.

[217] For the text of this jar, see Aldred, *Akhenaten King of Egypt*, 204.

[218] Davis, *The Tomb of Queen Tiyi*, pl. xxix, xxxii.

[219] Ibid., 23, 19.

[220] Ibid., 26–27, pl. xxii. See also George Daressy's study of the texts in the tomb, "Cercueil de Khu-n-Aten," *BIFAO* 12 (1916): 145–159.

[221] Hawass et al., "Ancestry and Pathology in King Tutankhamun's Family," 640.

[222] Ibid., 638–639.

[223] Ibid., 645.

recent scientific study of the later 18th Dynasty royal mummies leads Hawass and his colleagues to determine that the unorthodox appearance of the king and his family in artistic representations cannot be attributed to some genetic disorder, but to the Amarna artistic style.[224] It seems likely that we have not heard the last word on the DNA analysis and implications for the amarna royal family.

There have been those who all along believed that the unique Amarna style should be understood in some symbolic manner rather than being a naturalistic (or exaggerated portrayal of the king's pathologies). In her recent monograph on the Akhenaten colossi, Manniche has surveyed the scholarly discussion of the past 90 years since they came to light, and there is a stream of thought that associates the male figure of the king with feminine characteristics as reflecting the universal nature of Aten as sole creator (i.e., no consort!) who is father and mother, a position taken by Pillet who had worked with Chevrier in the 1925 discovery of the colossi at Karnak.[225] Because the king's name is recorded on the belt of the statues (less the so-called "sexless" colossus), the statue cannot be said to be only Aten.

While the peculiar figure of the king remains a subject of academic discussion, there seems to be a growing realization that the variety of crowns worn by the king is significant. Four of the *nemes*-crowns are topped off with standing *šw*-feathers[226] that are associated with the god Shu.[227] It will be recalled that "Shu" is embedded in the second part of the didactic name: "in his name of *šw* which is in the Aten." J. R. Harris further suggested that Tefnut, Shu's twin sister, and Shu were the first cosmic forces that Atum created, and that Nefertiti represents Tefnut in some of the statues.[228] Thus he theorizes that if the statues "represent Re-Harakhty (Aten) in different hypostases, as the cartouches (of the didactic name) may indicate, then one might postulate the symbolic expression both of the phases of the sun's aging and of the complementary principles of fecundity."[229]

This interpretation is worthy of consideration, and makes sense of the Shu-feathered crown. The problem, however, is that this theory rests on identifying one statue (i.e., the "sexless" one)—that is different from the others—with Nefertiti. As we have seen, some, like Robins, have questioned associating this statue with Nefertiti, thinking it represents Akhenaten like the other sandstone statues.[230] Nefertiti's name is nowhere

---

[224] Ibid., 644.

[225] M. Pillet, "L'art d'Akhenaton," in *Mélanges Mariette* (ed. J. Garnot; Cairo: IFAO, 1961), 91.

[226] Manniche, *The Akhenaten Colossi of Karnak*, 36–41.

[227] J. R. Harris, "Akhenaten or Nefertiti," *Acta Orientalia* 38 (1977): 5–10. Redford, *The Heretic King*, 102–104. Freed, "Art in the Service of Religion and the State," in *Pharaohs of the Sun: Akhenaten, Nefertiti, Tutankhamun*, 113. Manniche, *The Akhenaten Colossi of Karnak*, 108–110.

[228] Harris, "Akhenaten or Nefertiti," 10.

[229] Ibid., 10.

[230] Robins, "The Representation of Sexual Characteristics in Amarna Art," 37–38.

on this statue, only the double cartouches of Aten are engraved into the image. Furthermore, the crown is broken off, which precludes identifying it with Tefnut's iconography. In response to suggestions that the "sexless" statue was either Nefertiti or representing the king as a hermaphrodite, Redford demurs, "it need not be pointed out how ill-advised it is to read profound meaning into such a flimsy piece of evidence."[231]

In the end we will have to agree with Manniche's observation that "it would seem that now, some three thousand and five hundred years after the event, we will continue to live with the fact there is no final answer to our questions about the meaning of the colossi."[232] It is fair to say that Egyptologists and art historians will likely agree with Robins when she opines, "Since one of the functions of Egyptian art was to express religious ideas visually, it is highly probable that the change in the artistic representation of the king's figure was related to Amenhotep IV/Akhenaten's new religious ideas."[233]

IMPLICATIONS OF THE ATEN THEBAN TEMPLES

The inscriptions and decoration of the Aten temples do provide a window into Akhenaten's evolving religion. What is lacking, however, is a clear rationale for the radical shift toward the Aten while ignoring or rejecting the Amun-Re and other deities. Theological statements are made both by what is present and what is absent in the decorative schemes in the Theban Aten temples. The absence of the name of Amun on temples built within the Amun precinct at Karnak, except in some early instances of the king's initial name (which in many cases were replaced later by "Akhenaten"), is a powerful statement.

While Re-Harakhty's name stands at the heart of the didactic name of the Aten and is repeated hundreds of times in talatat and on the colossi, his actual image (falcon head on standing human figure) that was so prominent in the first year or two of Akhenaten's reign and in the earliest Aten temples (Figure 3.8) is all but gone in the talatat temples. In fact, only a few illustrations have been documented and they are small figures, not exceeding the height of a talatat (ca. 26 cm).[234] The disc that had been perched on Re-Harakhty's head with its rays emanating from it remains as the sole icon of Aten. The only divine images that survive in the Theban period—the uraeus, sphinx, griffin, baboon, and bull—are connected to ancient solar religion[235] (see Chapter 1).

---

[231] Redford, *The Heretic King*, 104.

[232] Manniche, *The Akhenaten Colossi of Karnak*, 115.

[233] Robins, "The Representation of Sexual Characteristics in Amarna Art," 36.

[234] Redford, *The Akhenaten Temple Project*, Vol. 1, 86, no. 8, 9.

[235] Redford, *The Heretic King*, 175.

In this chapter we have seen the significant development and transitions in Atenism. "Re-Harakhty who rejoices in his horizon in his name of light which is in the disc (Aten)" might be thought of as a new god, even God, but he is clearly rooted in the Heliopolitan solar religion of the Old Kingdom. As a testimony to complete devotion to Aten, Amenhotep IV changed his name to Akhenaten, "Beneficial to the Aten."

What was behind this radical change? How is it that Amun and the other deities fell out of favor? What prompted Akhenaten to abandon Thebes and the Karnak temples, which he had sought to transform into the Domain of Aten (*pr itn*), for a pristine new city in middle Egypt? To these questions we now turn.

His majesty stood in the presence of his father,
HOR-ATEN, as Aten's rays were upon him
AMARNA BOUNDARY STELA

Chapter 5

Finding Aten and Founding Akhet-Aten

ATENISM AND THEORIES OF RELIGIOUS EVOLUTION

IT IS EVIDENT that Akhenaten's religious devotion to the Aten went through several steps, as seen in the previous two chapters, and will go through yet another phase when it reaches its final and theologically most advanced form. That will occur after the move to Amarna during the final decade of his reign (ca. 1346–1336 B.C.). Initially, following William Murnane's understanding of the progression, Aten coexisted with the traditional cults, coupled with neglect, which was followed by "abandonment," and then culminating with "persecution."[1] This pattern seems be the result of theological reflection and the maturing (degeneration from the orthodox perspective!) of Akhenaten's thought. Egyptian history is indeed filled with pharaohs who favored one deity over others by building larger cult centers for one or another and inadvertently or intentionally downplaying other divinities. What Akhenaten did, however, with the Aten, right at the very time when Amun was at the peak of his power as the imperial god of Egypt, was unprecedented when initial neglect gave way to abandonment and then persecution.

From the standpoint of the history of religions, in the span of less than a decade (between about 1352–1346 B.C.) Akhenaten's religious-intellectual pilgrimage went

[1] William Murnane, "Observations on Pre-Amarna Theology during the Earliest Reign of Amenhotep IV," in *Gold of Praise: Studies on Ancient Egypt in Honor of Edward F. Wente* (eds. E. Teeter & J. Larson; Chicago: Oriental Institute, 1999), 303–312.

from polytheism, to henotheism or monolatry (i.e., the worship of one god while not denying the existence of other deities), to monotheism (the exclusive belief in one God). The point is that this process was not a lengthy evolutionary one that took centuries or longer. Concerning his start as a traditional "orthodox" Egyptian polytheist, Donald Redford recently observed that "at the very outset of the reign, the king seems to have shown no overt aversion to 'the gods.'"[2] So it is not as if he necessarily started with a monotheistic proclivity as far as the evidence goes. At the same time, one recognizes that Aten's status had been growing in royal circles during the reigns of his grandfather and father (see Chapter 3).

During the 19th century the academic study of religion(s) was influenced by evolutionary thought. It logically followed that if the biological record witnessed an evolution from simple life forms to complex (single cells to humans), societies, languages, cultures, and religion likewise developed over time. For pioneering anthropologists of religion, like E. B. Tyler (*Primitive Culture*, 1871) and James Frazer (*The Golden Bough*, 1890), animism and totemism were viewed as the most primitive religious expressions that after centuries (or millennia) of time would evolve into monotheism, having passed through the intervening stages.[3]

The evolutionary approach to the study of world religions was all but abandoned by the mid-20th century. Religionists came to reject the notion that a religion had to naturally progress through this predictable pattern. Hinduism and some traditional African religions, for example, after 5,000 years are still essentially polytheistic and animistic, and religions like Islam burst into a polytheistic culture of Arabia without going through the theoretically expected evolution. In other words, the evolutionary theory on how religions ought to develop did not square with the actual study of various religious traditions. For the most part today, historians of religion rightly reject the developmental model, although there are many biblical scholars who still follow 19th-century modes of thinking about religion (without realizing it?). They consider monotheism to be a late development in Israel (6th–5th century B.C.) and not a movement that began with Moses at the time of the exodus (ca. 15th–13th century B.C.). Put another way, some biblical scholars do adhere to the evolutionary model when it comes to the appearance of monotheism in ancient Israel, while supposedly rejecting the theoretical model.[4] We will return to this question and the relationship (if any) between Israelite monotheism and Atenism in Chapter 9.

---

[2] Donald Redford, "Akhenaten: New Theories and Old Facts," *BASOR* 369 (2013): 13.

[3] James Waller and Mary Edwardsen, "Evolutionism," in *The Encyclopedia of Religion* vol. 5 (ed. M. Eliade; New York: Macmillan, 1987), 214–218.

[4] For a review of this perspective, see Rainer Albertz, *A History of Israelite Religion in the Old Testament Period* I (Louisville: Westminster/John Knox Press, 1994), 61–62, and Mark Smith, *The Origins of Biblical Monotheism: Israel's Polytheistic Background and the Ugaritic Texts* (New York: Oxford University Press, 2001), 149–194.

The phenomenology of religion school developed as a distinct methodology out of 19th- and 20th-century philosophical circles. Franz Brentano laid the foundation for the phenomenology approach, but it was his student Edmund Husserl (1859–1938) whose writings advanced it further.[5] The aim of phenomenology was "to investigate and become more directly aware of phenomena that appear in immediate experience, and thereby allow the phenomenologist to describe the essential structures of these phenomena."[6] The critical word here is "experience." And this is a fundamental principle of the phenomenology of religion. Western academics have long been influenced by Enlightenment positivism and as a consequence have maintained a condescending attitude toward religious experience in their own day or when studying religion in the past. The scientific study of religion (*Religionswissenschaft*, as it was known in German) attempted to investigate religion as a dispassionate outsider whose analysis is "scientific," objective, and descriptive, rather than as an empathetic insider.[7] The phenomenological school in early 20th-century Europe offered an alternative approach to the prevailing *Religionswissenschaft* method. The phenomenological approach took religious experience seriously, striving to view religion as an insider (i.e., sympathetically). To be sure, there is a place for the critical eye of the "outsider" in the study of religion. But something is lost when the only approach used is supposedly "objective" and scientific, as sociological, psychological, and spiritual considerations are typically overlooked. Put another way, the tendency of the modern scientific perspective is to reject what is deemed irreconcilable with that worldview and what the investigator has not experienced.

Rudolf Otto's influential book *Das Heilige* (1917), which appeared in English as *The Idea of the Holy* in 1923, offered a more sympathetic approach to religious phenomena. Otto maintained that regardless of the religious tradition, the encounter with divinity, the *numinous* (the sacred/the holy), was a non-rational (not irrational!) or subjective experience.[8] He argued that "the holy" was unique to the realm of religion and defied rational or psychological explanations.[9] In other words, the disciplines of history, science, and psychology simply lacked the necessary tools for assessing religious experience. Otto coined the expression *mysterium tremendum* to define the feeling of fear and awe aroused in the person who encountered the

---

[5] Dagfinn Føllesdal, "Edmund Husserl," in *Routledge Encyclopedia of Philosophy*, (ed. Edward Craig; London/New York: Routledge, 1998), 574–588.

[6] Douglas Allen, "Phenomenology of Religion," in *The Encyclopedia of Religion*, vol. 11, 272–285.

[7] For a recent discussion of the "insider" and "outsider" approach to the study of religion, see Arvind Sharma, *To the Things Themselves: Essays on the Discourse and Practice of the Phenomenology of Religion* (Berlin/New York: de Gruyter, 2001), 1–10.

[8] Rudolf Otto, *The Idea of the Holy*, trans. J. W. Harvey (London: Oxford University Press, 1946), 6–7.

[9] Ibid., 5.

numinous.[10] A related term was *majestas*, that is, the sense of being overpowered by the sacred.[11] For a person to experience the numinous is to encounter "that which is quite beyond the sphere of the usual, the intelligible, and familiar."[12] This state, for Otto, is to experience "the wholly other" (*das ganz andere*), outside the sphere of the mundane world. To illustrate his ideas of encountering the holy and the human response to it, Otto cited examples from the Bible, such as Jacob's dream and vision at Bethel and God's appearance to Moses in the burning bush in Sinai. The human responses to these theophanies in the Bible are consistent with those of ancient and modern people. Otto's approach to religion provided the early 20th-century study of religion with a new and fresh way of understanding religion that was diametrically opposed to the mainstream of historians of religion of that era.

The Dutch Egyptologist and historian of religion Gerardus van der Leeuw in 1933 (1938 in English) authored a two-volume work that further advanced the phenomenological school.[13] Similar to Otto, van der Leeuw associated power, awe, and *tabu* with "the sacred." "The sacred" functioned "within boundaries" and was "exceptional."[14] For van der Leeuw, this was the object of religious encounter. The subject, of course, was the recipient of the encounter. Experience of "the sacred" was not something to be investigated in purely subjective terms, but must be studied in concert with historical research. He proposed that investigating phenomenology requires "perpetual correction by the most conscientious philological and archaeological research."[15]

Building upon the works of these European scholars, the French sociologist of religion Roger Caillois wrote *L'homme et le sacré* (1939), which appeared in English as *Man and the Sacred* (1959)[16] and focused on sacred and profane matters, but his works were less influential than those of Mircea Eliade.[17] Eliade promoted and popularized the phenomenological approach. His seminal works, especially *The Sacred and the Profane* (1957) and *Patterns in Comparative Religion* (1958), might be considered to be a defense of Otto's *Das Heilige*. He did this by offering countless examples of theophanies from the ancient Near East, Africa, Oceania, and India, describing how sacred space was established and typically protected by walls, and how

---

[10] Ibid., 12–14.

[11] Ibid., 19.

[12] Ibid., 26.

[13] Gerardus Van Der Leeuw, *Religion in Essence and Manifestation*, trans. J. E. Turner (Gloucester, MA: Peter Smith, 1967).

[14] Ibid. 47.

[15] Ibid. 67.

[16] Reprinted again recently: Roger Caillois, *Man and the Sacred* (Urbana/Chicago: University of Illinois, 2001).

[17] Eliade was a Romanian who spent many years in Paris before coming to the United States, where he was Professor of Religion at the University of Chicago. Thus he stands very much in the European tradition.

rituals grew out of the theophany and were practiced to renew the theophany in sacred time. He thereby demonstrated that the encounter with and response to "the holy" was universally experienced at various times in history. He coined the terms "hierophany" (sacred manifestations) and "kratophany" (manifestations of power) to describe numinous phenomena. For him, "every hierophany one examines is also an historical fact; every manifestation of the sacred takes place in some historical situation. Even the most personal and transcendent mystical experiences are affected by the age in which they occur," Eliade maintained, and "The Jewish prophets owed a debt to the events of history, which justified them and confirmed their message; and also the religious history of Israel, which made it possible for them to explain what they had experienced."[18]

Contrary to the view of Enlightenment positivism, phenomenologists—who do use a comparative method—are not dismissive of religious experience, nor do they seek a naturalistic explanation behind the encounter (even though there may be one) with the sacred, but seek to understand how the individual responds to the numinous, the sacred.

In Akhenaten's religion we seem to have the classic example of a response to the numinous, a hierophany that resulted in a change in religious focus, a new deity (or different form of an old one), different architecture, and most significantly the abandonment of the old holy city and its patron god, Amun, while retaining only the solar element (Re) of that divinity. The intention of the present research is to attempt to investigate Akhenaten's religion with the sensitivity of the phenomenologist and to employ comparative considerations. Consequently, one will view Atenism not merely as a vehicle to serve a political agenda designed to diminish the power of the establishment (Amun) priesthood, as some scholars had proposed in the mid-20th century. George Steindorff and Keith Seele, for example, considered a political/religious agenda as the motivation for the new religion or religious reforms. They spoke of "a bitter religious controversy with the priesthood of Amun at Thebes" and Akhenaten, a religo-political power struggle.[19] John Wilson, on the other hand, thought that controversy with the Amun priesthood arose because of Akhenaten's pacifism, which prompted him to pull back from maintaining or expanding the empire, which had been a boon to the Karnak priests who were enriched by foreign tribute and the booty of war.[20] More recently, David Silverman also has suggested that political considerations may have been a motivating factor in advancing Akhenaten's religious program, namely diminishing the clout of the

[18] Eliade, *Patterns in Comparative Religion*, 2.

[19] George Steindorff & Keith Seele, *When Egypt Ruled the East* (Chicago: University of Chicago, 1957), 80.

[20] John Wilson, *The Culture of Ancient Egypt* (Chicago: University of Chicago, 1951), 207.

powerful Amun priesthood.[21] There obviously were political benefits for Akhenaten when the Amun priesthood was reduced in stature and influence, but was that the impetus for the reforms, or was there some sort of encounter with the numinous?

The story of St. Paul in the New Testament is well known. An ardent opponent of the fledgling religious sect, Christianity, Paul had been a persecutor of the church (Acts 9:1–2, 21; Galatians 1:13, 23) and was on a mission to Damascus with the authorization of the religious leaders in Jerusalem to arrest Christians. Then it happened: "As he neared Damascus on his journey, suddenly a light from heaven flashed around him. He fell to the ground and heard a voice say to him, 'Saul, Saul, why do you persecute me?' 'Who are you, Lord?' Saul asked" (Acts 9:3–5). Paul would recount this experience with some regularity, and each time he did, he focused on what he believed was a divine manifestation. When reporting his story to Festus, the Roman governor, and Herod Agrippa (king of Judea, Samaria, and Galilee) while on trial decades later in Caesarea Maritima, he relates that "[a]t midday, O king, I saw on the way a light from heaven, brighter than the sun, that shone around me and those who journeyed with me" (Acts. 26:13). This "Damascus road experience" resulted in his conversion to Christianity. He was transformed from persecutor of Christianity to its strongest advocate in the first century A.D. The obvious question is, did Akhenaten have his own version of a "Damascus road experience"? Some sort of revelation? Aten shining on him in some remarkable or unique way that was taken to be an encounter with the numinous?

DID ATEN FIND AKHENATEN OR DID AKHENATEN FIND ATEN?

We may never know the impetus for the rise of Akhenaten's religious revolution, especially if a personal, divine encounter had occurred. Presently no text or artistic representation exists to offer an explanation. There may, however, be some significant hints that have heretofore not been considered adequately.

One aspect of the Aten theology as reflected in the hymns from Amarna tombs (see Chapter 8) is revelation through nature. The main medium of this manifestation, Vincent Tobin maintains, "is the sun disc itself in virtue of its very existence and also in virtue of the fact that its practical effects on the world and man."[22] Theologians refer to this as natural or general revelation, that is, revelation by nature that is accessible to anyone at any time and any place. As the Hebrew Psalmist frames it, "the heavens declare the glory of God, and the sky above proclaims his handiwork"

---

[21] David Silverman, "Divinities and Deities in Ancient Egypt," in *Religion in Ancient Egypt: Gods, Myths, and Personal Practice* (ed. Byron Shafer; Ithaca, NY: Cornell University Press, 1991), 4–75.

[22] Vincent A. Tobin, "Amarna and Biblical Religion," in *Pharaonic Egypt, the Bible and Christianity* (ed. S. Israeli-Groll; Jerusalem: The Hebrew University, 1985), 265.

(Psalm 19:1). This communication of nature is not audible: "there is no speech, nor are there words whose voice is not heard" (Psalm 19:3). This seems to imply that the speech from nature is "not fully comprehended" as would be a direct, audible message.[23] Tobin also sees in Amarna religion another more direct type of communication, which finds parallels in biblical religion, and that is revelation by "spoken word."[24] Theologians identify this type of revelation as "special," meaning a more direct or specifically focused revelation, an audible message or visible phenomenon. These two elements occur side by side in Psalm 19 where verses 1–6 focus on the general characteristics of the Creator that can be witnessed in the sky and sun, indeed in all nature.[25] The deity is merely identified as "god" (*'el*), the most general term for divinity, which occurs but once in the opening six verses, but in verses 7–14, as the focus shifts to the Law or Torah, the divine name YHWH, LORD occurs seven times. The implication is that in special revelation a more intimate and direct manifestation occurs. The suggestion advanced in this chapter is that Akhenaten, very early in his reign, experienced some sort of theophany out of which emerged the didactic name (see further Chapter 8).

In the previous chapter, the Theban temples of the Aten cult were introduced. The largest of the temples, the function of which was to celebrate the Sed-festival, was named *Gm(t) p3 itn*. Various grammatically based translations were offered due to the variant writings that have survived. It was suggested that either a passive (*sḏmw.f or sḏm.t[w].f*) form ("the Aten has been/is found") or the relative form ("that which the Aten found") were the most likely readings. The former would stress the discovery of the Aten, presumably by the king, whereas the second would lay stress on the object of the Aten's discovery, namely Akhenaten or the new sacred area designated for the Aten's precinct. Rather than having to choose between the two options, could the variant writings be introducing an intentional ambiguity to allow for this range of ideas? The position taken here is that the different spellings of *gm/gmt* are intended to stress both meanings: "the Aten has been/is found" (i.e., by Akhenaten) and "that which the Aten found" (i.e., Aten and/or the place where his sanctuary would be located).

Also, as noted in the previous chapter, *Gm(t) p3 itn* was also the name of one of the major sanctuaries at Akhet-Aten. Located within a massive temple complex surrounded by an enclosure wall (800 × 300 m; 2,624 × 984 ft) is *Gm(t) p3 itn,* also known as the long temple.[26] The long axial temple stretches ca. 207 × 30 meters

---

23 A. A. Anderson, *The Book of Psalms*, Vol. I (London: Marshall, Morgan & Scott, 1972), 168.

24 Tobin, "Amarna and Biblical Religion," 265,

25 For a further discussion of Psalm 19 and the role of general and special revelation therein, see James K. Hoffmeier, "'The Heavens Declare the Glory of God': The Limits of General Revelation," *Trinity Journal* 21 (2000): 17–24.

26 Barry Kemp, *The City of Akhenaten and Nefertiti: Amarna and Its People* (London: Thames Hudson, 2012), 87.

(ca. 623 × 100 ft), and is made up of six courts, each demarcated by a pylon or gateway. Like the temples at Karnak, this edifice is opened to the sky, with courts filled with offering tables, more than 1,700 according the Barry Kemp's calculations.[27] His ongoing work at Amarna has helped clarify the plan of this temple (see Figure 5.1).[28] 920 mud-brick altars were neatly arranged in the area outside the southern walls of the temple, and earlier excavators thought there were more altars on the north side, but Kemp has been unable to confirm this claim. If there were hundreds of altars on the north side, the original number could have exceeded 2,000 (Figure 5.2). The illustrations of this temple in the tombs of Akhenaten show scores of altars with foodstuffs piled high,[29] the same phenomenon that we saw in the Karnak talatat reliefs.[30] Why so many altars? For Kemp the vast number "is surely a symptom of obsession."[31]

Could the preoccupation with altars and offerings to Aten, not just at Amarna but also at Karnak, and persistent representations of them in the art, be intended to re-enact the sacred moment of his revelation? Did Akhenaten's original theophany occur while making an offering in a cultic context? This may explain what Kemp calls the king's "obsession." No king before or after established and furnished so

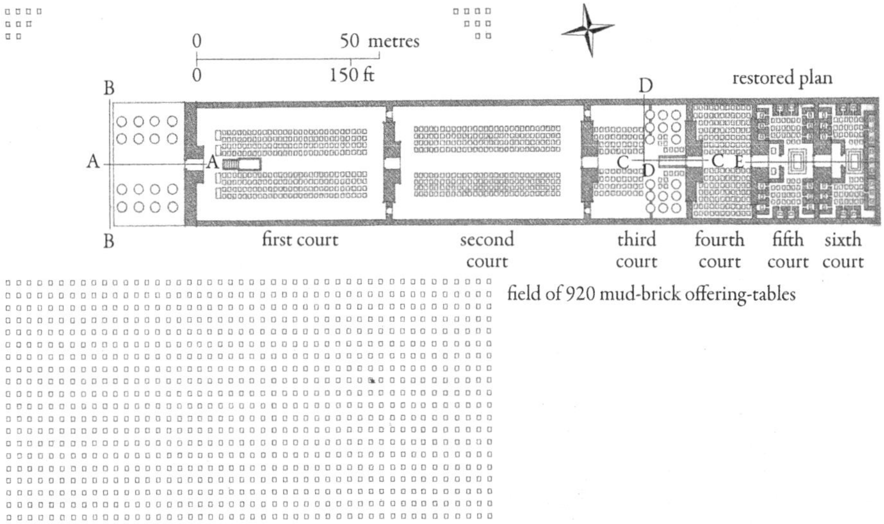

FIGURE 5.1 Barry Kemp's plan of *Gm(t) p3 itn* temple at Amarna. Barry Kemp, *The City of Akhenaten and Nefertiti: Amarna and Its People* (London: Thames Hudson, 2012), 90 (reprinted with permission of the author).

---

[27] Ibid. 92.

[28] Most recently, see Barry Kemp et al., "Tell el-Amarna, 2012–2013," *JEA* 99 (2013): 20–32.

[29] Norman de Garis Davies, *The Rock Tombs of El-Amarna*, Vol. IV (London: EEF, 1908), 1–6.

[30] Jocelyn Gohary, *Akhenaten's Sed-festival at Karnak* (London: Kegan Paul International, 1992), xxviii –xxxvi.

[31] Kemp, *The City of Akhenaten and Nefertiti*, 92.

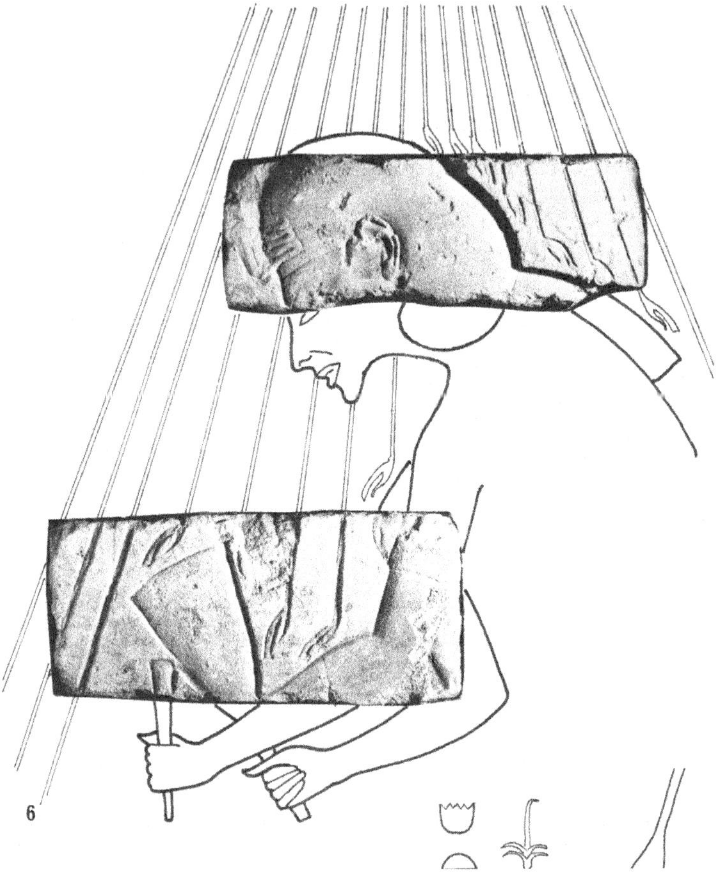

FIGURE 5.2 Akhenaten pounding a peg in some religious ceremony. Ray W. Smith & Donald Redford, *The Akhenaten Temple Project*, Vol. 1 (Warminster: Aris and Phillips, 1976), pl. 18, digitized by Joshua Olsen.

many altars and makes standing before an altar the primary focus of his decoration program in temples, not to mention the central place of this motif in the private tombs at Amarna.

The name *Gm ỉtn* is also found in a Nubian toponym and initially was thought to be associated with the Temple of Sesebi, located between the 2nd and 3rd Cataracts in present-day northern Sudan. While investigating the site of Sesebi in 1906, James Henry Breasted concluded that the New Kingdom temple was built by Amenhotep IV (prior to changing his name), complete with an open solar court, although many of the inscriptions and reliefs were erased or carved over by Seti I.[32] The name of the town site appears to have derived from the Aten temple. Under Taharka (690–664 B.C.),

[32] James Henry Breasted, "A City of Ikhenaten in Nubia," *ZÄS* 40 (1902/3): 106–113, and "Second Preliminary Report of the Egyptian Expedition," *AJSLL* 25, no. 1 (1908): 52–83.

the name of a city is "Amun (of) Gem Aten" somewhere in the region.[33] Breasted believed that Akhenaten's Theban temple by the same name stood behind the name of its Nubian counterpart.

Equating the name Gem Aten with Sesebi was challenged by Francis Ll. Griffith, who worked at Kawa, just over 100 kilometers (60 mi) south of Sesebi. He argued that Gem Aten rather was the name of a "little temple to Amun of Gematen and to the Sun-God Atum of Heliopolis, who is named on the foundation-scarab. Nothing attributable to his successor Akhenaten has been found."[34] Griffith's identification of Gematen with Kawa was accepted by A. M. Blackman and Herbert Fairman, who in the 1930s worked at Sesebi under the auspices of the Egypt Exploration Society. They mapped and did some excavation and epigraphic recording.[35] They did, however, recognize that the major fortification system and its temples within it were established by Akhenaten, although there may have been an earlier and smaller enclosure.[36]

Renewed work at Sesebi under the direction of Kate Spence and Pamela Rose confirms the earlier view that Akhenaten's building projects were from early in his reign, showing the pre-Amarna art style and using Amenhotep for the king's name.[37] Aten is presented iconographically as a falcon (Re-Harakhty?). To date, no inscriptional evidence has been found to secure the ancient name of Sesebi. Derek Welsby has recently argued regarding Kawa (following Griffith) that "epigraphic evidence indicates that in Old Egyptian, the town was called Gem Aten ('the Aten is perceived'); this strongly suggests that a settlement was founded (or refounded) there during the New Kingdom, either in the latter part of the reign of Amenhotep III or that of his son, Amenhotep IV . . ."[38]

It appears, then, that Griffith's identification of Gem Aten with a temple at Kawa is generally accepted, but inscriptional evidence from Kawa has not confirmed that, and Sesebi has thus far refused to reveal its Pharaonic era name. So the precise location of Gem Aten remains problematic, but it seems that somewhere in the 2nd through 3rd Cataract regions was an Aten temple built by Akhenaten, as Breasted thought and Wellesby allows (contrary to Griffith's proposal). It is tempting to

---

[33] Breasted, "Second Preliminary Report of the Egyptian Expedition," 82.

[34] F. L. Griffith in *The Temples of Kawa II: History and Archaeology of the Site* (ed. M. F. L. Macadam; London: Oxford University Press), 10.

[35] A. M. Blackman, "Preliminary Report on the Excavations at Sesebi, Northern Province, Anglo-Egyptian Sudan 1936–37," *JEA* 23 (1937): 145–151. H. W. Fairman, "Preliminary Report on the Excavations at Sesebi (Sudla) and 'Amarah West, Anglo-Egyptian Sudan, 1937–38," *JEA* 24 (1938): 151–156.

[36] Ibid.

[37] Kate Spence & Pamela Rose, "New Fieldwork at Sesebi," *EA* 35 (2009): 31–34. Kate Spence, Pamela Rose, et al., "Fieldwork at Sesebi, 2009," *Sudan and Nubia* 13 (2009): 38–45, and "Sesebi 2011," *Sudan and Nubia* 15 (2011): 34–38. I am grateful to Dr. Spence for sending me copies of these articles.

[38] Derek Welsby, "Kawa," *OEAE* 2, 226.

associate the open solar court temple at Sesebi with Gem Aten, but this will have to await new textual material.

The foregoing evidence means that there are at least three temples built by Akhenaten that include the verb *gmi*, "to find."[39] Akhenaten's attachment to the word *gmi* does not end with these temples. The establishment of the Aten's city, Akhet-Aten, at the site known in modern times as el-Amarna was marked by a series of boundary stelae that were intended to demarcate Aten's realm (Figure 5.3). In all, 15 stelae have been documented, three of which are on the western cliffs of the Nile

FIGURE 5.3 Boundary Stela S. Norman de Garis Davies, *The Rock Tombs of Amarna* V (London: EEF, 1908), pl. XXIX.

[39] *Wb* 5, 166.

Valley (A, B, and F) and 12 on the east, surrounding the actual city (J, K, L, M, N, P, Q, R, S, U, V, and X).[40] Three of the boundary slabs (K, M, and X) are called the "Early Proclamation" that commemorated the actual discovery of the site.[41]

Although the preservation of the texts are rather poor, William Murnane and Charles Van Siclen recently collated a new critical edition of the texts, offering some improved readings over the original copies made by Norman de Garis Davies some 80 years earlier.[42] Between these two works and comparing the versions, a majority of the inscription is legible, but there are many major lacunae. Dated to regnal year 5, Akhenaten recounts his personal involvement in the discovery of the location for the holy city and establishing its limits. The king claims

> On this day, when One (the king) was in Akhet-[Aten], his person (*ḥm.f*)[43] [appeared] on the great chariot of electrum—just like Aten, when he rises in his horizon and fills the land with the love and [pleasantness (?) of] the Aten. He set off on a good road [toward] Akhet-Aten, his place of the primeval event, which he made for himself to set within it daily, and which his son Waenre made for him—(being) his great monument which he found for himself; his horizon, [in which his] circuit comes into being where he is beheld with joy while the land rejoices and all hearts exult when they see him.[44]

There are several vital pieces of information in this paragraph that is dated to the early months of Akhenaten's fifth year. Until this point, Karnak Temple had been the place of creation (i.e., *st.f n(y)t sp tpy*—"his place of the primeval event"). The "holy of holies" of Karnak Temple was identified with this "place of the primeval event (of creation),"[45] it was Amun's realm. Now Akhenaten was going to establish this location at Aten's "place of the primeval event." In a sense, Akhenaten discovered the place that the sun had already discovered, a point made later in the proclamation (see below). It was at this "place of the primeval event" that the sun-god

---

[40] William Murnane & Charles Van Siclen, *The Boundary Stelae of Akhenaten* (London/New York: Kegan Paul International, 1993), 1.

[41] For translations of these inscriptions, see Murnane & Van Siclen, *The Boundary Stelae of Akhenaten*. William Murnane, *Texts from the Amarna Period in Egypt* (Atlanta: Scholars Press, 1995), 73–88. Miriam Lichtheim, *Ancient Egyptian Literature* II (Berkeley: University of California, 1976), 48–51.

[42] Norman de Garis Davies, *The Rock Tombs of El Amarna* V (London: Egypt Exploration Fund, 1908), pl. xxv–xliii. Murnane & Van Siclen, *The Boundary Stelae of Akhenaten*, chapters 3, 4.

[43] Murnane translates *ḥm.f*, traditionally rendered "his majesty," as "his Person." While the translation of *ḥm.f* as "his majesty" sounds archaic and rings of British monarchy, I am not sure how "his Person" is any improvement.

[44] Murnane, *Texts from the Amarna Period in Egypt*, 74.

[45] James K. Hoffmeier, *"Sacred" in the Vocabulary in Ancient Egypt* (Orbis Biblicus et Orientalis 59; Freiburg: Universitätsverlag, 1985), 173.

first manifested himself, revealing this place as holy.[46] Eliade observed that "a sacred place involves the notion of repeating the primeval hierophany which consecrated the place by marking it out, by cutting if off from the profane space around it,"[47] and the observance of the cult is how the theophany is maintained. The daily sunrise would indeed be a dramatic re-enactment of the original sacred event of creation.

Again, Eliade's observations about establishing sacred space are germane to the founding of Akhet-Aten. "So it is clear to what a degree the discovery—that, the revelation—of a sacred space possesses existential value for religious man . . . The discovery or projection of a fixed point—the center—is equivalent to the creation of the world."[48] Divine revelation (theophany) is discovered by an individual or group of people and becomes the basis for a new created order, a new creation, or in Egyptian parlance, "place of the primeval event." In the boundary stelae inscriptions of Akhenaten, all these elements are present: revelation, discovery, place of creation, leading to a temple or holy city. Re-establishing the place of the beginning of creation from Karnak to Akhet-Aten represents a radical, mythic paradigm shift that necessitated a compelling theophany.

The early proclamation continues by announcing that Akhenaten "founded (it) for him (Aten)" (*snṯ.f n.f*).[49] The word *snṯ* means "plan, plot out, found," and is determined by the looped rope-sign.[50] *Snṯ* has to do with laying out a plot of land with measuring ropes to establish the area of a temple, a building, or, as in this case, a city.[51] A scene from the Karnak talatat shows Akhenaten in a ceremony where he drives a stake into the ground with a mallet; possibly some sort of founding ceremony for an edifice in the Aten precinct, although a little known rite connected to the Sed-festival is also a possibility (Figure 5.1).[52] Regardless of the occasion for Akhenaten pounding the stake into the ground, such a ceremony was doubtlessly envisioned in the "Early Proclamation." It might even be argued that the purpose of the boundary stelae that surrounded Akhet-Aten did not just represent the limits of a political capital, but a sacred realm, cut off and holy. The initial city plan occupied only the eastern flood plain, east to the limestone cliffs that curve like a bow, the apex being at the point in the royal valley (i.e., where the royal tombs were quarried out). The geographical layout gives the impression that from the royal valley area the sun

[46] See discussion of this matter in Chapter 1.

[47] Eliade, *Patterns in Comparative Religion*, 368.

[48] Mircea Eliade, *The Sacred and the Profane* (New York: Harcourt Brace Jovanovich, 1959), 22.

[49] Murnane & Van Siclen, *The Boundary Stelae of Akhenaten*, 30, l. 2. I take *n.f* to be the dative + 3rd masc. suffix, not the reflexive as taken by Murnane, *Texts from the Amarna Period in Egypt*, 74. Akhet-Aten was founded for Aten, not the king.

[50] Alan H. Gardiner, *Egyptian Grammar* (London: Oxford University Press, 1969), 522, sign V-5.

[51] *Wb* 4, 177–178.

[52] Ray Smith & Donald Redford, *Akhenaten Temple Project*, Vol. 1 (Warminster: Aris & Phillips, 1976), pl. 18.

would shine (see further below) in the morning, with the rays fanning out in a triangular (pyramid) shaped pattern in the plain where the city was built, just like the iconic artistic representations of the Aten with its rays shining downward. With the subsequent addition of the secondary stela in the western cliffs, Akhet-Aten was expanded by around 124 square miles (400 sq km).[53]

It is only conjecture, but one wonders if the king while traveling on the Nile was passing by the area where Akhet-Aten would be established, and there experienced a further theophany. Cyril Aldred relates his own experience as he sailed downstream and passed Amarna. As seen from the Nile, one notices the break in the eastern cliffs caused by the aforementioned valley. Aldred described what he saw: "this gap in the cliffs forms a huge natural silhouette of the *ꜣḫt*-sign (𓈌) and suggests that its appearance determined not only the location of the place of the origin of the Aten but its name also, *ꜣḫt-ỉtn*—"the Horizon of the Aten."[54] The eastern horizon at sunrise at Amarna must have been a stunning panorama,[55] resulting in what Kemp has called a "devotional landscape" that would help erase any memory of Amun from Aten's realm.[56] Michael Mallinson, an architect who works with Kemp at Amarna, has suggested that the royal tomb in the valley served as the projection point that aligns with some of the stela and serves as the line along the axis of the great temple complex, including *Gm(t) pꜣ ỉtn* and on to Stela B on the western cliffs.[57] These observations suggest that the configuration and placement of the temples were intended to be oriented with the rising sun emerging from the gap in the mountain where in the early morning the rays would shine through, lighting the plain. This dazzling picture may have been the theophany of the sun that was seen as Aten founding this spot as claimed in Stela X, line 37 (see discussion below).

There may have been the attempt to capture the moment of the rising sun over the 𓈌-like formation at Amarna in the temple architecture at Akhet-Aten. Among the reliefs of the various temples at Akhenaten, some show the Aten-disc aligned centrally over the temple as if the pylons with the rays pouring down represent the two sides of the horizon (Figure 5.4a-b).[58]

One might imagine the royal flotilla going north from Thebes in search of the new home for Aten's city when, at sunrise, the Aten's rays burst forth from the eastern

---

[53] Kemp, *The City of Akhenaten and Nefertiti*, 32.

[54] Cyril Aldred, "The Horizon of the Aten," *JEA* 62 (1976): 184. For a good picture of this rock formation, see Kemp, *The City of Akhenaten and Nefertiti*, 102, fig. VII.

[55] Kemp, *The City of Akhenaten and Nefertiti*, 100–101. The picture dates to February 19, 2005.

[56] Ibid., 24.

[57] Michael Mallinson, "The Sacred Landscape," in *Pharaohs of the Sun, Akhenaten, Nefertiti, Tutankhamun* (eds. Rita Free, Yvonne Markowitz, & Sue D'Auria; Boston: Museum of Fine Arts, 1999), 72–79, see especially fig. 51 and map on p. 15.

[58] Davies, *The Rock Tombs of El Amarna* IV, pl. vi, xxix, xxx.

(a) (b)

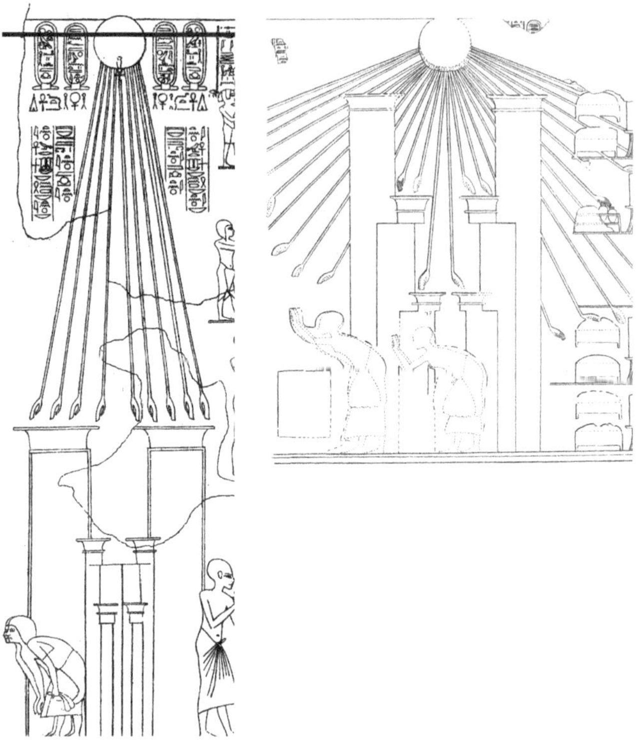

FIGURE 5.4 a. Aten shining through temple pylon. Norman de Garis Davies, *The Rock Tombs of Amarna* IV (London: EEF, 1908), pl. vi. b. Aten shining through temple pylon. Norman de Garis Davies, *The Rock Tombs of Amarna* VI (London: EEF, 1908), pl. xxix, xxx.

cliffs, showering the plain of Amarna with morning light. Perhaps such a view greeted Akhenaten, and that was all the revelation he needed. In his recent and lavishly illustrated book on Amarna, Kemp offers a dramatic picture in which the sun rises in the trough of the silhouetted mountain, with the sun aligning with the Small Aten temple.[59] Such a dramatic scene may well have inspired the name Akhet-Aten. The power of the morning light coming from the eastern horizon over the limestone Akhet-like formation, as Aldred described it, may be what the king is describing on the proclamation stela and what left a permanent impression on the king.

The "early proclamation" continues by detailing the offerings made by the king for his father, "Living Re-Harakhty who rejoices in his horizon in his name of light which is in the disc (Aten)." It included "bread, beer, long-and short-horned cattle, calves, fowl, wine, fruits, incense, all sorts of fresh green plants and everything good

[59] Kemp, *The City of Akhenaten and Nefertiti*, 100–101.

in front of the mountain of Akhet-Aten."[60] This lavishly abundant offering is a response to the appearance of Aten in the sky. In stela K line XV, immediately following the sacrifice list, it reads that the Aten "hovered over [his] place" (*ḥtp ḥr st.[f]*).[61] Here we have a verbal description of the ubiquitous offering scenes with the king (and often queen) standing before an altar piled high with various foods with the sun-disc directly overhead, while its rays cascade down on the cultic activity.

This offering is part of the king's response to the Aten's manifestation. Such a reaction of theophanies is normal and expected. Earlier in this study (Chapter 2), the manifestations of Min to the Vizier Amenemhet at the end of the 11th Dynasty in the Wadi Hammamat were mentioned. In one miraculous manifestation (*bi3t*) there was a mysterious appearance of a pregnant gazelle that approached with its eyes fixed on the men of the vizier's quarrying crew. Gazelles by nature are very shy and avoid humans, but this one approached them as if in a divinely induced trance and laid down on a nearby block. There she gave birth to her young.[62] This unexpected occurrence was interpreted by the expeditionary force as a manifestation of Min, directing them to the very rock that should be quarried for the king's sarcophagus lid. Their response to this *bi3* was to sacrifice the gazelle to Min. There was a second manifestation of Min recorded by Amenemhet in which an unexpected downpour filled a pool, thus providing much needed water for the workers. To commemorate these events "[c]alves were slaughtered, goats sacrificed, (and) incense was placed on fire," and a stela was carved into the face of the mountain "as a monument for his father Min of Coptos, lord of the highlands."[63]

Another memorable divine-human encounter in Egyptian literature is found in the Tale of the Shipwrecked Sailor from the Middle Kingdom. The sailor is the lone survivor of a ship consisting of an expeditionary force of 120 on the Red Sea, headed for a mining expedition, apparently to Sinai. The fortunate sailor ended up on a mystical island where he experienced a thunderous revelation, a kratophany (manifestation of power):

> Then I heard a thundering noise and thought, "It is a wave of the sea." Trees splintered, the ground trembled. Uncovering my face, I found it was a snake that was coming. He was of thirty cubits; his beard was over two cubits long. His body was overlaid with gold . . . Then he opened his mouth to me, while I was on my belly before him.[64]

[60] Murnane, *Texts from the Amarna Period in Egypt*, 74.

[61] Ibid., 74.

[62] Adrian De Buck, *Egyptian Reading Book* (Leiden: Netherlands Institute for Near Eastern Studies, 1970), 76–77.

[63] Ibid., 75.5.

[64] Miriam Lichtheim, *Ancient Egyptian Literature* I (Berkeley: University of California, 1975), 212.

The gigantic divine serpent spoke to the man, interrogating him about how he came to the island. Then the snake-god announced that the sailor would spend four months on the island, after which he would be rescued and returned home. His first reflex after this revelation was to make offerings:

> Stretched out on my belly I touched the ground before him; then I said to him: "I shall speak of your power to the king, I shall let him know of your greatness. I shall send you *ibi* and *ḥnkw* oils, laudanum, and incense of the temples . . . I shall slaughter oxen for you as burnt offering; I shall sacrifice geese to you."[65]

Making offerings and sacrifices is a very normal human response to a theophany, even the expected behavior. This is why the practice is also widely attested outside Egypt as well. At Ugarit (Ras Shamra on the Syrian coast), the Kirtu Epic (ca. 13th century) includes a divine encounter between king Kirtu and the head of the Syro-Canaanite pantheon, El ('Ilu). Tragically, Kirtu's family and wives all died, threatening his ability to perpetuate his line. Devastated by his calamity, Kirtu wept until sleep overwhelmed him:

> Sleep overcame him and he lay down,
> Slumber and he curled up.
> In a dream 'Ilu descended,
> In a vision, the father of mankind.
> He came near, asking Kirta:
> Who is Kirta that he should weep?[66]

He asks the deity to provide a son for him, and then El instructs Kirtu to make offerings:

> Enter [the shade of (your) tent]
> Take a lamb [in your hand],
> a sacrificial lamb [in] (your) right hand,
> a kid in both hands,
> all your best food.
> Take a fowl, a sacrificial bird
> Pour wine into a silver cup
> Honey into a golden bowl . . .

[65] Ibid., 214.
[66] Dennis Pardee, "The Kirtu Epic," in *COS* I, 334.

Raise your hands heavenward,
Sacrifice to the Bull, your father 'Ilu.
Bring down Ba'lu with your sacrifice . . .[67]

The Bible contains similar reports of how humans respond to encounters with the numinous. In the biblical patriarchal traditions of Genesis, erecting an altar (מִזְבֵּחַ—*mizbeaḥ*) typically follows divine appearances.[68]

Then the LORD appeared to Abram and said, "To your offspring I will give this land."

So he built there an altar to the LORD, who had appeared to him. (Gen 12:7)

Jacob's well-known vision occurred at Bethel (central hill country of Canaan) while traveling from Beer-sheba in the south to Harran in Mesopotamia (Gen 29:10–22). His initial response to the encounter was to erect a stone as a pillar (מַצֵּבָה—*maṣṣēḇâ*) and pour oil on it (vs. 18). Years later, according to the narrative, he made a pilgrimage back to Bethel to offer thanks to the LORD (Gen 35) and at that time he made an altar.

When Manoah and his wife, a childless couple, received a divine message via an angel that she would give birth to a son (Samson the judge), their reaction was to make an offering: "So Manoah took the young goat with the grain offering and offered it on the rock to the LORD . . ." (Judges 13:19).

The narrative about King David's discovery of the plot of ground to build a temple to the LORD of Israel has elements that are strikingly similar to the founding of Akhet-Aten: "The angel stretched out his hand toward Jerusalem to destroy it, the LORD relented from the calamity and said to the angel who was working destruction among the people, 'It is enough; now stay your hand.' And the angel of the LORD was by the threshing floor of Araunah the Jebusite. . . . David . . . saw the angel" (2 Samuel 24:16–17). This place was just north of Jebusite Jerusalem or "the City of David."[69] Then, at the urging of Gad the prophet (2 Samuel 24:18), he "built an altar to the LORD and offered burnt offerings and peace offerings" (2 Samuel 24:25). Then David purchased the land where the theophany occurred, which became the place where Solomon's temple would be built in the next decade.

---

[67] Ibid., 334.

[68] For a thorough study of the theophanies of Genesis 12–36, see the doctoral dissertation of my student William M. Pak, "Genesis 12–36: An Investigation of the Patriarchal Theophanies using a Phenomonological Approach," (Ph.D. dissertation, Trinity International University, 2012).

[69] Jebusites are the inhabitants of Jerusalem prior to David's conquest of the city. See Judges 1:21; 2 Samuel 5:6–9.

In the Chronicler's account of the theophany, after reporting on the incident and how David made a sacrifice there, the text adds: "Then David said, 'Here shall be the house of the LORD God and here the altar of burnt offering for Israel'" (1 Chronicles 22:1). In this example we see the important collocation of revelation, offering/sacrifice, and marking the sacred space with a temple.

The point of these examples is to demonstrate that Akhenaten's activities on his first visit to Amarna in the early boundary stelae are consistent with how humans throughout the Near East (and elsewhere) respond to a theophany. Making offerings is not only an expression of thanksgiving, but offerings also figure in the dedication and sanctifying of the area for the deity. The text of the boundary stelae continue by summoning his officers and troops, and Akhenaten addresses them, thereby disclosing more about the encounter:

> Behold Aten! The Aten wishes to have [something] made for him as a monument with an eternal and everlasting name. Now it is the Aten, my father, who advised (*mtr*) me concerning it, (namely) Akhet-Aten. No official had ever advised (*mtr*) me concerning it, to tell me [a plan] for making Akhet-Aten in this distant place. It is Aten, my father, [who advised (*mtr*) me] concerning it, so that it could be made for him as Akhet-Aten.[70]

The king begins his address to his officials by saying, as it were, "there He is," the immanent one. What follows seems to indicate that the Aten's wish (*ꜣby*) was communicated to Akhenaten. The key word is *mtr*, which occurs five times in the proclamation and likely a sixth time in the lacuna in this passage,[71] and it occurs yet again later in the decree.[72] It can be translated as "advise," as Murnane did. *Mtr*, however, could also be rendered as "inform" and "instruct."[73] The nuance is clear; Akhenaten did not get the inspiration for establishing the new holy city from mere mortals; rather he was "instructed" by Aten himself. The numerous references for *mtr* in this text make it abundantly clear that this is a central theme in the proclamation.

To stress the point that Aten was the one who instructed the king, the text changes the normal word order and places "the Aten" at the beginning of the clause.[74] This grammatical practice is called "fronting" or "topicalization,"[75] that is, "<u>it is Aten</u>, my

---

[70] Murnane, *Texts from the Amarna Period in Egypt*, 75.

[71] The phallus-sign in the word *mtr* is apparently preserved in stela M in Murnane & Van Siclen, *The Boundary Stelae of Akhenaten*, 21.

[72] See Murnane & Van Siclen, *The Boundary Stelae of Akhenaten*, 21–23.

[73] Leonard Lesko, *A Dictionary of Late Egyptian* 1 (Berkeley: BC Scribe, 1982), 253.

[74] Stela K XXI: Murnane & Van Siclen, *The Boundary Stelae of Akhenaten*, 21.

[75] James Hoch, *Middle Egyptian Grammar* (Mississauga, Ontario: Benben Publications, 1997), §§ 36–37.

father [who advised me] concerning it." Fronting "the Aten" is used again similarly in the following section.

The king continues his first person proclamation by saying,

> Behold, I did not **find** (*gm*) it provided with shrines or plastered with tombs or porticoes (?) . . . Behold, it is pharaoh, l.p.h.,[76] who **found it** (*gmt.s*), when it did not belong to a god, nor to a goddess; when it did not belong to a male ruler, not to a female ruler; when it did not belong to any people to do their business with it. [Its . . .] is not known, (but) **I found** it widowed . . . It is the Aten, my [father] who advised (*mtr*) me concerning it (saying), "Behold, [fill] Akhet-Aten with provisions—a storehouse for everything!" while my father, "Living Re-Harakhty who rejoices in his horizon in his name of light which is in the disc (Aten),"[77] who proclaimed (*sḏd*) to me, "It is to belong to my Person (*ḥm.i*), to be Akhet-Aten continually forever."[78]

Here there are three occurrences of the verb *gmi*, expressing that the king found or discovered the site that previously had not been the hallowed ground of any deity, nor had any previous monarch claimed it, and no shrines or temples had been established there. This virgin, "distant place" was found by Akhenaten, so he claims, having received some sort of divine communication or "proclamation" (*sḏd*) from the Aten. *Sḏd* is the causative form, *s* + *ḏd* (meaning say for "speak"), which when followed by the preposition *n* is translated "to speak to someone."[79] Simply put, the king claims that the Aten spoke to him directly, instructing him about his desire.

The idea, then, is that Aten had somehow expressed his desire for his own cult city, which led Akhenaten to discover the new holy city. Interestingly, toward the end of the proclamation, in a very broken section of the text—only preserved in Stela X line 37[80]—Aten himself is emphatically credited with the discovery of the city: "on the day when [the] Aten, my [father], . . . [for (?) the] Aten in [Akhet]-aten, this place which he himself **found** for himself (*gm.f n.f ḏs.f*)." This claim seems to reflect the meaning of the Aten temples (*Gm(t) pꜣ itn*).

At least seven times[81] in the text of early proclamation stelae Akhenaten claims that Aten instructed (*mtr*) him, that he spoke to him (*sḏd*) regarding his desire (*ꜣby*)

---

[76] Abbreviation for "life, prosperity & health" (Eg., *ꜥnḫ wḏꜣ snb*) that accompanies various royal and divine names and titles.

[77] Murnane, *Texts from the Amarna Period in Egypt*, 75, offers the abbreviated form of the didactic name, I have written it in totality.

[78] Ibid., 75.

[79] *Wb* 4, 395.

[80] See Murnane & Van Siclen, *The Boundary Stelae of Akhenaten*, 30.

[81] Given the many lacunae in the stelae, there could have been more occurrences that have not survived.

for a monument on which his name might live forever (*m mnw ḥr ▒ nḥḥ ḏt*).[82] These key terms and the king's response suggest that he believed he was following the divine disclosure he had received from Aten. There is no indication in the language to suggest that this directive came via a priestly oracle, but rather by direct revelation.

On the first anniversary of the founding of Akhet-Aten, the king returned, possibly on an inspection tour to see how the building program was progressing. He had to bivouac in a tent or pavilion made of heavy woven material (*ỉꜣmw n psš*),[83] apparently because the royal palace was not yet ready to be occupied.

This event is documented on eight of the boundary stelae and includes a brief summary of Akhet-Aten's founding:

> On this day one (the king) was in Akhet-Aten, in the pavilion of matting that his Person (*ḥm.f*) made in Akhet-Aten, the name of which is "Aten is Content." His Person, l.p.h., appeared mounted on the great chariot of electrum, like Aten when he rises in the horizon, having filled the Two Lands with his love. He set off on a good road toward Akhet-Aten on the first anniversary of its discovery (*gm*), which his Person, l.p.h., did in order to found (*snṯ*) it as a monument for the Aten, just as the father "Living Re-Harakhty who rejoices in his horizon in his name of light which is in the disc (Aten)"[84]—given life forever continually—commanded (*wḏ*) in order to make a memorial for himself in it.[85]

Here we again encounter the familiar terms that had appeared in the three early stelae, namely, discovery (*gm*) and the founding (*snṯ*) as a result of Aten's command (*wḏ*).

It is unfortunate that we have no comparable set of stelae from Thebes containing a complete proclamation announcing the rationale for his building program. One might expect that such a document would have shed light on the motivation behind Akhenaten's decision to make temples to Aten at Karnak and to move away from traditional Amun worship. (A possible clue, however, is found on the above-mentioned 10th Pylon blocks of Akhenaten's early speech, which is further treated below.)

The name of the temple *Gm(t) pꜣ ỉtn* may, as proposed here, provide an important indicator as to what may have stimulated the entire religious revolution. The use of

---

[82] Murnane & Van Siclen, *The Boundary Stelae of Akhenaten*, 20 (K xx).

[83] Murnane & Van Siclen, *The Boundary Stelae of Akhenaten*, 84–86. For a discussion of the meaning of *ỉꜣmw n psš*, see James Hoffmeier, "Tents in Egypt and the Ancient Near East," *SSEA Newsletter* VII, no. 3 (1977): 19. In this publication I wrongly wrote that this was Akhenaten's initial visit to Amarna rather than the anniversary of the founding a year later.

[84] Murnane offers the abbreviated form of the didactic name, Hor-Aten, but I have written it in totality.

[85] Murnane, *Texts from the Amarna Period in Egypt*, 75.

the verb *gmi* is unattested in temple names prior to Akhenaten.[86] The fact that it can be tied to no fewer than three Aten temples (Thebes, Nubia, and Akhet-Aten) seems to imply that not only did the Aten discover Akhenaten, but Akhenaten found Aten and so spent the most of his 17-year reign devoted to cultic activities for the sun-god who had revealed himself to the young king in some dramatic theophany. Now, thanks to the revelation described on the early proclamation, Akhet-Aten could be the new sacred place where Aten's creation of the cosmos began and would be his holy city.

FURTHER THOUGHTS ON DISCOVERY/FINDING OF DEITY

The argument made here is that the names of the several Aten temples, *Gm (t) p3 itn*, and the multiple occurrences of the verb *gmi,* (find/found) in the early proclamation on the Amarna stelae suggest that a significant discovery was made. The Aten had, it is argued, revealed itself in some dramatic way to Amenhotep IV, and that revelation began the radical religious shift. Then the "discovery" of Akhet-Aten to serve as the new holy city of Aten followed, some years later. This element of discovery, as pointed out by Eliade, is the discovery of the theophany. Finding deity or the deity finding a particular individual is at the heart of religious experience that spans cultures and time periods. Moreover, finding deity and sacred space are conceptually conjoined. To further illustrate how vital "discovery" is to theophany and the founding of sanctuaries, some examples from the Hebrew Bible are illustrative.

The Hebrew word is מָצָא (*māsā'*), whose basic meaning is "find" but also means "to meet accidentally."[87] This nuance certainly figures into theophanies. Moses does not go looking for God; rather he sees that the burning bush was not consumed and then investigates "this great sight" (Exodus 3:1–4). The divine announcement is: "the place (הַמָּקוֹם – *hammāqôm*) on which you are standing is holy ground" (3:5).

The divine encounter Jacob had, as reported in the book of Genesis, is a classic example cited by Otto (as previously noted) and numerous times by Eliade[88] to exemplify how theophanies work. Like Moses, Jacob did not seek God, but God appeared to him in a visionary dream and "the place (*hammaqôm*)" became Bethel, meaning "the house of God" (Genesis 28:10–17). Significantly, when the

---

[86] I am unaware of any complete catalogue of temple names in Egypt. Every temple in Egypt had a name, often including the name of the sanctuary's principal deity. I conferred with Richard Wilkinson, author of *The Complete Temples of Ancient Egypt* (London: Thames and Hudson, 2000), and he too knows of no catalogue of temple names. He also confirmed my belief that the verb *gmi* is not attested among temple names prior to Akhenaten.

[87] KB 619.

[88] Eliade, *The Sacred and the Profane*, 26, 37, and *Patterns in Comparative Religion*, 107, 228–231, 377, 437.

8th-century prophet Hosea reflected on the Bethel theophany, he introduced the term "find" to describe the encounter:

> He found (*māṣā'*) him at Bethel and talked with him there—the LORD God Almighty, the LORD is his name! (Hosea 12:4-5, NIV)

The phrase "he found him" is ambiguous, though commentators tend to think that the subject is God and the object Jacob. Douglas Stuart rightly observes that the "subject of the two could be Jacob."[89] The ambiguity may be intentional to allow for this range of possibilities, that is, Jacob found God and God found Jacob. These two elements of "discovery" are complimentary. Earlier in Hosea (9:10), God says, "Like grapes in the wilderness, I found (*māṣā'*) Israel." Who expects to find grapes in the wilderness (i.e., Sinai)? Therein lies the point. The divine discovery was totally unexpected, a complete surprise, like finding grapes in the desert.

"Finding" a person or place also carries with it the idea of divine selection or election. Psalm 89 speaks of King David's divine election in which God says: "I have exalted one chosen from the people. I have **found** David, my servant" (vss. 19–20). David, in turn, is credited in Psalm 132 with saying:

> he swore to the LORD
> and vowed to the Mighty One of Jacob,
> "I will not enter my house
> or get into my bed,
> I will not give sleep to my eyes
> or slumber to my eyelids,
> until I **find a place** (*'emᵉṣ' māqôm*) for the LORD,
> a dwelling place for the Mighty One of Jacob." (vss. 2–5)

As seen already, "the place" David found in Jerusalem was identified by theophany.

Boyo Ockinga has observed that this Hebrew Psalm portrays the pious and diligent king who deprives himself of sleep until he finds a suitable place to build a sanctuary, and that this motif is an adaptation of an Egyptian literary topoi for which he cites examples spanning from Amenhotep III to Ramesses III.[90] One such declaration is made of Seti I: "As for the good god (the king) who inclines to make monuments who spends the night watchful, he sleeps not, seeking to do that which is profitable. It is his majesty who gives the instructions, who leads the work in his

---

[89] Douglas Stuart, *Hosea-Jonah* (Waco, TX: Word Biblical Commentary, 1987), 191

[90] Boyo Ockinga, "An Example of Egyptian Royal Phraseology in Psalm 132," *Biblische Notizen* 11 (1980): 38–42.

monument (temple)."[91] Ockinga makes a compelling case because in all the Egyptian texts and Psalm 132, the *Sitz im Leben* is the same, the king is vigilant and sleep deprived (both using the same type of parallelism) in order to find the right spot to build a temple.

A final interesting point of comparison between Hebrew ideas of establishing a sanctuary and what is recorded on Akhenaten's boundary stelae is that Aten "desires to make [it] for him as a monument on which his name dwells forever and ever."[92] The idea that the Jerusalem temple was a place for the name of the LORD (YHWH) to reside is a prominent theme in Deuteronomy (nine occurrences). Similarly, according to these references, Moses instructed his people before they entered the promised land that "you are to seek the place the LORD your God will choose from among all your tribes to put his Name there for his dwelling" (Deuteronomy 12:5). "Name Theology" and the idea of a sanctuary in which the divine name dwells are central themes in the Old Testament.[93]

It is apparent from the boundary stelae that a theophany of Aten resulted in the founding of the new capital and its temples as a place for the deities "everlasting name." Could it be that a theophany at the outset of Akhenaten's reign was the motivating factor in the building of the Aten temple complex at Karnak?

THE DEATH OF THE GODS

In the foregoing sections one has argued, based upon Akhenaten's inscriptions and representations from Amarna, that standing behind Akhenaten's religious program was a theophany, a kind of conversion experience. This, in turn, was followed later by a divine directive to find a new holy place for Aten. It was also suggested that Akhenaten's texts indicate that his responses—making sacrifices and building sanctuaries—find striking parallels in the Near East and the Hebrew Bible. Having presented this case based upon the corpus of texts from Amarna, now it must be asked, are there any similar hints in the smaller body of texts of Amenhotep IV from Thebes to support this encounter-with-the-sun-disc-theory, beyond the name of the temple, *Gm(t) p3 itn*?

In Chapter 3 the intriguing speech of Amenhotep IV was discussed when treating "the earliest stages of Akhenaten's religion." We return now to that text in order

---

91 Ibid., 39.

92 Text in Murnane & Van Siclen, *The Boundary Stelae of Akhenaten*, 20 (K xx).

93 See Sandra Richter, *The Deuteronomistic History and the Name Theology*: lešakkēn šemô šam *in the Bible and the Ancient Near East* (Berlin: deGuyter, 2002); idem. "The Place of the Name in Deuteronomy," *Vetus Testamentum* 57 (2007): 342–366.

to examine it through the same lens that we used to look at the early proclamation, namely a phenomenological one.

Found in the secondary context of the 10th Pylon at Karnak, Redford has identified two inscribed sandstone blocks from the earliest buildings of Akhenaten in Thebes.[94] Their early date is not in dispute; they are carved in raised relief following the artistic tradition of Amenhotep III and the blocks are large (the one is 1.58 m long and the other 1.47 m long), executed before the standardizing of the talatat blocks that were used for building the east Karnak temples (treated in the previous chapter). They may date to Akhenaten's first year. Sadly these extremely important texts are damaged and other blocks that would have completed the inscription and scene are missing. Consequently we are presently deprived of the full extent of this royal proclamation. Redford has worked ingeniously with this limited source and has coaxed out some vital information.

The first inscribed block (ATP no. 30/70) contains some of Akhenaten's titulary and possibly he is identified as [First Prophet][95] of Re-Harakhty + didactic name without cartouche.[96] The end of line 4 and the beginning of 5 are partially lost, but *ḏd.f* is clear, meaning "he says/said." Apparently the deity speaks. Other than "those who do not" his words are not preserved. Following this break, the partially preserved line reads: "Lo Harakhty seated himself [▨ his form(?)] is [not] known [▨]."[97]

The second block (ATP no. X 1/5), Redford has suggested, contains a statement by the king, a royal address where the king "sits" (*ḥmst nsw*) to make proclamation to a group of courtiers and officials,[98] not unlike what was recorded on the early proclamation stela at Amarna (see above). In this block the king speaks to inform his court (*ḏd.i di.i rḫ.*[*tn*])—"I am speaking that I may inform [you] [...] [... the for]ms(?) of the gods."[99] Could it be that in the first block the Aten expresses his desire for a new cult or temple that is befitting of a deity whose "form" (*ḫpr*) is not known? That would in itself be a revolutionary concept in Egypt. The second block would recount how the faithful king carried out the divine wish by making the announcement of his intentions. The question that begs an answer is "why"?

---

[94] Donald Redford, "A Royal Speech from the Blocks of the 10th Pylon," *BES* 3 (1981): 87–102.

[95] I have rendered the title *ḥm nṯr tpy* as "High Priest" elsewhere in this volume. Both translations are acceptable. Alan Gardiner suggested that "the term 'high-priest' can conveniently be retained for 'first prophet,' if and when desired" (*Ancient Egyptian Onomastica* [London: Oxford University Press, 1947], 30–31*;).

[96] Redford, "A Royal Speech from the Blocks of the 10th Pylon," 89.

[97] Ibid., 89.

[98] Ibid., 96–97.

[99] Ibid., 97.

Akhenaten's declaration may provide some answers. He states that "[. . . their temples(?)][100] fallen to ruin" and seems to imply that the old deities (*nṯrw*) were ineffectual, while elevating, presumably the new Aten, "[. . . who himself gave birth] to himself, and no one knows the mystery of [. . .] he [go]es where he pleases, and they know not [his going. . . .]."[101] Murnane considers this fragmentary statement to be Amenhotep IV's "harangue (which) apparently contrasts the perishable images of orthodox deities with the uncreated and enduring nature of the solar orb."[102] It is as if the king is saying that the old deities had simply shut down (*ꜣbb*),[103] while the deity associated with this new temple was eternal.

In a detailed article just published in 2013 about the early phase of Atenism, Redford returns to these 10th Pylon inscriptions, stating that they are "a watershed in Akhenaten's Theban sojourn. The king herein is describing for the benefit of his court a determination, if not a downright revelation having to do with the cessation of activity on the part of all the gods save one."[104] Could this "revelation" be connected to what Re-Harakhty enunciates (that is missing) on the other block and harkens back to an original theophany? As we saw with the early proclamation at Amarna, the king searches for a new holy city for Aten in response to divine instruction (*mtr*) and Aten's communication (*sḏd*).

Claiming the deities of Egypt to be moribund is unprecedented. Statements about decaying state of the temples and cult statues forsaken, however, are well attested. Such claims were used to protest the treatment of the temples and cults by previous illegitimate rulers.[105] Given the extensive building projects of Akhenaten's father, especially for the glory of Amun-Re, it is inconceivable that Egypt's temples were neglected or disrespected by the great Amenhotep III!

The early stelae at Amarna report of some calamity or evil that had befallen Egypt, without specifying what had occurred. Akhenaten announces his intent to build

[100] Redford (ibid., 89–90) explains restoring "their temples" in the lacuna because the following word "fallen into ruin" (*ḏꜥm*) typically applies to building and temples in particular. On the use of the word, see Alan Gardiner, "On the Reading of 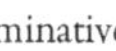," *ZÄS* 41 (1904), 71–76. When  is written with  determinative, it takes on the meaning "fallen into ruin" or dilapidated. So the reading "their temples" (i.e., of the gods) makes sense contextually and by virtue of the adjacent word .

[101] Ibid., 89–90.

[102] Murnane, *Texts from the Amarna Period in Egypt*, 31.

[103] See Redford's discussion, "A Royal Speech from the Blocks of the 10th Pylon," 95.

[104] Redford, "Akhenaten: New Theories and Old Facts," 14.

[105] Hatshepsut blamed the Hyksos for neglect that left temples in decay (see Donald Redford, "Textual Sources for the Hyksos Period," in *The Hyksos: New Historical and Archaeological Perspectives* [ed. E. D. Oren; Philadelphia: University Museum, 1997], 17). Akhenaten's own apostasy would later be viewed in the same manner in Tutankhamun's restoration stela. Tutankhamun states that when he was crowned, "the temples and cities of the gods and goddesses, starting from Elephantine [as far] as the Delta marshes . . ., were fallen into decay and their shrines were fallen into ruin, having become mere mounds overgrown with grass" (Murnane, *Texts from the Amarna Period in Egypt*, 213).

various temples and shrines at Akhet-Aten, including a burial place for the Mnevis Bull (*mn wr*), the sacred bull of Re the sun-god.[106] The inclusion of the Mnevis Bull burial might appear to be out of place, but Gardiner sees the inclusion of this Heliopolitan cult as "another sign how dependent the new Atenism was upon one of the oldest of Egypt's religious cults."[107] A litany of woe follows the announcement of the building projects:

> Now, as my father HOR-ATEN[108] lives! As for [. . .] in Akhet-Aten,
> it was worse than those which I heard in regnal year 4;
> it was worse than [those] which I heard in regnal year 3;
> it was worse than those which I heard [in regnal year 2;
> it was] worse [than those which I heard in regnal year 1]
> it was worse [than] those which (King) [Nebmaat]re heard;
> [it was worse than those which] (King) [OKHEPRURE (?) heard];
> it was worse [than] those which (King) MENKHEPERRE heard;
> [(and) it was] worse [than] those heard by any kings who had (ever)
> assumed the White Crown.[109]

This is a most puzzling and enigmatic statement. The break in the first line occurs precisely at the critical point in the sentence that would explain the problem (?) experienced at Akhet-Aten. The lacuna is large enough to fit possibly two words. Norman de Garis Davies thought the missing word was "priests," but adds a query (?).[110] This speculative restoration may have been reading into the passage the theory that a power struggle ensued between the Amun priests and Akhenaten and was the cause of the break between church and state and the founding of the new religion and its pristine holy city. Many now doubt this reading, including Aldred.[111]

What was the calamity that was "heard" (charges brought to the ears of the king?) annually by Akhenaten for four years, and also by three of his predecessors, back to Thutmose III (1479–1425 B.C.)? Whatever it was, "it was worse than" (*bỉn st r*) previously experienced. *Bỉn* also means wicked or evil.[112] So there is no doubt that Akhenaten is referring to some sort of calamity or strong opposition.

---

106 Stephen Quirke, *The Cult of Ra* (London: Thames & Hudson, 2001), 109.

107 Alan Gardiner, *Egypt of the Pharaohs* (London: Oxford University Press, 1961), 222.

108 Murnane uses this abbreviated form of the didactic name of Aten. Murnane, *Texts from the Amarna Period in Egypt*, 78.

109 Ibid., 78.

110 Davies, *The Rock Tombs of El-Amarna* V, 30.

111 Cyril Aldred, *Akhenaten King of Egypt* (London: Thames & Hudson, 1988), 50.

112 *Wb* 1, 442–443.

Nicholas Reeves points to the paragraph following the series of "worse than's" as offering a clue.[113] Though plagued with breaks in the text, it begins with the king speaking in the first person: "I heard a report in the mouth of an official . . ."[114] which picks up on the theme of the king hearing reports, and that they were "offensive things (*mr*)."[115] Four times in this paragraph the word *mr* occurs, signaling that this was a significant issue. The king continues: "As for the offensive things (*mr*) [. . .] in every mouth saying, 'I will commit an offense' [against the lord of Akhet]-Aten, my father, HOR-ATEN . . ."[116] Reeves sees this statement as pointing to the crux of the problem, namely that Akhenaten (and therefore Aten) was receiving some sort of push back against the coveted position of the upstart deity, and perhaps there had been a plot or an assassination attempt against the king.[117]

Unfortunately, we may never know exactly what Akhenaten was reporting on the Amarna boundary stela, but if there was opposition to the new cult (and that would not be surprising) that may have been a factor in the decision to abandon Thebes, despite the presence of the large "Domain of Aten" complex with its several temples. If this is the case, this part of the text offers no insight into what was behind the emergence of the king's Aten cult, but it might explain a cause for abandoning Thebes for Amarna.

Thus we are forced to rely upon the 10th Pylon inscriptions as the principal written source that best explains the rise of Aten in Thebes. Certainly most Egyptians and their clergy would hardly agree that the gods and goddesses of Egypt had somehow ceased to function. The phrase *ꜣbb.s n wꜥ m-ḫt sn.nw*—"they have ceased one after the other"—suggests a "progressive cessation" of the gods.[118] Not that the divinities ceased to exist, but ceased to function or ceased their "customary activities."[119] In his announcement, the king refers to the "[wri]tings of/and the inventory manual" of the gods, some sort of ancient record of the various deities and their functions. Recently Redford has shed additional light on this comment by proposing that the gods "have ceased operation, ceding place to one whose goings and form were not covered by the Great Inventory. There is an embryonic rejection here of all erstwhile normative regulations."[120]

Put another way, this newly revealed Aten is unlike any deity known in the annals and canons of Egyptian religious history. He "[who himself gave birth] to himself,

---

[113] Nicholas Reeves, *Akhenaten: Egypt's False Prophet* (London: Thames & Hudson, 2001), 110–111.

[114] Murnane, *Texts from the Amarna Period in Egypt*, 78. Text in Murnane & Van Siclen, *The Boundary Stelae of Akhenaten*, 26–27.

[115] Ibid., 78.

[116] Ibid., 78.

[117] Reeves, *Akhenaten: Egypt's False Prophet*, 111.

[118] Redford, "A Royal Speech from the Blocks of the 10th Pylon," 95.

[119] Ibid., 95.

[120] Redford, "Akhenaten: New Theories and Old Facts," 14.

and not one knows the mystery of [. . .]" and, as stated in the decree on the boundary stela, Aten was "the one who created (*ḳd*) himself with his own hands, whom no craft (*ḥmw*) knows."[121] Unlike the myriad deities whose forms (*ḫprw*) were known, as well as how their cult statues were to be made, no such formula existed for the sun-disc. If this was Akhenaten's understanding of Aten, then it is clear why he rendered the other deities ineffectual. According to the king's theology, Aten's form could not be replicated by an artisan, which may explain why there was a need for the lengthy didactic name, "Re-Harakhty who rejoices in the horizon in his name of light which is in the Aten." The name, rather than an image, communicated the essence of this divine light from the sun that reveals himself.

[121] Text in Murnane & Van Siclen, *The Boundary Stelae of Akhenaten*, 23.

Sole God beside whom there is no other

THE GREAT HYMN TO ATEN

Chapter 6

Aten Alone

THE FIRST FOUR years or so of Akhenaten's reign at Thebes seem to have been without hostility toward Amun, his temple, and the other gods of Egypt. The priestly establishment may have raised eyebrows as the Aten temples proliferated in Amun's domain, but there had been no overt attacks on Amun's temples or images, although perhaps there was benign neglect.

From the 9th Pylon at Karnak comes an offering list on a large sandstone block (1.94 × 1.05 × .22 m = 6ft 4 in × 3ft 5 in × 8.7/8 in), indicating that it is from the first year or two of Akhenaten's reign.[1] This list records that offerings were being made to "Aten on the offering-tables of Re' from Memphis to Diospolis (in the 17th Lower Egyptian nome)" by Amenhotep IV "to his father Re' as daily offers of every day in Memphis."[2] The second list on this block is devoted to "Re-Harakhty who Rejoices in the horizon in his name of Shu (or light) which is in the Aten."[3] These texts suggest that Re's altars were now receiving Aten's offerings from Memphis and into the Delta, which illustrates that the Aten cult was not restricted to Thebes, even in the earliest years of Akhenaten's reign (on other Aten temples, see below).

[1] Ramadan Saad & Lise Manniche, "A Unique Offering List of Amenophis IV Recently Found at Karnak," *JEA* 57 (1971): 70–72.

[2] Ibid, 70.

[3] Ibid., pl. XXXI A.

A papyrus letter found at Gurob in the Fayum contains a report from the steward (city manager) of Memphis, named Apy, that dates to "regnal year 5, third month of *prt* (winter or growing season), day 19" of Neferkheperure-waenre, Amenhotep.[4] This date means that the letter was recorded a month before the early proclamation at Amarna ("Regnal year 5, fourth month of *prt*, day 13").[5] It gives the impression that all is well in Memphis, no apparent crisis there. Apy reports:

> [This is] a communication [to my lord], l.p.h, to let One [i.e., the king] know that the temple of your father Ptah, South-of-his-Wall, the lord of Ankhtowy,[6] is prosperous and flourishing; that the house of Pharaoh, l.p.h., is in good order; that the palace complex of Pharaoh, l.p.h., is in good order; and that the quarter of Pharaoh, l.p.h. is in good order and security. The offerings of all the gods and goddesses who are on the soil of Memphis [have been issued] in full, and nothing therein has been held back, but is offered—pure, acceptable, approved and selected—on behalf of the life, prosperity and health of the King of Upper and Lower Egypt, who lives on Maat, the Lord of the Two Lands, NEFERKHEPRURE-WAENRE; the Son of Re, who lives on Maat, Amenhotep IV . . .[7]

Not only are the royal quarters in good running order, according to Apy, so is the temple of Ptah, the city's patron, and other gods and goddesses are receiving fully their proper offerings. This suggests that even while the move to Amarna was being planned, the temples of Memphis (the political capital) flourished. No pogrom had been launched against the divinities and their cults; rather they had continued to enjoy royal patronage. For some reason, it appears that this letter was never sent, as it was discovered along with its duplicate[8] (one would have been sent and the other archived at Memphis). While the letter suggests that all is well at Memphis with the cult centers of the various deities, the fact that it apparently was not sent may indicate that such a report had become moot.

---

[4] Francis Ll. Griffiths, *The Petrie Papyri: Hieratic Papyri from Kahun and Gurob* (London: Bernard Quaritch), pl. XXXVIII. Maj Sandman, *Texts from the Time of Akhenaten* (Brussels: Queen Elizabeth Foundation of Egyptology, 1938), 147–148, § CXIV.

[5] William Murnane & Charles Van Siclen, *The Boundary Stelae of Akhenaten* (London/New York: Kegan Paul International, 1993), 19.

[6] According to Jacobus van Dijk, this title of Ptah "probably refers to the area of the west bank of the Nile between the city and the necropolis in the desert," see "Ptah" in *OEAE 3*, 74.

[7] William Murnane, *Texts from the Amarna Period in Egypt* (Atlanta: Scholars Press, 1995), 50–51.

[8] Griffiths, *The Petrie Papyri: Hieratic Papyri from Kahun and Gurob*, pl. XXXVIII.

Building the vast temple complex to the Aten at Karnak would have required a huge labor force and major funding to achieve. To pull this off, resources had to be diverted from other projects, temples, and their estates. During the New Kingdom, temples had become major holders of land, animals, and manpower, thanks to the foreign campaigns of earlier kings and the tribute and taxes that had continued to pour in. Kings would redistribute taxes and tribute to the various temples as they saw fit.[9]

Among the Karnak talatat blocks studied by Claude Traunecker in the 1980s is a group that gives an impression of the vast numbers of individuals and materials involved in temple operations, even if they reflect an enlarged staff in connection with celebrating Amenhotep IV's Sed-festival.[10] The number of men exceeds 13,000. A major building operation would have required even greater numbers of workers and artisans.

Some idea of the numbers used in quarrying and mining expeditions help shed some light on the size of workforces that would be required for a major building project. The aforementioned quarrying expedition of the vizier Amenemhet on behalf of Montuhotep II in the 11th Dynasty included 3,000 men just to obtain a sarcophagus.[11] The figures 3,000 and 4,000 are the numbers of men involved in turquoise-mining missions to Sinai recorded on recently found inscriptions on the Red Sea site of 'Ain Sukhna.[12] Also from the 12th Dynasty comes a text from the reign of Senusert I, year 38 (ca. 1905 B.C.) that had a quarrying force of 17,000 workers.[13] These figures simply illustrate the numbers of workers used on quarrying expeditions, which in turn suggests that even higher numbers were required for major building endeavors. The focus of so much manpower on temple building for Aten at East Karnak, and shortly thereafter at Akhet-Aten, would surely have had some impact on refurbishing and adding to existing temples throughout Egypt.

Temples from all over Egypt would have had to contribute to Ahhenaten's Theban temple program, both for building and the ongoing operations. Among those named

---

9 Edward Bleiberg, "The Redistributive Economy in New Kingdom Egypt: An Examination of *B3k(t)*," *JARCE* 25 (1988): 157–168. Edward Bleiberg, *The Official Gift in Ancient Egypt* (Norman: University of Oklahoma Press, 1996), 100–103.

10 Claude Traunecker, "Donnés nouvelle sur le début au regne d'Amenophis IV et son oeuvre à Karnak," *JSSEA* 14, no. 3 (1984): 60–69. For a recent discussion of these texts, see Donald Redford, "Akhenaten: New Theories and Old Facts," *BASOR* 369 (2013): 18–20, and Murnane, *Texts from the Amarna Period in Egypt*, 30–31.

11 Adrian De Buck, *Egyptian Reading Book* (Leiden: Netherlands Institute for Near Eastern Studies, 1970), 75.9.

12 Gregory Mumford & Sarah Parcak, "Pharaonic Ventures into South Sinai: El-Markha Plain Site 346," *JEA* 89 (2003): 89.

13 Ian Shaw, "Quarries and Mines," *OEAE* 3: 103.

in the talatat offering list from Lower Egypt and Delta area are the temples of Horus at Athribis, Thoth of Hermopolis Parva,[14] Osiris of Busiris, Hathor of the Fields of Re (possibly Abu Sir), and all the way to Egypt's frontier town of Tjaru/Sile, where Horus was lord.[15] The list further includes the temples from southern Egypt, that is, the temples of Min of Coptos, Khnum of Esna, Hathor of Dendera, Nekhbit of El-Kab, and Khnum of Elephantine in Upper Egypt.[16] This offering list indicates that from one end of Egypt to the other, from the farthest north (Tjaru/Sile) to the most southerly city of Elephantine, temples were taxed. This means that taxes and income—operational expenses for these temples—were being directed to Aten temples from all over Egypt.

The Theban official Parennefer[17] (who had attended Amenhotep IV while a young prince) reports that the gods were receiving offerings, but "in superabundance are they measured for the Disc,"[18] clearly showing some favoritism. This text leads Donald Redford to opine that "Parennefer strongly implies that the diversion took place at the expense of the temples."[19] Perhaps the thought of building a new city to Aten was too much for the religious establishment, resulting in some sort of rebellion in Thebes while Akhenaten was out of town searching for what would be the new holy city, Akhet-Aten. Could this be the *bỉn* (evil thing) and *mr* (offensive thing) he heard while at Akhet-Aten (see Chapter 5)? The plan of leaving Thebes for Amarna in middle Egypt must have been hatched sometime in regnal year 4,[20] which signals the beginning of the second phase of Akhenaten's treatment of Amun and other deities, following William Murnane's understanding of the religious development—that is, abandonment.

What is becoming increasingly clear is that Akhenaten's temple-building efforts to Aten were not limited to the Theban area. Some edifices may have been built concurrently with the construction of the Aten temples at Karnak, while others may have been established after the move to Amarna. In the following section we will review the evidence for these Aten temples and shrines.

---

14 Not to be confused with Thoth of Hermopolis Magna in Upper Egypt, present-day Ashmunein.

15 Traunecker, "Donnés nouvelle sur le début au regne d'Amenophis IV et son oeuvre à Karnak," 63.

16 Ibid., 63.

17 This is the same Parennefer, who also had a tomb (#7) at Amarna.

18 Susan Redford, "Theban Tomb No. 188 (The Tomb of Parennefer): A Case Study of Tomb Reuse in the Theban Necropolis," 2 Vols. (Ph. D. diss., Pennsylvania State University, 2007), 63.

19 Redford, "Akhenaten: New Theories and Old Facts," 19.

20 On the dating see Redford, "Akhenaten: New Theories and Old Facts," 23. J. Van Dijk suggests a date early in the fifth year ("The Amarna Period and Later New Kingdom," *The Oxford History of Ancient Egypt* [ed. Ian Shaw; Oxford/New York: Oxford University Press, 2000], 269). That date coincides with the early proclamation. So the decision to seek a new holy city must have come some months earlier, probably in year 4.

OTHER ATEN TEMPLES

Nubia

Dokki Gel (Kerma)

Previous (Chapters 3 and 4) mention has been made of temples that Akhenaten completed at Soleb and Sesebi in Nubia that had been initiated by Amenhotep III. The Aten's imprint has been left elsewhere in Nubia. At the New Kingdom site of Dokki Gel (Kerma), Charles Bonnet discovered a partially preserved temple made of talatat blocks in 1999.[21] Though only the lowest course of undecorated blocks remains *in situ*, some decorated talatat were found.[22] One fragmentary talatat has the didactic name of Aten on it, carved within a cartouche.[23] It retains the word *šw*, pointing to a date between year 3, when the cartouche appears around the name, and year 9, when *šw* was dropped from the name.[24] Another block shows the head and lower portion of the crown of Nefertiti, although it was mutilated.[25] The missing blocks were either reworked or reused in later buildings, or they were transported elsewhere for a later construction.

Gebel Barkal

Farther to the south at Gebel Barkal, 960 kilometers (600 miles) south of Egypt's frontier town of Elephantine, talatat blocks have been recently investigated by Timothy Kendall.[26] Reisner documented stone structures in 1916 that were part of the "Great Temple of Amun," with small blocks that he measured at 52.5 × 26.5 × 22.5 cm.[27] Because no decoration or inscriptions identified these structures with Akhenaten or Aten, he apparently did not know at the time that the talatat was the signature building block of Akhenaten's temples. He identified one of the talatat edifices (B 500) as having been built by Ramesses II, although he thought the origins of the temple went back to the 18th Dynasty.[28] Kendall points to a sandstone fragment that contains the partial cartouche of Horemheb, whom he suggests may have dismantled the Aten temples (as was the case in Karnak and at Amarna) and ridded the site of the decorated

---

21 Charles Bonnet, "Kerma-Rapport préliminaire sur les campagnes de 1999–2000 et 2000–2001," *Kerma Soudan* XLIX (2001): 199–219.

22 Ibid., 208, fig. 10.

23 Dominique Valbelle, "Kerma—les inscriptions," *Kerma Soudan* XLIX (2001): 231, fig. 4.

24 Donald B. Redford, *Akhenaten the Heretic King* (Princeton, NJ: Princeton University Press, 1984), 186.

25 Valbelle, "Kerma—les inscriptions," 232, fig. 5.

26 Timothy Kendall, "Talatat Architecture at Jebel Barkal: Report of the NCAM Mission 2008–2009," Nubia & Sudan 13 (2009).

27 George Reisner, "The Barkal Temples in 1916," *JEA* 5 (1917): 213–227; idem, "The Barkal Temples in 1916, pt. II" *JEA* 5 (1918): 99–112.

28 Reisner, "The Barkal Temples in 1916," 218.

talatat.[29] The talatat blocks continued to be reused in the Kushite and Meroitic periods, and as recently as the 19th century in a local sheikh's tomb.[30] Rectangular piers found in association with Temple 500 leads Kendall to associate them with the piers found in the *Gm(t) p3 itn* complex at Karnak (see Chapter 4 and Figures 4.2b and 4.11), leading to the proposal that a sun-court styled temple like the Theban counterparts had originally been erected in front of the stunning mountain of Barkal.[31] He thinks that this temple was originally built early in Amenhotep IV's reign. There is some reason to think that the king's Sed-festival was celebrated at a number of locations, and this temple may have been built for this momentous occasion.

North of Thebes

Abydos

The sacred city of Osiris, Abydos is located 150 kilometers (93 miles) north of Thebes. There, within a structure of Ramesses II, a number of talatat were recovered. Twenty-six blocks were documented, of which seven were inscribed with reliefs of Akhenaten.[32] Initially these talatat were thought to have originated at Amarna, despite the fact that it was 250 kilometers (150 miles) upstream from Amarna. David Silverman, on the contrary, has suggested that these blocks were actually from a shrine or chapel located on site.[33] The key point in favor of this interpretation of the data is that two of the blocks contain what appears to be the name of this small edifice, based on the line "Aten lord of heaven and lord of earth who is in *ḳd.f 3ḫt///*."[34] This name *ḳd.f 3ḫt///* is not complete on either block, but is not attested elsewhere in the Akhenaten era corpus of inscriptions. The phrase means something like "he (who) forms the horizon . . ." Unless and until this name is attested elsewhere in a contemporary text, it seems safe to believe that these blocks came from an Aten structure at Abydos and that *ḳd.f 3ḫt* was part of its name.

Akhmim

At Akhmim, 60 km (37 miles) north of Abydos, other blocks of an Akhenaten structure have come to light. Queen Tiye seems to have had family connections

---

[29] "Talatat Architecture at Jebel Barkal," 8.

[30] Ibid., 2–12.

[31] Ibid., 14–15.

[32] William Kelly Simpson, *Inscribed Material from the Pennsylvanian-Yale Excavations at Abydos* (New Haven/Philadelphia: Peabody Museum/University of Pennsylvania Museum, 1995), 76–77.

[33] David Silverman, "The So-called Portal Temple of Ramesses II at Abydos," in *Akten des vierten internationalen Ägyptologen-Kongresses, München*, Vol. 2 (Hamburg: Helmut Buske Verlag, 1985), 269–277.

[34] Simpson, *Inscribed Material from the Pennsylvanian-Yale Excavations at Abydos*, 76–77, fig. 136, 137.

at Akhmim (see Chapter 3). It, therefore, may not be surprising to know that Akhenaten built there. In 1988, while dismantling a base for a statue of Ramesses II for rebuilding and consolidation, Egyptian Antiquities officials discovered some decorated blocks of a partial, large-scale scene showing an offering table with sun's rays pouring over it.[35] The blocks are of limestone, probably from local quarries, and not of talatat size, leading Yahia El-Masry to posit, based on the large scale of the scene, that the blocks may originally have been from a pylon.[36] The figure of Akehnaten in this scene had been intentionally destroyed, leaving questions of style and dating uncertain. At an earlier date at Akhmim, some sandstone talatat blocks were discovered,[37] indicating that there likely had been an Aten temple there. Presently, the relationship between the Aten temple and the large decorated façade is unknown since all the blocks in question were reused elsewhere on the site.

Assiut

Talatat blocks from an Aten temple were discovered at Assiut (300 km/180 mi north of Thebes) during construction work on a street in the late 1920s.[38] The blocks were apparently reused by Ramesses II after the Amarna period (as is the case elsewhere). The only publication of these blocks was a brief report with inadequate pictures, although Maj Sandman included the texts in her volume on Amarna period inscriptions.[39] The didactic name of Aten, with Re-Harakhty and *šw* elements included, is written on what appears to have been a relatively small temple, according to Sami Gabra, the excavator.[40] Since these blocks were reused, evidently in a Ramesside context, Cyril Aldred thought they originated in Amarna and were transported south to Assiut for reuse.[41] One talatat, however, apparently has the name of a sanctuary on it, "Firm is the Life of Aten" (*rwd ꜥnḫw itn*).[42] This name is not attested at Karnak or Amarna, which seems to argue in favor of this temple being one actually built at Assiut by Akhenaten.

---

[35] Yahia El-Masry, "New Evidence for Building Activity of Akhenaten in Akhmim," *MDAIK* 58(2002): 391–398.

[36] Ibid., 396–398.

[37] Ibid., 397–398.

[38] Sami Gabra, "Un Temple d'Aménophis IV a Assiout," *Chronique d'Égypte* 12(1931): 237–243.

[39] Maj Sandman, *Texts from the Time of Akhenaten* (Brussels: Queen Elizabeth Foundation of Egyptology, 1938), 161. Her text edition was apparently based on Gabra's rather inadequate transcriptions.

[40] Ibid., 243.

[41] Cyril Aldred, *Akhenaten King of Egypt* (London: Thames & Hudson, 1988), 87.

[42] Sandman, *Texts from the Time of Akhenaten*, 161 §CLXXIX.

Hermopolis Magna (Ashmunein)

At Hermopolis Magna, located on the western Nile Valley opposite Amarna, hundreds of inscribed talatat have been found.[43] The poorly preserved temple pylon of Ramesses II still contains inscribed blocks, but these, like all of those at Hermopolis, originated at Amarna and were transported to the west for reuse (Figure 6.1). Some contain portions

FIGURE 6.1 Ramesses II temple pylon at Hermopolis (Ashmunein). Photo James K. Hoffmeier.

[43] Günther Roeder and Rainer Hanke, *Ausgrabungen der Deutschen Hermopolis-Expedition in Hermopolis, Ober-Ägypten 1929–1939* (Hildesheim: Gerstenberg, 1959–1969), *Amarna-reliefs aus Hermopolis, Ausgrabungen der Deutschen Hermopolis-Expedition in Hermopolis 1929–1939*, vol. II & III (Hildesheim: Pelizeaus Museum, 1969 & 1978). John Cooney, *Amarna Reliefs from Hermopolis in American Collections* (New York: Brooklyn Museum, 1965).

FIGURE 6.2 Inscribed talatat embedded in temple pylon. Photo James K. Hoffmeier.

of texts and scenes (Figure 6.2). There is no evidence that an Aten temple had once stood at this important ancient site. In the desert cliffs of Tuna el-Gebel nearby Ashmunein, however, is where boundary Stela A is located (Figure 5.4 in Chapter 5).

Memphis

Apy, the Memphite official whose letter is dated to year 5 of Akhenaten, reported that cultic activities in Aten's name (along with other deities) were underway at the northern capital (see previous section). No specific mention was made of an Aten temple, however. It is clear that there was indeed a temple there, to judge from scattered talatat found in the Memphite region. About 40 years ago, Beatrix Löhr published a catalogue of various inscribed materials attributed to Akhenaten that originated in Memphis.[44] Most of these are now scattered in various museums and collections. Several limestone talatat were discovered by Petrie in 1913, near the Ptah Temple complex.[45] A couple of blocks depict cultic activities in a large temple court (like those at Karnak and Amarna), complete with altars piled high with offerings and bound sacrificial bovine.[46] One block shows a fairly large-scale portrayal of Nefertiti.[47] These reliefs give the impression that a large temple once stood in Memphis.

---

[44] Beatrix Löhr, "Aḫanjati in Memphis," *SÄK* 2(1975): 139–173.

[45] R. Engelback and W. M. F. Petrie, *Riqqeh and Memphis VI* (London: Bernard Quaritch, 1915), 32.

[46] Petrie, *Riqqeh and Memphis VI*, pl. LIV, no. 7, 8, 10.

[47] Ibid., no. 9.

A couple of intriguing Akhenaten era reliefs were found in excavations near the spot where the recumbent colossal statue of Ramesses II was before it was moved to the museum at Mit Rehineh, where it now reclines.[48] The Aten's name is all but obliterated, but clearly is written in a cartouche. The rays of the sun flow down on the royals not shown on that piece. The second block is notorious for the depiction of Akhenaten and a shorter male royal figure, possibly a young co-regent. They may be the recipient of Aten's glow in the other block. If this scene has been properly understood, it would suggest that they come from late in Akhenaten's reign.

Fragments of two back pillars of standing statues were also uncovered by Petrie at Memphis.[49] The quartzite piece contains the didactic name of Aten in a pair of cartouches (complete with Re-Harakhy and *šw*). The size of the cartouche (.60 m long) is evidence of a lifesize or larger image. The second statue piece is much smaller (25 × 8 × 13 cm) and has inscribed on it only the second cartouche of Aten's name, and it is the later form found after year 9, which reads "in his name of Re who comes in [or 'as'] Aten."[50] The former would date to regnal years 3–4 to 9, while the latter would fall in the period after year 9.

A further block from Memphis is worth mentioning because it contains the name of a temple. It also bears the double cartouches of the later form of the didactic name, plus the epithet, "the [great] living Aten, lord of jubilees and all that [Aten] encircles, lord of heaven and lord of earth in [Shad]e of Re ▨ (in Memphis?)."[51] Variations on this name are found at Amarna, associated with the names of Nefertiti and Meritaten. At Kom el-Nana in southern Amarna, a large structure was excavated in the 1930s, and has been the subject of renewed research by Barry Kemp and his team.[52] Fragments of texts have identified it as *šwt rʿ*, the "Sunshade of Re of Nefertiti." The name of this temple was known earlier, associated with Akhenaten's mother, Queen Tiye.[53] This same name is attested on other objects found at Memphis.[54]

A second temple name found in Memphis is *tꜣ Ḥwt pꜣ Ỉtn*, "the Mansion of the Aten."[55] Additionally, there is now textual evidence to tie this name to Memphis. The Theban necropolis the coffin of Hatiay includes the title "scribe of the granaries of

---

48 Percy Newberry, "Akhenaten's Eldest Son-in-law 'Ankhkeperure," *JEA* 14 (1928): 7–9.

49 Löhr, "Aḫanjati in Memphis," 148–152.

50 Ibid., 149.

51 Ibid., 152.

52 Barry Kemp, "The Kom el-Nana Enclosure at Amarna," *Egyptian Archaeology* 6 (1995): 8–9. Jacquelyn Williamson, "The 'Sunshade' of Nefertiti," *Egyptian Archaeology* 33 (2008): 5–8.

53 James Henry Breasted, "A City of Ikhenaton in Nubia," *ZÄS* 40 (1902/3): 111.

54 For these examples, see Valérlie Angenot, "A Horizon of Aten in Memphis?" *JSSEA* 35 (2008): 7–9.

55 Breasted, "A City of Ikhenaton in Nubia," 112. Löhr, "Aḫanjati in Memphis," 152–153.

the Mansion of Aten (*Ḥwt Itn*)," [56] which might initially incline one to consider a Theban location for this temple. A staff bearing the same name and title from the Memphite region, however, reads: "Hatiay . . . scribe of the granary . . . of the Mansion of Aten in Memphis (*Mn-nfr*). [57] Hatiay was likely buried or reinterred in Thebes.

In 2001 Alan Zivie cleared the tomb of an official named Râiay in the limestone escarpment at the entry of Saqqarra, the necropolis of Memphis, where other later 18th Dynasty officials were laid to rest. One of Râiay's titles was "scribe of the treasury of the Domain of Aten in Memphis" (*sš pr-ḥd n pr ỉtn m Mn-nfr*). [58] Perhaps as was seen already at Karnak and Amarna, *pr ỉtn* was the name of the large complex within which there were large temples and smaller chapels to the Aten.

A final name associated with Memphis needs to be considered. William Murnane pointed out that the name Akhet-Aten (or Akhet-en-Aten) was a toponym that was not only associated with the Amarna holy city, but also with Thebes. [59] He based this on inscriptions on granite altars found in the east Karnak Aten complex, which declare that Aten (early didactic name) was "residing in 'Rejoicing in Horizon of Aten (*ꜣḫt n ỉtn*) in Upper Egyptian Heliopolis, the great and primeval (place) of the Disk,'" concluding that Thebes was the "earliest 'Horizon of Aten.'" [60] Valérie Angenot has recently made a good case for the same epithet being attributed to Memphis. [61] Her evidence for this proposal includes a talatat discovered by Joseph Hekekyan in the early 1850s that is now in the Nicholson Museum in Sydney and recently was restudied by David Jeffreys, who in recent years has been excavating at Memphis. [62] This decorated block was found in the northeastern corner of the enclosure of the Ptah Temple in a section of wall of reused talatats. [63] The inscription is on a falcon-headed vessel that is surrounded by the sun's rays, which inclines one to think that the king and queen are engaged in a cultic act as Aten showers his light over them. The text includes the later didactic name of Aten in cartouches with the epithet "who resides in Akhet-en-Aten" (*ḥry-ỉb ꜣḫt n ỉtn*). [64]

---

[56] Alain Zivie, "Hataiay, Scribe du temple d'Aton à Memphis," in *Egypt, Israel, and the Ancient Mediterranean World: Studies in Honor of Donald B. Redford* (eds. G. N. Knoppers & A. Hirsch; Leiden: Brill, 2004), 224–231.

[57] Ibid., 224.

[58] Ibid., 227.

[59] William Murnane, "Observations on Pre-Amarna Theology during the Earliest Reign of Amenhotep IV," in *Gold of Praise: Studies on Ancient Egypt in Honor of Edward F. Wente* (eds. E. Teeter & J. Larson; Chicago: Oriental Institute, 1999), 304–305.

[60] Ibid., 304–305.

[61] Angenot, "A Horizon of Aten in Memphis?" 1–20.

[62] David Jeffreys, "An Amarna Period Relief from Memphis," in *Egyptian Art in the Nicholson Musem, Sydney* (eds. K. N. Sowada & B. G. Ockinga; Meditarch, 2006), 119–133.

[63] Ibid., 122.

[64] Ibid., 120–112, 125.

Then, too, Marten Raven and his colleagues recently discovered the tomb of Meryneith at Saqqara,[65] which contained an elegant statue of statue of Meryre and his wife.[66] Among the titles of Meryre is "scribe of the Domain of Aten in Akhet-Aten in Memphis" (*sš n Pr ỉtn m Mn-nfr*).[67] Reference to "Akhet-Aten in Memphis" is puzzling. Angenot proposes understanding this name as referring to Memphis, meaning that Akhet-Aten or Akhet-en-Aten applied to Amarna as well as Thebes and Memphis.[68] She rightly observes that while we think of Amarna/Akhet-Aten as a city, it is never written with the city determinative (⊗), which may suggest that in Akhenaten's mind Akhet-en-Aten/Akhet-Aten was not restricted to the limitations of a city. She offers two possible interpretations for this name: first, that it is a particular temple along with the other named ones at Memphis, or second, that "the expression *ꜣḫ.t ỉtn* is a generic denomination for all the cultic places in which the Aten was worshipped."[69] The latter option seems like a better explanation for the multiple applications of this name at different locations.

These blocks and texts, especially with various Aten temple names, demonstrate that there was a sizable Aten complex at Memphis, likely with several smaller chapels associated with it.

Heliopolis

It is not surprising that there is evidence for Aten temples at Heliopolis, the very city of the sun that in many ways provided inspiration for Akhenaten. In 1967 a gaping hole opened in a street in Matariya, a suburb of Cairo and part of ancient Heliopolis. Some antiquities were visible, resulting in further excavations in the area. Among the finds were a number of inscribed Amarna period objects.[70] One interesting object was a votive stela of Neferrenpet of *ỉwnw* in the Amarna style, but it is Osiris who is the giver of the offering![71] At nearby Ain Shams ("spring of the sun") a fragment of a hand from a statue was uncovered in a later tomb that had the double cartouche with the earlier didactic name of Aten on the wrist.[72] Also from Fatimid Cairo (10th century A.D.) in Bab el-Nasr, some decorated talatat blocks were found,[73] while

[65] M. Raven et al. "Preliminary Report of the Leiden Excavations at Saqqara, Season 2001: The Tomb of Meryneith," *JEOL* 37 (2001–2002): 71–89.

[66] Apparently the name Meryneith was taken after the end of the Amarna revolution.

[67] Raven et al. "Preliminary Report of the Leiden Excavations at Saqqara," 82.

[68] Angenot, "A Horizon of Aten in Memphis?" 10–20.

[69] Ibid., 19.

[70] Hassan Bakhry, "Akhenaten at Heliopolis," *Cd'É* 47 (1972): 55–67.

[71] Ibid., 56–57.

[72] Ibid., 60.

[73] Ibid., 61–61.

17 blocks from various Pharaonic periods were documented in the minaret of the el-Hakim ibn Amr Mosque (A.D. 990–1010). One of these is an important talatat that contains the name of one of the Memphite Aten temples, namely *wṯs ỉtn m ỉwn n rꜥ* ("Uplifting Aten in Heliopolis of Re").[74] Little can be said about this temple or whether there were multiple sanctuaries there, but excavations at Matariya have recently begun with a partnership between Dietrich Raue of the University of Leipzig and Aimen Ashmawy of the Ministry of Culture for Antiquities. Early news indicates that some "Amarna Period blocks" were collected from secondary use.[75]

By reviewing the data of Aten temple materials from Nubia to Heliopolis in the Delta, it is clear that Akhenaten's building program for the Aten was not limited to Thebes, followed by Amarna, but in keeping with the recurring theme in texts of "that which the Aten encircles," Aten could be and should be worshiped everywhere because his light was universal. So it is not surprising that there now may be evidence for an Amarna period temple even in northern Sinai, thanks to the investigations at Tell el-Borg between 1999 and 2008.[76]

An Aten Temple in North Sinai?

In 1998, the author led a small team to reconnoiter in northern Sinai, east of the Suez Canal, between Qantara East and Pelusium to the northeast. We were interested in identifying a New Kingdom site that was part of Egypt's eastern frontier defense system. Work had already been ongoing at Tell Hebua I since the mid-1980s by Mohamed Abd el-Maksoud. A massive fort was discovered there, and in 1999 a 13th-century B.C. statue was discovered with a dedication to "Horus Lord of Tjaru (Sile)."[77] This discovery seems to confirm that Hebua was Egypt's long sought east frontier capital and entry point from western Asia. The writer had thought for nearly a decade that Hebua was indeed ancient Tjaru/Sile, so this confirmation was most welcomed.[78]

---

[74] Labib Habachi, "Akhenaten in Heliopolis," in *Zum 70. Geburstag von Herbert Ricke* (Wiesbaden: Franz Steiner Velag, 1971), 35–45.

[75] See "Heliopolis (Matariya)," *Egyptian Archaeology* 41 (2112): 31.

[76] For reports of the earliest investigations, see James K. Hoffmeier, "Tell el-Borg in North Sinai," *Egyptian Archaeology* 20, no. Spring (2002): 18–20. James K. Hoffmeier & Mohamed Abd el-Maksoud, "A New Military Site on 'the Ways of Horus'—Tell el-Borg 1999–2001: A Preliminary Report," *JEA* 89 (2003): 169–197.

[77] For reports on the early work at Hebua, see Mohamed Abd el-Maksoud, "Une nouvelle forteresse sur la route d'horus: Tell Heboua 1986 (North Sinai)," *CRIPEL* 9 (1987): 13–16. Mohamed Abd el-Maksoud, *Tell Hebuoa—1981–1991* (Paris: Éditions Recherche sur les Civilisations, 1998). Mohamed Abd el-Maksoud, "Tjarou, Porte De L'oriente," in *Le Sinaï durant l'antiquité et le moyen age* (eds. C. Bonnet & D. Valbelle; Paris: Errance, 1998), 61–65. For the publication of the statue, see Mohamed Abd el-Maksoud & Dominique Valbelle, "Tell Héboua-Tjarou l'apport de l'épigraphie," *R d'É* 56 (2005): 18–20.

[78] James K. Hoffmeier, *Israel in Egypt* (New York: Oxford University Press, 1996), 185–187.

In 2005 a second inscription was uncovered in the temple precinct at Hebua and it too had the name of Tjaru/Sile inscribed on it.[79] By confirming the identification of Hebua and its several sites (four areas have been identified, numbered I–IV)[80] as the northeastern border town of Tjaru/Sile, it is apparent that settlements east and south of this point are technically outside of Egypt.

Located 10 kilometers (6 mi) east of the Suez Canal at Qantara East and 2.5 kilometers (1.55 mi) and approximately 2 kilometers (1 mi, 425 yds) north of the El-Arish road is Tell el-Borg, which is situated 5 kilometers (3 mi) east-southeast of Hebua II. Excavations directed by the author resulted in the discovery of two New Kingdom Forts, the earlier one from the mid-late 18th Dynasty (ca. 1450/1425 to 1325 B.C.), while the latter dates from the end of the Amarna Period into the 20th Dynasty (ca. 1325 to 1180 B.C.).[81] One of the surprises that awaited us was the significant amount of Amarna period remains.[82]

In Field II, the area on the south side of the "tell," and thought to be a public space area, contained three robber pits that were investigated. Once the wind-blown sand was removed, limestone blocks of various sizes lay in the holes; among them were undecorated talatat blocks. Once the jumble of blocks left by the recent robbers was cleared, a large stone-lined cistern or well was revealed (Figure 6.3).[83] The five steps lead down into the cistern and they were made of talatat; the first four steps were made up of a pair of talatat. The fifth step is made up of three parallel talatats. None of the exposed surfaces was inscribed; we did not, however, dislodge them to inspect the undersides. Situated in the walls of the cistern were other random talatat blocks. In all, more than 20 of these unique Akhenaten temple limestone blocks were noted in this structure. Clearly this water facility utilized reused blocks from a dismantled Aten temple.

Additional talatat blocks were found reused in the Ramesside period fort situated (Field IV) about 200 meters (650 ft) south of the stone-lined cistern.[84] In the

---

[79] Abd el-Maksoud & Valbelle, "Tell Héboua-Tjarou l'apport de l'épigraphie," 7–8.

[80] Abd el-Maksoud, *Tell Hebuoa—1981–1991* (Paris: Éditions Recherche sur les Civilisations, 1998), 15.

[81] Hoffmeier & Mohamed Abd el-Maksoud, "A New Military Site on 'the Ways of Horus'—Tell el-Borg 1999–2001." James K. Hoffmeier, "Tell el Borg on Egypt's Eastern Frontier: A Preliminary Report on the 2002 and 2004 Seasons," *JARCE* 41 (2004): 85–103.

[82] For a review of the architectural, inscriptional, and ceramic evidence for the Amarna period at Tell el-Borg, see James K. Hoffmeier & Jacobus van Dijk, "New Light on the Amarna Period from North Sinai," *JEA* 96 (2010): 191–205.

[83] Hoffmeier & Mohamed Abd el-Maksoud, "A New Military Site on 'the Ways of Horus'—Tell el-Borg 1999–2001," 180–184, pl. xi.

[84] Between the fortification area and the cistern a Nile distributary was discovered, meaning that it divided the site into north and south sectors; see J. K. Hoffmeier and S. O. Moshier, "New Paleo-Environmental Evidence from North Sinai to Complement Manfred Bietak's Map of the Eastern Delta and Some Historical Implications," in *Timelines: Studies in Honour of Manfred Bietak* (Orientalia Lovaniensia Analecta 149; vol. 2; ed. E. Czerny, I. Hein, and H. Hunger, D. Melman, A. Schwab; Paris: Uitgeverij Peeters, 2006) 170. Stephen O. Moshier and Ali El-Kalani, "Late Bronze Age Paleogeography along the Ancient Ways of Horus in Northwest Sinai, Egypt," *Geoarchaeology* 23, no.4 (2008): 450–473.

FIGURE 6.3 Field II cistern with reused talatats (Tell el-Borg). Photo James K. Hoffmeier.

foundation of the largely destroyed foundations of the Ramesside era moat, both whole blocks and others that had been cut vertically in half had been reused in the foundations of this defensive feature in Field IV (Figure 6.4). A second stone cistern was found inside the west-most wall of the Ramesside fort. It too utilized plain talatat blocks.[85]

Then, too, in the gate area of the same fort (Field V) three talatat blocks were actually uncovered in their original reused context in the foundation of the limestone gate (Figure 6.5).[86] Moreover, several other talatat from the original gate (which had been robbed out in ancient times) were among the scatter of pieces of limestone from the gate's destruction. The name of Ramesses II (1279–1213 B.C.) was found on many of the remaining fragments, and there are two witnesses to Merneptah's name (1213–1203 B.C.); a lone limestone shard contained the double cartouche Ramesses III (1184–1153 B.C.). The evidence suggests that although this fort was likely built in the immediate aftermath of the Amarna Period (possibly by Horemheb 1323–1295 B.C.), the stone gate was from a later phase, likely built by Ramesses II.[87]

---

[85] Hoffmeier, "Tell el Borg on Egypt's Eastern Frontier: A Preliminary Report on the 2002 and 2004 Seasons," 99–103 & Fig. 18.

[86] James K. Hoffmeier, "The Gate of the Ramesside Period Fort at Tell el-Borg, North Sinai," in *Ramesside Studies in Honour of K. A. Kitchen* (ed. M. Collier & S. Snape; Bolton: Rutherford Press), 207–219.

[87] Ibid., 212–213.

FIGURE 6.4 Talatat blocks in foundation of moat (Tell el-Borg). Photo James K. Hoffmeier.

One of the talatat blocks found in the gate contained hieroglyphs, but the limestone was extremely friable. Only a few signs could be read (Figure 6.6). A small fragment of a royal male figure wearing a *khat* or bag-crown was found that could depict one of Akhenaten's ephemeral successors (Figure 6.7). A study of this piece by Earl Ertman and the author tentatively posited that the unnamed royal was possibly Ankhkheperure on stylistic grounds.[88] In support of this suggestion, this little known ruler's cartouche was found impressed on a wine amphora jar handle that was discovered in the stone-lined cistern from Field II (Figure 6.8a).[89] The second

[88] James K. Hoffmeier, "Amarna Period Kings in Sinai," in *Egyptian Archaeology* 31 (2007): 38–39. James K. Hoffmeier & Earl Ertman, "A New Fragmentary Relief of King Ankhkheperure from Tell el-Borg (Sinai)?" *JEA* 94 (2008): 296–302.

[89] Hoffmeier & Mohamed Abd el-Maksoud, "A New Military Site on 'the Ways of Horus'—Tell el-Borg 1999–2001," 180–181.

FIGURE 6.5 Talatat blocks in foundation trench of gate (Tell el-Borg). Photo James K. Hoffmeier.

FIGURE 6.6 Inscribed (but illegible) talatat in gate area of fortress (Tell el-Borg). Photo James K. Hoffmeier.

FIGURE 6.7 Talatat fragment with head of an Amarna king (Tell el-Borg). Photo James K. Hoffmeier.

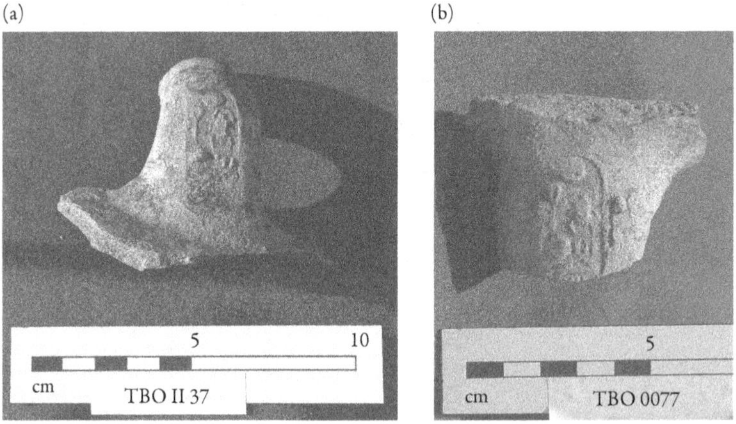

FIGURE 6.8 a. Ankhkheperure jar handle was discovered in Field II (Tell el-Borg). Photo James K. Hoffmeier. b. Ankhkheperure jar handle was discovered in Field IV (Tell el-Borg). Photo James K. Hoffmeier.

Ankhkheperure jar handle was discovered in Field IV from the final phase of the 18th Dynasty fort (more on this below) (Figure 6.8b).[90]

A third inscribed talatat found among the gate debris contains the deeply carved and painted cartouche of Ramesses II (Figure 6.9). The right side of the cartouche interrupts a beautiful Aten-disc. The uraeus is clearly visible at the bottom of the disc in keeping with its placement on the orb in the era of Akhenaten.[91] It is likely that plaster had covered the earlier decoration so as to allow the new Ramesside

[90] Ibid., 180.

[91] On this iconographic development, see Donald Redford, "The Sun-Disc in Akhenaten's Program," *JARCE* 13(1976): 55.

FIGURE 6.9 Talatat with Aten-disc with Ramesses II's cartouche superimposed (Tell el-Borg). Photo James K. Hoffmeier.

inscription to replace it. As often is the case, in time, and perhaps during the stress of dismantling the gate, the plaster fell out, revealing the earlier Aten-disc.

These several reused inscribed blocks, along with around three dozen uninscribed talatat found at Tell el-Borg, require an explanation as to their presence at this remote desert location. There are no sources of limestone in the area, and the closest quarries are nearly 200 kilometers (120 mi) to the southwest, in the Cairo area. Three possible scenarios present themselves. First, the talatat blocks came from a dismantled Aten temple in a Delta site like Memphis or Heliopolis, which would have been shipped to Tell el-Borg via the recently discovered Nile distributary that passed by the site.[92] Second, there might have been an Aten Temple at nearby Tjaru. It is 5 kilometers from Tell el-Borg to Hebua II and 6–7 kilometers to Hebua I. Given that this fortified city was so vital to Egypt's defense and military operations in Western Asia throughout the New Kingdom, one might expect an Aten temple to have stood there in the Amarna Period. After more than 20 years of work, no talatat blocks have been found at either Hebua I or II. These are extremely large sites and vast tracks remain to be investigated, so evidence for a possible Aten temple may yet appear.

[92] Hoffmeier and Moshier, "New Paleo-Environmental Evidence from North Sinai to Complement Manfred Bietak's Map of the Eastern Delta and Some Historical Implications," 170. Moshier and El-Kalani, "Late Bronze Age Paleogeography along the Ancient Ways of Horus in Northwest Sinai, Egypt," 450–473.

The third possibility is that the talatat came from a temple at Tell el-Borg itself that would have been dismantled like other Aten temples on Horemheb's orders. As it turns out, two clay seal impressions (bullae) from papyrus documents and the bezel of a ring were discovered at Tell el-Borg with Horemheb's name on them.[93] It is evident that Horemheb was active at Tell-el-Borg, and as we have suggested, he possibly built the second fort at Tell el-Borg (probably with a mud-brick gate) before Ramesses II erected the limestone gate.[94]

In the course of eight seasons of excavations at Tell el-Borg, we found no clear evidence for the location of a limestone Aten temple, although we thought that a small mud-brick temple might have once stood in Field II in the area 40–75 meters east of the stone-lined cistern where numerous talatat had been identified. In this area a number of larger granite blocks and fragments were found, including a 12.34-ton granite block (uninscribed), a travertine (alabaster) block, and scores of broken pieces of limestone. This concentration of elite type stone is highly suggestive of a temple area, but no talatat blocks were found in the vicinity.

The most impressive architectural feature discovered at this site was a moat, the foundations of which were made of red (fired) brick (Figure 6.10), not to be confused

FIGURE 6.10 Field IV Moat with fired brick foundations (Tell el-Borg). Photo James K. Hoffmeier.

[93] Hoffmeier & van Dijk, "New Light on the Amarna Period from North Sinai," 202–203, 204, figs. 17–19.

[94] Hoffmeier, "The Gate of the Ramesside Period Fort at Tell el-Borg, North Sinai," 207–216.

with the Ramesside Period moat that employed reused talatats (Figure 6.4). In Field IV (area 2) the section of moat was 7.7 meters (25.25 ft) wide at the top, 2.65 meters in depth from the current surface and 3 meters wide at the bottom. Eight courses of fired bricks formed the foundations of the inside and outside parallel walls, on top of which mud-brick walls were laid onto the basal sand at approximately a 45-degree angle. The defense walls that would have stood inside the moat wall are completely denuded. An approximately 20-meter (65 ft) long section of this moat was laid bare south of the gate area, but the moat was not completed.

Clearing the contents of the massive moat proved challenging indeed, as tons of sand and stone had to be removed. Some of the contents of the fill were valuable in answering questions about the history of the fort and the date when it was filled, and unexpectedly it pointed to the Amarna Period. Just as digging began in a new square, and close to the surface (Field IV, Unit D 12, Locus 2) the top layer of fill of the moat produced a large quantity of broken potsherds. Included in this deposit was a second wine amphora jar handle with the name of Ankhkheperure on it (Figure 6.8b). Since this layer represented the final materials dumped into the moat, the contents should date quite close to the period of the filling. The identity of Ankhkheperure remains a problem. It could be the throne name of Nefertiti or Smenkhkare; the latter monarch possibly ruled after the death of Akhenaten and before the accession of Tutankhamun.[95] The fact that at Tell el-Borg there are two witnesses to this short-lived ruler is remarkable indeed. The inclusion of one of these in the fill at the top of this moat demonstrates that the filling occurred just after the death of Akhenaten. Furthermore, the pottery discovered in this square proves that the moat did not fill naturally over a long period of time, but was intentionally filled after Akhenaten's death (ca. 1336 B.C.).[96]

At a lower level in the moat, another stamped amphora jar handle was found. Although the name was partially lost, the first element in the cartouche is *ỉtn*, meaning that the name is likely that of Akhenaten himself![97] This impression is the only occurrence of this king's name among the remains at Tell el-Borg (Figure 6.11). Interestingly, the name of Akhenaten's mother, the dowager queen Tiye, occurs on a steatite ring found in the eastern cemetery area.[98]

---

[95] For a recent review of the different theories, see Aidan Dodson, *Amarna Sunset: Nefertiti, Tutankhamun, Ay, Horemheb and the Egyptian Counter-Reformation* (Cairo/New York: American University Press, 2009), 27–52.

[96] Hoffmeier & van Dijk, "New Light on the Amarna Period from North Sinai," 204.

[97] Ibid., 198–199.

[98] Hoffmeier, "Tell el Borg on Egypt's Eastern Frontier: A Preliminary Report on the 2002 and 2004 Seasons," 107–109, fig. 26.

FIGURE 6.11 Stamped jar handle with Akhenaten's name (Tell el-Borg). Photo James K. Hoffmeier.

The reason for the intentional filling was that the 18th Dynasty fort had been compromised, likely by flooding that wiped out the western and part of the northern walls and moat of the fort in these areas.[99] A new fort was immediately planned and constructed and placed directly east of the first fort, with the west or back end of the second fort overlapping with part of the front or east wall of the earlier fort. To accomplish this rebuilding, the moat of the 18th Dynasty was purposefully filled with debris that included mud clods (from bricks?), potsherds, and fragments of limestone in the sandy matrix. What was most unexpected was to discover that a large section of the moat was filled with crushed limestone fragments and chunks of larger blocks, apparently from talatats (Figure 6.12). This area was carefully excavated, revealing the actual top of the heap of the crushed stone (Figure 6.13). Each fragment was carefully examined for any decorations. One feature that was noticed was that some limestone fragments had traces of blue and yellow paint. These colors are common with temple ceilings, blue being the sky and yellow being the stars. In fact, a number of such decorated pieces were found in this area, including one large block that was found on the banks of the adjacent canal (apparently dug up when the canal was excavated) (Figure 6.14). While it is known that Aten temples were largely opened to the sky, it has not been established if the undersides of the small roofed sections were decorated to represent the sky, as was the practice in other temples (Figure 4.11 in Chapter 4).[100] At this point, one cannot determine whether or not the star-decorated ceiling pieces from the moat were from an Aten temple.

The probing question is, what was the limestone temple debris doing in the fill of the temple? As noted above, stone of any sort had to be shipped from the Nile Valley and thus was costly, and explains why stone was reused elsewhere in Egypt, but especially at a remote location like Tell el-Borg. It is therefore inconceivable that

[99] James K. Hoffmeier, "Recent Excavations on the 'Ways of Horus': The 2005 and 2006 Seasons at Tell el-Borg," *ASAE* 80 (2006): 262–263.

[100] For examples of roofed sections of Aten temples, see reconstructions in Barry Kemp, *The City of Akhenaten and Nefertiti, Amarna and Its People* (London: Thames & Hudson, 2012), 49, 78, 92, 95. Robert Vergnieux & Michel Gondran, *Aménophis et les Pierres du Soleil* (Paris: Arthaud, 1997), 85, 94–95, 125.

FIGURE 6.12 Pile of limestone chips filling the 18th Dynasty moat, looking south (Tell el-Borg). Photo James K. Hoffmeier.

FIGURE 6.13 Pile of limestone chips filling the 18th Dynasty moat, looking east (Tell el-Borg). Photo James K. Hoffmeier.

FIGURE 6.14 Ceiling block with stars carved on limestone ceiling block (Tell el-Borg). Photo James K. Hoffmeier.

the limestone blocks were purposefully crushed just to use as fill for the moat. Limestone was just too valuable for that! Being a desert environment, sand was easily accessible and the most logical choice for filling the moat in order to provide a solid surface for building walls for the new fort.

Consequently it is tempting to interpret the presence of the limestone debris as coming from a destroyed temple. To be sure, temple blocks were typically reused, even in religious centers like Thebes, but this was not to desecrate but to incorporate the old "sacred" material into the new.[101] It is well established that after the Amarna kings passed from the scene, Horemheb was responsible for dismantling and destroying the Aten temples, and that he and his successors (Ramesses II in particular) reused the blocks (see Chapter 4). As we have shown earlier in this chapter, we have ample evidence for Horemheb's activities at Tell el-Borg, and it has been suggested based on chronological and stratigraphic considerations that it was likely under Horemheb that the second fort was constructed.[102] These factors lead to the plausible, though tentative, hypothesis that

[101] Gun Björkman, *Kings at Karnak: A Study of the Treatment of the Monuments of Royal Predecessors in the Early New Kingdom* (Upsala: Acta Universitatis Upsaliensis, 1971).

[102] James K. Hoffmeier et al., *Excavations in North Sinai: Tell el-Borg* I (Winona Lake: Eisenbrauns, 2013), chapters 5 & 6.

FIGURE 6.15 Seal impression of Neferneferuaten on wine jar hand (Tell el-Borg). Photo James K. Hoffmeier.

the destroyed temple had been devoted to the Aten cult, that Horemheb demolished the temple, and that some of the wreckage was used to fill the moat of the early fort, while preserved blocks were used in other building projects on the site by succeeding kings.

Thus far we have shown that we have evidence for several Amarna era kings, Akhenaten, Ankhkheperure, and Horemheb, the last ruler of the 18th Dynasty.[103] But that is not all that this military site has yielded from the Amarna age. One of the most provocative finds was a jar seal impression with the name of *Nfr-nfrw-ỉtn 3ḫ.t n ḥy.s*, "Nefer-neferu-aten who is beneficial to her husband"[104] (Figure 6.15). It was discovered in Field VI (Area 2, Square A, Locus 002), within a large garbage pit, which was apparently unwittingly dug into an earlier tomb during the very end of the 18th Dynasty or early 19th Dynasty. This impression provides virtually the only complete, more or less undamaged and un-usurped example of this intriguing name, the existence of which was rediscovered some years ago by Marc Gabolde.[105]

The identity of this female royal figure continues to be debated. Gabolde himself thought it might be Akhenaten's eldest daughter Meritaten,[106] while James Allen has suggested it was Neferneferuaten Jr.[107] Despite their arguments to the contrary, it might be simply that it is Nefertiti herself, whose name was changed. Recently Aidan Dodson has agreed that Neferneferuaten was Nefertiti, but speculates that she jointly ruled with Tutankhamun.[108] This joint rule seems questionable. It is more likely that her new name, coupled with the epithet "who is

---

[103] Hoffmeier & van Dijk, "New Light on the Amarna Period from North Sinai," 191–205.

[104] For a discussion of the orthography of the name, see Hoffmeier & van Dijk, "New Light on the Amarna Period from North Sinai," 110–112.

[105] Marc Gabolde, *D'Akhenaton à Toutânkhamon* (Lyon: Université Lumière-Lyon 2 1998), 153–157.

[106] Gabolde, *D'Akhenaton à Toutânkhamon*, 183–185; idem, "Under a Deep Blue Starry Sky," in *Causing His Name to Live: Studies in Egyptian Epigraphy and History in Memory of William J. Murnane* (eds. P. J. Brand & L. Cooper; Leiden/Boston: Brill, 2009), 120.

[107] J. P. Allen, "The Amarna Succession," in *Causing His Name to Live*, 9–20, particularly 18–19.

[108] Dodson, *Amarna Sunset*, 42–46.

beneficial to her husband," signals the elevation of Nefertiti's status to co-regent, "her husband" being Akhenaten.[109]

Other members of the Amarna royal family discovered at Tell el-Borg include Tutankhamun (i.e., Neb-kheperu-re), whose cartouche was stamped on an amphora jar handle and on the base of another amphora: both were found in the cistern in Field II. The name of Ay, Tutankhamun's successor, was also discovered in the Field VI pit where the Neferneferuaten seal impression was found.[110] It is this same Aye in whose tomb at Amarna the Great Hymn to Aten was recorded. The presence of this series of Amarna royal figures, even the more obscure members, means that this frontier fort was functioning throughout the entire Amarna period, beginning with Tiye, Amenhotep III's great queen, from the outset of the Amarna period, to Horemheb, the destroyer of the Aten's domains, which marked the end of the era. This unbroken chain from circa 1360 to 1300 provides ample evidence that there could have been an Aten temple at the site, and Horemheb's presence may explain how and under what circumstances the Aten temple was destroyed and why blocks were accessible for reuse and the rubble from the destruction available for fill in the moat.

If this explanation of the facts is correct, then there was an Aten temple at Tell el-Borg just beyond the frontier town and fort at Tjaru. This marks the north-most point where an Aten temple briefly flourished. The temple and the troops at the fort were supplied with wine in large amphorae as the Amarna royal names on the jars demonstrate. Among the finds from the palace of Malkata in western Thebes, were 68 wine jar dockets from vineyards of the "western Nile" in the northwest Delta, indicating that this vintage was "highly prized."[111] During the Amarna period, wine from this area came under the domain of the House of Aten. In Tutankhamun's tomb, the label "Sweet wine of the House of Aten, L. P. H., of the Western River" is found on at least a dozen wine dockets.[112]

Tjaru/Sile was also renowned for its fine sweet wines. At Malkata six dockets with wine of Tjaru were recorded by W. C. Hayes,[113] and more have since been

---

[109] J. R. Harris, "Neferneferuaten," *GM* 4 (1973): 15–17; idem, "Neferneferuaten Regnans," *Acta Orientalia* 35 (1974): 11–21. Julia Samson, "Nefertiti's Reality," *JEA* 63 (1977): 88–97. Nicholas Reeves, *Akhenaten: Egypt's False Prophet* (London: Thames and Hudson, 2001), 169–173.

[110] Hoffmeier, "Recent Excavations on the 'Ways of Horus': The 2005 and 2006 Seasons at Tell el-Borg," 261–262, fig. 23.

[111] William C. Hayes, "Inscriptions from the Palace of Amenhotep III," *JNES* 10 (1951): 88–89, fig. 4 no. 5, fig. 6 nos. 51–52, fig. 7 nos. 74–76, fig. 25 (J, K) and possibly fig. 29 (FFF). Wine from Tjaru is attested on jar sealings and wine dockets dating to Years 28 and 36.

[112] Jaroslav Cerny, *Hieratic Inscriptions form the Tomb of Tut'ankhamun* (Oxford: Oxford University Press, 1965), 1–3.

[113] Hayes, "Inscriptions from the Palace of Amenhotep III," 89.

documented.[114] Tjaru wine labels from Akhenaten's year 13 and 15 were also found at Amarna.[115] Then, too, a docket in Tutankhamun's tomb, dated to year 5, reads "Sweet wine of the House-of-Aten [of] Tjaru."[116]

Just a short distance from Tutankhamun's tomb in the Valley of the Kings (KV 62) a burial (KV 63) was only discovered in 2005–2006. Among the contents of the tomb was an amphora with a hieratic inscription that also mentions wine from Tjaru, and like the one from Tutankhamun's time, it is also dated to year 5.[117] Consequently, Otto Schaden, who discovered KV 63 (that lacks any royals names on the objects found therein), posits that the two year 5 vintages from Tjaru/Sile both date in Tutankhamun's reign. These two texts demonstrate that there was a temple estate of *pr-ỉtn* in the Tjaru region, and possibly that an Aten temple built by Akhenaten flourished just beyond the most northeastern province. Akhenaten's talatat blocks and the presence of so many luminaries of the Amarna Period at Tell el-Borg lead one to think that there was an Aten temple there, but this will have to remain a provisional suggestion.[118]

There is one more sign of Akhenaten's presence at Tell el-Borg. On the north side of the Ramesside fort lay a section of moat (Field V, Area 2) that paralleled the section found on the south side where the talatat blocks were found in the foundations. In the northern moat a wide range of limestone blocks were incorporated, but none was clearly identifiable as a talatat block. The variety of foundational materials ranged from crushed limestone pieces to doorjambs 1.40 meters (4 ft 7 in) long.[119] In all, the remains of seven inscribed doorjambs were laid in the foundations of the moat, with their texts facing down. Three were complete. Two of the jambs bear the cartouche of *ꜥ3 ḫprw rꜥ*, the prenomen of Amenhotep II (1427–1400 B.C.). Of the remaining jambs, four have the nomen (Amenhotep, divine ruler of Heliopolis) inscribed, although in some cases the name *ỉmn* is hacked out of the cartouche (Figure 6.16a–c), a sure sign of Atenist iconoclasm. In other instances, the divine

[114] A. Leahy, *Excavations at Malkata and the Birket Habu 1971–1974*, IV: *The Inscriptions* (Warminster: Aris & Phillips, 1978), pl. 15 ([XII]) and 16 (XIII).

[115] H. W. Fairman and J. Cerny, in J. Pendlebury, *The City of Akhenaten* III (London: EES, 1951), 165, pl. 89 no. 123. T. E. Peet & C. L. Woolley, *The City of Akhenaten* I (London: EES, 1923), pl. 63 (N).

[116] Cerny, *Hieratic Inscriptions from the Tomb of Tut'ankhamun*, 22 no. 8.

[117] Verbal communication from Otto Schaden. A picture and translation of the text is found in Otto Schaden, "KV 63: An Update," *KMT* 18, no. 1 (2007): 22.

[118] Because *pr itn* was also found at Thebes, Amarna, and Memphis, one has to allow the possibility that Tjaru vineyards was owned and managed by one of these temples.

[119] James K. Hoffmeier & Ronald D. Bull, "New Inscriptions Mentioning Tjaru from Tell el-Borg," *Rd'É* 56 (2005), 79–94. Hoffmeier, "Recent Excavations on the 'Ways of Horus': the 2005 and 2006 Seasons at Tell el-Borg," 260–261, figs. 17–18.

(a) (b) (c) (d)

FIGURE 6.16 a. Limestone doorjamb with defaced Amenhotep II cartouche and epithet of Amun (Tell el-Borg). Photo James K. Hoffmeier. b. Limestone doorjamb with defaced Amenhotep II cartouche (Tell el-Borg). Photo James K. Hoffmeier. c. Limestone doorjamb with defaced Amenhotep II cartouche (Tell el-Borg). Photo James K. Hoffmeier. d. Limestone doorjamb with defaced epithet of Amun (Tell el-Borg). Photo James K. Hoffmeier.

name Amun (written in the epithet "beloved of Amun") is obliterated (Figure 6.16a & d). Occasionally the iconoclasts missed the name of Amun (Figure 6.16d). While Amun's names in the epithet "beloved of [Amun]-Re lord of the thrones of the two lands" was removed, but the sun-disc was not molested (Figure 6.16a & d). It was only the Amun part of the name Amun-Re that was problematic.

These doorjambs clearly had been incorporated into an important building in the first fort and were still functioning when the attempt was made to systematically remove Amun's name (except for a few cases, probably due to the haste with which the names were expunged). Even though Amenhotep II was Akhenaten's great-grandfather, his cartouches were not spared, but the sun-discs were preserved. The sky goddess Nut's name was carved into two of the blocks (Figure 6.16b), but they were left intact. So the excising was aimed solely at Amun on these blocks. This attack, as we shall see in the next chapter, was not limited to this remote location. What was the motivation for this program of removing Amun's name, and what does this tell us about Akhenaten's religious convictions? Are these characteristics of a monotheist? These questions will be the subject of the next chapter.

The great living Aten who is in jubilee, the lord of all that the Disc (*itn*) encircles, lord of heaven, lord of earth

THE TOMB OF PARENNEFER (AMARNA)

Chapter 7

Is Atenism Monotheism?

THE DEATH OF THE GODS

A fragmentary hymn sung on the occasion of the Sed-festival by the children of the king is found on blocks from the *Gm(t) p3 itn* temple at Karnak. It refers to Re and the gods (*nṯrw*).[1] Even though this paean likely dates to sometime in year 3 or 4 when Aten's temples were flourishing in east Karnak, the use of the word "gods" here in Aten's temples is unexpected. Anthony Spalinger observed that "it is significant that at this early stage worship of the Sun-disc did not preclude the other deities in Egypt."[2] There is a definite "polytheistic flavor," but he rightly associates that with the very nature of the traditional *ḥb sd* rituals, the context for this song.[3] It therefore could well be that the archaic traditions associated with the Jubilee were such that they would not be excluded, and thus he was not making a theological affirmation by allowing the word *nṯrw* to be used. Be it a vestige of polytheism or an archaism in the ceremony (the position favored here), it was only a short time later when the gods would be eradicated.

The plural writing of "gods" also occurs on an early relief (from Karnak?) in the epithet "Shu, son of Re, father of the gods" (*šw s3 rʿ it nṯrw*) (Figure 3.9 in

[1] Anthony Spalinger, "A Hymn of Praise to Akhenaten," in *The Akhenaten Temple Project*, Vol. 2 (ed. D. Redford; Toronto: Akhenaten Temple Project/University of Toronto Press, 1988), 29–30.

[2] Ibid., 30.

[3] Ibid., 32.

Chapter 3).[4] Unfortunately, the context of this inscription is unknown, but it must be admitted that in the first year or two (no more)—the likely dating of this block—referring to "the gods" was still permissible.

The letter from the Memphite official Apy in Akhenaten's fifth year, drafted just about five weeks before the date on the early boundary stelae at Amarna (see Chapter 6), signaled that the temple of Ptah and those of other deities in the capital were functioning normally. Nine months earlier (in year 4), a graffito was etched in the quarry area of Wadi Hammamat by an expedition that had been dispatched by Akhenaten to obtain *bḫn*, graywacke[5] stone for a statue of the king. The leader of the expedition was none other than the high priest of Amun, named May.[6] Minimally, this reference suggests that while the Aten temples in Karnak were functioning, the adjacent Amun temple was still operational with the high priest who had been appointed by Amenhotep III when he was still in office.[7] The fact that the cleric who had been the most influential and powerful in the land was leading a quarrying expedition to the remote Wadi Hammamat was certainly not a promotion for the pontiff, and was likely a humiliating assignment. Surely this ignoble mission presaged a change in fortunes for Amun, his temple, and his priesthood.

The persecution of Amun and the other gods of Egypt was about to begin. A precise date for the iconoclastic pogrom is not known, nor do we possess a decree announcing the new initiative. Henry Fischer has proposed that iconoclasm occurred very early, believing that the mutilation of the penis on the reliefs of Min on the Senusert I chapel at Karnak was the result of Atenism.[8] Because these blocks were incorporated into the construction of the 3rd Pylon by Amenhotep III, he reasons that the mutilation was an anti-Amun action. To connect this disfiguring with Akhenaten's action requires a long co-regency, which we have shown is implausible, and it is hard to believe that the desecration against Amun would have been tolerated while Amenhotep III was alive. Then, too, all the other signs of iconoclasm at Karnak point to the final years before the move to Amarna.

---

[4] Baudouin van de Walle, "Survivances mythologiques dans les coiffers royales de l'epoque atonienne," *Cd'É* 55 (1980): fig. 1.

[5] Though some have thought that *bḫn* could be basalt, J. R. Harris (*Lexicographical Studies in Ancient Egyptian Minerals* [Berlin: Academie-Verlag, 1961], 78–81) is probably right in arguing that the stone is graywacke from the Wadi Hammamat.

[6] The text is in Georges Goyon, *Nouvelles inscriptions rupestres du Wadi Hammamat* (Paris: Imprimerie Nationale, 1957), pl. 25. Translation in William Murnane, *Texts from the Amarna Period in Egypt* (Atlanta: Scholars Press, 1995), 68.

[7] Donald Redford, "The Identity of the High-priest of Amun at the Beginning of Akhenaten's Reign," *JAOS* 83 (1963): 240–241.

[8] Henry Fischer, "An Early Example of Atenist Iconoclasm," *JARCE* 13 (1976): 131–132.

One signal of change was that Amenhotep IV dropped his birth name and adopted Akhenaten, "serviceable to the Aten." Even when the Aten temples were being made in years 2–3, the name "Amenhotep" was initially carved into the talatat. But a major operation began to erase that name on the Aten temples, replacing it with "Akhenaten."[9] Since it was suggested that the Sed-festival may have marked the occasion of the name change of the king (see Chapter 4), this may have provided the impetus to begin the purge. Alternatively, it may have been initiated in the aftermath of the "evils" and "offensive things" alluded to on the Boundary Stela at Amarna[10] (see Chapter 5).

Jacobus van Dijk thinks that the name change may mark the start of the iconoclasm: "probably at that same time as this name change took place, the traditional gods were banned completely and a campaign was begun to remove their names and effigies (particularly those of Amun) from monuments."[11] Donald Redford sees the vindictive action as a parting shot that began with the move to Amarna: "Amun became anathema."[12] No royal decree survives in which the king unveiled his intent to close temples and rid Egypt of Amun and the gods. The evidence that a campaign was initiated to eradicate the gods, however, is unequivocal.

Were the temples actually closed down by edict? Or did the diversion of resources and manpower to the Aten cult at Karnak, and then at Akhet-Aten, simply deprive the temples of their lifeblood, forcing them to close down? Either scenario is possible; the available evidence is not clear on the matter. All one can do is point to the "Restoration Stela" of Tutankhamun, which was usurped in turn by Horemheb, who carved his name over that of his predecessor. Even allowing for the possibility of hyperbole in the text, the implication is that the other temples were dysfunctional for a period of time, and due to the lack of the requisite cultic activities, the gods and goddesses ceased to function. The restorer king claims to have

> repaired what was ruined as a monument lasting to the length of continuity (i.e. throughout eternity), and having repelled disorder throughout the Two Lands, so that Maat rests [in her place] as he causes falsehood to be an abomination and the land to be like its primeval state.

---

9 For example, see Donald Redford, *Akhenaten: The Heretic King* (Princeton, NJ: Princeton University Press, 1984), 140–141. Idem, *The Akhenaten Temple Project*, Vol. 2, Fig. 12.

10 Murnane, *Texts from the Amarna Period in Egypt*, 78.

11 Jacobus van Dijk, "The Amarna Period and Later New Kingdom," in *The Oxford History of Ancient Egypt* (ed. Ian Shaw; Oxford/New York: Oxford University Press, 2000), 270.

12 Donald Redford, "Akhenaten: New Theories and Old Facts," *BASOR* 369 (2013): 25.

> When his Person (*ḥm.f*) appeared as king, the temples and the cities of the gods and goddesses, starting from Elephantine [as far] as the Delta marshes . . . , were fallen into decay and their shrines were fallen into ruin, having become mere mounds overgrown with grass. Their sanctuaries were like something that had not come into being and their buildings were a footpath—for the land was in rack and ruin. The gods were ignoring this land: if an army [was] sent to Djahy to broaden the boundaries of Egypt, no success did come to all; if one prayed to a god, to ask something from him, he did not come at all; and if one beseeched any goddess in the same way, she did not come at all. Their hearts were weak because of their bodies and they destroyed what was made.[13]

The king goes on to report that he specifically restored the cult images of Amun of Thebes and Ptah at Memphis, re-establishing proper cultic functions, saying that he

> endowed (them) with possessions forever; instituting divine offerings for them, consisting of regular daily sacrifices; and proving their food offerings on earth.
>
> He gave more than what had existed before, surpassing what had been done since the time of the ancestors: he installed lay priests and higher clergy from among the children of the officials of their cities, each one being the "son-of-a-man"[14] whose name is known; he multiplied their [offering tables], silver, copper and bronze, there being no limit to [anything]; he filled their workrooms with male and female slaves from the tribute of His Person's (the king's) capturing.[15]

The text continues to state how Tutankhamun lavished gifts and provisions on the temples.

Scholars normally and appropriately question this genre of text in which a new king castigates his ancestors for neglect of temples in order to legitimize himself. But given the fact that there is so much evidence for Akhenaten's neglect and iconoclasm, and because the cost of building the massive Aten complexes at Karnak, at Amarna (not to mention the palaces, administrative buildings, and domestic quarters), and at locations from Nubia to north Sinai, it does not stretch credulity to believe that

---

[13] William Murnane, *Texts from the Amarna Period in Egypt*, 212–213.

[14] This expression (*sꜣ* s) literally means "a son of a man," but idiomatically means "a well-born man" or "a man of noble birth" (R. O. Faulkner, *A Concise Dictionary of Middle Egyptian* [Oxford: Oxford University Press, 1962], 205–206).

[15] Murnane, *Texts from the Amarna Period in Egypt*, 213.

the temples of other deities were deprived, either intentionally or unintentionally. The fact that the "Restoration Stela" was found in the temple of Amun at Karnak, which certainly suffered more than any other temple did, lends credibility to the claims that the temples needed to be restored.[16] Furthermore, if indeed the temples of Egypt were so neglected and had images marred, what better genre of text to use than this "Time of Troubles" motif?[17]

The traditional view that the temples were neglected, defunded, and possibly shut down, and that the priests (especially of Amun) were left without a royal sponsor, seems supported by the circumstantial evidence. Not only would the temple institutions have been reeling from the loss of revenue, but, as Ronald Leprohon points out, the economy of Egypt probably was harmed significantly by the redirection of resources to the Aten Temples at Karnak and the immense building efforts at Akhet-Aten.[18] The "two main themes" found in Tutankhamun's restoration stela, Leprohon avers, are the restoration of the temples and re-establishment of their proper function, and, second, the reinstatement of "the old priestly families, who had been displaced during the Amarna period. . . ."[19] The point that old orders of priests had been marginalized or dismissed is further underscored in Horemheb's coronation inscription dating from 13 to 14 years after Akhenaten's death,[20] and following Tutankhamun's restoration efforts, all of which seems to imply that the restitution program took more than a decade. Horemheb's claims in the coronation inscription include:

> Then did his Person [= the king] sail downstream with the statue of Re-Horakhty, and he reorganized this land, restoring its customs to those of the time of Re. From the Delta marshes down to the Land of the Bow [= Aswan region] he renewed the gods' mansions and fashioned all their images, they being distinguished from what had existed formerly and surpassing in beauty from what he did with them. So that Re rejoiced when he saw them—they having been found wrecked from an earlier time. He raised up their temples and created their statues each in their exact shape, out of all sorts of costly gemstones. When he had sought out the gods' precincts which were in ruins in this land, he refounded them just as they had been since the time of the first primeval age,

---

[16] Aidan Dodson, *Amarna Sunset: Nefertititi, Tutankhamun, Ay, Horemheb, and the Egyptian Counter Reformation* (Cairo/New York: American University in Cairo Press, 2009), 64.

[17] Redford, *Akhenaten: The Heretic King*, 208.

[18] Ronald J. Leprohon, "The Reign of Akhenaten Seen Through the Late Royal Decrees," in *Mélanges Gamal Eddin Mokhtar* (ed. Paule Posener-Kriéger; Cairo: Institut français d'archéologie orientale du Caire, 1985), 94–96.

[19] Ibid., 99.

[20] The publication of the text, translation, and commentary were offered by Alan H. Gardiner, "The Coronation of King Ḥaremḥeb," *JEA* 39 (1953): 13–31.

> and he instituted divine offerings for them, as regular daily sacrifices—all the vessels of their temples being modeled out of gold and silver. And he equipped them with the lay priests (*wꜥbw*) and lector priests (*ḥry ḫbw*) from the pick of the home troops, assigning them fields and herds, being equipped on all sides, so that they might rise early to pay homage to Re at dawn every day. . . .[21]

Like Tutankhamun after his coronation in Thebes, Horemheb embarked on a tour to visit temples throughout Egypt. Sir Alan Gardiner, who originally published this text, is surely on point to say that "nothing could have been more important than to conciliate the priesthood of Amen-Re."[22] It is evident from this statement that Horemheb was associating himself with the old orthodoxy by refurbishing temples and reinstating clerics; in addition, perhaps to ensure their loyalty, the king appointed lector priests from the military ranks as he, too, had been the top general under Akhenaten and Tutankhamun.[23] His actions seem to have paid off, as Gardiner concluded that "public opinion acquitted him of all taint of Atenism."[24]

The claims of Tutankhamun and Horemheb argue strongly that the former religious order was in shambles, a testimony to the thoroughness of Akhenaten's aggressive actions (in some instances) against various cults and the overt neglect of others, coupled with religious reforms and heavy investment in the new Aten temples. Let us now examine examples of the iconoclasm and their implications.

THE PERSECUTION OF AMUN

No one who has studied this era would disagree with the statement that the Amun cult suffered the greatest losses and that this deity was the focal point of Atenist persecution.

The contrast between the Aten and his minimalist iconography and lack of human symbolism (save the hands at the end of the solar rays) and Amun, who is typically shown in human form (Figures 2.2, 2.4–2.7 in Chapter 2), could not be more striking. What is clear is that the program of desecration of texts and images spanned from Nubia in the south and north and east to Sinai, thanks to the recent discoveries at Tell el-Borg (see Chapter 6). Such a thorough program of annihilation required a massive effort. Van Dijk is surely correct to say that the widespread nature of the iconoclasm and its thoroughness represented "a Herculean task that

---

21 Murnane, *Texts from the Amarna Period in Egypt*, 232–233.

22 Gardiner, "The Coronation of King Ḥaremḥeb," 22.

23 Alan H. Gardiner, "The Memphite Tomb of General Ḥaremḥeb," *JEA* 39 (1953), 3–12. G. T. Martin, *The Memphite Tomb of Horemheb, Commander-in-Chief of Tut'ankhamûn* I (London: Egypt Exploration Society, 1989).

24 Gardiner, "The Coronation of King Ḥaremḥeb," 21.

can only have been carried out with the support of the army."[25] Critical to the success of Akhenaten's religious agenda was the support of the military, which by every measure stayed loyal to the king and had a very visible presence at Amarna.[26] Whether or not the military as a whole bought into Akhenaten's religious agenda we cannot say; nevertheless, it was the muscle that enforced his ideology.

Mention was made in the previous chapter that the name of Amun was erased from limestone doorjambs of Amenhotep II at Tell el-Borg, a recently discovered military site in northwestern Sinai. The same is true of scenes and inscriptions in temples in Nubia that were associated with fortresses and temples over 3,220 km (2,000 miles) to the south of the eastern frontier, and virtually everywhere between.

The Gebel Barkal Stela of Thutmose III, so named because it was discovered by the sacred mountain at Napata in Nubia, bears witness to the results of the Atenists' chisels. Amun's name was regularly hacked out (seven times in all),[27] and in four instances "Amun-Re" and his epithet "Lord of the Thrones of the Two Lands" were entirely erased."[28] The wrath of Aten was only limited to Amun on this stela, while other deities' names were not touched, for example Montu, Thoth's name in Thutmose, and even the title "all the gods" (*nṯrw nbw*) was retained.

Also in Nubia is the temple of Amada, built by Hatshepsut and Thutmose III, with decorations by Amenhotep II.[29] Amun's name was hammered out of many of the latter king's cartouches, and in other instances, the name and epithet were removed, for example "Amun-Re Lord of the Thrones of the Two Lands"; in other examples, his image appears to be reworked (i.e., restored after defacing).[30] In one case, the epithet "Amun-Re Lord of the Thrones of the Two Lands, the Great God, Lord of the Sky" was carefully chiseled out.[31] In some cases, the texts were restored, probably by Seti I, whose name is also found on the temple.[32] Hathor's name was also erased in several instances, but her image was spared.[33] The name of Khnum of Elephantine was violated, but his image beneath the text was untouched.[34] The images of the deities were by and large not disturbed, which is curious, as if attacking

---

[25] Van Dijk, "The Amarna Period and Later New Kingdom," 270.

[26] On the military during the Amarna period, see Emmeline Healey, "Akhenaten and the Armed Forces," (Ph.D. diss., Monash University, 2012), idem., "The Decorative Program of the Amarna Rock Tombs: Unique Scenes of the Egyptian Military and Police," in *Egyptology in Australia and New Zealand 2009* (eds. C. M. Knoblauch & J. C. Gill; Oxford: BAR International Series 2355, 2012).

[27] *Urk*. IV, 1227.10, 15, 17; 1228.12; 1237.17; 1238.8; 1241.4.

[28] *Urk*. IV, 1234.1; 1236.7; 1239.5, 16.

[29] Paul Barguet et al., *Le Temple D'Amada*, Vol. 3, 4 (Cairo: Centre for Documentation, 1967).

[30] Ibid., C 3, F 9, 11–14, G 9–11, H 1–6, 7–9, 12, I 1–4.

[31] Ibid., J 9–10.

[32] Ibid., figs. B 5, 6.

[33] Ibid., C 6, 8, 25, P 11–13.

[34] Ibid., C 27.

the name was sufficient to do the job. This may be due to the fact that in Egyptian thought, one's name was a vital part of one's personhood, and hence to eradicate the name was to damn the person or deity to oblivion.

Egyptologists distinguish between the practice of usurpation (i.e., one king replacing his name over that of an earlier monarch) and what is called *damnatio memoriae* (i.e., damning the memory).[35] In the former, a later king is identifying himself with the early monarch, while in the second type, the motivation is intended to eradicate the memory of an infamous individual. Akhenaten's motives were patently clear, namely to stamp out Amun in particular, as well as other deities, as the following examples illustrate.

The Gebel es-Silseleh quarries north of Aswan, the source for the talatat blocks for the Theban Temples of Akhenaten, are the location of one of Akhenaten's earliest inscriptions.[36] The text reports on the expedition to obtain the great benben-stone for Re-Harakhty-Aten at Karnak (see discussion in Chapter 4). At this early stage, perhaps year 1 or early in 2 at the latest, the image of Amun-Re was included, along with several epithets of that deity and a declaration (*d̠d mdw*) by him. Once the purge against Amun began, this image was hammered out and his name and epithets were removed, including the king's own name, Amenhotep.[37] Even his father's name, Amenhotep III, was not sacrosanct in his own temples, and not even monuments in his funerary temple were spared![38] In the parts of Luxor Temple built by Akhenaten's father, numerous images of Amun were wiped out (see Figure 7.1).

Tremendous efforts to erase Amun can be seen in the obelisks of Hatshepsut at Karnak. Standing 29.56 m (96 feet) tall, these obelisks had the figure of Amun removed from the pyramidion at the top, along with the divine titles. The relief was subsequently re-carved, probably by Seti I at the beginning of the 19th Dynasty (Figure 2.10 in Chapter 2).

The Annals of Thutmose III, which were carved on the walls that surround the Holy of Holies of the Amun-Re temple at Karnak, consistently have Amun's name removed, but the names of other deities (e.g., Montu, Re and Horus) are untouched.[39]

---

[35] Alan Schulman may be the first to use this Latin expression in Egyptology; see "Some Remarks on the Alleged 'Fall' of Senmut," *JARCE* 8 (1970): 29–48. On the distinction between usurpation and *damnatio memoriae*, see Peter Brand, "Usurpation of Monuments," in *UCLA Encyclopedia of Egyptology* (ed. Willeke Wendrich; Los Angeles, 2010), http://digital2.library.ucla.edu/viewItem.do?ark=21198/zz0025h6fh. See also Richard Wilkinson, "Controlled Damage: The Mechanic and Micro-History of the *Damnation Memoriae* Carried Out in KV-23, the Tomb of Ay," *Journal of Egyptian History* 4 (2011): 129–147. I am grateful to Professor Wilkinson for sending me a copy of this article.

[36] Georges Legrain, "Les Stèles d'Aménôthès IV à Zernik et à Gebel Silseleh," *ASAE* 3 (1902): 259–266.

[37] Ibid., 263.

[38] *Urk.* IV, 1657.6, 15; 1658.3; 1687.1; 1685.4; 1701.3, 11, 16; 1702. 8, 16; 1703.6.

[39] For a few examples, see *Urk.* IV, 651–659.

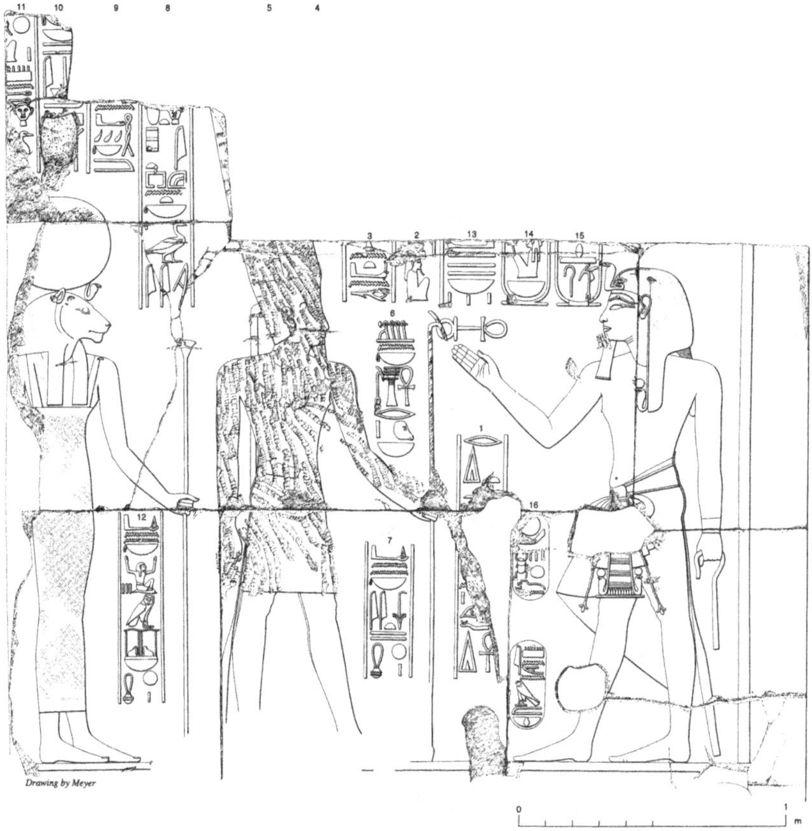

FIGURE 7.1 Defaced image of Amun (Luxor Temple). Epigraphic Survey, *Reliefs and Inscriptions at Luxor Temple*, Vol. 2 (Chicago: The Oriental Institute, 1998), pl. 149.

Amun's name was deleted from the Sphinx Stela of Amenhotep II at Giza, but the names of other deities were not (e.g., Montu, Reshep, Astarte, Horus).

Amun and his various epithets are the focus of the Atenist revenge on monuments everywhere, such as "Amun-Re King of the Gods,"[40] "Amun-Re Foremost of Karnak,"[41] "Amun-Re Lord of the Thrones of the Two Lands,"[42] and "Amun-Re Lord of the Thrones of the Two Lands, Foremost of Karnak."[43]

Even private tombs were not exempt from desecration. The Vizier Ramose's tomb experienced attacks on Amun's name,[44] but when it was written as "Amun-Re," the sun-disc was sometimes preserved.[45] The name of Amun and his titles, such as

[40] *Urk.* IV, 1692.9.

[41] *Urk.* IV, 1684.9.

[42] *Urk.* IV, 1704.13; 1711.17.

[43] *Urk.* IV, 1672.7; 1714.6.

[44] *Urk.* IV,1778.1, 7.

[45] *Urk.* IV, 1779.3; 1780.3. In the case where the epithet "Amun-Re Lord of the Thrones of the Two Lands" occurs, even the disc was erased (*Urk.* IV, 1780.7).

"Amun-Re Lord of the Thrones of the Two Lands," may be obliterated in the tomb of Djeserkare-Senb (no. 38 in the Theban Necoropolis).[46] The tomb of Neb-Amun in western Thebes witnessed the removal of the name of Amun, while preserving the sun-disc (◎),[47] while in other cases "Amun" was even erased from the tomb owner's name. This practice is documented elsewhere in the cases of Amenemopet and Amunnakht.[48] On a stela of the shipbuilder Iunna, there is a list with the names of a dozen ships for which he was the carpenter (*ḥm*).[49] One of Akhenaten's sharp-eyed henchmen noticed that two of the boats included the name Amun, and so the divine name was carved out.[50]

As has already been shown, other deities could be targeted for desecration, but this was applied very inconsistently. Apart from solar deities, whose names seem to be exempted, a number of deities elsewhere experienced Atenism's zealotry. Hathor and Khnum have already been mentioned, and we can add many other gods and goddesses to the list: Amun-Re Ka-Mutef,[51] Montu,[52] and even Mut's name were scratched out in the cartouche of Mutemwia (Akhenaten's grandmother!).[53] Mut was the consort of Amun.

One of the more salient practices of Aten's iconoclasts was the desecration of writings of the plural forms of deity, 𓊹𓊹𓊹 (*nṯrw*), "the gods."[54] In Neb-Amun's tomb in western Thebes, the lines "the gods who are in heaven and earth," along with the "gods who are in the Netherworld," were deleted.[55] In the next line, the name of the god Re was preserved, along with the sun-disc sign (◎), but the seated male anthropomorphic deity sign (𓀭) was scratched out, an action that seems to reflect Atenism's aversion for associating the human form with the deity. It must be recalled that after about year 3 or 4, Aten never is shown in human form.

At Deir el-Bahri in Hatshepsut's mortuary temple, the word 𓊹𓊹𓊹 was periodically erased.[56] Amenhotep III's buildings at Luxor Temple were especially hard hit. Many examples of the defilement of Amun, his title, and the cartouches of Akhenaten's

[46] *Urk.* IV, 1638.1.

[47] *Urk.* IV, 1625.4, 5, 9.

[48] *Urk.* IV, 1604.14, 18.

[49] *Urk.* IV, 1630–1632.

[50] *Urk.* IV, 1631.2; 1632.1.

[51] *Urk.* IV, 1674.17; 1683.5; 1687.25.

[52] *Urk.* IV, 1693.1; 1695.6.

[53] *Urk.* IV, 1715.2.

[54] *Urk.* IV, 1657.7; 1690.2.

[55] *Urk.* IV, 1628.7.

[56] *Urk.* IV, 216.9. Another possible case of iconoclasm is in the writing of *p3wt nṯrw*, the primeval gods (*Urk.* IV, 298.8). Since Amun-Re's name is untouched in the same inscription, this erasure may not be iconoclasm. Without actually examining the inscription, I cannot be sure of the nature of the lacuna.

father have already been cited. The word *nṯrw* was also attacked in the expression "all the gods," but the adjective *nbw* was sometimes spared.[57]

In other cases, such as in the tomb of Ramose, even the adjective *nbw* ("all the gods") was removed.[58] The fact that Ramose's tomb had the name of Amun, his titles, and the plural writing for "gods" hammered out is not surprising since this tomb was being decorated during the final years of Amenhotep III and into the reign of Amenhotep IV, and it is in this tomb that we see an early example of the Amarna style reliefs (see Chapter 3). So the artisans who were executing the Amarna-type scenes may well have been the defilers of Amun and "the gods" in that tomb.

The eradicating of the plural references to deity, some have suggested, was aimed solely at the Theban triad, Amun, Mut and Khonsu.[59] There is, however, no evidence to support this contention, and the fact that the names of other deities were wiped out (as noted earlier) militates against this limited understanding of *nṯrw* and its removal in many instances.

Finally, another interesting case of iconoclasm was directed against the name of Karnak Temple, *ipt swt*. Several examples of this are found at Luxor Temple.[60] The attempt to obliterate the name of Karnak Temple, the domain of Amun-Re, makes sense since Akhenaten was in the process of remaking Thebes as the Domain of Aten (*pr itn*) and the Horizon of Aten (*3ḫt n itn*).

What is the purpose and significance of this nationwide program to wipe out the name and image of Amun and those of other deities? Was this merely an act of revenge, or was it a theological statement? Words and hieroglyphs have magical force and are potent in Egyptian thought.[61] The efforts to expunge the names and images of Amun, those of other deities, and the plural references to "gods" carried with them the idea of magically eradicating that which is erased, damning the name, individual, or deity to oblivion.[62]

It is maintained here that Akhenaten's iconoclasm was making a theological statement that points in the direction of Atenism being monotheistic. Before this matter is addressed further, we need to examine other developments in Atenism that occurred with the move to Amarna.

---

[57] *Urk.* IV, 1695.14; 1696.18; 1699.18.

[58] *Urk.* IV, 1778.12, 19.

[59] Orly Goldwasser, "The Essence of Amarna Monotheism," in *In.t ḏr.w—Festschrift für Friedrich Junge* (eds. Gerald Moers et al.; Göttingen: Seminar für Ägyptologie und Koptologie, 2006), 269–270.

[60] *Urk.* IV, 1684, 9–10; 1697.18; 1698.1; 1699.14.

[61] Richard Wilkinson, *Symbol and Magic in Egyptian Art* (London: Thames & Hudson, 1994), 183.

[62] On magical practices, especially dealing with rendering enemies powerless, see Robert K. Ritner, *The Mechanics of Egyptian Magical Practice* (Chicago: The Oriental Institute, 1993), 113–136.

ATENISM'S FINAL STAGE

The move to the new Akhet-Aten witnessed the final developments of Atenism. The most significant one was yet another change to the didactic name of Aten. At this point, the name had already gone through two steps. First was the didactic name that appears as early as year 1 or early year 2 of Akhenaten: "Re-Harakhty who rejoices in his horizon in his name of light (or Shu) which is in the disc (Aten)" (see Chapter 3). This name was then placed in a pair of cartouches, (Re-Harakhty who rejoices in the horizon) (in his name of light which is in the Aten), perhaps as an outcome of the Sed-festival celebrated likely in regnal year 4 (see Chapter 4). Some time after taking up residence at Amarna, possibly around year 9, additional changes occurred.[63] These changes must signal some sort of evolving theological understanding of the deity.

The new didactic name still appears in a pair of cartouches as before, but now reads (*ʿnḫ rʿ ḥḳ3 3ḫt ḥʿy m 3ḫt*) (*m rn.f m rʿ ỉt ỉỉ m ỉtn*) (see Figure 7.2). Cyril Aldred correctly noted that scholarly differences remain on how to translate this name,[64] largely because variant readings are possible. He offers "Live Re, the Ruler of the Horizon, rejoicing in the Horizon in his aspect of Re the Father who returns

FIGURE 7.2 Final didactic name of Amun on bronze fragment from a door (Neues Museum Berlin). Photo James K. Hoffmeier.

---

[63] For some examples, see Norman de Garis Davies, *The Rock Tombs of El-Amarna* vol. 4 (London: EEF, 1906), pl. xx, xxii, xxvii, xxxi.

[64] Cyril Aldred, *Akhenaten King of Egypt* (London: Thames & Hudson, 1988), 278.

as the sun-god [the Aten]."[65] This translation requires one to read *tỉ* as a metathesized writing for *ỉt* meaning "father."[66] Like Aldred, Erik Hornung tentatively rendered this word "father," but places a "?" after it, reflecting his uncertainty.[67] Many years ago, Gunn recognized that "father" was a frequent appellation for the sun-god in texts at Amarna,[68] and thus would make sense in the new revised name. Redford reads *tỉ* as *ỉt* and translates the name as "Living Re, Ruler of the Horizon, Rejoicing in the Horizon in His Name of Re, the Father, who has come as the Sun-disc."[69] The translation of Reeves is quite similar.[70]

The translation of *ỉỉ* has also been variously rendered. "Return" or "come" are standard, somewhat literal translations. A more idiomatic and appropriate nuance of "come," in the sense of "appearing" or "manifesting," is "Re who is manifested in the Aten."[71]

There is a variant on the didactic name that has no parallels. Discovered early in the 20th century, it reads (*ḥr 3ḫty ḥꜥy m 3ḫt*)(*m rn.f m 3ḫ m ỉtn*),[72] "Harakhty who rejoices in the horizon in his name being glorious (or becoming spirit) in Aten." Noticeably, "Re" is missing at the beginning of the name, which is attested elsewhere, but the addition of *3ḫ* is peculiar. Alternatively, Alessandro Bongioanni considers the possibility that this version of the name was a transitional compromise between the first and second names.[73] This is an interesting suggestion that would garner more support if another example or two of this version were attested. Since this is the only documented case of this variant,[74] one wonders if this writing represents a scribal error, a conflation of Aten and Akhenaten's names.

---

[65] Ibid., 278.

[66] For writings, see Maj Sandman, *Texts from the Time of Akhenaten* (Brussels: Queen Elizabeth Foundation of Egyptology, 1938), 162.10, 14; 163.5, 15, 20; 164.15; 165.5, 20.

[67] Erik Hornung, *Akhenaten and the Religion of Light*, trans. D. Lorton (Ithaca, NY: Cornell University Press, 1999), 76.

[68] Battiscombe Gunn, "Notes on the Aten and His Names," *JEA* 9 (1923): 175–176.

[69] Redford, *Akhenaten: The Heretic King*, 186.

[70] Nicholas Reeves, *Akhenaten: Egypt's False Prophet* (London: Thames and Hudson, 2001), 116.

[71] A rather different understanding of this epithet is advanced by Alessandro Bongioanni ("Considerations sur les 'nomes' d'Aten et la nature du rapport souverain-divinite a l'epoque amarnienne," *GM* 68 [1983]: 46–47), who thinks that ⊙ in the second cartouche should not be read as Re, but a writing for *šwtỉ*, followed by *ỉỉ m ỉtn*, and he translates this line as "la manifestation visible de l'esprit divin qui arrive en tant qu'Aten." This rather expansive definition of *šwty* is questionable, and it fails to explain why is never written, only ⊙. He does point to variant writings where *3ḫ* replaces what he reads as *šwtỉ ỉỉ* as semantically related. This is not a particularly convincing explanation, although he may be on the right track in thinking that this phrase has to do with the idea of how the manifestation of the deity occurs.

[72] Sandman, *Texts from the Time of Akhenaten*, 162, § CLXXXII.

[73] Bongioanni, "Considerations sur les 'nomes' d'Aten et la nature du rapport souverain-divinite a l'epoque amarnienne," 47.

[74] Based on a survey of Sandman's *Texts from the Time of Akhenaten*.

The most striking feature of the revised didactic name is that the names of "Harakhty" and "Shu" were stripped out,[75] a deletion that was meant to remove any doubt that Aten is connected to these gods. The homonymous word *šw*, Jan Assmann notes, means that "light" but could be read as the god Shu, and now this understanding was unacceptable.[76] (On the meanings of "shu" and the depiction of Shu on an early block form Karnak, see Chapter 3 and Figure 3.9). Despite the strong solar and Heliopolitan associations that Re-Harakhty had, only Re—the generic term for the sun—remains. Redford has framed this final step in the refinement of Atenism that is reflected not only in the final form of the name, but also in the elimination of many solar symbols in the art, observing, "Gone was Re-Harakhty the falcon, the *ḫprr*-beetle, the Ennead with Atum at its head, *Bḥdty* the winged sun-disc, the solar boat, the *Himmelsfahrt*, Apophis, myth and its use in magic, and a host of other mechanisms and images, read as referential icons."[77] These factors suggest to Redford that even classic Heliopolitan images suffered in this final expression of his Aten theology. This final form of the name also seems to signify that the sun-disc alone is God, and the energy, light, and rays that emanate from the disc are ways in which this deity manifested himself (see further in Chapter 8).

WHAT IS MONOTHEISM?

That question seems easy enough. Monotheism is the worship of one deity, but so is henotheism or monolatry.[78] "Henotheism" was a term coined in the 19th century by Friedrich Schelling and F. Max Müller to describe a faith community that worships a single deity, which coexists with other gods and goddesses; nor is the worshiper of that one divinity intolerant toward other deities. Some have called this "rudimentary monotheism."[79] On the other hand, monotheism has an exclusive dimension to it: "there is no God but God," as the Muslim "Shahada," or confession, declares. The "oneness" of God is also a central tenet of monotheism,[80] and is echoed in the

[75] Redford, *Akhenaten: The Heretic King*, 186. Aldred, *Akhenaten King of Egypt*, 19–20.

[76] Jan Assmann, *The Search for God in Ancient Egypt* (Ithaca, NY: Cornell University Press, 2001), 210.

[77] Donald Redford, "Akhenaten: New Theories and Old Facts," *BASOR* 369 (2013): 27.

[78] Originally these terms had different nuances, but in recent literature tend to be used interchangeably, especially by Biblical and Near Eastern scholars not familiar with History of Religions methods and definitions; see Michiko Yusa, "Henotheism," in *The Encyclopedia of Religion*, 2nd edition (ed. L. Jones; Detroit: Macmillan, 2005), 3913.

[79] Ibid., 3913.

[80] Theodore Ludwig, "Monotheism," in *The Encyclopedia of Religion*, 2nd edition (ed. L. Jones; Detroit: Macmillan, 2005), 6155.

ancient Israel's "Shema"—"Hear, O Israel: The LORD our God, the LORD is one" (Deut. 6:4;[81] see Chapter 8).

Egyptologists who have specialized in Amarna religion differ on how to interpret Atenism. While in recent years there has been a tendency to consider Akhenaten's religion to be monotheistic, there have been those who reject this interpretation of the data.[82] In his highly respected book, *Egyptian Religion*, Siegfried Morenz maintained: "It is quite clear that, even in his early radical phase, Amenophis IV was in no sense an advocate of simple monotheism. On the contrary, what he proposed was precisely a Trinitarian formula."[83] Morenz's idea of Akhenaten's Trinitarianism is that it consists, as the didactic name suggests, of Re-Harakhty, Shu, and Aten, with Akhenaten being their son. Written originally in 1960, Morenz seems to ignore the fact that Re-Harakhty and Shu were removed from the didactic name after the move to Amarna (see previous section). The data now seem to suggest that Atenism became more radical and intolerant as it developed during the first decade of Akhenaten's reign, and not the other way around as Morenz implied.

More recently, Nicholas Reeves has taken the nature of Atenism in a slightly different direction, opining that "Akhenaten's much-vaunted worship of a single god was nothing of the sort; it was ancestor-worship writ large, emphasizing the divine power of kingship with a will and determination not demonstrated since the days of the pyramids."[84] Although Reeves opts for a shorter co-regency, he nevertheless accepts Raymond Johnson's theory of the divinized Amenhotep III becoming the "Dazzling Aten" and Akhenaten's god.[85] This book has argued against this connection, especially in the light of the total absence of Amenhotep III in the Sed-festival of Akhenaten depicted in the *Gm(t) p3 ỉtn* Temple at Karnak (see Chapter 4).

Then, too, there are those who have noticed that Akhenaten, along with Nefertiti, whose prominence in cultic activities is on par with the king, and Aten form a triad, a holy family of sorts with which Egyptians were already familiar.[86] Hornung spoke

---

[81] While many scholars maintain that the Shema is a monotheistic affirmation, Nathan McDonald in a recent monograph has attempted to argue against this understanding (in this author's opinion, unsuccessfully); see Nathan MacDonald, *Deuteronomy and the Meaning of "Monotheism"* (Forschungen zum Alten Testament, 2. Reihe, 1; Tübingen: Mohr Siebeck, 2003). MacDonald's position is extreme in rejecting monotheistic affirmations in Deuteronomy.

[82] Edwin Yamauchi offers a recent survey of scholars who hold that Akhenaten was a monotheist, as well as those who believe he was not; see "Akhenaten, Moses, and Monotheism," *Near East Archaeological Society Bulletin* 55 (2010): 1–15.

[83] Siegfried Morenz, *Egyptian Religion*, trans. Ann Keep (Ithaca, NY: Cornell University Press, 1973), 147.

[84] Reeves, *Akhenaten: Egypt's False Prophet*, 118.

[85] Ibid., 71–73.

[86] John Foster, "The New Religion," in *Pharaohs of the Sun: Akhenaten, Nefertiti, Tutankhamun* (eds. R. Freed et al.; Boston: Museum of Fine Arts, 1999), 107. John Wilson thought in terms of "two gods," Akhenaten and his family and Aten (*The Culture of Egypt* [Chicago: University of Chicago Press, 1951], 223), but that could be easily reconfigured as Akhenaten, Nefertiti, and Aten.

of "a divine trinity" made up of Akhenaten, Nefertiti, and Aten.[87] At Karnak the family threesome (father, mother, and son) of Amun, Mut, and Khonsu was well known, as were Ptah, Sekhmet, and Nefertum at Memphis; then there was perhaps the best-known triad of Osiris, Isis, and Horus.[88] This is, obviously, a different kind of trinity than what Morenz understood. Nevertheless, these views about Akhenaten's religion indicate that not all accept Atenism to be monotheistic.

Obviously, one must look at all relevant data and recognize that in the course of the first decade of Akhenaten's reign, Atenism went through several critical phases, which may only be called "monotheism" in the final years at Thebes and with the move to Amarna. We return to William Murnane's three phases of Akhenaten's religion, namely (1) the coexistence between Aten and Amun and other deities, marked by neglect; (2) subsequent abandonment (Amun's name dropped from the king's cartouche and the desertion of Thebes); and (3) persecution, which involved the aggressive program to destroy Amun and the gods by erasing their names, defacing their statues and various images, and closing temples.[89]

This third phase, it might be suggested, is the sure sign of monotheism. The recent studies on monotheism by Assmann have been helpful in this regard.[90] All Near Eastern religious traditions emphasize the role of the creator god in the origins of the cosmos, and invariably, it is the creator god who is the head of the pantheon. Assmann observes that "the primacy of the one god over all other gods is grounded in creatorship" and that "this highest god, who alone is uncreated, is called kheper-djesef (literally, 'who originated by himself')."[91] What this epithet reveals is that in Egypt it was impossible to conceive of even the creator god as being eternal.

Often creation myths of the ancient Near East contain theogony, that is, a mythic explanation for the origin of the creator god, the first deity. Typically in monotheism, theogony is absent, as God is eternal. The Hebrew creation story, for example, promptly begins with "in the beginning God created the heavens and earth" (Gen. 1:1), assuming the existence of the deity and offering no theogony. Similarly in Islam,

---

[87] Hornung, *Akhenaten and the Religion of Light*, 57.

[88] Erik Hornung, *Conceptions of God in Ancient Egypt*, trans. John Baines (Ithaca, NY: Cornell University Press, 1982), 217–218.

[89] William Murnane, "Observations on Pre-Amarna Theology during the Earliest Reign of Amenhotep IV," in *Gold of Praise: Studies on Ancient Egypt in Honor of Edward F. Wente* (eds. E. Teeter & J. Larson; Chicago: Oriental Institute, 1999), 303–316.

[90] Jan Assmann, *Re und Amun: Die Krise des polythestischen Weltbilds im Ägypten der 18.–20. Dynastie* [OBO 51; Fribourg: Universitätsverlag, 1983] = *Egyptian Solar Religion in the New Kingdom: Re, Amun and the Crisis of Polytheism*, trans. A. Alcock (London/New York: Kegan Paul International, 1995); idem, *Moses the Egyptian: The Memory of Egypt in Western* Monotheism (Cambridge, MA: Harvard University Press, 1997); idem, *Of God and Gods: Egypt, Israel, and the Rise of Monotheism* (Madison: University of Wisconsin Press, 2008).

[91] Assmann, *Of God and Gods*, 61.

there is no theogony in the Qur'an. It will be suggested later (see Chapter 8) that the expression "self-created," which was initially applied to any creator gods, became a monotheistic claim when used in reference to Aten.

A second characteristic of monotheism for Assmann is a tendency toward violence and iconoclasm: "monotheistic violence, conversely, is directed against paganism—typically against the 'pagan within'—and not against political enemies."[92] The persecution of Amun and the gods of Egypt is a classic illustration of this violent feature, a point acknowledged by Assmann: "The iconoclastic actions of Akhenaten, who closed the Egyptian temples, smashed the cult-images, erased the names of the gods—especially Amun—consequently [have] to be classified [not][93] as internal but extrasystemic because they were directed against the traditional polytheism of Egypt."[94]

To these considerations, other points can be added. Sixty years ago, Louis Zabkar noticed that divine determinatives were not used to write the name of Aten, nor is he ever called a god (*nṯr*).[95] More recently, Orly Goldwasser has further investigated the writings of *ỉtn*, pointing out that the standard determinatives or classifiers normally attached to the names of deities (𓀭, 𓊹 and 𓅆) are not used in writings of Aten.[96] This omission represents a significant departure from the tradition for writing the name of a deity, and therefore must be signifying something different about Aten. Goldwasser offers an obvious yet brilliant explanation for this orthographic peculiarity unique to the Amarna period:

> I would like to suggest that the thinking of Amarna religion deliberately [does] not add a [GOD] classifier after the word Aten, because their revolutionary doctrine has actually cancelled the options for a "category of gods." Putting any [GOD] classifier after the combination *ỉtn* would mean that the Aten is the chosen one, but still *one among the many*. It would still be an "example of," or one option of the superordinate [GOD]—just like the good old gods of the earlier times.[97]

She goes on to note that even the use of 𓊹 in connection with Aten is particularly unexpected, since this hieroglyph is the most ancient sign for "god" and is devoid of

[92] Ibid., 29.

[93] There seems to be a printing error in this sentence. Because of the disjunctive used after the word "internal" it logically follows that the sentence requires a negative before "internal." This omission was confirmed by email from Jan Assmann (10/2/2013) after I wrote to inquire.

[94] Ibid., 31.

[95] Louis Zabkar, "The Theocracy of Amarna and the Doctrine of the Ba," *JNES* 13 (1954): 87–101.

[96] Goldwasser, "The Essence of Amarna Monotheism," 267–279.

[97] Ibid., 275.

any anthropomorphic or zoomorphic associations that were so offensive to Atenism. Since the earliest texts of Akhenaten used 𓊹 and 𓀭 signs, for example the Prisse d'Avennes drawing (Figure 3.9), the omission in later texts demonstrates that a significant theological shift had occurred. Strengthening this point, she shows that the deity sign (𓀭) occurs in writings of Aten during Amenhotep III's reign before Akhenaten and after him during Horemheb's kingship.[98] The exclusion of these signs during Akhenaten's reign, Goldwasser proposes, represents "a conscious organized effort, which aimed at the canceling of the possible existence of 'other examples' of 'other gods'—by canceling the very options of a category."[99] The writing of Aten without divine markers leads Goldwasser to conclude that Amarna theology approached "mature monotheism"—associated with the Jewish faith from the 6th century B.C. onward.[100]

CONCLUDING THOUGHTS

What has been suggested here and in previous chapters is that Akhenaten's religion went through several stages of development. It began with some sort of theophany (very early in the king's reign, or even possibly while still a young prince) and the development of the first didactic name. The royal announcement from the 10th Pylon blocks seem to advance the idea that something had gone wrong with the current religious order and the gods themselves (see Chapter 5, section "The Death of the Gods"). The Sed-festival of Amenhotep IV and Aten resulted in the establishment of Aten as king (his names appear in cartouches) and the change of his name (perhaps at the same time or shortly thereafter), in which "Amun" was dropped from his name. The search for and discovery of the new holy city for Aten, Akhet-Aten, marked the abandonment of Amun's realm, which seems to closely coincide with the iconoclasm against Amun, other deities and the "gods" (see Chapter 6). When these factors are tallied and we consider the fact that Akhenaten and the royal family are only ever shown adoring and making offerings to Aten, this certainly looks like monotheism. There is yet another corpus of material to consider that permits one to plumb the depths of Atenism, and that is the Aten Hymns from the tombs of Akhenaten's officials at Amarna. These might be considered a monotheistic manifesto, the subject of the next chapter.

---

[98] Ibid., 276.

[99] Ibid., 276.

[100] Ibid., 276. Goldwasser evidently adheres to the view of many Hebrew Bible scholars that monotheism is an exilic development in the Jewish community.

The Great Hymn to the Aten is an eloquent and beautiful statement of the doctrine of the one god.

MIRIAM LICHTHEIM[1]

Chapter 8

The Hymns to Aten

A Monotheistic Manifesto

THE HYMNS TO the Aten carved on the walls of private tombs at Amarna are widely hailed for their poetic beauty and their theological profundity. The so-called Great Hymn, recorded in the tomb of Ay,[2] is the longest of the poems. There are five witnesses to the "Shorter Hymn" and a host of even shorter hymns and prayers in the same tomb group.[3] It is the longer "Great Hymn" that has attracted the most attention. "Of all the monuments left by this unparalleled revolution," James Henry Breasted considered the hymns to Aten to be "by far the most remarkable."[4] In the view of Ronald J. Williams, "the great Hymn to Aten is a major document of the new faith as well as a fine example of the Egyptian poetic genius."[5] The late John Foster, a brilliant specialist in Egyptian literature and poetry in particular, probably offered the most effusive praise of the Great Hymn, believing it is "one of the most remarkable documents in all of ancient Egyptian history—and, indeed, in all of the ancient world."[6]

---

1 Miriam Lichtheim, *Ancient Egyptian Literature* II (Berkeley: University of California Press, 1976), 89.

2 Transcriptions of the text are available in Norman de Garis Davies, *The Rock Tombs of El-Amarna*, vol. 4 (London: EEF, 1906), pl. XXVII; Maj Sandman, *Texts from the Time of Akhenaten* (Brussels: Queen Elizabeth Foundation of Egyptology, 1938), 93–96.

3 Sandman, *Texts from the Time of Akhenaten*, 10–15.

4 James Henry Breasted, *A History of Egypt* (London: Hodder & Stoughton, 1921), 371.

5 Ronald J. Williams, "The Hymn to Aten," in *Documents from Old Testament Times* (ed. D. W. Thomas; New York: Harper & Row Publishers, 1958), 145.

6 John L. Foster, "The Hymn to Aten: Akhenaten Worships the Sole God," *Civilizations of the Ancient Near East* III (ed. J. Sasson; New York: Charles Schribner, 1995), 1754.

Norman de Garis Davies, the great epigrapher of the Amarna tombs, thought that the shorter hymns and prayers were "culled from the Royal Hymn (i.e. the 'Great Hymn') or echoing its thoughts."[7] The latter suggestion makes sense since it appears that Akhenaten himself was either the composer or the mind behind it that a scribe transformed it into the poem. In line 12 of the Hymn, Akhenaten appears to be the speaker, directing his words to Aten: "you are in my heart, there is no other who knows you except your son, Neferkheperure waen-Re"—*iw.k m ib.i wn.k ky rḫ tw wpw-ḥr s.k* (*nfr ḫprw rʿ wʿ n rʿ*)|.[8] Then, too, some think that Akhenaten may be the actual speaker of the entire hymn based on the use of "he says" (*ḏd.f*) as the Hymn begins (line 2). After introducing the recipient of the adoration (*dw3*) to be Aten (in the early didactic form), the names of Akhenaten and Nefertiti follow (all in line 1). Line 2 begins with "he says" (*ḏd.f*). The only masculine antecedents are either the Aten or the king, and given that Aten is the focus of the Hymn, the king must be the speaker. Based on this factor, William Murnane believed that Akhenaten by default is the speaker.[9] Miriam Lichtheim, however, thought that the Hymn was composed by the king to be recited by the tomb owner, hence Ay is the subject of the verb *ḏd*.[10]

The point may be a moot one because the king clearly had a hand in the composition of the hymns(s), that is, the words may originally have been those of the king, but in the context of the tomb, it was the courtier who was offering the words as his poem of praise. That the Hymn was from the mind or pen of the king is further implied within the Hymn itself. Indeed, Ay does use the word *sb3yt*, "teaching" or "instruction"[11] of the king in texts from his tomb. In a prayer Ay introduces himself as "God's father, the Vizier and Fanbearer on the right of the King" who "brought him up" (*sḫpr.n.f*) or instructed him.[12] Based on such a claim, it may be, as Erik Hornung has suggested, that Ay was an influential teacher, a "guru of the young reformer."[13] A few lines later in the text in Ay's tomb, the picture reverses itself; now Akhenaten is the

---

7 Davies, *The Rock Tombs of El-Amarna*, vol. 4, 26.

8 Sandman, *Texts from the Time of Akhenaten*, 95.16.

9 William Murnane, *Texts from the Amarna Period in Egypt* (Atlanta: Scholars Press, 1995), 200 n. 7.

10 Lichtheim, *Ancient Egyptian Literature* II, 100, n. 1. Kenneth Kitchen also believes that the tomb owner, Ay, is the speaker, even adding Ay's name and titles into his translation, although they are written below the text of the Hymn and are technically not a part of the Hymn (*Poetry of Ancient Egypt* [Josered, Sweden: Paul Åstroms Förlag, 1999], 251). It may be a logical inference to think Ay is speaking, but his name is not actually in the text of the Hymn.

11 *Wb* 4, 85–86. For a more detailed study of *sb3yt*, see Nili Shupak, *Where Can Wisdom Be Found? The Sages Language in the Bible and in Ancient Egyptian Literature* (OBO 120; Fribourg: University of Fribourg Press, 1993), 31–34.

12 *Sḫpr* is frequently rendered "fostered" (Murnane, *Texts from the Amarna Period in Egypt*, 111; Lichtheim, *Ancient Egyptian Literature* II, 94), but could also mean "bring up" and "educate" (Raymond Faulkner, *A Concise Dictionary of Middle Egyptian* [Oxford: Oxford University Press, 1962], 240).

13 Erik Hornung, *Akhenaten and the Religion of Light*, trans. D. Lorton (Ithaca, NY: Cornell University Press, 1999), 60.

teacher and Ay the disciple: "I practiced my lord's teaching (*nb.ỉ iry.ỉ sb3yt.f*), I live in the praise of his Ka."[14] Later in the same prayer, Ay again speaks of the king's teaching: "How fortunate is the one who hears your teaching of life" (*w3ḏ.wy p3 sḏm sb3yt.k n ꜥnḫ*).[15] This line echoes the sentiments found in other didactic or wisdom literature.[16]

There is wide agreement that the Amarna hymns, especially the "Great Hymn," sought to communicate the theological dogma of the religious revolution,[17] likely through liturgical use in the cult. One concurs with Lichtheim, who declared: "The doctrine of the Aten as taught by the king was undoubtedly recorded in many writings. But it has survived in only two forms: in the statements of the king on the boundary stela, and in the hymns and prayers inscribed in the tombs of the courtiers."[18]

Building on Lichtheim's understanding of these written sources, and combining that with the interpretation of the early proclamation on the first three boundary stelae offered previously (see Chapter 5), it seems that the Amarna proclamation was a sort of "Declaration of Independence" from Amun and Thebes as it lays the theological foundation for the new religion and its requisite Holy See. The hymns, on the other hand, served as the liturgical and didactic constitution designed to advance the theology of Atenism through its dogma.

THE DATE OF THE ATEN HYMNS

The diachronic study of the first decade of Akhenaten's reign revealed dramatic changes in the new religion, including innovations in iconography and alterations to the didactic name of the Aten, which reflected his evolving theological thought (see Chapters 3–7). While there is a tendency to think of the Aten hymns as reflecting the zenith of Akhenaten's theological development, Atenism's ultimate expression, there is reason to suppose that they may actually date to the period before the final phase of Atenism that occurred in the king's ninth year (see Chapter 7). Of the five versions of the Short Aten Hymn, those in the tombs of Apy and Tutu use the pre-year 9 form of the didactic name,[19] whereas in the texts in the tombs of Any, Meryre, and Mahu the later didactic name occurs: (Living Re, Ruler of the Horizon, Rejoicing in the Horizon)(in His Name of "Re," the Father, who has come [or appears] as the

[14] Sandman, *Texts from the Time of Akhenaten*, 92.2–3.

[15] Ibid., 92.8.

[16] In Amenemope, see Chapter 1, ll. 9–11 (Lichtheim, *Ancient Egyptian Literature* II, 149) and in the Hebrew Bible, see Proverbs 22:17–18.

[17] To cite only a few sources, see John Wilson, *The Culture of Egypt* (Chicago: University of Chicago Press, 1951), 222–229; Vincent A. Tobin, "Amarna and Biblical Religion," in *Pharaonic Egypt, the Bible and Christianity* (ed. S. Israelit-Groll; Jerusalem: The Hebrew University, 1985), 234. Lichtheim, *Ancient Egyptian Literature* II, 89.

[18] Lichtheim, *Ancient Egyptian Literature* II, 90.

[19] Ibid., 10.13, 17.

Sun-disc). In the Tomb of Ay the writings of the early didactic name in cartouches is used in the Great Hymn and in the other prayers and paeans.[20]

The use of the early form of the didactic name points to a composition date prior to the final change to the name. It stands to reason that the tombs of senior officials like Ay, Apy, and Tutu began work on their tombs almost immediately upon settling at Akhet-Aten. Tombs completed a few years later (after year 9) employed the final form of the Aten's name, but the hymns show no other signs of later insertions or redactions that reflect the ultimate theological stance.

There is another element in the Short Hymns that may point to a composition date for the songs. The cultic nature of the hymns are evident from lines 10–11: "Singing, chanting and joyful shouting are in the open court of the Mansion of the Benben (*Ḥwt bnbn*) and in every temple in Akhet-Aten . . . food and offerings are presented within it."[21] No doubt the hymns under discussion here and others like them were chanted in the Aten temples as offerings were made. The presentation of offerings is the most prominent theme on the scenes from Karnak and Amarna.[22] The writing of the temple *Ḥwt bnbn* employs the obelisk or *bnbn*-stone signifier (𓉶), as it is written in the name of the same temple at Karnak (see Chapter 4, § section "The Names of the Aten Temples Revealed").

The temple *Ḥwt bnbn* at Akhet-Aten apparently may not have included a *bnbn*-stone within the sanctuary despite the name. Thirty years ago, Redford called attention to the fact that there seemed to have been a change in the shape of the *bnbn* in *Ḥwt bnbn* at Akhet-Aten.[23] The archaeologists who worked in the "Great Temple," a descriptive name used by 20th-century investigators for *Pr itn* (House of Domain of Aten) and *Ḥwt bnbn*, have found no trace of an obelisk or even foundation stones for one within the temple, even though its name would suggest one was present like its earlier counterpart at Karnak.[24] Despite the name, which is typically written with the 𓉶 sign, there is surprisingly no corresponding depiction of a *bnbn*-stone in the temple reliefs of *Ḥwt bnbn*. Barry Kemp has recently pointed out that "none of the pictures carved in the tombs at Amarna show an obelisk, even though some of them include detailed renderings of Aten temples."[25] He points to an example where *Ḥwt bnbn* is

[20] Ibid., 90.15; 93.9.

[21] Sandman, *Texts from the Time of Akhenaten*, 13.9–14.4.

[22] For a discussion of the various types of offerings, see Cathie Speiser, *Offrandes et purification à l'époque amarnienne* (Turnhout, Belgium: Brepols, 2010).

[23] Donald Redford, Akhenaten: the Heretic King (Princeton, NJ: Princeton University Press, 1984), 72.

[24] Barry Kemp, *The City of Akhenaten and Nefertiti: Amarna and Its People* (London: Thames & Hudson, 2012), 82–83.

[25] Ibid., 82–83.

written with the stela determinative (), suggesting that one should not expect an exact correspondence between writing, the reliefs, and what is discovered archaeologically.[26]

This observation may be true in some cases, but there is another possible, tantalizing explanation for the absence of the Heliopolitian solar symbol in the Amarna temple. While it is true that many writings of *Ḥwt bnbn* in inscriptions at Amarna use the expected  sign (especially the multiple occurrences in the Short Hymn), there are some other noteworthy variants. The tomb of Tutu has three different writings. First there is an occurrence where *bnbn* with the house sign () is determinative, and in a different inscription no indicator is used at all.[27] The third occurrence of *bnbn* is in the Short Hymn in the very passage quoted above, which refers to the cultic activities in the open court of *Ḥwt bnbn*. In this instance the *bnbn*  sign was included.[28] A careful examination of Davis's edition of the text of the Short Hymn in Tutu's tomb, however, shows that the vertical  sign was carefully scratched out, leaving just the surrounding hieroglyphs . This erasure was also noted in Sandman's edition of the Short Hymn in Tutu's tomb.[29] It is as if some literate and astute observer (Tutu himself?) saw the text and had the obelisk-sign removed to reflect the reality of architecture of this temple. The example in Tutu's tomb is not an isolated one. Another case of erasing the obelisk is also found in the tomb of Panehsy, where one can clearly see the careful and intentional elimination of the vertical *bnbn* sign.[30]

In view of the lack of archaeological evidence for an obelisk in *Ḥwt bnbn* temple at Amarna—not even so much as a foundation or platform for one has been found,[31] and no indication of the sacred solar emblem in the scenes of the temples in the decorated tombs of Akhet-Aten—could it be that either the temple never had a *bnbn*-stone or, perhaps more likely, that it was removed after the year 9 purge of the last vestiges of other deities, including their names, images, and emblems? Once again, Redford's earlier quoted statement describing the aftermath of the final phase of Atenism is especially germane here: "Gone was Re-Harakhty the falcon, the *ḫprr*-beetle, the Ennead with Atum at its head, *Bḥdty* the winged sun-disc, the solar boat, the *Himmelsfahrt*, Apophis, myth and its use in magic, and a host of other mechanisms and images, read as referential icons."[32] Perhaps just as

---

[26] Ibid., 83.

[27] Davies, *The Rock Tombs of El-Amarna* vol. 6 (London: EEF, 1906), pl. XIV, S. ceiling inscription & XV, left jamb, l. 3.

[28] Ibid., pl. XVI, l. 10.

[29] Sandman, *Texts from the Time of Akhenaten*, 13.16.

[30] Davies, *The Rock Tombs of El-Amarna*, vol. 2 (London: EEF, 1905) pl. xxi, left-most vertical column.

[31] Kemp, *The City of Akhenaten and Nefertiti*, 82.

[32] Donald Redford, "Akhenaten: New Theories and Old Facts," *BASOR* 369 (2013): 27.

these other traditional solar icons had to go, so did the *bnbn*-stone even while the name *Ḥwt bnbn* was retained.

The point of the foregoing lengthy treatment of the variant writings of *Ḥwt bnbn* is to propose that the writings that include 𓉵 may simply reflect the orthography of the name that was standardized during the years at Thebes (or the earliest years at Amarna) when the hymn was written. This theory, when combined with the use of the early form of the didactic name written in cartouches, might indicate that the Great Hymn and the shorter hymns were composed near the end of the stay in Thebes or early in the Amarna sojourn. This may mean that these doctrinal confessions do not reflect the post–year 9 era when Atenism had attained its final form. The Aten hymns, nevertheless, contain the most profound theological statements that have survived. One wonders what the Great Hymn would have looked like had it been composed in the final year or two of Akhenaten's reign? Even if we allow that the Great Hymn and the shorter ones may not completely reflect the final form of Atenism, they remain the primary sources to access the nuances of Akhenaten's theology.

TRANSLATIONS OF THE ATEN HYMNS

Thirty years ago, in a valuable study of Amarna theology, Vincent Tobin lamented that he found existing English translations of the Great Aten Hymns to be "unsatisfactory," so he offered his own rendition.[33] True enough, in 1984 available translations tended to use more archaic (King James-ish) language. These classical translations include those of Breasted,[34] John Wilson,[35] Ronald Williams,[36] and William Kelly Simpson.[37] An English edition of the same hymn by Miriam Lichtheim, published in 1976, remains an excellent translation (Tobin's disclaimer notwithstanding) in the view of the writer and many other scholars. In fact, it was recently reprinted in 1997 in a new anthology of texts, *The Context of Scripture*.[38]

In addition to Tobin's and Licthheim's translations, there are now available many more recent wonderful English translations of the shorter hymns and the Great Hymn.

[33] Tobin, "Amarna and Biblical Religion," 234–237.

[34] Breasted, *A History of Egypt*, 371–376.

[35] John Wilson, "The Hymn to the Aton," in *Ancient Near Eastern Literature Relating to the Old Testament* 3rd ed. (ed. J.B. Pritchard; Princeton, NJ: Princeton University Press, 1969), 369–371.

[36] Williams, "The Hymn to Aten," 142–148.

[37] William Kelly Simpson, "The Hymns to the Aten," in *The Literature of Ancient Egypt: An Anthology of Stories, Instructions, and Poetry* (eds. R. O. Faulkner et al.; New Haven: Yale University Press, 1973), 289–295.

[38] Miriam Lichtheim, "The Great Hymn to the Aten," in *The Context of Scripture* Vol. I (eds. W. W. Hallo & K. L. Younger; Leiden: Brill, 1997), 44–46.

John Foster provided a rather free rendering of the Great Hymn in 1992,[39] which in turn was reprinted with comments in the very useful four-volume *Civilizations of the Ancient Near East.*[40] Foster produced yet another, less idiomatic translation in his *Hymns, Prayers, and Songs* in the SBL Writings from the Ancient World Series in 1995.[41] Also in the same year and in the same series is William Murnane's *Texts from the Amarna Period in Egypt*, which includes his translations of the shorter and longer hymns.[42] A translation of the Great Hymn was also included in a lesser known anthology of poetic texts by Kenneth Kitchen that was published in Sweden in 1999.[43] One advantage of Kitchen's edition is that a transliteration of the Egyptian text is available on the opposite page of the translation.

In order to see the translations of the abridged and long versions together, Murnane's translations are offered here with a transliteration of key terms.

The Short Hymn:

> Adoration of **Heka-Aten**,[44] . . . You appear (*ḫꜥꜥ*) beautifully (*nfrw*), O living **Aten** (*itn ꜥnḫ*), lord of eternity dazzling (*tḫn*), fair, powerful. The love (*mrw*) of you is great and extensive. Your rays (*stwt*) reach the eyes of all you created (*ḳmꜣ*), and your bright hue revives (*sꜥnḫ*) all hearts when you have filled the Two Lands with love (*mrw*) of you, O august god who constructed himself by himself (*ḳd sw ḏs.f*)—maker (*iri*) of every land, creator (*ḳmꜣ*) of what is on it: namely, people, all sorts of long- and short-horned cattle, all trees and what grows on the ground—they live (*ꜥnḫ*) when you rise (*wbn*) for them.
>
> You are the mother and father of all you make (*irr*). When you rise (*wbn*), their eyes see by means of you. When your rays (*stwt*) have illuminated (*ḥḏ*) the entire land, all heart(s) rejoice at seeing you manifest (*ḫꜥi*) as their lord. When you set in the western horizon of heaven, they repose in the fashion of those who are dead, heads covered, noses obstructed, until the occurrence of your rising (*wbn*) at dawn from the eastern horizon of heaven, their arms are in adoration of your Ka: when you have revived (*sꜥnḫ*) all hearts with your beauty (*nfrw*), one lives (*ꜥnḫ*); and when you give forth your rays (*stwt*), every land is in festival. Singing, chanting and joyful shouting are in the courtyard

[39] John L. Foster, *Echoes of Egyptian Voices: An Anthology of Ancient Egyptian Poetry* (Norman: University of Oklahoma Press, 1992), 5–10.

[40] John L. Foster, "The Hymn to Aten: Akhenaten Worships the Sole God," in 1751–1761.

[41] John L. Foster, *Hymns, Prayers, and Songs: An Anthology of Ancient Egyptian Lyric Poetry*, SBL Writings from the Ancient World Series (Atlanta: Scholars Press, 1995), 102–107.

[42] Murnane, *Texts from the Amarna Period in Egypt*, 112–116 (Great Hymn) and 157–158 (Shorter Hymn).

[43] Kitchen, *Poetry of Ancient Egypt*, 249–260.

[44] Abbreviated writing of the later didactic name of Aten.

of the Mansion of the Benben (*Ḥwt Bnbn*), in the place of truth in which you have become content. Food and provisions lie within it, while your son is pure in doing what you praise.

O **Aten** (*itn*), who lives (*ʿnḫ*) in his appearances (*ḫʿyw*)! All that you make is dancing in front of you, and as for your august son, his heart exults with joy. O living (*ʿnḫ*) **Aten,** who is born in the sky daily, that he might give birth (*msy*) to his august son, Waenre, just like himself, without ceasing—the son of Re who raises up his beauty, Neferkheperure-waenre.

I am your son, who is effective for you and raises up your name.

Your might and your power are established in your hear. You are the living (*ʿnḫ*) **Aten**: continuity is your image, for you made the distant (*w3t*) sky in order to rise (*wbn*) in it and see all you make (*iry*)—while you are one (*iw.k wʿ.ti*), but with millions of lives (*ʿnḫ*) in you, in order to make them live (*ʿnḫ*). The breath of life (*ʿnḫ*) penetrates into noses when your rays (*stwt*) are seen. All sorts of flowers are continually alive (*ʿnḫ*), growing on the ground and made to flourish, because of your rising (*wbn*): they grow drunk at the sight of you, while all sorts of cattle are prancing on their legs. Birds which were in the nest are aloft in joy, their wings which were folded are spread in adoration to the living (*ʿnḫ*) **Aten**, the one who makes (*irr*) them all . . ."[45]

Now a translation of the Great Hymn in the tomb of Ay:

Adoration of **Hor-Aten** (early didactic name in cartouches)

Beautiful you appear (*ḫʿy*) from the horizon of heaven, O living **Aten** who initiates life (*ʿnḫ*)—for you are risen (*wbn*) from the eastern horizon and have filled every land with your beauty (*nfrw*); for you are fair, great, dazzling (*tḫn*) and high over (*k3.ti*) every land,
And your rays (*stwt*) enclose the lands to the limit of all you have made (*irt*);
For you are Re, having reached their limit and subdued them your beloved son;
For although you are far away (*w3*), your rays (*stwt*) are upon the earth and you are perceived.

When your movements vanish and you set in the western horizon,
The land is in darkness, in the manner of death.

[45] Murnane, *Texts from the Amarna Period in Egypt*, 158–159.

(People), they lie in bedchambers, heads covered up, and one eye does not see its fellow.
All their property is robbed, although it is under their heads, and they do not realize it.
Every lion is out of its den, all creeping things bite.
Darkness gathers, the land is silent.
The one who made them is set in his horizon.
(But) the land grows bright (*ḥḏ*) when you are risen (*wbn*) from the horizon,
Shining (*psd*) in the **orb** (*itn*) in the daytime, you push back the darkness and give forth your rays (*stwt*).
The Two Lands are in festival of light[46]—
Awake and standing on legs, for you have lifted them up:
Their limbs are cleansed and wearing clothes,
Their arms are in adoration at your appearing (*ḫꜥꜥ*).
The whole land, they do their work:
All flocks are content with their pasturage, trees and grasses flourish,
Birds are flown from their nests, their wings adoring your Ka;
All small cattle prance upon their legs.
All that fly up and alight, they live (*ꜥnḫ*) when you rise (*wbn*) for them.
Ships go downstream, and upstream as well, every road being open at your appearance.
Fish upon the river lead up in front of you, and your rays (*stwt*) are within the Great Green (sea).

(O you) who brings into being foetuses in women, who make fluid in people.
Who gives life (*sꜥnḫ*) to the son in his mother's womb, and calms him by stopping his tears;
Nurse in the womb, who gives breath to animate (*sꜥnḫ*) all he makes (*iri*)
When it descends from the womb to breathe on the day it is born (*msw*)—
You open his mouth completely and make (*iri*) what he needs.
When the chick is in the egg, speaking in the shell,
You give him breath within it to cause him to live (*sꜥnḫ*);
And when you have made (*iri*) his appointed time for him, so that he may break himself out of the egg, he comes out of the egg to speak at his appointed time and goes on his two legs when he comes out of it.

[46] Only the sign 𓇶 is written, which normally serves as a determinative associated with the rising and shining sun, so the exact word remains uncertain.

How manifold it is, what you have made (*iry*), although mysterious in the face (of humanity),
O sole god (*p3 nṯr wꜥ*), without another beside him (*nn ky ḥr///f*)!
You create (*ḳm3*) the earth according to your wish, being alone (*iw.k wꜥ*)—
People, all large and small animals, all things which are on earth, which go on legs, which rise up and fly by means of their wings,
The foreign countries of Kharu and Kush, (and) the land of Egypt.
You make the inundation from the underworld, and you bring it to (the place) you wish in order to cause the subjects to live (*sꜥnḫ*),
In as much as you made (*iri*) them for yourself, their lord entirely,
who is wearied with them,
The lord of every land, who rises (*wbn*) for them, the **orb** (*itn*) of daytime, whose awesomeness is great! (As for) all distant countries, you make their life (*ꜥnḫ*):
You have granted an inundation in heaven, that it might come down for them
And make (*iry*) torrents upon the mountains, like the Great Green, to soak their fields in their locale(s).

How functional are your plans, O lord of continuity!
An inundation in heaven, which is for the foreigners (and) for all foreign flocks which go on legs; (and) an inundation when it comes from the underworld for the Tilled Land (= Egypt), while your rays (*stwt*) nurse every field:
When you rise (*wbn*), they live (*ꜥnḫ*) and flourish for you.
You make (*iri*) the season in order to develop (*sḫpr*) all you make (*iri*):
The Growing season to cool them, and heat so that they might feel you.

You made (*iri*) heaven far away (*w3.ti*) just to rise (*wbn*) in it, to see all you make,
Being unique (*wꜥ.ti*) and risen (*wbn*) in your aspects of being as "living (*ꜥnḫ*) **Aten**" – manifest (*ḫꜥi*), shining (*psd*), far (yet) near (*w3.ti ḫn.ti*).
You make millions of developments from yourself, (you who are) a oneness (*wꜥy*): cities, towns, fields, the path of the river.
Every eye observes you in relation to them, for you are **Aten** of the daytime above the earth (?).You have travelled just so that everybody might exist.
You create (*ḳm3*) their faces so that you might not see [your]self [as] the only (thing) which you make (*irt*).[47]

---

[47] Murnane, *Texts from the Amarna Period in Egypt*, 113–115.

THE THEOLOGY OF THE ATEN HYMNS

Since the early 20th century, scholars who have studied the Great Hymn have proposed that it was arranged by thematic units. Because their lengths vary, the units do not correspond to the eleven vertical lines of texts.[48] Breasted, for instance, isolated 12 themes: (1) The Splendor of Aten, (2) Night, (3) Day and Man, (4) Day and the Animals and Plants, (5) Day and the Waters, (6) Creation of Man, (7) Creation of Animals, (8) The Whole Creation, (9) Watering the Earth, (10) The Seasons, (11) Beauty Due to Light, and (12) Revelation.[49] Foster also identified 12 parts.[50] More recent translators of the text divided the Hymn into different sections, such as Lichtheim, who has eight parts,[51] while Kitchen divided the hymn into just six sections.[52] Kitchen identifies the themes as follows: Sections 1 and 2 focus on sunrise and sunset, the brilliance and light of Aten by day and the death by night. Section 3 concentrates on sunrise and the way creation responds to it, while section 4 is dominated by Aten's role as the creator of humans and animals. The fifth section has a universal emphasis; Aten's care is for all humanity, regardless of race or region. The sixth and final part deals with how Aten rules the seasons of the year.[53]

Foster offers an interesting theological analysis of the Great Hymn, identifying the attributes of this God following categories familiar in Systematic (Christian) Theology. The characteristics he deduces from the text are: (1) God is one, (2) God is alone, (3) God is the creator of the universe, (4) God is Alpha and Omega, the span of Time, (5) God is Universal, (6) God is love, (7) God is light, (8) God is beauty, (9) God is father, and (10) God is within.[54]

The various studies of the Great Hymn, from Breasted's down to the recent ones of Kitchen and Foster, all have merit and offer valuable insights into the themes and theology promoted within text itself. What is offered here is a more linguistic-based analysis that seeks to identify major themes through the terminology used and frequency of occurrence within the hymns. This approach will reveal that certain words are used in more than one "section," suggesting that a micro-analysis is best suited to uncover the theological agenda of Atenism. It stands to reason that the use and distribution of words and expressions offer rhetorical keys to understanding the

---

[48] Davies, *The Rock Tombs of El-Amarna*, vol. 6, XXVII.

[49] Breasted, *A History of Egypt*, 371–376.

[50] Foster, "The Hymn to Aten," 1751–1753.

[51] Lichtheim, *Ancient Egyptian Literature* II, 96–99.

[52] Kitchen, *Poetry of Ancient Egypt*, 250–260.

[53] Ibid., 260.

[54] Foster, "The Hymn to Aten: Akhenaten Worships the Sole God," 1755–1758.

author's intent in writing a piece of literature.[55] What were these hymns seeking to teach, communicate, and emphasize? What attributes and actions of the deity are stressed? To answer these questions, frequently occurring adjectives and verbs will be examined. Though some terms do not occur frequently, they fit into the semantic range of other terms that are repeated and therefore are significant to consider together (e.g., words for creation).

First of all, the word or name Aten occurs six times each in the short and long versions,[56] respectively, with each paean preceded by an introduction that begins with the didactic name, various epithets, and an announcement that Akhenaten and Nefertiti are the celebrants. Clearly Aten is the subject of the hymns. The most frequently occurring attribute of the Aten found in the hymns is the word "live" (*ꜥnḫ*) and the causative form (*sꜥnḫ*), meaning to make live or revive, which is closely connected to the idea of creation. He is the "living Aten," a widely used epithet found in tomb and temple inscription alike. Cleary the "living Aten" makes things live, brings things to life (*sꜥnḫ*). *Sꜥnḫ* occurs four times in the Great Hymn and three times in the shorter versions, while *ꜥnḫ* occurs 11 times in the short hymn and four in the long one. Why the shorter edition has so many more occurrences of *ꜥnḫ* than its longer counterpart is surprising, but when combined (*ꜥnḫ* + *sꜥnḫ*) the total number in the two hymns is 22. Therefore, the word *ꜥnḫ* (with its causative form *sꜥnḫ*) is the most dominant word in the hymns. The conclusion is inescapable: Aten is the living and life-giving deity, and this is the central doctrine of Amarna theology to judge from frequency of terminology. This should be not unexpected since *ꜥnḫ* (☥) is the first word-sign written in the early and later didactic names of Aten, which clearly signals the priority of this characteristic.

Speaking of creation of animal life, the shorter hymn concludes by addressing the deity as "the living Aten, the one who makes (*irr*) them all." It is the living Aten who creates life; in this instance the verb *iri* is used.[57] The word *iri* is widely used as a synonym for "create." Ten occurrences are found in the great hymn and three in the shorter form, 13 in all, making it the second most dominant verb in the corpus. The Short Hymn describes Aten as the "august god who constructed himself (*ḳd sw ḏs.f*)—maker (*iri*) of every land, creator (*ḳmꜣ*) of what is on it."[58] Here three

---

[55] Such approaches are now being successfully used in prose literature in biblical studies, but equally apply to poetry. For a recent example with references, see Robert Bergen, "Word Distribution as Indicator of Authorial Intention: A Study of Genesis 1:1–2:3," in *Do Historical Matters Matter to Faith* (eds. J. Hoffmeier & D. Magary; Wheaton: Crossway, 2012), 201–218.

[56] With reference to the occurrences in the five short versions, a term may occur in all editions, but only one is counted in the totals given in this analysis.

[57] *Irr* is the writing for the imperfective active participle. This form is used to stress that this is ongoing or repeated action.

[58] Murnane, *Texts from the Amarna Period in Egypt*, 158.

terms for "create" (*ḳd*, *iri*, & *ḳm3*) appear together, demonstrating that they are synonymous. While Murnane renders *ḳd* as "constructed," an appropriate meaning in architectural contexts, a more fitting sense in this context is "form;" *ḳd* is associated with the activity of the potter who fashions or creates vessels.[59] Lichtheim's rendering, "August God who fashioned himself,"[60] better captures the essence of this important concept, which will be explored in more detail in the following section.

The verb *ḳd* is followed by the reflexive pronoun *sw* and is made emphatic with the addition of the element *ḏs.f*,[61] which most literally means he "gives birth to himself (by) himself," or perhaps more idiomatically it might be rendered "gives birth to his very self." This same emphatic reflexive form occurs elsewhere, including with an alternative expression from another text in the tomb of Ay that describes the "living Aten" as one "who gives birth to his very self everyday" (*ms sw ḏs.f rʿ nb*).[62]

Msi, the normal word used for women giving birth, also means "shape" or "form."[63] It occurs once in each version of the hymns. The Short Hymn uses all four words for a total of eight occurrences (*iri* = 4x, *ḳm3* = 2x, *ḳd* = 1x, *msi* = 1x), while the Great Hymn twice uses *msi*, once alongside *ḳm3* (which occurs twice), and then there are the 10 instances of *iri*, for a total of 14 "creation" terms. Together the two poetic units employ four different words in the semantic range for creation for a total of 22 occurrences. The rich vocabulary associated with creation and the large number of occurrences highlight the importance of this theological precept in Amarna theology.

The doctrine of creation naturally lends itself to universalist ideas, which scholars as early as Breasted recognized. It is worth noting that there is a close connection between creation, the creator acting alone, and the broader world. The Great Hymn in line 9 declares:

> You create (*ḳm3*) the earth according to your wish, being alone (*iw.k wʿ*)—
> People, all large and small animals, all things which are on earth, which go on legs, which rise up and fly by means of their wings,
> The **foreign countries of Kharu and Kush**, (and) the land of Egypt . . .
> **The lord of every land**, who rises (*wbn*) for them, the orb (*itn*) of daytime, whose awesomeness is great! (As for) **all distant countries**, you make (*ir*) their life (*ʿnḫ*).[64]

[59] *Wb* 5, 78–80.

[60] Lichtheim, *Ancient Egyptian Literature* II, 91.

[61] Alan Gardiner, *Egyptian Grammar* (London: Oxford University Press, 1969), §35.

[62] Sandman, *Texts from the Time of Akhenaten*, 89.4.

[63] *Wb* 2, 137.

[64] Murnane, *Texts from the Amarna Period in Egypt*, 114.

In imperial Egypt it would be unthinkable to consider "wretched" (*ḫs*) Kharu (Syria/Canaan) and Kush (Nubia), a favorite way of referring to Egypt's foreign neighbors,[65] as equal to Egypt. If one, however, holds to a single creator deity, as Akhenaten affirmed, then it stands to reason that the sole creator not only made Egypt, but also distant lands and peoples everywhere the sun rose and set. Aten was indeed "lord of every land." It was suggested in Chapter 1 ("When the Sun Ruled Egypt") that solar religion by its very nature had latent universalist propensities because wherever Egyptian kings moved their armies or sent trade missions, be it north to Hatti (Anatolia) or Mitanni (northern Mesopotamia), or south to Nubia or even distant Punt (somewhere in the Djibouti-Somalia region?), the same sun was present. It was universal.

The third major theme that emerges from this word-based analysis of the hymns is the expected attributes of the sun and how it manifests itself. Here, too, there is a robust vocabulary. Both hymns begin with "you appear," the verb being *ḫꜥi*, which also means "rise" and "shine,"[66] and also "appear in glory."[67] In the hymns, a verbal form *ḫꜥi* is used consistently, occurring three times in each. Semantically related to *ḫꜥi* is the term *wbn*, which also can be rendered "rise" and "shine,"[68] and is found seven times in the long hymn and five times in the short version. Closely related are other words for shine, bright, and dazzle: *tḥn* and *ḥḏ* (once each in both hymns), and *psd* (twice in the Great Hymn). The various references to the sun appearing or shining in the horizon (*ꜣḫt*) and dispelling darkness (*kkw*) suggest the possibility that these hymns were used at dawn when the sun reveals itself, and brings light and life to all creation. The importance of the horizon is not just that the sun appears there first each day, but, as James Allen points out, it is where the gods are born in the Pyramid Texts.[69]

The rising Aten shoots forth his rays, an iconic image in temple and tomb art of the period. *Stwt*, the word for the sun's rays, is found among the Karnak talatat to describe the spindly arms (rays) of the Aten.[70] This word occurs frequently in the Aten hymns: four occurrences in the short and five in the long versions. Combining

---

65 For a brief discussion of this concept, see Stuart T. Smith, *Wretched Kush* (London/New York: Routledge, 2003), 1–3.

66 *Wb* 3, 239.

67 Faulkner, *A Concise Dictionary of Middle Egyptian*, 185–186. Orly Goldwasser, "The Aten Is the 'Energy of Light': New Evidence from the Script," *JARCE* 46 (2010): 161–162.

68 Wb 1, 292–293.

69 James Allen, "The Cosmology of the Pyramid Texts," in *Religion and Philosophy in Ancient Egypt* (ed. W. K. Simpson; New Haven, CT: Yale Egyptological Studies 3, 1989), 17.

70 Edmund Meltzer, "Glossary of Amenophis IV-Akhenaten's Karnak Talatat," in *The Akhenaten Temple Project*, Vol. 2 (ed. D. B. Redford; Toronto: Akhenaten Temple Project/University of Toronto Press, 1988), 107.

these terms about the sun's manifestations, there are a total of 33 occurrences of these terms.

In a recent analysis of these terms, Orly Goldwasser has shown that all these words are dominated by the same classifier sign, namely a variation of the sun-disc with extending rays ().[71] A new hieroglyph was established in Akhenaten's day that sometimes replaces the earlier sign associated  that was used with words like *wbn*, *stwt*, and *ḫʿi*. It is a miniature version of the iconography of the Aten, a disc whose rays terminate with hands (), and was designed to accommodate the thought behind this word. She concludes that this sign, with the disc and rays, was intended to show the commonality of these words, and that shared aspect was "the energy of light."[72] One germane observation that Goldwasser makes is that never is this sign used as a determinative for Aten, which, she maintains, demonstrates that Aten was not merely the sun-disc.[73] Aten, rather, is the source of light and power by which he reveals something of his character to his creation on earth.

This daily reappearing of Aten, shining and extending his rays, is what causes plants to grow and animals and humans to spring to life and adore the sun, a motif found in both hymns. This image is dramatically portrayed in a badly damaged relief in Akhenaten's tomb. The king and queen are depicted in the center of the scene within the temple, adoring Aten as he rises over the mountain on the eastern horizon on the left side of the tableau, and immediately below the sun within the mountainous area, fowl flap their wings and animals prance, just as the hymns describe (Figure 8.1).[74]

Obviously, the fact that Aten manifests himself daily in the sun's journey from eastern to western horizons was a re-enactment of the primeval theophany that occurred at creation (and in some way is connected to the theophany experienced by the king). This is why Mircea Eliade maintained that to the religious individual "every event, simply by happening, by taking place in time, is a hierophany, a 'revelation.'"[75]

The fourth major dogma of the Amarna hymns is theologically the most novel, namely the monotheistic nature of Aten. Because of the influence of the modern, scientific view of the world, most people today consider the rising sun to be simply a recurring rotation of the earth, a phenomenon of nature. The Amarna hymns give

---

[71] Goldwasser, "The Aten Is the 'Energy of Light': New Evidence from the Script," 159–165.

[72] Ibid., 162–164.

[73] Ibid., 164.

[74] Geoffrey Martin, *The Royal Tomb at El-Amarna, Part 2, the Reliefs, Inscriptions and Architecture* (London: EES, 1989), pl. 34.

[75] Mircea Eliade, *Patterns in Comparative Religion* (New York: Meridian, 1958), 396.

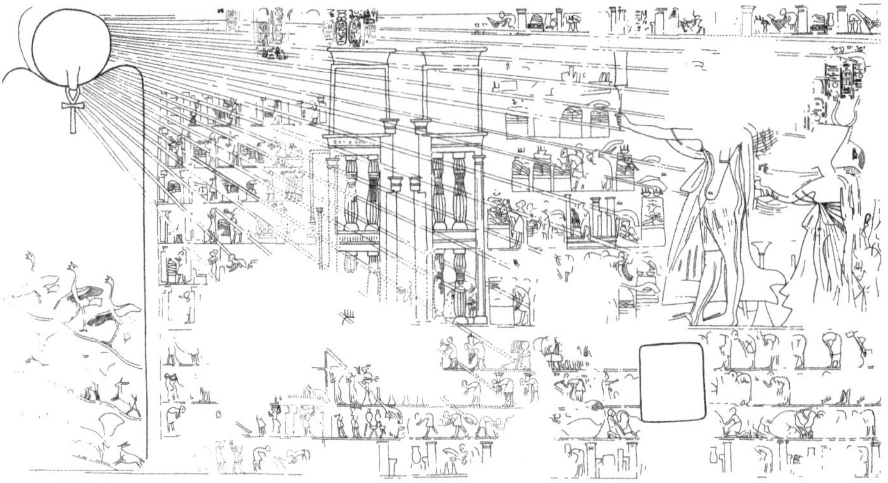

FIGURE 8.1 Sun rising over Akhetaten, with animals responding to its rays and temple to the right with Akhenaten and Nefertititi adoring Aten. Geoffrey T. Martin, *The Royal Tomb at el-Amarna* (London: Egypt Exploration Society), pl. 34.

the impression that the rising sun was much more than that. It was, in fact, a manifestation of God, the creator. It was a daily theophany: something to be celebrated, a moment for worship. The sun appears **alone** in the sky. This visual reality is possibly behind the claims in the hymns to the oneness of the Aten. The shorter hymn declares: "You are the living (*ʿnḫ*) Aten . . . for you made the distant (*w3t*) sky in order to rise (*wbn*) in it and see all you make (*iry*)—while you are one (*iw.k wʿ.ti*)." Here *wʿ* is a stative verb, that is, Aten is in the state or condition of being one or alone.[76] Lichtheim clearly sees this as a monotheistic claim, capitalizing "one"—"you are One."[77] Four times *wʿ* occurs in the hymn in the tomb of Ay. The first two are found in the same couplet:

> O sole god (*p3 nṯr wʿ*), without another beside him (*nn ky ḥr///f*)!
> You create (*ḳm3*) the earth according to your wish, being alone (*iw.k wʿ*)

In the first instance *wʿ* is an attribute of god Aten, "one" instead of many, coupled with the clause that there is no one beside him, is a monotheistic claim. The second relevant passage in the Great Hymn reads:

> Being unique (*wʿ.ti*) and risen (*wbn*) in your aspects of being as "living (*ʿnḫ*) Aten"—manifest (*ḫʿi*), shining (*psd*), far (yet) near (*w3.ti ẖn.ti*).

---

[76] James Hoch, *Middle Egyptian Grammar* (Mississauga: Benben Publications, 1997), §82.
[77] Lichtheim, *Ancient Egyptian Literature* II, 92.

You make millions of developments from yourself, (you who are) a oneness (*wꜥy*).

In both of these passages, *wꜥ* is in the stative form, signifying Aten as "being" one or alone. Both of these claims of "oneness" or acting "alone" occur in the broader context of creation. Thus Aten is in the state of "oneness"; as creator this was not achieved in collaboration with other deities or personified forces of nature.

While the claim of deity being "one" or "alone" is attested as early as the Old Kingdom in Egypt (see next section), and by itself is not likely a monotheistic claim in the 3rd Millennium, whereas with Akhenaten in the 14th century, the focus is monotheistic. Erik Hornung argues this point: "Not until the radical change in thought under Akhenaten does the epithet 'unique' (*wꜥ*) acquire the meaning with which we are familiar; the truly unique God Aten does not tolerate the existence of gods other than himself."[78] Jan Assmann believes that the claims found in this hymn show that Akhenaten was the "first to formulate the principle of exclusive monotheism."[79] It is this "exclusive" element, with its iconoclastic zeal (see Chapter 7) that separates monotheism from henotheism. Louis Zabkar's earlier treatment of Amarna religion likewise recognized this factor, opining that this epithet ("Sole God, without another beside him"), while applied to other deities (e.g., Amun-Re, Harakhty), "the Amarna zealots expressed the idea of the exclusive nature of their god in a more categorical way: Aton is 'the living Aton beside whom there is no other.'"[80]

The confession in the Great Hymn that Aten is "without another except him" (*nn ky wpw-ḥr* [//].*f*)[81] also occurs in a third even shorter hymn to the "living Aten," found in three different Amarna tombs (Ay, Maryre, and Huya).[82] It reads, "Living Aten, there is no other except him" (*nn ky wpw-ḥr.f*).[83]

This exclusionary clause presages the affirmations of the 8th century Hebrew prophet Hosea who declared:

> But I am the LORD your God from the land of Egypt;you know **no God but me**, and **besides me there is no savior** (Hos. 12:4).

---

[78] Erik Hornung, *Conception of God in Ancient Egypt: The One and the Many* (Ithaca, NY: Cornell University Press, 1982), 186.

[79] Jan Assmann, *Of God and Gods: Egypt, Israel, and the Rise of Monotheism* (Madison: University of Wisconsin Press, 2008), 81.

[80] Louis Zabkar, "The Theocracy of Amarna and the Doctrine of the Ba," *JNES* 13 (1954): 93.

[81] The writer's translation.

[82] Sandman, *Texts from the Time of Akhenaten*, 6–9.

[83] Ibid., 7.7.

The same perspective is expressed in the prophecy of Isaiah:

> For thus says the LORD,
> who created the heavens
> (he is God!),
> who formed the earth and made it
> (he established it;
> he did not create it empty,
> he formed it to be inhabited!):
> "I am the LORD, and **there is no other**." (Isa. 45:18)
>
> Who told this long ago?
> Who declared it of old?
> Was it not I, the LORD?
> And **there is no other god besides me**,
> a righteous God and a Savior;
> **there is none besides me** (Isa. 45: 21–22).[84]

The Amarna hymns, like the later Hebrew prophets, could affirm the creed "there is no god but God." Both accomplish this view by denying the existence of other deities.

The fifth and final major doctrine embedded in the Amarna hymns is the transcendence and imminence of Aten. According to the Great Hymn, he is "high (*ḳ3*) over every land."[85] The concept of being high or distant is further addressed by use of the word *w3*, meaning "distant" or "far away."[86] Twice in the Great Hymn *w3* is used to advance this idea: "For although you are far away (*w3*), your rays (*stwt*) are upon the earth and you are perceived," and "You made (*iri*) heaven far away (*w3.ti*) just to rise (*wbn*) in it, to see all you make." So although Aten is distant in the sky, when he rises or shines (*wbn*) he is visible, and principally, his rays (*stwt*) are the primary vehicle of revelation, a concept also endorsed in the shorter hymns: "Your rays (*stwt*) reach the eyes of all you created (*ḳm3*)." This belief is actualized in the ubiquitous

[84] The weight of biblical scholarship considers Isa. 39–66 to be the work of an anonymous exilic prophet (6th century) and not from the pen of Isaiah of Jerusalem in the 8th century. Hence the passage quoted here, according to the prevailing view, reflects the full maturation of monotheistic thought in Israel. Here is not the place to critique the majority view, but not to the theological sophistication of Deutero-Isaiah and its monotheistic view as the reason for this late dating, I maintain, is ill-founded. Hosea is 8th century in date and uses similar language to what is found in Isa. 45.

[85] Ibid., 93.14.

[86] *Wb* I, 245–246.

usage of the Aten's rays in virtually every scene at Thebes and Amarna; it illustrated the imminence of this transcendent God.

Based on the assumption that frequently occurring terms in the corpus (provided in the two renowned poetic Aten hymns) offer clues to the major doctrines of Amarna theology, the analysis presented here suggests that five major doctrines emerge (this is not to say that other themes are not present): (1) Aten is the living and life-giving deity; (2) Aten is the universal creator, maker of heaven and earth, all lands, rivers, seas, people, animals and vegetation; (3) Aten manifests his power daily from sunrise to sunset through the visible disc and its rays; (4) Aten alone is God, there is no other; and (5) Aten is transcendent and yet immanent, he is high and distant, yet accessible, and reaches out to nourish and sustain creation in all its forms.

The short and Great versions of the Aten hymns reveal some common themes and vocabulary; however, the two contain different terminology and emphasis (as the foregoing analysis shows). The differences make it difficult to believe that the short hymn is merely an abridged version of the longer hymn or that the Great Hymn is an expansion of the shorter hymn. Rather they appear to be two different paeans that share common solar themes, while differences in vocabulary and frequency of occurrences of key terms (e.g., *ꜥnḫ* occurs 11 times in the Short Hymn and only 4 times in the Great Hymn; 10 occurrences of *iri* in the Great Hymn and only 4 in short hymn), suggest that the two Aten hymns were separate compositions.

ANTECEDENTS TO THE HYMN TO ATEN

The readers familiar with Egyptian literature will recognize that some of the central ideas expressed in the Amarna hymns are not novel. While the hymns convey a new theological perspective and further develop monotheistic principles, they employ the traditional language associated with solar or Heliopolitan theology. Even de Garis Davies, when he published the Amarna hymns in 1903, called attention to certain elements that would have been known prior to Akhenaten's time and were associated with traditional solar worship, and noted "the hymns and prayers to the Aten do not contain a great deal that is unique."[87]

Since de Garis Davies made these observations there has been intense study of other solar hymns, especially early (pre-Akhenaten) Theban recensions.[88] Solar language used in

---

[87] Norman de Garis Davies, *The Rock Tombs of El-Amarna* vol. 1 (London: EEF, 1903), 46.

[88] T. George Allen, "Some Egyptian Sun Hymns," *JNES* 8(1949): 349–355; H. M. Stewart, "Some Pre-'Amarnah Sun-Hymns," *JEA* 46(1960): 83–90; idem, "Traditional Egyptian Sun Hymns of the New Kingdom," *Bulletin of the Institute of Archaeology* 6 (1966): 29–74. Jan Assmann, *Ägyptische Hymnen und Gebete* (Zürich: Artemis, 1975); idem, *Egyptian Solar Religion in the New Kingdom: Re, Amun, and the Crisis of Polytheism* (London: Kegan Paul International, 1995).

the Pyramid Texts of the Old Kingdom is also found in the Amarna hymns, as will be shown below. And Amarna thought has been detected in Coffin Texts in passages like Spell 255, as observed by Gertrud Thausing,[89] David Lorton,[90] and others. H. M. Stewart[91] observed that sun-hymns enjoyed a rising popularity in the 18th Dynasty, and that the universalist dogma of the Amarna hymns can be seen in Pap. Boulaq 17 from the time of Amenhotep II,[92] as well as in the hymns on the Suty and Hor stela from the time of Amenhotep III.[93] Let us now investigate some of the antecedent themes or motifs and language that are found in the Amarna hymns.

Autogenesis

The expression in the Short Hymn that Aten created himself—"august god who formed himself" (*ḳd sw ḏs.f*)—has already been introduced. In Egyptian cosmogonic thought, a number of deities are credited with creating the cosmos. These include Ptah, Amun, and Re/Atum.[94] The creator gods used various methods and material to complete their task. When it came to explaining the origin of the creator god, theogony, the texts never claim that the creator god always existed. The concept of a deity being eternal, that is, not having a beginning or end, was apparently incomprehensible to the ancient Egyptian priests and clergy. Their solution was to explain that the creator god somehow created or formed himself.

In PT §§1040 the king who identified with the sun-god is described as existing (*ḫpr*) before the other gods: "I was born (*msi*) in the Abyss before the sky existed (*ḫpr*), before the earth existed (*ḫpr*), . . . I am one of this great company who was born aforetime in On."[95] Alternatively, the sun-god is saluted as self-created in PT §1587: "Hail to you, Atum. Hail to you, [Khoprer] the Self-created."[96] In this spell, Atum/Khoperer "brought himself into being," or "shaped" or "formed himself" (*ḫpr ḏs.f*).

---

[89] Gertrud Thausing, "Amarna-Gedanken in Einem Sargtext," in *Festschrift für Prof. Dr. Viktor Christian Gewidmet von Kollegen un Schülern zum 70. Geburtstag* (ed. Kurt Shubert; Vienna: Notring der Wissenschaftlichen Verbände Österreichs, 1956), 108–110.

[90] David Lorton, "God's Beneficent Creation: Coffin Texts Spell 1130, the Instructions for Merikare, and the Great Hymn to the Aton," *SÄK* 20 (1993): 125–155.

[91] Stewart, "Some Pre-'amarnah Sun-Hymns," 84–85.

[92] For a recent translation of this hymn, see Foster, *Hymns, Prayers, and Songs: An Anthology of Ancient Egyptian Lyric Poetry*, 56–65.

[93] Texts in *Urk.* I, 1943–1947. See translations, see Lichtheim, *Ancient Egyptian Literature II*, 86–98. Murnane, *Texts from the Amarna Period in Egypt*, 27–28.

[94] For a useful review of these various deities and the modes of creation, see Siegfried Mornz, *Egyptian Religion* (Ithaca, NY: Cornell University Press, 1973), 159–182.

[95] R. O. Faulkner, *The Ancient Egyptian Pyramid Texts* (Oxford: Clarendon Press, 1969), 173.

[96] Ibid., 238.

The Coffin Texts carry on the tradition of the self-created sun-god from the earlier Pyramid Texts. For instance, CT Spell 335 reads: "I was Re in his first appearance (*ḫꜥw tpw*) when he rises (*wbn*) in the horizon. I am the great one who created himself" (*ḫpr ḏs.f*).[97] The deceased is transformed into "the soul of Shu, the self-created god" in CT Spell 75, and then this epithet occurs five more times in the same spell.[98] Khopri, a manifestation of the sun-god, is also "self-created" (*ḫpr ḏs.f*),[99] an obvious wordplay on his name. Alternatively, the word *ḳd* (as in Short Hymn), coupled with the reflexive pronouns *sw ḏs.f*, is found in early Coffin Text Spell 601, "I am Re-Atum who formed himself by himself"—*ink rꜥ-itm ḳd sw ḏs.f.*[100]

The doctrine of self-creation continues in the New Kingdom. Amun-Re is described as one "who bore himself" (*ms sw*) on an early 18th Dynasty stela.[101] An interesting variation of this autogenesis language occurs in the hymn to the sun-god on the Suty and Hor stela that dates to the reign of Amenhotep III, only a decade or two before the Amarna age.[102] Re/Khopri is described as "one who fashioned yourself, shaping your own body, one who was born without being born"—*ptḥ tw, nbi.k ḥꜥw.k, mss iwty ms.tw.f.*[103] This translation is somewhat literal, while Lichtheim's translation of this last line captures the sense more idiomatically: "Creator uncreated."[104] There is an unmistakable pun on the name of the craftsman-creator god Ptah, used perhaps in a polemical way to elevate the sun-god above the Memphite creator god. Kitchen renders this line as "A Ptah are you, you mould your own body, a fashioner (of others), (but) not himself fashioned."[105] By using the verb *ms*(*i*), the metaphor for birth is in view, normally understood to mean fathered by a male and borne by a mother. But with the sun-god, he was self-generated.

A second hymn on the Suty and Hor Stela praises "Aten of day" and the same expression is applied. He is the "Beetle who raised himself. He created himself without being born" (*ḫprr sṯs sw ḏs.f, ḫpr ḏs.f iwty ms.tw.f*).[106]

It appears that the Aten theologians (or Akhenaten himself) comprehended theogony in same manner as did earlier solar theology from the Old Kingdom, and the Aten hymns were heirs to the same terminology and thought. Heliopolitan

---

97 My translation based on the texts in Adriaan de Buck, *The Egyptian Coffin Texts* IV (Chicago: University of Chicago Press, 1951), 185–189.

98 Rami Van der Molen, *A Hieroglyphic Dictionary of the Egyptian Coffin Texts* (Leiden: Brill, 2000), 382–383.

99 Adriaan de Buck, *The Egyptian Coffin Texts* V (Chicago: University of Chicago Press, 1957), 175d.

100 Adriaan de Buck, *The Egyptian Coffin Texts* VI (Chicago: University of Chicago Press, 1959), 216h.

101 Stewart, "Traditional Egyptian Sun Hymns of the New Kingdom," 63.

102 *Urk.* IV, 1944. 1–2.

103 *Urk.* IV, 1944. 1–2.

104 Lichtheim, *Ancient Egyptian Literature II*, 87.

105 Kitchen, *Poetry of Ancient Egypt*, 243.

106 *Urk.* IV, 1945–1946.

influence in the formation of early Atenist theology is uncontested (as we have shown), although there appears to have been an estrangement between Heliopolis and Amarna after Akhenaten's year 9, as noted in the previous chapter.

There is also a close connection between a deity being self-created and the idea of being "one" or "alone" (discussed in the next section), as seen in Coffin Text Spell 335: "I was alone (*wnn.i wꜥ.kwi*). I was Re in his first appearance (*ḫꜥw tpw*) when he rises (*wbn*) in the horizon. I am the great one who created himself" (*ḫpr ḏs.f*).[107]

The language of self-creation was originated with the sun-god in the Old Kingdom and it continued into the New Kingdom. It had to do with the creator god originating on his own, hence "alone" or "one" (*wꜥ*), without the aid of another deity. It is easy to see how this concept is pregnant with monotheistic potential.

The Epithet wꜥ

It has been argued above that this epithet is a monotheistic claim in Amarna thought. *Wꜥ*, however, is also associated with the sun-god in the Pyramid Texts a thousand years earlier. It is attributed of Re in PT §853: "Hail to you, unique one (*wꜥ*) who endures every day."[108] The resurrected king, who is identified with the sun-god, is called *nṯr ꜥ3 wꜥ.ti*, "great god, who is one (or unique)"[109] in PT §§1616c.[110] The implication in the Pyramid Texts may be that when Re-Atum created himself, he was alone, but then created other deities, and hence was the Creator. Put another way, the creator sun-god in the Old Kingdom and later was the first in a sequential sense, not the exclusive or only divinity.

The epithet *wꜥ*, both as an adjective and a verb, is also applied to the sun-god in the Coffin Texts. Just above, a portion of CT 355 was partially quoted. The whole line says "I am Re, I was alone (or one) (*wnn.i wꜥ.kwi*), I was Re in his first appearance (*ḫꜥw tpw*) when he rises (*wbn*) in the horizon. I am the great one who created himself" (*ḫpr ḏs.f*).[111] The moon too stands alone in the sky at night, and hence is "the One who shines (*psd*) and rises (*wbn*) as the moon."[112] In this spell the idea of self-creation and *wꜥ* are closely related, and we see the terms familiar to us from the Aten hymns for the sun shining, which will be dealt with in the next section.

---

[107] My translation based on Adriaan de Buck, *The Egyptian Coffin Texts* IV, 185–189.

[108] Faulkner, *The Ancient Egyptian Pyramid Texts*, 152. There is a second occurrence of *wꜥ* in the same spell (§854).

[109] *Wꜥ.ti* is a stative expressing the state or condition of this deity. It is worth noting that the stative form is also used in the Short Hymn (Sandman, *Texts from the Time of Akhenaten*, 15.4–6).

[110] Faulkner, *The Ancient Egyptian Pyramid Texts*, 243.

[111] de Buck, *The Egyptian Coffin Texts* IV, 185–188.

[112] Adriaan de Buck, *The Egyptian Coffin Texts* II (Chicago: University of Chicago Press, 1938), 64.

The idea of oneness or sole god abounds in the New Kingdom, too. The Theban stela of Yamunedj, an official who served Thutmose III, contains a hymn which opens with a statement about Re's nature: "Hail to you Re, lord of eternity, One without exception (or exclusively unique)"—*wꜥ ḫr ḫw.f.*[113] The same phrase is found in the Suty and Hor Stela. After the affirmation of Re's self-generation ("self-made you fashioned your body, Creator uncreated"), the next line reads "one without exception" or "exclusively unique"—*wꜥ ḫr ḫw.f.* [114] Hornung, however, has cautioned that the use of *wꜥ* is not necessarily a monotheistic claim before Amarna and that other deities (such as the Semitic goddess Qodeshu) are said to be "*wꜥ*."[115] So one must be careful when seeking to discern the theological meaning of *wꜥ* as an epithet of a deity.

Another consideration is that when *wꜥ* is applied to a deity prior to Akhenaten's day, that divinity is surrounded by references to other deities, especially the citations in the Pyramid and Coffin texts. So plainly, prior to Akhenaten, this epithet was not making a monotheistic claim. In a hymn to Amun-Re in Papyrus Boulaq 17, the deity is called "exclusively unique one among the gods" (*wꜥ ḫr-ḫw.f m-m nṯrw*).[116] This fuller expression seems to imply that Amun-Re is the number one god among the gods, head of the pantheon rather than the only God. In the case of Aten, other gods are absent (after the early years of his reign) and, as we saw in Chapter 7, Aten's iconoclasts destroyed images of Amun and other deities (they had ceased to exist!), as well as the writing of their names and, most relevantly, plural writings for "gods" were purged. Consequently, Akhenaten's use of the word *wꜥ* shares the monotheistic affirmation in the Hebrew Shema: "Hear, O Israel: The LORD our God, the LORD is one" (Deuteronomy 6:4).

The Sun Appears (ḫꜥi), Rises (wbn), Brightens (ḥḏ) and Shines (psd)

The variety of terms associated with the rising and shining sun noted in the Aten hymns is well attested in earlier literature as well. *Ḫꜥi* and *wbn*, prominent words in the Aten hymns to describe the blazing sun in the horizon, are also found in the Pyramid and Coffin Texts to describe the appearing or rising of the sun or the resurrected king. "I appear (*ḫꜥi*) as Nefertum, as the lotus-bloom which is at the nose of Re; he will issue from the horizon daily" (PT §266a-b).[117] A coronation and

113 *Urk*. IV, 942.11–13. On this meaning of the compound preposition *ḫr ḫw.f*, see Gardiner, *Egyptian Grammar*, 133.

114 *Urk* IV. 1944.3.

115 Hornung, *Conception of God in Ancient Egypt*, 185–186.

116 For text, see Maria Luiselli, *Der Amun-Re Hymnus des P. Boulaq 17* (P. Kairo CG 58038) (Wiesbaden: Harrassowitz Verlag, 2004). Translation in Foster, *Hymns, Prayers, and Songs*, 64.

117 Faulkner, *The Ancient Egyptian Pyramid Texts*, 61.

enthronement ritual for the resurrected king requires him to wash himself "when Re appears (*ḫꜥi*), when the great Ennead shines (*psd*)," which continues by claiming that when "Re is in the horizon (*ꜣḫt*) . . . the Two Lands shine" (*psd*).[118] Like the sun, "the King has appeared (*ḫꜥw*) again in the sky, He is crowned as Lord in the horizon (*ꜣḫt*)" (PT §409).[119]

These well-known terms abound in the Coffin Texts. For example, "he rises (*wbn*) daily when he issues from his egg which the god who went up shining(?)[120] fashioned" (CT II, 36).[121] In part II of Coffin Text Spell 335, Aten is mentioned along with the expected language: "O Re who are in your egg, rising (*wbn* or *psd*)[122] in your disc (*itn*) and shining (*wbn* or *psd*) in your horizon, swimming in your firmament, having no equal among the gods, sailing over the Supports of Shu, giving the winds with the breath of your mouth, illumining (*sḥḏ*) the Two Lands with your sunshine . . ."[123] (for a discussion of Aten in this important text, see Chapter 3).

These terms appear regularly in the hymns of the New Kingdom, before and after the Amarna period, but especially in solar hymns leading up to the Amarna period.[124] The hymns of the stela of Suty and Hor contain such language. "Adoring Amun when he rises (*wbn*) as Re-Harakhty," . . . Hail to Re, beautiful everyday, rising (*wbn*) dawn without ceasing," . . . "your hues dazzle (*tḥn*) more than its (the sky) expanse."[125] The focus of praise in the second hymn on the same stela is "Aten of day."[126] The full array of solar language found in the Amarna hymns occur here, namely *ḫꜥꜥ*, *sḥḏ*, and *wbn* (2x).

The Response of Creation to the Rising Sun

Both the short and long hymns contain lengthy sections describing how nature responds to the sun when it rises, and then how, when the Aten sets and darkness sets in, it is as if the world is dead until the next day.

---

118 Kurt Sethe, *Die Altaegyptischen Pyramidentexte* (Spruch 1–468), (Leipzig: J. C. Hinrichs, 1908), §370 & 372.

119 Faulkner, *The Ancient Egyptian Pyramid Texts*, 82.

120 This word is *pri*, meaning to go out or proceed, but determined with the shining sun sign 𓇶.

121 R. O. Faulkner, *The Ancient Egyptian Coffin Texts* I (Warminster: Aris & Phillips, 1973), 84.

122 Seven witnesses of this spell use *wbn* and five *psd*, which shows how semantically close these words are to each other. Cf. Adriaan de Buck, *The Egyptian Coffin Texts* IV (Chicago: University of Chicago Press, 1951), 292c.

123 Faulkner, *The Ancient Egyptian Coffin Texts* I, 261.

124 Stewart, "Some Pre-ʿAmarnah Sun-Hymns," 86; idem, "Traditional Egyptian Sun Hymns of the New Kingdom," 40–41, 48–71; Jan Assmann, *Sonnenhymnen in thebanischen Gräbern* (Mianz: P. von Zabern, 1983), 81, 97, 103, 104, 138, 139, 146, 251 (these references are all pre-Amarna).

125 *Urk*. IV, 1943–1944.

126 *Urk*. IV, 1945.2–1946.9.

> All sorts of flowers are continually alive (*ʿnḫ*), growing on the ground and made to flourish, because of your rising (*wbn*): they grow drunk at the sight of you, while all sorts of cattle are prancing on their legs. Birds which were in the nest are aloft in joy, their wings which were folded are spread in adoration to the living (*ʿnḫ*) **Aten**, the one who makes (*irr*) them all . . ."[127]

These lines, however, are reminiscent of earlier cosmological statements in the Coffin Texts. Spell 80 states, "He rises (*wbn*) everyday in the eastern horizon," followed by this important statement:

> There live falcons and ducks, jackals moving to and fro,
> pigs in the desert, hippos in the marsh, people, grain,
> crocodiles and fish, fish in the water which is in the Nile
> according to the command of Atum that I may lead them
> and cause them to live by this my mouth. (CT II, 42b–43b)

From earlier in the 18th Dynasty are the hymns on Papyrus Bulaq XVII, one of which contains a list of animals and how they are cared for by their creator, Amun-Re. Though the animals are different, the idea is similar to what is seen in the Aten hymns:

> Who creates the pastures for the animals and food-plants for mankind
> Who provides for fishes in the River and for birds who mount the sky;
> Who offers breath to all who are unborn, brings life to the offspring of the worm,
> Provides for gnats, insects and fleas as well,
> Supplies the field mice in their burrows and cares for all the bird-shapes in the trees.[128]

The terminology associated with the sun's rising and shining, which impacts the earth and all that live on it, is used repeatedly in the Aten hymns and hearkens back to earlier sources such as the Pyramid Texts, while some of the attributes of Aten are developed in the Coffin Texts (see Chapter 3, section "Aten before Atenism"), and earlier 18th Dynasty hymns continue using the earlier terminology and motifs. The Aten hymns had an existing body of literature, motifs and vocabulary relating to the sun-god, and Akhenaten or his poets drew heavily upon it.

---

127 Murnane, *Texts from the Amarna Period in Egypt*, 159.

128 Foster, *Hymns, Prayers, and Songs*, 62.

CONCLUSIONS

It is evident that the Aten hymns, while advancing Akhenaten's monotheistic theology, relied on the received solar language to do so. In some cases, especially with the word "one" or "only" (*wʿ*), new and exclusive nuance is intended. One might expect a new dynamic religious expression like Atenism to inspire novel language and metaphors. Atenism, however, opted for traditional language. This move has some advantages, for one can link what is known from past religious experience to something new that springs from it. By way of analogy, in the narrative of Exodus 3, in which the revelation of the divine name YHWH is disclosed to Moses, the deity introduces himself as "the God of Abraham, the God of Isaac, and the God of Jacob" (3:6), and then Moses is instructed to say to the Hebrews, "the LORD (YHWH), the God of your fathers, the God of Abraham, the God of Isaac, and the God of Jacob, has sent me to you. This is my name forever and thus I will be remembered through all generations" (3:15). Clearly an earlier manifestation or understanding of God is used as the springboard to introduce the new name and a fuller revelation of God Yahweh. Exodus 6:2–3 explains this development by stating: "God spoke to Moses and said to him, 'I am the LORD. I appeared to Abraham, to Isaac, and to Jacob, as God Almighty, but by my name the LORD I did not make myself known to them.'"

The revelation of the divine name YHWH, as traditionally understood, occurred sometime in the Late Bronze Age or New Kingdom (13th century B.C.), but Abraham and the ancestors of Israel are thought to have lived centuries earlier[129]—four centuries according to the Bible (Gen. 15:13; Exod. 12:40–41). The point is that there is a conscious attempt to link a past religious understanding (or revelation) of the deity with a new manifestation or expression. The later revelation clarifies, explains, or expands the earlier tradition.

As was observed previously, solar theology hearkens back to the Old Kingdom when Re/Atum was the most powerful deity for centuries (Chapter 1), but then other deities (such as Amun) grew in importance in the subsequent era (Chapter 2). With Akhenaten solar religion, which had been on the ascendency during the 15th century B.C., there was a revival of the old Heliopolitan theology (Chapter 3), expressed as Atenism. Aten was not just the sun-disc; rather he had a lengthy didactic

---

[129] There is an ongoing debate among biblical historians concerning the dating of the exodus era and whether it is even a historical event. Regarding the dating problem, among those who maintain that there was a historical exodus, see Kenneth Kitchen, *On the Reliability of the Old Testament* (Grand Rapids, MI: Eerdmans, 2003), 307–312; Bryant Wood, "The Rise and Fall of the 13th Century Exodus-Conquest Theory," *JETS* 48 (2005): 475–489; James K. Hoffmeier, "What Is the Biblical Date for the Exodus? A Response to Bryant Wood," *JETS* 50 (2007): 225–247.

name that went through three stages (see Chapters 3, 4, 7) that explained who Aten was: "Re-Harakhty who rejoices in the horizon in his name of light which is in the Aten" (Figure 3.8 in Chapter 3), after which the lengthy name was written within a pair of cartouches (Figure 3.11 in Chapter 3), which beginning around Akhenaten's year 9 was stripped of any possible association with other gods and became "Living Re, Ruler of the Horizon, Rejoicing in the Horizon in His Name of 'Re, the Father, who is manifested in the Aten the Sun-disc'" (Figure 7.2 in Chapter 7). Akhenaten's god, Aten, then, represents a more complete, intimate and direct revelation of the old sun-god, Re. All the various attributes of the gods are bound up in the One. "You are Re" . . . "sole god, without another beside him," as the Great Hymn claims.

The investigation of the Aten hymns, when coupled with the expansive building of temples to Aten and the iconoclastic practices witnessed in Thebes and throughout Egypt, leaves little doubt that Akhenaten's encounter with Aten developed into a monotheistic faith in the 14th century B.C. If the Hebrew exodus occurred in the next century, obvious questions have been raised concerning the possible influence of Atenism on biblical religion. Consequently, as Edwin Yamauchi has recently observed, "the striking fact of a monotheism in Egypt and in Israel in roughly the same time period has attached an attempt to posit an influence of the former on the latter, either directly or indirectly."[130] A possible connection between Atenism and Yahwism must be examined in more detail, and this will be the final act of the drama being played out in this book.

[130] Edwin Yamauchi, "Akhenaten, Moses, and Monotheism," *Near East Archaeological Society Bulletin* 55 (2010): 9.

God is three of all gods:
Amun, Re, Ptah, without any others
LEIDEN HYMN TO AMUN

I am the LORD your God from the land of Egypt;
you know no God but me, and besides me there is no savior.
It was I who knew you in the wilderness,
in the land of drought
HOSEA 13:4–5

Chapter 9

The Influence of Atenism in Egypt and the Bible?

THE FINAL YEARS of Akhenaten's reign and the years following his death in 1336 B.C. remain full of uncertainty and intrigue.[1] It remains a matter of debate whether Queen Nefertiti served as co-regent toward the end of Akhenaten's reign or served independently as ruler for a brief period. Mention was made earlier of our discovery in north Sinai of a wine jar seal with the name *Nfr-nfrw-ỉtn 3ḫ.t n hy.s* "Nefer-neferu-aten who is beneficial to her husband" (see Chapter 6 and Figure 6.15).[2] Coupled with Nefertiti's later name, this epithet suggests that she reigned along with her husband, Akhenaten.[3] Akhenaten's immediate successor appears to have been Smenkhkare, also known as Ankhkheperure, whose identity remains uncertain. He or she (Nefertiti?) may have been co-regent and/or successor,[4] a reign that seems not to have lasted more than a few years.

[1] The following recent studies review the various theories and investigate the immediate successors of Akhenaten: Rolf Krauss, *Das Ende der Amarnazeit* (Hildesheimer Ägyptologische Beiträge, 1978); James Allen, "The Amarna Succession," in *Causing His Name to Live: Studies on Egyptian Epigraphy and History in Memory of William J. Murnane* (eds. L. Cooper & P. Brand; Leiden: Brill, 2009), 9–20. Aidan Dodson, *Amarna Sunset: Nefertititi, Tutankhamun, Ay, Horemheb and the Egyptian Counter Reformation* (Cairo/New York: American University Cairo Press, 2009).

[2] James K. Hoffmeier & Jacobus van Dijk, "New Light on the Amarna Period from North Sinai," *JEA* 96 (2010): 110–112.

[3] Marc Gabolde, *D'Akhenaton à Toutânkhamon* (Lyon: Université Lumière-Lyon 2 1998), 153–157.

[4] For some of the various identities of the successor/s of Akhenaten, see J. R. Harris, "Neferneferuaten," *Göttinger Miszellen* 4 (1973): 15–17. Julia Samson, "Akhenaten's Successor," *Göttinger Miszellen* 32 (1979): 53–58; idem, "Akhenaten's Coregent Ankhkheperure-Neferneferuaten," *Göttinger Miszellen* 53 (1982): 51–54; idem, "Neferneferuaten-Nefertiti 'Beloved of Akhenaten,' Ankhkheperure Neferneferuaten 'Beloved of Akhenateon,' Ankhkheperure Smenkhkare 'Beloved of the Aten,'" *Göttinger Miszellen* 57 (1982): 61–67. Marc Gabolde, *D'Akhenaten à Toutankhamon*.

In the Amarna tomb of an official named Mery-re II (Tomb 2), King Ankhkheperure Smenkhkare is shown beside his queen, Meritaten (Akhenaten and Nefertiti's eldest daughter),[5] which might indicate a brief rule at Akhet-Aten. At Thebes a hieratic graffito in the Tomb of Pa-Re contains a prayer directed to Amun and is dated to regnal year 3 of Ankhkheperure-Neferneferuaten.[6] Whether or not this ruler is the aforementioned Smenkhkare-Ankhkheperure is not the concern of the present study, but rather to show that shortly after Akhenaten's reign the Thebans were directing petitions to Amun, and beyond the ruler's name and epithets, Aten is conspicuously absent from this text. When Akhenaten passed away, his remains were sealed in his pink granite sarcophagus. It was decorated with the Aten and its descending rays, along with the didactic name and he was buried (initially?) in the royal tomb at Amarna. This tomb was desecrated: scenes and inscriptions were smashed, while the sarcophagus was savagely bashed to pieces.[7] Thanks to the restoration work of Geoffrey Martin, the sarcophagus was pieced together and now is on display outside the Cairo Museum (west side) (Figure 9.1).

Within a few years, the mysterious Tutankhamun ruled from Memphis, so reports the "Restoration Stela,"[8] indicating that Akhet-Aten had been abandoned as the capital. He altered his name from Tut-ankh-aten, his birth name, as did his wife; Ankhesenpaaten became Ankhesenamun.[9] While some objects from Tutankhamun's tomb have the earlier name on them, the magnificent golden throne chair contains both forms of his name, and Aten hovers over the figures of the king and queen with its iconic extended rays (Figure 9.2). This throne apparently was reworked several times for different rulers, Tutankhamun being the last.[10] This leads some to believe that there was a brief period of détente between Aten and Amun early in Tutankhamun's reign before the complete rejection of the former.[11] Donald Redford also sees no immediate turn against the new status quo when Akhenaten died, noting that "no temple of the Sun-disc was closed, their reliefs hacked out, or their priesthoods disbanded and slaughtered. There was no sudden *damnatio*

[5] Norman de Garis Davis, *The Rock Tombs of Amarna* II (London: Egypt Exploration Society, 1905), pl. xli.

[6] Alan Gardiner, "The Graffito from the Tomb of Pere," *JEA* 14 (1928): 10–11. For an recent translation, see William Murnane, *Texts from the Amarna Period in Egypt* (Atlanta: Scholars Press, 1995) 207–208.

[7] Geoffrey T. Martin, *The Royal Tomb at El-ʿAmarna*. I. *The Objects* (London, Egypt Exploration Society 1974); idem, *The Royal Tomb at El-ʿAmarna*. II. *The Reliefs, Inscriptions, and Architecture* (London: Egypt Exploration Society 1989).

[8] In the stela, the king resides in the palace of Thutmose I, which is in Memphis (Murnane, *Texts from the Amarna Period in Egypt*, 213).

[9] Donald Redford, *Akhenaten the Heretic King* (Princeton, NJ: Princeton University Press, 1984), 207; Dodson, *Amarna Sunset*, 49–52.

[10] Nicholas Reeves, *The Complete Tutankhamun* (London: Thames & Hudson, 1995), 184–185.

[11] David Silverman, Josef Wegner, & Jennifer Wegner, *Akhenaten and Tutankhamun: Revolution and Restoration* (Philadelphia: University of Pennsylvania Museum, 2006), 165–166.

(a)

(b)

FIGURE 9.1 Akhenaten's pink granite coffin (Cairo Museum). Photo Boyo Ockinga.

memoriae of Akhenaten, Nefertiti, and those associated with them."[12] The reason for the name "Restoration Stela," is because of Tutankhamun's claim that he restored and refurbished dilapidated temples throughout Egypt (for translation of this passage, see Chapter 7). And Tutankhamun was active building in Thebes and Karnak specifically. One temple he built was made of reused Akhenaten talatat, suggesting

[12] Redford, *Akhenaten the Heretic King*, 207.

FIGURE 9.2 Close-up of Tutankhamun's gold throne showing the royal couple under Aten and its rays (Cairo Museum). Photo James K. Hoffmeier.

that the dismantling of Aten temples began with him (late in his reign?), continued under Ay (his successor), but that Horemheb appears to have done the yeoman's share of the work of destroying the Aten temples across Egypt.[13]

While it is evident that Tutankhamun was responsible for re-establishing the old polytheistic orthodoxy, with Amun-Re reinstated as "king of the gods" once again, his connection to Akhenaten and the Amarna heresy meant that he had to go the extra mile in his efforts to mollify the old order and show his *bona fides* as a reformer. New images of Amun and his consort Amunet were executed at his command, in which the likenesses of Tutankhamun and Ankhesenamun served as the models; they were placed at the heart of Karnak Temple (Figure 9.3a–b).[14] His restoration stela was subsequently usurped by Horemheb,[15] who himself had been a general of Akhenaten, so as to deprive Tutankhamun of the credit he deserved for the restoration and

[13] For a comprehensive analysis of Tutankhamun's temples and monuments in Thebes, see W. Raymond Johnson, "An Asiatic Battle Scene of Tutankhamun from Thebes: A Late Amarna Antecedent of the Ramesside Battle-Narrative Tradition," (Ph.D. diss., University of Chicago, 1992).

[14] Silverman, Wegner, & Wegner, *Akhenaten and Tutankhamun: Revolution and Restoration*, 168, fig. 152; Nicholas Reeves, *The Complete Tutankhamun*, 27; Dodson, *Amarna Sunset*, 77.

[15] Murnane, *Texts from the Amarna Period in Egypt*, 212.

FIGURE 9.3 a. Statue of the god Amun using Tutankhamun's face (Karnak Temple). Photo James K. Hoffmeier. b. Statue of the goddess Amunet using Ankhesenamun face (Karnak Temple). Photo James K. Hoffmeier.

obviously to distance himself from the previous royal family.[16] In Horemheb's reign, hostility toward Akhenaten and the Amarna heresy was no longer restrained. Aten's temples were systematical demolished and the talatat blocks were reused in building projects (thereby completely obscuring them) of Horemheb and his successors, especially Ramessses II (see Chapter 4).

Seti I (1294–1279 B.C.) actively restored many damaged monuments. Where Amun's name had been erased, Seti I's scribes recarved the texts (e.g. Figure 2.10 in Chapter 2). Moreover, when he had a list of his predecessors inscribed on the walls of his temple at Abydos, there was a hiatus between Amenhotep III and Horemheb, intentionally omitting the names of Akhenaten, Smenkhkare, Tutankhamun, and Ay, as if they had never ruled.[17]

In the Ramesside story known as the "Quarrel between Apophis and Seqenenre," the former ruler being the Hyksos king and the latter being his Theban counterpart, a curious criticism of Apophis is made.[18] The derogatory accusation is that the

[16] For a survey of the history and career of Horemheb, see Charlotte Booth, *Horemheb: The Forgotten Pharaoh* (Chalford: Amberley, 2009).

[17] James K. Hoffmeier, "King Lists," in *COS* I, 69–70.

[18] For the text, see Alan H. Gardiner, *Late-Egyptian Stories* (Brussels: Édition de la Fondation Égyptologique Reine Élisabeth: 1932), 85–89.

Hyksos king "adopted Seth for himself as lord, and he refused to serve any god that was in the entire land ex[cept] Seth."[19] Seth, of course, was an Egyptian deity who corresponds to Baal of the Semitic world.[20] Orly Goldwasser recently explained that the offense of the Hyksos is not that they worshiped Seth, "but the fact that the Hyksos ruler did not worship *any other god* in the entire land *except* Seth."[21] The use of the word "except" (*wpwt*) is the same exclusionary word used by Akhenaten to describe Aten (see Chapter 8). Jan Assmann has suggested that behind the charge of heterodoxy against the Hyksos were "dislocated Amarna reminiscences."[22] The idea is that the bitter and recent memories of the Atenist heresy were unfairly equated with the Hyksos. Goldwasser, on the contrary, argues that the memory of the Hyksos religious practice "was an authentic—not superimposed or artificially projected—ideological affinity . . . The Amarna king and the Hyksos king may have shared a genuine religious otherness."[23]

Goldwasser's observations are quite intriguing. It is difficult, even after four decades of excavations at Tell el-Dab'a, to know if Apophis worshiped only one deity; however, the main temple of Avaris was the precinct of Baal/Seth, which thrived throughout the Hyksos period and was even restored in Tutankhamun's and Horemheb's reign.[24] The negative attitude towards the worship of one deity is on display in the "Quarrel between Apophis and Seqenenre," and Egypt after Akhenaten viewed monotheism as a heresy. The short duration of the Amarna sacrilege, coupled with a quick return to polytheistic orthodoxy, and the iconoclasm directed at Akhenaten, his successors, and the Aten temples and tombs at Amarna are testimony to the attempt to eradicate every memory of this embarrassing interlude of Egyptian history.

It was impossible to completely rewrite history, however, and there were instances when individuals needed to refer back to events that occurred in the Amarna period. For example, the tomb of Mes, or Mose, contains the record of a legal dispute dated to the end of Horemheb's reign in which the plaintiff seeks to gain control of property inherited "in the time of the enemy (*ḫrw*) of Akhet-Aten."[25] Though around 40

---

[19] Edward Wente, "The Quarrel of Apophis and Seknenre," *The Literature of Ancient Egypt* (eds. W. K. Simpson et al.; New Haven, CT: Yale University Press, 1973), 78.

[20] Hermann Te Velde, "Seth," in *OEAE* 3, 269–270.

[21] Orly Goldwasser, "King Apophis of Avaris and the Emergence of Monotheism," in Timelines Studies in Honour of Manfred Bietak, Vol. II, eds. Ernst Czerny et al.; Leuven: Peeters, 2006), 130 (emphasis is Goldwasser's).

[22] Jan Assmann, *Moses the Egyptian: The Memory of Egypt in Western Monotheism* (Cambridge, MA: Harvard University Press, 1997), 28.

[23] Goldwasser, "King Apophis of Avaris and the Emergence of Monotheism," 131–132.

[24] Manfred Bietak, "Zur Herfungt des Seth von Avaris," *Ägypten und Levante* 1 (1990): 9–16. An inscription of Horemheb on a door linter from Seth temple has been discovered, see Manfred Bietak, *Avaris: The Capital of the Hyksos* (London: The British Museum, 1996), 77.

[25] Murnane, *Texts from the Amarna Period in Egypt*, 240–241.

years after the death of Akhenaten, this court proceeding could not avoid referring to an event during Akhenaten's reign, but the witnesses could not bring themselves to utter Akhenaten's name. He is simply dubbed, "the enemy of Akhet-Aten."

A second case where an event from this fateful period is recalled comes from a tax record of the Ramesside period. The death date of one [. . .] nakht is requested. The answer was that "he died in regnal year nine of the rebellion (*sby*)."[26] The word *sby* could be translated "rebellion" or "rebel."[27] In either case, the attitude toward Akhenaten more than 50 years later was visceral. The antipathy toward Akhenaten precluded uttering his name.

Since Akhenaten's religion died with him and members of his immediate family were quick to drop the name "Aten" from their personal names, it is fair to say that the officials and people had no interest in perpetuating the cause. The idea of monotheism, however, may have left its imprint on the priests and theologians of Egypt. The Leiden Hymn from the Ramesside period contains a virtual Trinitarian description of the three most prominent deities, Amun, Re, and Ptah:

God is three of all gods:
  Amun, Re, Ptah, without any others.
Hidden his name as Amun;
  He is Re in features, his body is Ptah.
Their cities on earth endure to eternity—
  Thebes, Heliopolis, Memphis, forever.[28]

The presence of such theological supposition by some Amun priests may be Akhenaten's greatest legacy within Egypt. Even if this reflects a genuine triune conception of deity within a century of Akhenaten's death, it was limited to certain priestly elites, and it did not mean the end of the multitude of cults and the overshadowing of any gods and goddesses of Egypt. This consideration may be why John Wilson regarded the Leiden Hymn as "syncretistic" rather than monotheistic.[29]

Given the realities of the aftermath of the Amarna heresy in Egypt, it seems inconceivable that the Hebrews and the development of Yahwism were influenced directly by Atenism. The issue that must be considered is whether the Hebrews were in Egypt, and if so, when.

---

[26] Ibid., 241.

[27] Alan Gardiner, "A Later Allusion to Akhenaten," *JEA* 24 (1938): 124.

[28] John Foster, *Hymns, Prayers, and Songs: An Anthology of Ancient Egyptian Lyric Poetry* (Atlanta: Scholars Press, 1995), 77.

[29] John Wilson, *The Culture of Egypt* (Chicago: University of Chicago Press, 1951), 228.

CHRONOLOGICAL AND HISTORICAL ISSUES

When Sigmund Freud's book *Moses and Monotheism* was published (1939), the assumption of most Western scholars was that the Hebrews had been an enslaved population that was liberated by Moses and Yahweh, the God who had revealed himself to Moses, who then became the recipient of the laws given at Sinai. Freud theorized that Moses was actually the vizier or priest of Akhenaten, which would explain the connection between the monotheism of Atenism and Yahwism. He speculated, "I venture now to draw the following conclusion: if Moses was an Egyptian and if he transmitted to the Jews his own religion, then it was that of Ikhnaton, the Aton religion."[30] Most biblical scholars and Egyptologists have dismissed this suggestion as fanciful; after all, if there was a historical Moses among the Hebrews, how would he end up in such a prestigious office? Then, too, the pharaohs with whom Moses dealt in the book of Exodus give no indication of any affinity for Moses. He fled for fear of his life from the first pharaoh to the land of Midian (Exod. 2:11–15). While living as a refugee in Midian, the narrative reports that he had a theophany in which Yahweh revealed himself and his name (Exod. 3:1–15). Moses then returned to Egypt, where he approached the new king with the demand of Yahweh, "let my people go," to which pharaoh responds, "Who is the LORD (YHWH) that I should obey his voice" (Exod. 5:2). This memorable encounter hardly sounds like a pharaoh who is a devotee of God, be he called Aten or Yahweh.

One reason for others to reject any Egyptian connection between Atenism and Israelite religions is a chronological gap between the supposed date of the exodus. The dates for Akhenaten's reign are established, although a slight range exists among historians. The low chronology of Kenneth Kitchen dates his reign to 1353–1336 B.C.,[31] while Donald Redford, a proponent of the high chronology, opts for 1377–1360 B.C.[32] It is true that during the last 30 years, Israel's origins in Egypt have been increasingly dismissed by Old Testament scholars and Syro-Palestinian and biblical archaeologists. The author has dealt at length with these issues in two monographs and maintains that while there is no direct evidence to prove the exodus, the Egyptian linguistic and cultural background details in the Exodus narratives suggest a historical origin for Israel in Egypt that is most plausible.[33] Those who maintain a historical exodus date the Exodus to ca. 1447 B.C. (the early

---

[30] Sigmund Freud, *Moses and Monotheism* (New York: Alfred A. Knof, 1939), 33.

[31] Kenneth Kitchen, "Egypt, History of (Chronology)," in *ABD* 2, 329.

[32] Redford, *Akhenaten the Heretic King*, 13.

[33] For a discussion of the trends regarding the Hebrew sojourn in and exodus from Egypt, see James K. Hoffmeier, *Israel in Egypt* (New York: Oxford University Press, 1996), chapters 1 & 2, idem *Ancient Israel in Sinai*.

date) or ca. 1270 B.C.,[34] and a few scholars would push the exodus to as late as the 12th century B.C.[35]

The 15th century date would place Moses and the exodus nearly a century before Akhenaten's reign. The 13th century date, favored by the author, falls a generation or two after Akhenaten, while the early 12th century B.C. date is nearly a century and a half after the Amarna period. Since the dating of the era of Moses and the exodus remains unfixed, some scholars maintain that one cannot *a priori* dismiss a connection between two traditions. William Propp, for example, has recently revived the debate, proposing "that Atenism influenced Israel, remains viable. While I do not claim that it is correct, I insist that it is sufficiently plausible to be entertained by critical scholars, alongside or in conjunction with other possibilities."[36] He may have a point that the reasons for the knee-jerk negative response to Freud is that he was an amateur, not an academic trained in biblical and Near Eastern languages, and that his theory was overly specific in trying to identify Moses as a high priest or vizier who had a direct connection to Akhenaten.[37] Propp is not dismissive of the possibility of some sort of influence of Atenism, suggesting that it "is not ludicrous and is yet to be disproved."[38]

More recently, Edwin Yamauchi has also returned to the question of the possible relationship between "Akhenaten, Moses, and Monotheism," which is the title of his essay.[39] He, too, sees the chronological overlap between the two figures as a problem for establishing a direct connection between Atenism and Moses. He concludes, as did W. F. Albright 40 years earlier, that if there was any influence, it was indirect. They found it noteworthy that both "monotheistic" religions originate within less than a century of each other within Egypt, leading Albright to affirm that "it is very likely that Moses was familiar with vestigial remains of the Aten cult."[40] As was noted above, the Leiden Hymn to Amun-Re does contain hints of monotheism that may have lingered from Atenism in the Ramesside era. Some have seen the traces of the Great Hymn to Aten in Psalm 104 as a testimony to the Hebrew poet drawing from Akhenaten's theology.

---

[34] For a recent view of the debate, see Bryant Wood, "The Rise and Fall of the 13th-Century Exodus-Conquest Theory," *JETS* 48 (2005): 475–489, and James K. Hoffmeier, "What Is the Biblical Date for the Exodus? A Response to Bryant Wood," *JETS* 50, no. 2 (2007): 225–247.

[35] Gary Rendsburg, "The Date of the Exodus and Conquest/Settlement: The Case for the 1100s," *VT* 42 (1992): 510–527.

[36] William Propp, "Monotheism and 'Moses': The Problem of Early Israelite Religion," *Ugarit-Forshungen* 31 (1999): 539.

[37] Ibid., 537–539.

[38] Ibid., 574.

[39] Edwin Yamauchi, "Akhenaten, Moses, and Monotheism," *Near East Archaeological Society Bulletin* 55 (2010): 1–15.

[40] William F. Albright. "Moses in Historical and Theological Perspective," in *Magnalia Dei: The Mighty Acts of God* (eds. F. M. Cross et al.; Garden City, NY: Doubleday, 1976), 129.

THE GREAT HYMN TO ATEN AND PSALM 104

As early as 1905, the Egyptologist James Henry Breasted drew attention to similarities between these Egyptian hymns and Psalm 104.[41] As time went on, he became more convinced of a dependence of the Hebrew poem upon the Aten hymn. In the second edition of his *History of Egypt* he declared, "The one hundred and fourth Psalm of the Hebrews shows a notable similarity to our hymn both in the thought and sequence . . ."[42]

In the early 1930s he went so far as to claim that the Aten hymn "reveals to us the source of the Hebrew Psalmist's recognition of the gracious and goodness of God in the maintenance of his creatures."[43] In that volume he offered his translation of the hymn in one column and what he deemed to be the similar sections of the Hebrew Psalm in the second column. He saw the points of overlap being Psalm 104:20–26 and parts of lines 4–7 in the Hymn to Aten. The point is that the areas of similarity between the two works represent relatively small portions of the respective paeans. In John Wilson's translation of the Aten hymn, he saw additional similarities between Psalm 104:11–14 and the end of line 5 and beginning of 6 in the hymn.[44] Adding these verses to the picture would mean that 15 verses out of 35 find similarities in the Hymn to Aten. At best this means only portions or snippets of the Aten hymn made their way into the Hebrew Psalm, and not in the order in which they occur in the Egyptian original. Here the verses are laid out for comparative purposes, using Wilson's translation:[45]

The Great Hymn	Psalm 104 (King James Version)
Every lion is come forth from his den; All creeping things, they sting. Darkness is a shroud, and the earth is in stillness, for he who made them rests in his horizon (l. 4) At daybreak, when thou arisest on the horizon,	21 The young lions roar after their prey, and seek their meat from God. 20 Thou makest darkness, and it is night: wherein all the beasts of the forest do creep forth. 22 The sun ariseth, they gather themselves together, and lay them down in their dens.

[41] James H. Breasted, *A History of Egypt* (New York: Scribner, 1905), 371–374.

[42] James H. Breasted, *A History of Egypt* (London: Hodder & Stoughton, 1921; 2nd ed.) 371.

[43] James H. Breasted, *The Dawn of Conscience* (New York: Scribners, 1933) 368.

[44] John Wilson, "The Hymn to the Aton," in *Ancient Near Eastern Texts Relating to the Old Testament* (ed. J. B. Pritchard, NJ; Princeton: Princeton University Press, 1969; 3rd ed.), 370.

[45] Ibid., 370–371. Wilson, *The Culture of Egypt*, 228.

When thou shinest as the Aton by day,

(l. 5) All the world, they do their work.

All beasts are content with their pasturage;
Trees and plants area flourishing.
The birds which fly from their nests,
Their wings are (stretched out) in praise to thy *ka*.

How manifold it is, what thou has made!
(l. 8) Thou didst create the world according to thy desire, whilst thou wert alone:
All men, cattle, and wild beasts,
Whatever is on earth, going upon (its) feet,
And what is on high, flying with its wings . . .
Everyone has his food, and his time of life is reckoned.

(l. 9) For thou has set a Nile in heaven,
That it may descend for them
(l. 10) and make waves upon the mountains,
Like the great green sea,
To water their fields and their towns.

(l. 10) Thou makest the season in order to rear all that thou has made

The word came into being by thy hand,
According as thou has made them.
When thou has risen they live,
When thou settest they die

[23]Man goeth forth unto his work and to his labour until the evening.
[11]They give drink to every beast of the field: the wild asses quench their thirst.
[12]By them shall the fowls of the heaven have their habitation, which sing among the branches.
[13]He watereth the hills from his chambers: the earth is satisfied with the fruit of thy works.

[24]O Lord, how manifold are thy works! in wisdom hast thou made them all: the earth is full of thy riches.
[14]He causeth the grass to grow for the cattle, and herb for the service of man: that he may bring forth food out of the earth;

[27]These wait all upon thee; that thou mayest give them their meat in due season.
[6]Thou coveredst it with the deep as with a garment: the waters stood above the mountains.
[10]He sendeth the springs into the valleys, which run among the hills.

[19] He appointed the moon for seasons: the sun knoweth his going down.

[30]Thou sendest forth thy spirit, they are created: and thou renewest the face of the earth.
[29]Thou hidest thy face, they are troubled: thou takest away their breath, they die, and return to their dust.

Many biblical scholars from the 1930s through early 1960s concurred with Breasted's position. Problems on the connection between the two pieces of literature abound. First, it is apparent that if the Aten hymn was the source, the verses were randomly extracted and were used in a very different order. Second, in recent decades, scholars have been more cautious about seeing a direct connection because of the time gap between the two pieces of literature and the geographical distance between Israel and Amarna in Egypt. Those scholars who are inclined to see some sort of dependency of the Hebrew psalm on the Aten hymn(s) seem to overlook the fact that Akhet-Aten, the decade-long capital of Akhenaten where the texts were recorded, was abandoned shortly after the king's death. Furthermore, the tombs in which the hymns were recorded apparently were not actually used by Akhenaten's officials because of the abandonment of the city around 1335 B.C. Then too, there are no surviving papyrus or ostraca copies of the Amarna hymns to suggest that they were copied and studied by later generations of scribes, which would have been the case if it had attained some sort of canonical status. These factors notwithstanding, there are those who maintain a dependence between the two because the similarities are in their minds too striking to ignore or unlikely to be purely coincidental.

Thus a bridge linking the two sources was proposed, namely a Canaanite, Ugaritic, or Phoenician intermediary source. Mitchell Dahood, for instance, followed the lead of George Nagel[46] in believing that "it would be more prudent to envisage an indirect Egyptian influence through Canaanite mediation, more specifically through Phoenician intervention."[47] Moreover, he detected what he believed to be the presence of Canaanite and Egyptian elements that had been thoroughly Hebraized.[48] Storm-god imagery (Canaanite) and Egyptian literary motifs were detected in Psalm 104 by Peter Craigie.[49] Leslie Allen concurred, suggesting that the combination of Egyptian and Ugaritic elements were "a clue as to the means whereby a knowledge of Egyptian cosmological motifs became known to Israel."[50] What Allen meant by that is that there must have been some sort of Levantine intermediary between Egypt of the 14th century B.C. and the period of Israel's divided monarchy (i.e., prior to 586 B.C.) when the Hebrew psalm was composed. To those who hold this view, this is the only way to address the problem of the geographical and chronological propinquity.

---

[46] George Nagel, "À propos des rapports du psaume 104 avec les textes égyptiens," in *Festschrift für Alfred Bertholet* (eds. Otto Eissfeldt et al.; Tübigen, 1950).

[47] Mitchell Dahood, *Psalms III, 101–150* (New York: Doubleday, 1970) 33.

[48] Peter Craigie, "The Comparison of Hebrew Poetry: Psalm 104 in the Light of Egyptian and Ugaritic Poetry," *Semitics* 4 (1974) 9–24.

[49] Ibid., 10–21.

[50] Leslie Allen, *Psalms 101–150* (Waco, TX: Word, 1983), 30.

Building on the ideas of the dual emphasis of solar and storm-god language, Paul Dion offered an expanded investigation of these themes in Psalm 104.[51] He maintains that it "derived from the traditions of Egypt and of Syria, in reclaiming for the God of Israel an important part of the "common theology of the Ancient Near East."[52] Dion's reference to "the common theology of the ancient Near East," borrows from the classic expression from the title of Morton Smith's seminal article from 1952.[53] Smith was responding to what might be called a pan-Ugaritization of Old Testament studies, in which biblical scholars were trying to explain too much in the Hebrew Bible as being influenced by Canaanite religious literature. He, rather, saw certain commonalities in worldview, ideas of kingship and how nature functions that give rise to a common theology.[54] Most relevant to the issue at hand, namely the dependency of Psalm 104 on the Aten hymn(s), Smith concludes that "parallels between theological material in the OT and in 'Ancient Near Eastern Texts' cannot be taken off hand as indicating any literary dependence, common sources, or cultural borrowing."[55] It is curious, then, that Dion appeals to Smith's idea of common theology because he confidently asserts that "the religious and literary phenomenon represented in a privileged fashion by the great Aten hymn somehow did come to the attention of the biblical writer. There is simply no alternative explanation for the concentration of contacts between these two poems heaped up in vv. 19–30."[56] Furthermore, he asserts that the Hebrew poet had a "source of inspiration, and used it," and speaks of "his Amarnian source."[57]

J. Glen Taylor made a thorough investigation of solar imagery that is applied to Yahweh in the Hebrew Bible.[58] Perhaps the most memorable example is in the priestly prayer of Numbers 6:

> The LORD bless you and keep you;
> the LORD make his face to shine upon you and
> be gracious to you. (vss. 24–25)

---

[51] Paul Dion, "YHWH as Storm-God: The Double Legacy of Egypt and Canaan as Reflected in Psalm 104," *ZAW* 103 (1991): 43–71.

[52] Ibid., 44.

[53] Morton Smith, "The Common Theology of Ancient Near East," *JBL* 71 (1952): 135–147.

[54] Ibid., 137–147.

[55] Ibid., 146.

[56] Dion, "YHWH as Storm-God: The Double Legacy of Egypt and Canaan as Reflected in Psalm 104," 59.

[57] Ibid., 62, 65.

[58] J. Glen Taylor, *Yahweh and the Sun: Biblical and Archaeological Evidence for Sun Worship in Ancient Israel* (Sheffield: JSOT Press, 1993).

Naturally, Taylor treats Psalm 104, and he contends that there was no direct borrowing by the Psalmist, but that some sort of borrowing did occur, declaring "there can be no doubt that the poetic imagery of storm and sun which the psalmist borrowed has been brought into conformity with the distinctive theological outlook of ancient Israel."[59] He rightly recognizes that the Hebrew Psalmist does not equate Yahweh with the sun. Indeed the sun and moon, and all God's creation, are celebrated as "his works" (מַעֲשָׂיו) in Psalm 104:31, thus clearly distinguishing the creator from creation. This is no small matter.

While biblical scholars have tended to look for similarities between the two hymns, A. A. Anderson cogently observes "we must not neglect the striking differences."[60] The most "striking" difference between the Hebrew Psalm and the Hymn to Aten lies in their different understanding of the sun. For Akhenaten, the Aten or sun-disc was the vehicle through which direct revelation occurs, whereas in Hebrew thought, the sun was created by God; the sun, moon, and stars are "his works" and are never equated with God. In Hebrew thought, the sun and heavenly host can be vehicles of proclaiming the glory of God in some general way (see Chapter 8), whereas for Akhenaten, the sun-disc was the mode of direct or special revelation. These are the most fundamental differences that are hard to reconcile if there was some direct borrowing of the "Amarnian" theology by the Hebrew poet.

A LEVANTINE INTERMEDIARY SOLAR HYMN?

One explanation for the parallels between the Egyptian and Hebrew hymns is that there must have been some sort of West Semitic copy or version of the Aten hymn that was preserved and accessible to the Psalmist centuries later. This scenario is certainly plausible, but we lack an Ugaritic or Phoenician text that would approximate the hypothetical mediating document. Hence the position of Nagel, Dahood, Craigie, Allen, Taylor, and others rests on the *argumentum ex silentio*; they must conjure up a literary "missing link." Ronald Williams, who translated the Aten hymn for *Documents from the Old Testament Times* and was a respected Hebrew Bible scholar, addressed the chronological and geographical problems, saying:

> we may wonder how a Hebrew poet, more than half a millennium later, could have become acquainted with the central document of a religion which later ages execrated and sought to obliterate from their memory. Despite the complete eclipse of Atenism after the death of Akhenaten, however, its influence

[59] Ibid., 226.

[60] A. A. Anderson, *The Book of Psalms* 2 (London: Marshal, Morgan & Scott, 1972), 718.

remained in art and literature, and many of the ideas contained in the Aten Hymn, itself dependent on earlier models as we shall see, found expression in later religious works.[61]

In the present study, we have already investigated what Williams called the "earlier models" (Chapter 8), but need to examine some "later religious works." In the succeeding Ramesside era (ca. 1294–1100 B.C.), solar hymns continue to use this type of language. A Leiden Papyrus from around the time of Ramesses II states[62]

He rises (*wbn*) for them . . . all trees (*snw*) sway to and fro
at seeing him . . . fishes jump up from the water and dart in their
pools because of his love. All flocks (*ꜥwt*) leap (*ṯbhn*)
because of him. Birds dance with their wings.[63]

The theme of the response of nature to the sun, well known in the Aten hymns, was noted in the Coffin Texts (Chapter 8). The so-called monotheistic hymns on the recto of Pap. Chester Beatty No. IV, which date to the end of the 19th Dynasty, also paint a similar word picture. "Flocks and herds (*ꜥwt mnmnt*) turn to you, flying things leap (*ṯbhn*) for you. All vegetation turns to your beauty."[64]

The expression *i͗3wt/ꜥwt nbt ṯbhn* is first attested in the Aten hymns, and the word *ṯbhn* is not known in Egyptian literature until the Amarna hymns.[65] This suggests a possible influence of the Aten hymns on this 19th Dynasty hymn. If so, this is the only uniquely Amarna expression one can detect in later literature, whereas it has been shown that most of the solar imagery in the "Aten hymns" have antecedents from the Middle and Old Kingdoms (Chapter 8).

Hymns to the sun-god outlive the New Kingdom, and they continue to use the traditional solar language and motifs of earlier periods. First, the Book of the Dead, Chapter 15, contains paeans to Re and Osiris, and these span from the 18th Dynasty down to the Greco-Roman period with little appreciable change.[66] The title of this chapter is "Worshiping Re when he rises (*wbn*) in the eastern horizon

---

[61] D. Winton Thomas (ed.), *Documents from the Old Testament Times* (Nashville: Thomas Nelson, 1958), 148–149.

[62] A. H. Gardiner, "The Hymns to Amon from a Leiden Papyrus," *ZÄS* 42 (1905): 112–142.

[63] The Amun Hymns on Pap. Leiden I 344, verso, have been freshly translated in German with a comprehensive commentary by the late Jan Zandee, *Der Amunhymnus des Papyrus Leiden I 344, verso III Vols.* (Leiden: Rijksmuseum van Oudheden, 1992). This important study continually points to earlier parallels from these hymns.

[64] A. H. Gardiner, *Hieratic Papyri in the British Museum*, Vol. II (London: British Museum, 1935), Pl. 16.

[65] *Wb* V, 364.

[66] R. O. Faulkner, *Book of the Dead* (London: British Museum, 1985), 40–41. Chapter 15 of the BD is attested for the 18th, 19th, 21st Dynasties and Ptolemaic period in T. G. Allen's *The Book of the Dead* (Studies in Ancient Oriental Civilization 37; Chicago: Oriental Institute, 1974), 12–26.

of the sky" . . . Hail to you when you come (*ỉỉ*) as Khepri, Khepri being the one who creates (*ḳmꜣ*) the gods. When you appear (*ḫʿỉ*) you rise (*wbn*), shining (*psd*) (for) your mother." . . . "They have seen Re in his appearing (*ḫʿʿ*), his rays (*stwt*) flooding the lands . . . illuminating (*ḥḏ*) the land at his birth daily."[67] Another hymn is to Re in Book of the Dead 15 is adored as the Aten: "Hail to you, O Re when you rise . . . O Sun-disc (*ỉtn*), Lord of the sunbeams (*stwt*), who shines forth (*psd*) from the horizon everyday: may you shine (*psd*) in the face of N (the deceased) . . ."[68]

The solar terminology in these hymns is identical with what is present in the Aten hymns, solar hymns from the earlier 18th Dynasty, and all the way back to the Old Kingdom Pyramid Texts. And *ỉỉ*, it was noted (see Chapter 8), was the term introduced in the final form of Aten's didactic name. What is missing from BD 15 is the list of animals created by the deity, or their response to the rising sun, that is found at Amarna. From the Greco-Roman period, however, the temple of Khnum at Esna provides a litany to Khnum-Re that includes:

> He has fashioned gods and men,
> He has formed flocks and herds;
> He made birds as well as fishes,
> He created bulls and engendered cows.[69]

Another hymn from the same temple reads:

> You are Ptah-Tatenen, creator of creators . . .
> He feeds the chick in the nest in its time,
> He makes its mother eject it in time,
> He made mankind, created gods,
> He fashioned flocks and herds.
> He made birds, fishes, and reptiles all . . .[70]

These lines share motifs and language with the Aten hymns, but also the Coffin Texts. The fact that earlier solar images have survived into the Greco-Roman period is well known. Louis Zabkar pointed out that not only were Ptolemaic period temples patterned after New Kingdom architectural plans, but the liturgical texts follow

---

[67] Translation based on the text edition of E. A. W. Budge, *The Book of the Dead* (London: British Museum, 1895), 1–3.

[68] Faulkner, *Book of the Dead*, 41.

[69] Miriam Lichtheim, *Ancient Egyptian Literature* III (Berkeley: University of California Press, 1980) 112.

[70] Ibid., 113.

earlier ones with only minimal change.[71] At Philae Temple there are texts dating to Ptolemy II Philadelphus (284–246 B.C.), and yet some of the liturgies are from the New Kingdom. Part of the hymn to Atum-Khepri in Room X in the Temple of Philae, Zabkar observed, comes from the opening of Pyramid Text Spell 600 (§§1652–1653).[72] He argues that these texts were available to the scribes in the temple library and were written on papyri.

This continuity into the late period is not surprising since during the Kushite and Saite periods (715–525 B.C.) these rulers looked back on the Middle and Old Kingdoms for inspiration in art and literature.[73] There are examples of the entire artistic and textual repertoires of Old Kingdom tombs being lifted and copied in 26th Dynasty tombs.[74] The Saite period, late 7th and 6th century B.C., has been called the "Saite Renaissance" in which ancient texts were copied and utilized. Nicolas Grimal states that Psammetichus I continued, like the Kushite kings, to emphasize more "nationalistic" art by returning to Old Kingdom and Middle Kingdom artistic sources."[75] With this Kushite-Saite renaissance period, Pyramid Texts reappear on coffins and in tombs of this period and occasionally in tombs down to Dynasty 30 (4th century B.C.).[76] The Pyramid Texts spells were copied directly from the Old Kingdom pyramids themselves. The Pyramid of Unas as Saqqara seems to have been the inspiration for the texts used in the Memphite region. In his 2009 Brown University dissertation, Ramadan Hussein observed: "the Lower Egyptian cemeteries exhibit different levels of interest in the Pyramid Texts. The largest portion of Saite copies is attested in the shaft-tombs clustered around the pyramid of Unas."[77]

It is true that Akhenaten's successors attempted to stamp out his memory and his heretical theology. But solar religion and the traditional language associated with it, and Aten or sun-disc itself, were not censored or rejected. It was the particular theology of exclusiveness that Akhenaten attached to old solar religion and his brand of monotheism and his persecution of Amun and other deities that made him the heretic and the enemy of the polytheistic orthodoxy.

---

[71] Louis Zabkar, "Adaptation of Ancient Egyptian Texts to the Temple Ritual at Philae," *JEA* 66 (1980):127–136.

[72] Ibid., 130.

[73] Nicholas Grimal, *A History of Ancient Egypt* (Oxford: Blackwells, 1992), 355–356.

[74] John Wilson, *The Culture of Ancient Egypt* (Chicago: University of Chicago Press, 1951), 294–295.

[75] Nicolas Grimal, *A History of Ancient Egypt*, 355.

[76] For sources of late period Pyramid Texts, see T. G. Allen, *Occurrences of Pyramids Texts with Cross Indexes of These and Other Egyptian Mortuary Texts* (Chicago: The Oriental Institute, 1950), 13–21.

[77] Ramadan B. Hussein, "The Saite Pyramid Texts Copies in the Memphite and Heliopolitan Shaft-Tombs: A Study of Their Selection and Layout" (Ph.D. diss., Brown University, 2009), quote from Abstract.

When the foregoing post-Amarna hymns are considered, several conclusions regarding the hymns to Aten and their influence in Egypt and Israel are in order:

1. The Aten hymns draw heavily on solar language and motifs from earlier periods.
2. Solar hymns with traditional solar language and motifs continue after the Amarna period, down to the Greco-Roman period.
3. The latest manifestations of this literature do not contain evidence of significant redaction; rather, the scribes faithfully transmitted the literature of the New, Middle and Old Kingdoms.
4. The foregoing evidence demonstrates that throughout the 1st millennium, Egyptian solar hymns could in some form have been available to Hebrew writers. Thus the chronological gap between the Aten hymns and Psalm 104, whenever it was written during the 1st millennium, disappears since the two are chronologically mediated by post-Amarna period solar hymns. This means that later Egyptian solar literature and hymns may have influenced the Hebrew Psalmist, but likely not the Aten hymns themselves.
5. Therefore there is no need to fill this gap with a hypothesized Semitic intermediary.

The fact that there is no chronological gap between Egyptian sun-hymns and the Hebrew Psalm, and in the absence of any evidence for a Canaanite-Phoenician intermediary, the theory of a Semitic link between the Aten hymns and Psalm 104 can safely be abandoned.

CONCLUSIONS ON PSALM 104 AND THE ATEN HYMNS

There is no philosophical reason to reject some influence from Egypt on Psalm 104. The chronological gap between the 14th century B.C. when the Aten hymns were composed (for which there are no later extant copies) and the presumed 9th–7th century date for the composition of the Hebrew Psalm has posed a problem. The notion that the principal ideas and motifs were passed on in a Semitic version via Phoenicia (Byblos is especially known for having direct contact with Egypt for centuries) has been shown to be unnecessary in view of the fact that the same solar imagery and language lived on in the Book of the Dead and various liturgical texts in Egypt down to the Ptolemaic period, and thus theoretically there could have been some direct connection, although how that would have happened remains a mystery.

Nearly 30 years ago, the author participated in a conference at the University of Toronto in which a question was raised by a member of the audience asking about the relationship between the Aten hymn and Psalm 104.[78] One of the speakers, the late Klaus Baer, professor of Egyptology at the University of Chicago, offered a rather humorous but insightful answer. He memorably explained that most investigators who do comparative studies of the two pieces of literature have the King James Version in one hand, and in the other, John Wilson's somewhat King James–like translation of the Great Hymn to Aten from the *Ancient Near Eastern Texts* volume (see above in this chapter). Due to the archaic English used in both translations, he suggested, a false impression is given of a direct connection between the two poems. Baer then suggested that when the Aten hymn is read in Egyptian and Psalm 104 in Hebrew, the similarities fade. He has a point, for most biblical scholars who have compared the two pieces of literature have not been experts on Egyptian language and literature.

The literary or thematic parallels between the two hymns strike one as being rather banal. When the sun rises, life on earth springs into action and humans do their work. When the sun sets, humans rest, while certain nocturnal animals prowl looking for food. The sun and moon serve to mark the passing of time and seasons. Not surprisingly, some version of a sun-god is attested across the Near East. In Sumer, he was known as Utu, while the standard Semitic word for sun, *šmš*, is the name of the sun-god (Shamash) in Babylon as well as in the Levant,[79] and this same word for sun in the Hebrew Bible (שֶׁמֶשׁ), including Psalm 104. Indeed, there is no culture in the ancient Near East for which the phenomena of nature were not common, and for whom the sun did not play a central religious role; thus these "similarities" likely reflect "the common theology" of the eastern Mediterranean world, to return to Morton Smith's axiom. These common cosmological themes fit under what Smith called a "general pattern."

In the absence of convincing evidence for some sort of direct connection between the Amarna hymns or later solar literature and the Hebrew Psalmist, or some Semitic intermediary document by which this material reached Israel, it seems best to conclude for the present that the "parallels" between Amarna hymns to Aten and Psalm 104 should be attributed to "the common theology" and the "general pattern." Should some new text be discovered that offers a mechanism for explaining a connection between the two literary traditions, scholars would certainly welcome that, and where needed, one would happily revise the position taken here.

---

[78] This was during a panel discussion at the end of the annual Meeting of the Society for the Study of Egyptian Activities, November 1984.

[79] Helmer Ringgren, *Religions of the Ancient Near East* (London: SPCK, 1973), 56–59.

MONOTHEISM IN ISRAEL

The origin of Israel's religion has been the subject of hot debate for nearly two centuries. Here is not the place to review thoroughly the history of that debate, but to merely sketch some of the contours so as to allow a basis for studying the Hebrew Bible tradition alongside Atenism.

There are several problems that have led to the protracted academic deliberations. One, of course, is a matter of definition (for our working definition, see Chapter 7), especially where to draw the line between monotheism and henotheism (or monolatry), a challenge also for Egyptologists in understanding Atenism. The second major complication lies in the conflict between theoretical reconstructions of the composition of the Pentateuch or Torah by critical biblical scholars and what the biblical tradition actually claims. Since the 19th century, under the influence of evolutionary theory applied to the religion of Israel, sophisticated ideas like monotheism and covenant were believed to be developments from the end of Old Testament history. The Babylonian exile of Judah and its attendant trauma and dislocation are thought to serve as the crucible out of which monotheism finally emerged in the 6th century B.C.[80] Wellhausen asserted: "Monotheism was unknown to ancient Israel. . . . It would only be from the time of the Babylonian exile that the concept was alive. Around that time, it suddenly emerges that he [Yahweh] not only controls but also created the lands and seas, with all their abundance, the heavens and their host."[81]

---

[80] Wellhausen, Julius, *Prolegomena to the History of Ancient Israel* (Gloucester: Peter Smith, 1883), 417–420. For some standard works on Israelite Religion, see William F. Albright, *Yahweh and the Gods of Canaan* (Winona Lake: Eisenbrauns, 1968). Yehezkel Kaufmann, *The Religion of Israel: From Its Beginnings to the Babylonian Exile*, trans. Moshe Greenberg (New York: Schocken Books, 1972). Helmer Ringgren, *Israelite Religion*, trans. David E. Green (Philadelphia: Fortress Press, 1966). Georg Fohrer, *History of Israelite Religion*, trans. David Green (Nashville: Abingdon, 1972). Frank Moore Cross, *Canaanite Myth and Hebrew Epic* (Cambridge, MA: Harvard University Press, 1973). Some of his earlier ideas are updated and discussed afresh in Frank Moore Cross, *From Epic to Canon: History and Literature in Ancient Israel* (Baltimore/London: The Johns Hopkins University Press, 1998). Mark S. Smith, *The Early History of God: Yahweh and the Other Deities in Ancient Israel* (San Francisco: Harper & Row, 1990). Rainer Albertz, *A History of Israelite Religion in the Old Testament Period*, trans. John Bowden, 2 vols., vol. I: *From the Beginnings to the End of the Monarchy* (Louisville, KY: Westminster John Knox Press, 1994), 3–17. Susan Niditch, *Ancient Israelite Religion* (New York/Oxford: Oxford University Press, 1997). Mark S. Smith, *The Origins of Biblical Monotheism: Israel's Polytheistic Background and the Ugaritic Texts* (Oxford/New York: Oxford University Press, 2001). Othmar Keel & Christoph Uehlinger, *Gods, Goddesses, and Images of God in Ancient Israel*, trans. Thomas H. Trapp (Minneapolis: Fortress Press, 1998). Patrick D. Miller, *The Religion of Ancient Israel* (Louisville, KY: Westminster John Knox Press, 2000). Beth Alpert Nakhai, *Archaeology and the Religions of Canaan and Israel* (Boston: ASOR Books, 2001). Ziony Zevit, *The Religions of Ancient Israel: A Synthesis of Parallactic Approaches* (London/New York: Continuum, 2001). Richard S. Hess, *Israelite Religions* (Grand Rapids: Baker, 2007).

[81] Julius Wellhausen, *Israelitische und Jüdische Geschichte* (9th ed.; Berlin: de Gruyter, 1958), 29–30, translation in Stephen Cook, *The Social Root of Biblical Yahwism* (Atlanta: Society of Biblical Literature, 2004), 4.

With regard to "covenant" (Heb. *bᵉrîṯ*), it is now known that this word was universally used in the making of treaties across the Near East in the 2nd millennium B.C.[82] In fact, the word *bᵉrîṯ* is even used as a Semitic loan-word in 13th-century Egyptian texts.[83] So the use of this term in Genesis, Exodus, and Deuteronomy simply cannot be viewed as a late development.

Critical biblical scholars today by and large, while claiming that they no longer adhere precisely to Wellhausen's four source hypothesis and his dating of those sources (Yahwist of the 9th century, the Elohist of the 8th century, Deuteronomist of the 7th century, and Priestly of the 6th century), still in fact hold to some sort of evolutionary understanding of Israelite origin.[84] A new factor that has contributed to perpetuating the evolutionary model is the rejection by historical minimalists of the Bible story of Israel's national origin, namely that a group of Hebrew pastoralists migrated to Egypt, lived there for some centuries, followed by the exodus, the Sinai wilderness period, and the Sinaitic Covenant, culminating with military conquest in the land of Canaan two generations later.[85] Consequently, many biblical scholars and archaeologists now maintain that because there was no sojourn in Egypt, there was no exodus. As a result, Israel's origin as a people and their religious traditions require a new explanation. The current theory, which has captured the imagination of many scholars, is that "Israel" was originally an indigenous people group in Canaan.[86] There was a process of a long struggle with its Canaanite identity and its deities, El, Baal, Ashereh, and Astarte. Then, in some inexplicable way, this group attached itself to the god Yahweh[87] (although he is not attested in the Canaanite pantheon or in any Canaanite/Ugaritic literature!). According to this view, the struggle between this god and the other Canaanite deities was not as the Bible presents it, apostasy against "the LORD your God from the land of Egypt; you know no God but me, and besides me there is no savior. It was I who knew you in

---

[82] K. A. Kitchen, "Egypt, Ugarit, Qatna and Covenant," *Ugarit Forschungen* 11 (1979): 453–464.

[83] James Hoch, *Semitic Words in Egyptian Texts of the New Kingdom and Third Intermediate Period* (Princeton, NJ: Princeton University Press, 1994), 108–109, §135.

[84] E.g. Michael Coogan, "Canaanite Origins and Lineage," in *Ancient Israelite Religion: Essays in Honor of Frank Moore Cross* (P. D. Miller et. al. eds.; Philadelphia: Fortress, 1987), 115–124. Robert Gnuse, *No Other Gods: Emergent Monotheism in Israel* (Sheffield: Sheffield Academic Press, 1997). Mark Smith, *The Origins of Biblical Monotheism*.

[85] For a review of the literature on this subject and a critique, see Hoffmeier, *Israel in Egypt*; idem, *Ancient Israel in Sinai: The Evidence for the Authenticity of the Wilderness Tradition* (New York: Oxford University Press, 2005/2011).

[86] For a review of the various theories, see Richard Hess, "Early Israel in Canaan: A Survey of Recent Evidence and Interpretations," *Palestine Exploration Quarterly* 125 (1993): 125–142, and Hoffmeier, *Israel in Egypt*, 25–33.

[87] E.g. Saul Olyan, *Asherah and the Cult of Yahweh in Israel* (Atlanta: Scholars Press, 1988). Mark Smith, *The Early History of God: Yahweh and Other Deities in Ancient Israel* (San Francisco: Harper & Row, 1990).

the wilderness, in a land of drought," to quote the 8th century prophet Hosea (Hos. 13:4–5). Rather, as Mark Smith frames it, "it is precisely this conflict that produced the differentiation of Israelite religion from *its Canaanite heritage* during the second half of the monarchy."[88]

The major obstacle with the claim that Israel originated within Canaan is that there is no convincing explanation for the origin of Yahweh. The Pentateuch, the prophets, and the Psalms, when speaking of Israel's origins, focus invariably on Egypt, Sinai, and the wilderness.[89] So, according to this revisionist view, the god Yahweh evolved out of Canaanite culture and religion, and then Yahweh became the national deity and only in the end of biblical history did the Jews become authentically monotheistic. Some biblicists believe that the movement toward a Yahweh-only theology may have begun as early as the 8th century prophets, with Hezekiah's reforms playing a decisive role in centralizing the cult (2 Kings 18; 2 Chron. 29–30), followed by Josiah's reforms in the late 7th century (2 Kings 22–23), which is consistent with the preaching of 8th-century prophets like Hosea, Micah, and Amos,[90] who likely represented "a prophetic minority."[91]

Another reason that this evolutionary model continues is that it comports with the Axial Movement theory of religious development. The Zoroastrian 18th-century scholar A. H. Anquetil-Duperron had advanced the theory that in the centuries leading up to 500 B.C. there was a convergence of charismatic leaders, Zoroaster, Buddha, the Hebrew prophets, and Greek philosophers, across Asia to Europe, that led to "a great revolution for humankind."[92] The *Achsenzeit* (Axial Age) theory was further advanced by Karl Jaspers (who actually coined the term *Achsenzeit*)[93] and others who saw a breakthrough occurring in this era, from which monotheism emerged. Because this theory, too, is evolutionary, it has been criticized along with other more recent developmental schemes. In his recent study, *The Social Roots*

---

88 Smith, *The Early History of God*, xxxi. Emphasis is that of this writer.

89 For a review of the biblical literature, see James K. Hoffmeier, "'These Things Happened': Why a Historical Exodus is Essential for Theology," in *Do Historical Matters Matter to Faith: A Critical Appraisal of Modern and Postmodern Approaches to Scripture* (eds. James K. Hoffmeier & Dennis R. Magary; Wheaton: Crossway, 2012) 99–134.

90 Stephen Cook, *The Social Roots of Biblical Yahwism* (Atlanta: Society of Biblical Literature, 2004). Also a good critique of the late development of monotheism in Israel, see Simon Sherwin, "Did the Israelites Really Learn Their Monotheism in Babylon?" in *Israel: Ancient Kingdom or Late Invention* (ed. D. I. Block; Nashville: B & H Academic), 257–281.

91 Bernhard Lang, *Monotheism and the Prophetic Minority* (Atlanta: Almond Press, 1983).

92 For a treatment of this subject, see Jan Assmann, *Of God and Gods: Egypt, Israel, and the Rise of Monotheism* (Madison: University of Wisconsin, 2008), 76–78. Karl Woschitz, "Axial Age," *Religion Past and Present*, Vol. 1 (ed. H. D. Betz, et. al.; Leiden: Brill, 2007), 531.

93 Karl Jaspers, *The Origin and Goal of History* (New Haven, CT: Yale University Press, 1953).

of Biblical Yahwism, Stephen Cook offers a fitting critique of the old evolutionary model to explain the rise of monotheism in Israel: "one can defend nineteenth-century scholars' embrace of the developmental thesis as appropriate to their times, because of the contemporary dominance of Hegel's and Darwin's ideas of progress, evolution, and becoming. It is harder to view the current espousal of this thesis charitably, given the atrocities of the twentieth century and late-modern critiques of the idea of humanity's general religious ascent."[94]

The state of Pentateuchal studies is currently in flux,[95] and regarding the old consensus that consolidated around Wellhausen's views, John Van Seters has recently described that state of the art as being in "chaos rendered by the demise of the older consensus."[96] And this has had its impact on how the origins of Israel's religion is interpreted.

No one would argue that both the biblical text itself and archaeological data from Iron Age Israel show (bull cults, Asherah figures, etc.)[97] that Yahweh was the only deity worshiped in Israel and that other gods and goddess were not worshiped at different times and places. Indeed, the Hebrew Bible repeatedly speaks of Israel's recidivism and worshiping "other gods." Even in the "era" of Moses in the Sinai Wilderness, immediately after the grand theophany of Yahweh at Mt. Sinai (Exodus 19), a golden calf was molded and celebrated with offerings (Exod. 32). Moses reportedly demolished it (Exod. 32:20), in keeping with the first two commandments:

> I am the LORD your God, who brought you out of the land of Egypt, out of the house of slavery. You shall have no other gods before me. You shall not make for yourself a carved image, or any likeness of anything that is in heaven above, or that is in the earth beneath, or that is in the water under the earth. You shall not bow down to them or serve them . . ." (Exod. 20:3–5)

Moreover, even Joshua, Moses's successor, is reported to have spoken to the Israelites soon after entry into the land of Canaan in a covenant renewal ceremony at Shechem and indicated that the ancestors of Israel worshiped other deities.

---

[94] Cook, *The Social Roots of Biblical Yahwism*, 9.

[95] For recent developments in Pentateuchal criticism and its origins and dating, see Thomas B. Dozeman & Konrad Schmidt (eds.), *A Farwell to the Yahwist? The Composition of the Pentateuch in Recent European Interpretation* (Atlanta: Society of Biblical Literature, 2006). Thomas B. Dozeman, Thomas Römer, and Konrad Schmidt (eds.), *Pentateuch, Hexateuch or Enneateuch? Identifying Literary Works in Genesis through Kings* (Atlanta: Society of Biblical Literature, 2011).

[96] John Van Seters, *The Pentateuch: A Social-Science Commentary* (Sheffield: Sheffield Academic Press, 1999), 19.

[97] For recent discoveries on early Israelite polytheism, see Zevit, *The Religions of Ancient Israel*; Hess, *Israelite Religions*, Chapters 7–9; William Dever, *Did God Have a Wife?: Archaeology and Folk Religion in Ancient Israel* (Grand Rapids, MI: Eerdmans, 2005).

> And Joshua said to all the people, "Thus says the LORD, the God of Israel, Long ago, your fathers lived beyond the Euphrates, Terah, the father of Abraham and of Nahor; and they served other gods . . ." (Josh. 24:2)

Joshua complained that they continued to be entangled in pagan practices:

> Now therefore fear the LORD and serve him in sincerity and in faithfulness. Put away the gods that your fathers served beyond the River and in Egypt, and serve the LORD. And if it is evil in your eyes to serve the LORD, choose this day whom you will serve, whether the gods your fathers served in the region beyond the River, or the gods of the Amorites in whose land you dwell. But as for me and my house, we will serve the LORD. (Josh. 24:14–15)

Ever since Martin Noth's seminal work in 1943, scholars have viewed Joshua as a part of the work of the Deuternomistic History, compiled in the 7th century B.C. in Jerusalem.[98] Thus the narratives are largely a retrospective viewed through the lens of the reforms of Josiah. Robert Boling and G. E. Wright, however, regarded this Shechem pericope to be "pre-Deuteronomic,"[99] while in his recent monograph on the origins of monotheism in Israel, André Lemaire suggests that the Shechem episode "is probably also historical," but, in his view, the account portrays monolatry (i.e., henotheism), not strictly monotheism.[100]

The point argued here is that there was an official or orthodox view of Yahweh the God of the Exodus and Sinai that the prophets promoted, but that there was persistent tension between "biblical Yahwism," to use Cook's term, and popular religion's syncretistic tendency to intermingle Yahwism with local Canaanite cults.[101] Fifty years ago, Norman Snaith commented on this fusion: "It is the fact of the existence of the one and only High God from the beginning which leads scholars to see monotheism, or traces of monotheism at all stages of Israelite history . . . but this does not preclude low-god cults at that particular time."[102] "Popular religion" and state or official religion are not always the same, but typically coexist. It has been shown in New Kingdom Egypt that popular religion in the village of Deir

---

[98] Martin Noth, *Ueberlieferungsgeschectliche Studien* (Tübingen: Max Niemeyer, 1943), the English version of which is *The Deuteronomistic History* (Sheffield: JSOT Press, 1981).

[99] Robert Boling & G. Ernest Wright, *Joshua: A New Translation with Introduction and Commentary* (Garden City, NY: Doubleday, 1982), 533.

[100] André Lemaire, *The Birth of Monotheism: The Rise and Disappearance of Yahwism* (Washington, DC: Biblical Archaeology Society, 2007), 31–32.

[101] On popular religion, see Dever, *Did God Have a Wife?: Archaeology and Folk Religion in Ancient Israel.*

[102] Norman Snaith, "The Advent of Monotheism in Israel," *Annual of Leeds University Oriental Society* 5 (1963–1965): 112.

el-Medineh (Western Thebes) included the major deities of state religion, who were worshiped among the people of this community, but that the cults of other local deities not attached to the major state-sponsored temples were also venerated by the villagers.[103] The picture with Israel is surely the same, namely, that the official religion of Israel—with its first cult center in Shiloh[104] but later in Jerusalem—was Yahwism. After all, the temple was called "the house of Yahweh" (בֵּית יְהוָה). Indeed, there are more than 230 references to this expression in the Old Testament. Popular religion, with its local "high places" (בָּמוֹת/בָּמָה), was a perennial problem for orthodoxy in Israel and Judah during the monarchy, but Yahweh's dominance was clear, as evidenced by the choice of personal names used in the Hebrew Bible. One study has shown that of the 466 theophoric names, 89 percent are Yahwistic while only 11 percent are pagan.[105] Lest one think that the biblical data are slanted to reflect positively on devotion to Yahweh, an analysis of theophoric names from available epigraphic (extra-biblical) sources by Jeffrey Tigay revealed that 557 cases use some form of divine name Yahweh, whereas only 35 employ clearly identifiable "pagan" names, which is 6.3 percent.[106] Personal names are a good indicator of the deities venerated by the parents giving the names.

Although not the current prevailing view among biblical scholars, there is a stream of thought following scholars like Yehezkel Kaufmann,[107] Helmer Ringren,[108] William F. Albright,[109] Georg Fohrer,[110] and recently Lemaire,[111] that trace the origins of Israel's religion to the southern desert (Midian or Sinai) and the theophany of Yahweh to Moses.

The reason for looking for Israel and Yahweh's origin in Sinai or Midian is that among the geographical lists at the Temple of Amenhotep III at Soleb in Nubia are references to names of various Bedouin or desert tribes (Egyptian Shasu), including the Shasu land of 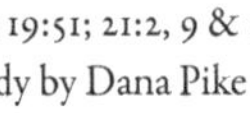, which reads *yhw3*.[112] These names were also recopied at

[103] Ashraf Iskander, *Popular Religion in Egypt during the New Kingdom* (Hildesheim: Gerstenberg, 1988), Chapter 6.

[104] E.g. Josh. 18:1, 8–10; 19:51; 21:2, 9 & 12; Judges 18:31; 21:12, 19, 21; 1 Sam. 1:3, 9.

[105] An unpublished study by Dana Pike cited by Jeffrey Tigay, *You Shall Have No Other Gods: Israelite Religion in the Light of Hebrew Inscriptions* (Atlanta: Scholars Press, 1985), 7.

[106] Ibid., 47–63.

[107] Yehezkel Kaufmann, *The Religion of Israel from Its Beginnings to the Babylonian Exile*, 223–242.

[108] Ringgren, *Israelite Religion*, 28–40.

[109] Albright, *Yahweh and the Gods of Canaan*; idem, *From Stone Age to Christianity: Monotheism and the Historical Process* (Baltimore, MD: The Johns Hopkins Press, 1946), 196–207.

[110] Georg Fohrer, *History of Israelite Religion* (Nashville: Abdingdon Press, 1972), 66–101.

[111] Lemaire, *The Birth of Monotheism*, 24–34.

[112] H.W. Fairman, "Preliminary Report On the Excavations at 'Amrah West, Anglo-Egyptian Sudan, 1938–9," *JEA* 25(1939): 139–44.

the nearby 'Amrah temple of Ramesses II in the 13th century B.C.[113] Egyptian *yhw3* linguistically corresponds to Hebrew YHWH. This toponym led some scholars to think that it points to a geographical territory where a cult for Yahwa existed in the 14th century B.C.[114]

This interpretation is strengthened by the proximity of Seir in the same list. Genesis 32:3 indicates that Seir is one and the same as Edom, or is some part of it or adjacent to it: "Jacob sent messengers before him to his brother Esau in the land of Seir, the country of Edom." Other passages in Genesis associate the two names: "So Esau settled in the hill country of Seir; Esau is Edom. These are the descendants of Esau, ancestor of the Edomites, in the hill country of Seir" (Exod 36:8–9).

The proximity of Seir and *yhw3* in the Soleb and 'Amrah geographical lists support the theory that Yahweh may have had his origin in the area of northeastern Sinai or the southern Arabah. This area, in turn, is associated with the home of the Kenites,[115] who are associated with the in-laws of Moses (Judg. 1:16).

Thus this Egyptian evidence seems to support the view that this is the very region where the Bible suggests Moses encountered Yahweh and where the Israelite encamped in the wilderness during the period 1350–1250 B.C.

From the perspective of the historian of religion, especially the phenomenologist, theophany is always foundational to a religion. The Sinai theophany is no exception. Memorable is the 9th-century story of Elijah and the prophets of Baal on Mt. Carmel in northern Israel. Yahweh's prophet challenges the followers of Baal to "call upon the name of your god, and I will call upon the name of the LORD, and the God who answers by fire, he is God" (1 Kings 18:24). At the end of the competing calls for a divine manifestation by the Baal prophets, Elijah called on Yahweh and "then the fire of the LORD fell and consumed the burnt offering and the wood and the stones and the dust, and licked up the water that was in the trench. And when all the people saw it, they fell on their faces and said, 'The LORD, he is God; the LORD, he is God'" (vss. 38–39). "The fire of the LORD" here surely evokes memories of the Sinai kratophany with its "thunders and lightnings" (Exod. 19:16). Noteworthy is the juxtaposition of this Mt. Carmel theophany (1 Kings 18) and Elijah's pilgrimage to Horeb (i.e., Sinai), where he experienced a numinous encounter at "the mount of God" (1 Kings 19:8).

The Mt. Carmel episode well illustrates the tug-of-war between Yahweh and local (Canaanite) deities, but also suggests that despite the invitation for Baal to reveal

---

[113] Raphael Giveon, "Toponymes Ouest-Asiatiques à Soleb," *VT* 14 (1964): 239–255.

[114] Bernhard Grdseloff, "Édôm, D'arès Les Sources Egyptiennes," *Revue de l'histoire juive d'Egypte* 1 (1947): 69–99. Raphael Giveon, *Les Bédouins Shosou Des Documents Égyptiens* (Leiden: Brill, 1971) 28. Donald Redford, *Egypt, Canaan, and Israel in Ancient Times* (Princeton, NJ: Princeton University Press, 1992), 272–273.

[115] Grdseloff, "Édôm, D'arès Les Sources Egyptiennes," 79ff.

himself, there was none. Commenting on the contest between Elijah and the prophets of Baal, Simon DeVries proposes that Elijah's statement "the god who answers by fire, he is God" (1 Kings 18:24) indicates that "early Israel believed not in a theoretical but a practical monotheism, i.e. that the only god who counts as real is the one who acts, who has power to help his people."[116]

CONCLUDING THOUGHTS

In this study it has been suggested that in the middle of the 14th century B.C. Akhenaten advocated a monotheistic expression of solar religion, namely Atenism. In Chapter 5, based on the language and terminology used on the boundary stela at Amarna, the idea was advanced that Akhenaten was the recipient of some sort of theophany, a revelation of the sun god (Aten) that was repeated in connection with the discovery of the site in middle Egypt to build his holy city, Akhet-Aten (Chapter 5). Then, after the move to that new capital, a third and unequivocally monotheistic form of Aten's didactic name was introduced, (Living Re, Ruler of the Horizon, Rejoicing in the Horizon in His Name of "Re, the Father, who has come as the Sun-disc") which involved the removal of the names of Shu (meaning light or the deity by that name) and Horus (from Harakhty) so as to convey one and only one God (Chapter 7). The names of Amun and other gods, and the plural writing for "gods," were erased in many tombs, stelae, obelisks, and temples. The early appearance of Aten as a man with the head of the falcon with the sun-disc on its head soon disappears, with only the sun-disc and its rays surviving as the official icon. The Aten hymns seem to serve as the official dogma of this "sole god."

Akhenaten must be considered the founder of Atenism. However, his monotheistic religion lacked a committed group of disciples or followers who carried on the tradition, copied, compiled, and canonized his teaching (*sb3yt*) for future generations. Egypt was clearly not prepared to give up its gods for the One, and officials like the priests Meryre and Panehsy, and high officials like Ay and Horemheb, must have realized that they were swimming against the current, and so abandoned Aten, opting for Amun-Re and traditional religion.

With regard to Axial Movement theory and Atenism, Assmann has observed that "ancient Egyptian evidence invites us to modify the Axial Age theory in two respects that are of some importance to our general search for the roots of monotheism."[117] He suggests that one needs to consider "smaller-scaled transformations" as influential on a culture, rather than major movements and the role that "breakdown

---

[116] Simon DeVries, *1 Kings* (Waco, TX: Word Books, 1985), 228.

[117] Assmann, *Of God and Gods*, 78.

and breakthrough" play in cultural and religious transformation to monotheism. When it comes to Israel, however, Assmann falls in step with the prevailing view among biblical scholars that even though Israel's founding "story is *set* in Egypt at a time strangely proximate to that of Akhenaten and his monotheistic revolution, that is, in the fourteenth century or thirteenth century B.C.E. However, it *was told* at a much later time, in the seventh through fifth centuries, and in Judaea and Babylon at the time of the Babylonian exile and Persian domination."[118]

What Atenism demonstrates is that even though it was only a blip on the radar of religious history, the "breakthrough" had occurred, to borrow Assmann's term. This means that there is no reason *a priori* to dismiss the idea of Mosaic monotheism or Yahwistic monotheism as originating in the century following Akhenaten. Here, too, an individual, Moses, reportedly experienced a theophany which the ancient Hebrews who had been in Egypt witnessed at Mt. Sinai/Horeb (Exod. 19–20), and which led to the establishment of a cult (with a movable shrine at first) and a body of teachings (the Book of the Covenant, Exod. 24:7).[119] While it appears that some or even many in early Israel were not prepared to follow Yahweh alone and his cult that had no images, some followed a more syncretistic form of Yahwism. Nevertheless, Mosaic monotheism had followers who perpetuated the religion, such as Joshua, Samuel, Elijah, Isaiah, and other prophets and priests like Jehoida and Hilkiah (2 Kings 11 & 22), and transmitted the tradition and added to it over time. It may be that beginning with reformer kings like Hezekiah (late 8th century) and Josiah (7th century), and through the preaching of prophets and priests and scribes, during and after the exile, a monotheist faith in Yahweh was no longer debated or challenged in the Jewish community. Standing behind these later reforms is the God Yahweh, who was believed to have delivered the Hebrews from Egypt, and the Sinai revelation. The latter is recalled in the Song of Deborah, thought to be among the oldest poetic works in the Old Testament,[120] "The mountains quaked before the LORD, even Sinai before the LORD, the God of Israel" (Judg. 5:5).

The fact that Atenism was a monotheistic religion does not prove that Mosaic Yahwism, possibly originating in the following century, was also monotheistic, but from the perspective of the historian of religion, there is no reason to deny that possibility. This is not to say that there was any direct or indirect influence of one upon the other, but Atenism does demonstrate that a long evolution from animism to monotheism, as early anthropologists of religion of the 19th century maintained

---

[118] Ibid., 86. The emphasis is Assmann's.

[119] Hoffmeier, *Ancient Israel in Sinai*, chapter 9.

[120] Frank M. Cross & David N. Freedman, *Studies in Ancient Yahwistic Poetry*. Vol. 21, *SBL Dissertation Series* (Missoula: Society of Biblical Literature, 1975), 1–14.

and some biblical scholars still advocate, is not a viable model to explain the origins of monotheism. True monotheism normally requires a theophany (or the belief in one), a charismatic leader, and followers to sustain and transmit the traditions and doctrines. This seems to be the pattern behind monotheistic faiths that survived: Moses and ancient Israel's religion and later Judaism; Zarathushtra and Zoroasterism; Jesus and Christianity; and Mohammed and Islam. Why Atenism ultimately did not survive beyond the lifetime of its founder is that it lacked the adherents to perpetuate the belief. So the sun set on Akhenaten's monotheistic religious experiment so that it is a footnote in history, but indeed an important one—the first one to advocate one God, the universal creator and sustainer of all life.

BIBLIOGRAPHY

Abd el-Maksoud, Mohamed, "Une nouvelle forteresse sur la route d'horus: Tell Heboua 1986 (North Sinai)," *CRIPEL* 9 (1987) 13–16.

Abd el-Maksoud, Mohamed, *Tell Heboua—1981–1991*, Paris: Editions Recherche sur les Civlisations, 1998.

Abd el-Maksoud, Mohamed, "Tjarou, Porte De L'oriente," *Le Sinaï durant l'antiquité et le moyen age* (eds. C. Bonnet and D. Valbelle), Paris: Errance, 1998, 61–65.

el-Maksoud, Mohamed Abd, and Dominique Valbelle, "Tell Héboua-Tjarou l'apport de l'épigraphie," *Rd'É* 56 (2005) 18–20.

el-Maksoud, Mohamed Abd, and D. Valbelle, "Tell Héboua: Sur le décor et lépigraphie des elements architectoniques découverts au cours des campagnes 2008–2009 dans la zone centrale due *Khétem* de Tjarou," *Rd'É* 62 (2011) 1–39.

Albertz, Rainer, *A History of Israelite Religion in the Old Testament Period*, trans. John Bowden, 2 Vols. Vol. I: *From the Beginnings to the End of the Monarchy*, Louisville, KY: Westminster John Knox Press, 1994.

Albright, William F., *From Stone Age to Christianity: Monotheism and the Historical Process*, Baltimore: The Johns Hopkins Press, 1946.

Albright, William F., *Yahweh and the Gods of Canaan*, Winona Lake, IN: Eisenbruans, 1968.

Albright, William F., "Moses in Historical and Theological Perspective," *Magnalia Dei: The Mighty Acts of God* (eds. F. M. Cross, et al), Garden City, New York: Doubleday, 1976, 120–131.

Aldred, Cyril, "The Beginning of the El-ʿAmārna Period," *JEA* 45 (1959) 19–33.

Aldred, Cyril, "The Horizon of the Aten," *JEA* 62 (1976) 184.

Aldred, Cyril, *Akhenaten King of Egypt*, London: Thames & Hudson, 1988.

Allen, Douglas, "Phenomenology of Religion," *The Encyclopedia of Religion*, Vol. 11 (ed. M. Eliade), New York: Macmillan, 1987, 272–285.

Allen, James P., "The Cosmology of the Pyramid Texts," *Religion and Philosophy in Ancient Egypt* (ed. W. K. Simpson), New Haven, CT: Yale Egyptological Studies, 3, 1989, 1–28.

Allen, James P., *The Ancient Egyptian Pyramid Texts*, Atlanta, GA: Society of Biblical Literature, 2005.

Allen, James P., "The Amarna Succession," *Causing His Name to Live: Studies in Egyptian Epigraphy and History in Memory of William J. Murnane* (eds. P. J. Brand and L. Cooper), Leiden/Boston: Brill, 2009, 9–20.

Allen, Leslie C., *Psalms 101–150*, Waco, TX: Word, 1983.

Allen, T. George, "Some Egyptian Sun Hymns," *JNES* 8 (1949) 349–355.

Allen, T. George, *Occurrences of Pyramid Texts with Cross Indexes of These and Other Egyptian Mortuary Texts*, Chicago: The Oriental Institute, 1950.

Allen, T. George, *The Book of the Dead or Going Forth by Day. Ideas of the Ancient Egyptians Concerning the Hereafter as Expressed in Their Own Terms*, Chicago: University of Chicago Press, 1974.

Anderson, A. A., *The Book of Psalms*, Vol. 1, London: Marshall Morgan & Scott, 1972.

Anderson, A. A., *The Book of Psalms*, Vol. 2, London: Marshall, Morgan & Scott, 1972.

Arnold, Dieter, *Building in Egypt: Pharaonic Stone Masonry*, New York/Oxford: Oxford University Press, 1991.

Arnold, Dieter, "Royal Cult Complexes of the Old and Middle Kingdoms," *Temples of Ancient Egypt* (ed. B. Shafer), Ithaca, NY: Cornell University Press, 1997, 31–85.

Asselbergs, Henri, "Ein merwürdiges Relief Amenophis' IV. im Louvre-Museum," *ZÄS* 58 (1923) 36–38.

Assmann, Jan, *Ägyptische Hymnen und Gebete*, Zürich: Artemis, 1975.

Assmann, Jan, *Sonnenhymnen in thebanischen Gräbern*, Mainz: P. von Zabern, 1983.

Assmann, Jan, "Akhanyati's Theology of Light and Time," *Proceedings of the Israel Academy of Sciences and Humanities*, VII, no. 4, Jerusalem: Israel Academy of Sciences and Humanities, 1992, 143–176.

Assmann, Jan, *Egyptian Solar Religion in the New Kingdom: Re, Amun and the Crisis of Polytheism* (trans. A. Alcock), London/New York: Kegan Paul International, 1995.

Assmann, Jan, *Moses the Egyptian: The Memory of Egypt in Western Monotheism*, Cambridge, MA: Harvard University Press, 1997.

Assmann, Jan, *Of God and Gods: Egypt, Israel, and the Rise of Monotheism*, Madison: University of Wisconsin Press, 2008.

Assmann, Jan, *The Search for God in Ancient Egypt*, Ithaca, NY: Cornell University Press, 2011.

Badawy, Alexander, *A History of Egyptian Architecture* I, Cairo: Misr Studio, 1954.

Baines, John, and Jaromír Málek, *Atlas of Ancient Egypt*, New York: Facts on File, 1980.

Bakhry, Hassan, "Akhenaen at Heliopolis," *Cd'E* 47 (1972) 55–67.

Barguet, Paul, "L'Obélisque de Saint-Jean-de-Latran dan le temple de Ramsès à Karnak," *ASAE* 50 (1950) 269–280.

Barguet, Paul, *Le Temple d'Amon-Rê à Karnak, essai d'exégèse*, Cairo: IFAO, 1962.

Barguet, Paul, et al, *Le Temple d'Amada*, Vols. 3 and 4, Cairo: Centre for Documentation, 1967.

Barnes, Deborah, "'Fragile X' Syndrome and Its Puzzling Genetics," *Science* 243 (1989) 171–172.

Bárta, Miroslav, "In Mud Forgotten: Old Kingdom Paleoecological Evidence from Abusir," *Studia Quaternaria* 30, no. 2 (2013) 75–82.

Bátra, Miroslav, and A. Bezdek, "Beetles and the Decline of the Old Kingdom: Climate Change in Ancient Egypt," *Proceedings of the Conference Held in Prague (June 11–14, 2007)*, Prague: Charles University, 2008, 215–224.

Baud, Michel, "The Old Kingdom," *A Companion to Ancient Egypt* I, Vol. 36 of *Blackwell Companions to the Ancient World* (ed. Alan B. Lloyd), Oxford: Wiley-Blackwell, 2010, 63–80.

Beckerath, J. von, *Handbuch der ägyptischen Königsnamen*, Mainz: Philipp von Zabern, 1999.

Bell, Lanny, "Luxor Temple and the Cult of the Royal *Ka*," *JNES* 44 (1985) 251–294.

Bergen, Robert, "Word Distribution as an Indicator of Authorial Intention: A Study of Genesis 1:1–2:3," *Do Historical Matters Matter to Faith* (eds. J. Hoffmeier and D. Magary), Wheaton, IL: Crossway, 2012, 201–218.

Berman Lawrence, "Overview of Amenhotep III and His Reign," *Amenhotep: Perspectives on His Reign* (eds. D. O'Connor and E. Cline), Ann Arbor: University of Michigan Press, 1998, 1–26.

Bianchi, Robert, "New Light on the Aton," *GM* 114 (1990) 35–41.

Bietak, Manfred, "Zur Herfungt des Seth von Avaris," *Ägypten und Levante* 1 (1990) 9–16.

Bietak, Manfred, *Avaris: The Capital of the Hyksos*, London: The British Museum, 1996.

Björkman, Gun, "Egyptology and Historical Method," *Orientalia Suecana* 13 (1964) 9–33.

Björkman, Gun, *Kings at Karnak: A Study of the Treatment of Monuments of Royal Predecessors in the Early New Kingdom*, Upsala: Acta Universitatis Upsaliensis, 1971.

Blackman, A. M., *Middle Eastern Stories. Bibliotheca Aegyptiaca*, Vol. 2, Brussels: Foundation Égyptologique Reine Élizabeth, 1932.

Blackman, A. M., "Preliminary Report on the Excavations at Sesebi, Northern Province, Anglo-Egyptian Sudan 1936–37," *JEA* 23 (1937) 145–151.

Bleiberg, Edward, "The Redisributive Economy in the New Kingdom Egypt: An Examination of *B3k(t)*," *JARCE* 25 (1988) 157–168.

Bleiberg, Edward, *The Official Gift in Ancient Egypt*, Norman: University of Oklahoma, 1996.

Boling, Robert, and G. Ernest Wright, *Joshua: A New Translation with Introduction and Commentary*, Garden City, NY: Doubleday, 1982.

Bongioanni, Alessandro, "Considerations sur les 'nomes' d'Aten et la nature du rapport souverain-divinite a l'epoque amarnienne," *GM* 68 (1983) 43–51.

Bonhême, Marie-Ange, and Annie Forgeau, *Pharaon: Les secrets du pouvoir*, Paris: Armand Colin, 1988.

Bonnet, Charles, "Kerma-Rapport préliminare sur les campagnes de 1999–2000 et 2000–2001," *Kerma Soudan* XLIX (2001) 199–219.

Booth, Charlotte, *Horemheb: The Forgotten Pharaoh*, Stroud' Gloustershire: Amberley, 2009.

Borchardt, Ludwig, "Ein Onkel Amenophis' IV. als Hoherpriester von Heliopolis," *ZÄS* 44 (1907) 97–98.

Borghouts, J. F., "Divine Intervention in Ancient Egypt and its Manifestation *(b3w)*," *Gleanings from Deir el-Medinah* (eds. R. J. Demarée and J. J. Janssen), Leiden: Netherlands Institute for Near Eastern Studies, 1982, 1–70.

Brand, Peter, "Usurpation of Monuments," *UCLA Encyclopedia of Egyptology* (ed. Willeke Wendrich), Los Angeles: 2010 [http://digital2.library.ucla.edu/viewItem.do?ark=21198/zz025h6fh]

Breasted, James Henry, "The Philosophy of a Memphite Priest," *ZÄS* 39 (1901) 39–54.

Breasted, James Henry, "A City of Ikhenaten in Nubia," *ZÄS* 40 (1902–03) 106–113.

Breasted, James Henry, *A History of Egypt from the Earliest Times to the Persian Conquest*, New York: Scribner, 1905.

Breasted, James Henry, "Oriental Exploration Fund of the University of Chicago: Second Preliminary Report of the Egyptian Expedition," *AJSLL* 25, (1908), no.1, 1–130.

Breasted, James Henry, *A History of Egypt from the Earliest Times to the Persian Conquest*, 2nd ed., London: Hodder & Stoughton, 1921.

Breasted, James Henry, *The Dawn of Conscience*, New York: Scribners, 1933.

Brock, Edwin, "Archaeological Observations in East Karnak, 2002–2003," *forthcoming*.

Bryan, Betsy, *The Reign of Thutmose IV*, Baltimore: The John Hopkins Press, 1991.

Bryan, Betsy, "The 18th Dynasty before the Amana Period (c. 1550–1352 B.C.)," *The Oxford History of Ancient Egypt* (ed. Ian Shaw), Oxford: Oxford University Press, 2000, 207–264.

Buck, Adriaan de, *The Egyptian Coffin Texts*, Chicago: University of Chicago Press, 1935–1962.

Buck, Adriaan de, "La Litterérature et la politique sous la douzième dynastie," *Symbolae ad jus et historian antiquitatis perinetes Juli Christiano van Overn dedicate* (eds. M. David, B. A. van Groigen, and E. M. Neijers), Leiden: Brill, 1946, 1–28.

Buck, Adriaan de, *Egyptian Reading Book; Exercises and Middle Egyptian Texts*, 3rd. ed. Leiden: Nederlands Instituut voor het Nabjje Oosten, 1970.

Budge, E. A. W., *The Book of the Dead*, London: British Museum, 1895.

Burridge, Alwyn, "Akhenaten: A New Perspective, Evidence of a Genetic Disorder in the Royal Family of the 18th Dynasty Egypt," *JSSEA* 23 (1993) 63–74.

Caillois, Roger, *Man and the Sacred*, Urbana/Chicago: University of Illinois, 2001.

Callender, Gae, "The Middle Kingdom Renaissance (c. 2055–1650 B.C.)" *The OxfordHistory of Ancient Egypt* (ed. Ian Shaw), Oxford: Oxford University Press, 2000, 137–171.

Caminos, Ricardo Augusto, *The New-Kingdom Temples of Buhen*, London: Egypt Exploration Society, 1974.

Caminos, Richardo Augusto, and T. G. H. James, *Gebel es-Silsilah* I, London: Egyptian Exploration Society, 1963.

Carter, Howard, and Percy Newberry, *The Tomb of Thoutmôsis IV*, London: Archibald Constable, 1904.

Centre, Franco-Égptien d'Étude des Temples de Karnak, http://www.cfeetk.cnrs.fr/

Černý, Jaroslav, *Hieratic Inscriptions from the Tomb of Tut'ankhamun*, Oxford: Oxford University Press, 1965.

Chappaz, Jean-Luc, "Le Prmier édifice d'Amenophis IV à Karnak," *BSEG* 8 (1983) 13–45.

Chappaz, Jean-Luc, "Un Nouvel Assemblage de Talâtât: une paroi du *Rwḏ-mnw* D'Aton," *Cahiers de Karnak* VIII (1987) 81–121.

Chevrier, Henri, "Rapport sur les travaux de Karnak (mars-mai 1926)," *ASAE* 26 (1926) 119–130.

Chevrier, Henri, "Rapport sur les travaux de Karnak (novembre 1926–mai 1927)," *ASAE* 27(1927) 134–153.

Coogan, Michael, "Canaanite Origins and Lineage," *Ancient Israelite Religion: Essays in Honor of Frank Moore Cross* (eds. P. D. Miller, et al.), Philadelphia: Fortress Press, 1987.

Cook, Stephen, *The Social Root of Biblical Yahwism*, Atlanta, GT: Society of Biblical Literature, 2004.

Cooney, John, *Amarna Reliefs from Hermopolis in American Collections*, New York: Brooklyn Museum, 1965.

Cottevielle-Giraudeet, Rémy, *Rapport sur les fouilles de Médamoud (1932): Les reliefs d'Aménemphis IV Akhenaten*, Cairo: Institut Français d'Archéologie Orientale, 1936.
Craigie, Peter, "The Comparison of Hebrew Poetry: Psalm 104 in the Light of Egyptian and Ugaritic Poetry," *Semitics* 4 (1974) 9–24.
Cross, Frank Moore, *Canaanite Myth and Hebrew Epic*, Cambridge, MA: Harvard University Press, 1973.
Cross, Frank Moore, *From Epic to Canon: History and Literature in Ancient Israel*, Baltimore/London: The John Hopkins University Press, 1998.
Cross, Frank Moore, and David Noel Freedman, *Studies in Ancient Yahwistic Poetry*. SBL Dissertation Series, Vol. 21, Missoula, MT: Society of Biblical Literature, 1975.
Cruz-Uribe, Eugene, "Another Look at an Aton Statue," *GM* 126 (1992) 29–32.
Cumming, Barbara, *Egyptian Historical Records of the Later Eighteenth Dynasty*, Westminster: Aris & Phillips, 1984.
Dahood, Mitchell, *Psalms III, 101–150*, New York: Doubleday, 1970.
Daressy, Georges, *Notice explicatie des ruins du temple de Louxor*, Cairo: Impremerie Nationale, 1893.
Daressy, Georges, "Cercueil de Khu-n-Aten," *BIFAO* 12 (1916) 145–159.
David, A. Rosalie, *The Ancient Egyptian: Religious Beliefs and Practices*, London: Routelege & Kegan Paul, 1982.
Davies, Norman de Garis, *The Rock Tombs of El-Amarna*, Vol. 1–6, London: Egypt Exploration Fund, 1903–1908.
Davies, Norman de Garis, "Akhenaten at Thebes," *JEA* 9 (1923) 132–152.
Davies, Norman de Garis, *The Tomb of the Vizier Ramose*, London: Egypt Exploration Society, 1941.
Davis, Theodore, *The Tomb of Queen Tiyi*, London: Constable and Co., Ltd., 1910.
Dever, William, *Did God Have a Wife? Archaeology and Folk Religion in Ancient Israel*, Grand Rapids, MI: Wm. B. Eerdmans Publishers, 2005.
DeVries, Simon, *1 Kings*, Waco, TX: Word Books, 1985.
Dijk, Jacobus van, "The Amarna Period and the Later New Kingdom," *The Oxford History of Ancient Egypt* (ed. Ian Shaw), Oxford: Oxford University Press, 2000, 265–307.
Dijk, Jacobus van, "Ptah," *The Oxford Ecyclopedia of Ancient Egypt*, Vol. 3, Oxford: Oxford University Press, 2001, 74–76.
Dijk, Jacobus van, "A Colossal Statue Base of Nefertiti and Other Early Atenist Monuments from the Precinct of the Goddess Mut in Karnak," *The Servant of Mut: Studies in Honor of Richard Fazinni* (ed. S. D'Auria), Leiden: Brill, 2008, 246–252.
Dion, Paul, "YHWH as Storm-God: The Double Legacy of Egypt and Canaan as Reflected in Psalm 104," *ZAW* 103 (1991) 43–71.
Dodson, Aidan, "Crown Prince Djhutmose and the Royal Sons of the Eighteenth Dynasty," *JEA* 76 (1990) 87–96.
Dodson, Aidan, *Amarna Sunset: Nefertiti, Tutankhamun, Ay, Horemheb and the Egyptian Counter-Reformation*, Cairo/New York: American University Press, 2009.
Donohue, V. A., "*Pr nfr*," *JEA* 64 (1978) 143–148.
Doresse, M., "Les temples atoniens de la region thébaine," *Orientalia* 24 (1955) 113–130.
Doresse, M., "Observations sur la publication des blocs des temples atoniens de Karnak: The Akhenaten Temple Project," *GM* 46 (1981) 45–79.

Dorman, Peter, "The Long Coregency Revisited: Architectural and Iconographic Conundra in the Tomb of Kheruef," *Causing His Name to Live: Studies in Egyptian Epigraphy and History in Memory of William J. Murnane* (eds. P. J. Brand, and L. Cooper), Leiden/Boston, 2009.

Dozeman, Thomas B., and Konrad Schmidt, *A Farewell to the Yahwist? The Composition of the Pentateuch in Recent European Interpretation*, Atlanta, GA: Society of Biblical Literature, 2006.

Dozeman, Thomas B., Thomas Römer, and Konrad Schmidt (eds.), *Pentateuch, Hexateuch or Enneateuch? Identifying Literary Works in Genesis through Kings* Atlanta, GA: Society of Biblical Literature, 2011.

Eliade, Mircea, *Patterns in Comparative Religion*, New York: Meridian, 1958.

Eliade, Mircea, *The Sacred and the Profane*, New York: Harcourt Brace Javanovich, 1959.

Emery, Walter B., *Archaic Egypt*, Baltimore: Penguin, 1961.

Engelbach, R., and W. M. F. Petrie, *Riqqeh and Memphis VI*, London: Bernard Quaritch, 1915.

Epigraphic Survey, *Medinet Habu V, The Temple Proper*, pt. 1, Chicago: University of Chicago, 1957.

Epigraphic Survey, *Medinet Habu VI, The Temple Proper*, pt. 2, Chicago: University of Chicago, 1965.

Epigraphic Survey, *The Tomb of Kheruef, Theban Tomb no. 192*, Chicago: Oriental Institute, 1980.

Epigraphic Survey, *The Battle Reliefs of Seti I*, Chicago: Oriental Institute, 1986.

Erman, Adolf, and Hermann Grapow, *Wörterbuch der Ägyptischen Sprache*, 5 Vol., Leipzig: J. C. Hinrichs'sche, 1926–1931.

Fairman, Herbert W., "Preliminary Report on the Excavations at Sesebi (Sudla) and 'Amārah West, Anglo-Egyptian Sudan, 1937–38," *JEA* 24 (1938) 151–156.

Fairman, Herbert W., "Preliminary Report on the Excavations at 'Amārah West, Anglo-Egyptian Sudan, 1938–9," *JEA* 25 (1939) 139–144.

Fairman, Herbert W., "Once Again the So-Called Coffin of Akhenaten, *JEA* 47 (1961) 25–40.

Faulkner, R. O., *A Concise Dictionary of Middle Egyptian*, Oxford: Oxford Univeristy Press, 1962.

Faulkner, R. O., *The Ancient Egyptian Pyramid Texts*, Oxford: Clarendon Press, 1969.

Faulkner, R. O., "The Admonitions of an Egyptian Sage, *The Literature of Ancient Egypt* (ed. W. K. Simpson, et al.), New Haven, CT: Yale University Press, 1973, 210–219.

Faulkner, R. O., "The Teaching of Ammenemes I to His Son Sesostris," *The Literature of Ancient Egypt* (W. K. Simpson, et al. eds.), New Haven, CT: Yale University Press, 1973, 193–197.

Faulkner, R. O., *The Ancient Egyptian Coffin Texts* III, Warminster: Aris & Phillips, 1978.

Faulkner, R. O., *The Book of the Dead*, London: British Museum, 1985.

Feucht, Erika, "The *Ḫrdw n k3p* Reconsidered," *Pharaonic Egypt: The Bible and Christianity* (ed. S. Israelit-Groll), Jerusalem: Magnes Press, 1985.

Finnestad, Ragnhild Bjeere, *The Image of the World and Symbol of the Creator: On the Cosmological and Iconological Values of the Temple of Edfu*, Wiesbaden: O. Harrasowitz, 1985.

Fischer, Henry, "An Early Example of Atenist Iconoclasm," *JARCE* 13 (1976) 131–132.

Fohrer, Georg, *History of Israelite Religion*, trans. David Green, Nashville: Abingdon, 1972.

Foster, John L., *Echoes of Egyptian Voices: An Anthology of Ancient Egyptian Poetry*, Norman: University of Oklahoma Press, 1992, 5–10.

Foster, John L., *Hymns, Prayers, and Songs: An Anthology of Ancient Egyptian Lyric Poetry*, Atlanta, GA: Scholars Press, 1995.

Foster, John L., "The Hymn to Aten: Akhenaton Worships the Sole God," *Civilizations of the Ancient Near East*, Vol. III (ed. J. Sasson), New York: Charles Scribner, 1995, 1751–1761.

Foster, John L., "The New Religion," *Pharaohs of the Sun: Akhenaten, Nefertiti, Tutankhamun* (eds. R. Freed et al.), Boston: Museum of Fine Arts, 1999, 97–109.

Føllesdal, Dagfinn, "Edmund Husserl," *Routledge Encyclopedia of Philosophy* (ed. Edward Craig), London/New York: Routledge, 1998, 574–588.

Franke, Detlef, "Amenemhet of Beni Hasan," *The Oxford Encyclopedia of Ancient Egypt*, Vol. 1, Oxford: Oxford University Press, 2001, 67–68.

Frankfort, Henri, *Ancient Egyptian Religion*, New York: Columbia University Press, 1948.

Frankfort, Henri, *Kingship and the Gods*, Chicago: University of Chicago Press, 1948.

Fransden, P. J., "Aspects of Kingship in Ancient Egypt," *Religion and Power: Divine Kingship in the Ancient World and Beyond* (ed. Nicole Brisch), Chicago: The Oriental Institute, 2008, 47–73.

Freed, Rita, "Art in the Service of Religion and the State," *Pharaohs of the Sun: Akhenaten, Nefertiti, Tutankhamun* (eds. Rita Freed, Yvonne Markowitz, and Sue D'Auria), Boston: Museum of Fine Arts, 1999, 110–129.

Freed, Rita, et al., *Pharaohs of the Sun: Akhenaten, Nefertiti, Tutankhamun*, Boston: Museum of Fine Arts, 1999.

Freud, Sigmund, *Moses and Monothesism*, New York: Alfred A. Knof, 1939.

Friedman Florence, "The Underground Relief Panels of King Djoser at the Step Pyramid Complex," *JARCE* 32 (1995) 1–42.

Friedman, Florence, "Notions of Cosmos in the Step Pyramid Complex," *Studies in Honor of William Kelly Simpson* Vol. 1 (ed. Peter der Manuelian), Boston: Museum of Fine Arts, 1996, 337–351.

Gabolde, Luc, *Monuments décorés en bas relief aux noms de Thoutmosis II et Hatschepsout à Karnak*, Cairo: IFAO, 2005.

Gabolde, Marc, *D'Akhenaton à Toutânkhamon*, Lyon: Université-Lyon 2, 1998.

Gabolde, Marc, "Under a Deep Blue Starry Sky," *Causing His Name to Live: Studies in Egyptian Epigraphy and History in Memory of William J. Murnane* (eds. P. J. Brand and L. Cooper), Leiden/Boston: Brill, 2009, 109–120.

Gabra, Sami, "Un Temple d'Aménophis IV a Assiout," *Cd'E* 12 (1931) 237–243.

Gardiner, Alan H., "On the Reading of ," *ZÄS* 41 (1904) 71–76.

Gardiner, Alan H., "The Hymns to Amon from a Leiden Papyrus," *ZÄS* 42 (1905) 112–142.

Gardiner, Alan H., *The Admonitions of an Egyptian Sage*, Leipzig: J. C. Hinrichs, 1909.

Gardiner, Alan H., "The Graffito from the Tomb of Pere," *JEA* 14 (1928) 10–11.

Gardiner, Alan H., *Late-Egyptian Stories*, Brussels: Édition de la Foundation Égyptologique Reine Élisabeth, 1932.

Gardiner, Alan H., *Hieratic Papyri in the British Museum*, Vol. II, London: British Museum, 1935.

Gardiner, Alan H., "A Later Allusion to Akhenaten," *JEA* 24 (1938) 124.

Gardiner, Alan H., "Horus the Beḥdetite," *JEA* 30 (1942) 23–36.

Gardiner, Alan H., "Davies Copy of the Great Speos Artemidos Inscription," *JEA* 32 (1946) 43–56.

Gardiner, Alan H., *Ancient Egyptian Onomastica* II, London: Oxford University Press, 1947.

Gardiner, Alan H., T. E. Peet, and J. Černý, *The Inscriptions of the Sinai* I, London: Egypt Exploration Society, 1952.

Gardiner, Alan H., T. E. Peet, and J. Černý, *The Inscriptions of the Sinai* II, London: Egypt Exploration Society, 1955.
Gardiner, Alan H., "The Memphite Tomb of General Ḥaremḥeb," *JEA* 39 (1953) 3–12.
Gardiner, Alan H., "The Coronation of King Ḥaremḥeb," *JEA* 39 (1953) 13–31.
Gardiner, Alan H., "The So-called Tomb of Queen Tiye," *JEA* 43 (1957) 10–25.
Gardiner, Alan H., *Egypt of the Pharaohs*, Oxford: Oxford University Press, 1961.
Gardiner, Alan H., *Egyptian Grammar*, 3rd ed., Oxford: Oxford University Press, 1969.
Giveon, Raphael, "Toponymes Ouest-Asiatiques à Soleb," *VT* 14 (1964) 239–255.
Giveon, Raphael, *Les Bédouins Shosou Des Documents Égyptiens*, Leiden: Brill, 1971.
Gnuse Robert Karl, *No Other Gods: Emergent Monotheism in Israel*, Sheffield:, Sheffield Academic Press, 1997.
Gohary, Jocelyn, *Akhenaten's Sed-festival at Karnak*, London: Kegan Paul International, 1992.
Goldwasser, Olry, "*'Itn*—the 'Golden Egg' (CT IV 292b-c [B9C[a]]," *Essays on Ancient Egypt in Honour of Hermann te Velde* (ed. J. Van Dijk), Gronigen: Styx Publications, 1997, 79–83.
Goldwasser, Orly, "The Essence of Amarna Monotheism," *in.t d̲r.w – Festschrift für Friedrich Junge* (eds. Gerald Moers et al.), Göttingen: Lingua Aegyptia, Seminar für Ägyptologie und Koptologie, 2006.
Goldwasser, Orly, "King Apophis of Avaris and the Emergence of Monotheism," *Studies in Honor of Manfred Bietak*, Vol. II (eds. Ernst Czerny et al.), Leuven: Peeters, 2006, 129–133.
Goldwasser, Orly, "The Aten Is the 'Energy of Light': New Evidence from the Script," *JARCE* 46 (2010) 159–165.
Goyon, Georges, *Nouvelles inscriptions rupestres du Wadi Hammamat*, Paris: Imprimerie Nationale, 1957.
Grandet, Pierre, "Weights and Measures," *The Oxford Encyclopedia of Ancient Egypt*, Vol. 3 (ed. Donald B. Redford), Oxford: Oxford University Press, 2001, 493–495.
Grdseloff, Bernard, "Édôm, D'arès Les Sources Egyptiennes," *Revue de l'histoire juive d'Egypte* 1 (1947) 69–99.
Griffith Francis Ll., *The Petrie Papyri: Hieratic Papyri from Kahun and Gurob*, London: Bernard Quaritch, 1898.
Griffith Francis Ll., "The Jubilee of Akhenaten," *JEA* 5 (1918) 61–63.
Griffith, Francis Ll., *The Temples of Kawa. Oxford University Excavations in Nubia. Volume II, History and Archaeology of the Site* (ed. M. F. L. Macadam), London: Oxford University Press, 1949, 1–10.
Grimal, Nicolas-Christophe, *La Stèle Triomphale de Pi(ankh)y au Musé du Caire*, Cairo: IF 1981.
Grimal, Nicolas-Christophe, *A History of Ancient Egypt*, Oxford: Blackwell, 1992.
Gunn, Battiscombe, "Notes on the Aten and his Names," *JEA* 9 (1923) 168–176.
Habachi, Labib, *Tell Basta*. Supplément aux Annales du Service des antiquités de l'Égypte; Cahier, Vol. 22, Cairo: Impr. de l'Institut français d'archéologie, 1957.
Habachi, Labib, "Akhenaten in Heliopolis," *Zum 70. Geburstag von Herbert Ricke*, Wiesbaden: Franz Steiner Velag, 1971, 35–45.
Habachi, Labib, *The Obelisks of Egypt: Skyscrapers of the Past*, Cairo: American University Press, 1984.
Harris, J. R., *Lexicographical Studies in Ancient Egyptian Minerals*, Berlin: Academie-Verlag, 1961.

Harris, J. R., "Neferneferuaten," *GM* 4 (1973) 15–17.

Harris, J. R., "Neferneferuaten Regnans," *Acta Orientalia* 35 (1974) 11–21.

Harris, J. R., "Akhenaten or Nefertiti," *Acta Orientalia* 38 (1977) 5–10.

Harris, James E., and Kent Weeks, *X-Raying the Pharaohs*, New York: Charles Scribner's Sons, 1973.

Harris, James E., "The Mummy of Amenhotep III," *Gold of Praise: Studies on Ancient Egypt in Honor of Edward F. Wente* (eds. Emily Teeter and John Anderson), Chicago: Oriental Institute, 1999, 163–174.

Hawass, Zahi, et al., "Ancestry and Pathology in King Tutankhamun's Family," *JAMA* 303, no. 7 (February 17, 2010), 638–647.

Hawass, Zahi, "King Tut's Family Secret," *National Geographic* 218, no. 3, September 2010 34–60.

Hayes, William C., "Inscriptions from the Palace of Amenhotep III," *JNES* 10 (1951) 35–56, 82–112, 156–183, 231–242.

Healey, Emmeline, "The Decorative Program of the Amarna Rock Tombs: Unique Scenes of the Egyptian Military and Police," *Egyptology in Australia and New Zealand 2009* (eds. C. M. Knoblauch and J. C. Gill), Oxford: BAR International Series 2355 (2012) 27–39.

Healey, Emmeline, "Akhenaten and the Armed Forces," Ph.D. diss., Monash University, 2012.

Helck, Wolfgang, *Die Prophezeihung des Nfr.tj. Textzusammenstellung*, Wiesbaden: Harrassowitz, 1970.

Helck, Wolfgang, *Egyptian Historical Records of the Later Eighteenth Dynasty*, Fasc. 4, translated from W. Helck, Urkunden der 18. Dynastie, Heft 20. by Benedict G. Davies, Warminster: Aris & Phillips, 1992.

Henri, Fankfort, *Ancient Egyptian Religion*, New York: Columbia University Press, 1948.

Hess, Richard S., "Early Israel in Canaan: A Survey of Recent Evidence and Interpretations," *Palestine Exploration Quarterly* 125 (1993) 125–142.

Hess, Richard S., *Israelite Religions: An Archaeological and Biblical Survey*, Grand Rapids, MI: Baker Academic, 2007.

Hoch, James, *Semitic Words in Egyptian Texts of the New Kingdom and Third Intermediate Period*, Princeton, NJ: Princeton University Press, 1994.

Hoch, James, *Middle Egyptian Grammar*, Mississauga, Ontario: Benben Publications, 1997.

Hodge, Carleton, "Akhenaten: A Reject," *Scripta Mediterranea* 2 (1981) 17–26.

Hoffmeier, James K., "Tents in Egypt and the Ancient Near East," *SSEA Newsletter* VII, no. 3 (1977) 13–28.

Hoffmeier, James K., "The Possible Origins of the Tent of Purification in the Egyptian Funerary Cult," *SAK* 9 (1981) 167–177.

Hoffmeier, James K., "Genesis 1 & 2 and Egyptian Cosmology," *JANES* 15 (1983) 39–49.

Hoffmeier, James K., *'Sacred' in the Vocabulary of Ancient Egypt*, Orbis Biblicus et Orientalis 59; Freiburg: Universitätsverlag, 1985.

Hoffmeier, James K., "The Chariot Scenes," *The Akhenaten Temple Project*, Vol. 2 (ed. Donald B. Redford), Toronto: Akhenaten Temple Project/University of Toronto Press, 1988, 34–45.

Hoffmeier, James K., "The King as God's Son in Egypt and Israel," *Papers Presented in Memory of Ronald J. Williams*, *JSSEA* 24 (1994) 28–38.

Hoffmeier, James K., *Israel in Egypt*, New York/Oxford: Oxford University Press, 1996.

Hoffmeier, James K., "Are there Regionally Based Theological Differences in the Coffin Texts," *The World of the Coffin Texts: Proceedings of the Symposium Held on the Occasion of the 100th Birthday of Adriaan de Buck, Leiden, December 17–19, 1992* (ed. Harco Willems), Leiden: Nederlands Instituut voor het Nabjje Oosten, 1996, 45–54.

Hoffmeier, James K., "'The Heavens Declare the Glory of God': The Limits of General Revelation," *Trinity Journal* 21 (2000) 17–24.

Hoffmeier, James K., "Abydos List," *Context of Scripture*, I, Leiden: Brill, 2002, 68–71.

Hoffmeier, James K., "King Lists," *Context of Scripture*, I, Leiden: Brill, 2002, 69–70.

Hoffmeier, James K., "Turin Canon" *Context of Scripture*, I, Leiden: Brill, 2002, 71–73.

Hoffmeier, James K., "Understanding Hebrew and Egyptian Military Texts: A Contextual Approach," *Context of Scripture*, III, Leiden: Brill, 2002, xxxi–xxvii.

Hoffmeier, James K., "Tell el-Borg in North Sinai," *Egyptian Archaeology* 20 (Spring 2002), 18–20.

Hoffmeier, James K., "Tell el-Borg on Egypt's Eastern Frontier: A Preliminary Report on the 2002 and 2004 Seasons," *JARCE* 41 (2004) 85–103.

Hoffmeier, James K., *Ancient Israel in Sinai: The Evidence for the Authenticity of the Wilderness Tradition*, New York: Oxford University Press, 2005/2011.

Hoffmeier, James K., "Recent Excavations on the 'Ways of Horus': The 2005 and 2006 Seasons at Tell el-Borg," *ASAE* 80 (2006) 257–259.

Hoffmeier, James K., "Amarna Period Kings in Sinai," *Egyptian Archaeology* 31 (2007) 38–39.

Hoffmeier, James K., "What Is the Biblical Date for the Exodus? A Response to Bryant Wood," *JETS* 50 (2007) 225–247.

Hoffmeier, James K., "Deities of the Eastern Frontier," *Scribe of Justice: Egyptological Studies in Honour of Shafik Allam* (eds. Z. A. Hawass, Kh. A. Daoud, and R. B. Hussein), Cairo: Supplement aux Annales du Service des Antiquities de l'Egypte, Cahier 42, 2011, 197–216.

Hoffmeier, James K., "The Gate of the Ramesside Period Fort at Tell el-Borg, North Sinai," *Ramesside Studies in Honour of K. A. Kitchen* (eds. M. Collier and S. Snape), Bolton: Rutherford Press, 2011, 207–219.

Hoffmeier, James K., "'These Things Happened': Why a Historical Exodus Is Essential for Theology," *Do Historical Matters Matter to Faith* (eds. J. Hoffmeier and D. Magary), Wheaton, IL: Crossway, 2012, 99–134.

Hoffmeier, James K., *Excavations in North Sinai: Tell el-Borg* I, Winona Lake, IN: Eisenbrauns, 2014.

Hoffmeier, James K., and Ronald D. Bull, "New Inscriptions Mentioning Tjaru from Tell el-Borg, North Sinai," *RdÉ* (2005) 79–94.

Hoffmeier, James K., and Jacobus van Dijk, "New Light on the Amarna Period from North Sinai, *JEA* 96 (2005) 191–205.

Hoffmeier, James K., and Mohamed Abd el-Maksoud, "A New Military Site on 'the Ways of Horus'—Tell el Borg 1999–2001: A Preliminary Report," *JEA* 89 (2003) 169–197.

Hoffmeier, James K., and Earl Ertman, "A New Fragmentary Relief of King Ankhkheperure from Tell el-Borg (Sinai)?" *JEA* 94 (2008) 296–302.

Hoffmeier, James K., and S. O. Moshier, "New Paleo-Environmental Evidence from North Sinai to Complement Manfred Bietak's Map of the Eastern Delta and some Historical Implications," *Timelines: Studies in Honour of Manfred Bietak*, Orientalia Lovaniensia Analecta 149; Vol. 2 (eds. E. Czerny, I. Hein, H. Hunger, D. Melman, and A. Schwab), Paris: Uitgeverij Peeters, 2006, 165–174.

Hollis, Susan T., "Tales of Magic and Wonder from Ancient Egypt," *Civilizations of the Ancient Near East*, Volumes III & IV, Peabody, MA: Hendrickson Publishers, 2000, 2255–2264.

Hornung, Erik, *Conceptions of God in Ancient Egypt: The One and the Many*, trans. John Baines, Ithaca, NY: Cornell University Press, 1982.

Hornung, Erik, *Akhenaten and the Religion of Light*, trans. D. Lorton, Ithaca, NY: Cornell University Press, 1999.

Hussein, Ramadan B., "The Saite Pyramid Texts Copies in the Memphite and Heliopolitan Shaft-Tombs: A Study of Their Selection and Layout," Ph.D. diss., Brown University, 2009.

Iskander, Ashraf, *Popular Religion in Egypt during the New Kingdom*, Hildesheim: Gerstenberg, 1988.

Jaspers, Karl, *The Origin and Goal of History*, New Haven, CT: Yale University Press, 1953.

Jeffreys, David, "The topography of Heliopolis and Memphis: Some Cognitive Aspects," *Stationen. Beiträge zur Kulturegeschichte Ägyptens, Rainer Stadelmann gewidment*, Mainz-am-Rein: P. von Zabern, 1998, 63–71.

Jeffreys, David, "An Amarna Period Relief from Memphis, *Egyptian Art in the Nicholson Museum, Sydney* (eds. K. N. Sowada and B. G. Ockinga), Meditrach, 2006, 119–133.

Johnson, W. Raymond, "The Deified Amenhotep III as the Living Re-Horakhty: Stylistic and Iconographic Considerations," *VI Congresso Internazionale di Egittologia Atti* (eds. Gian Zaccone and Tomaso di Netro), Turin: International Association of Egyptologists, 1992.

Johnson, W. Raymond, "An Asiatic Battle Scene of Tutankhamun from Thebes: A Late Amarna Antecedent of the Ramesside Battle-Narrative Tradition," Ph.D. diss., University of Chicago, 1992.

Johnson, W. Raymond, "Amenhotep III and Amarna: Some New Considerations," *JEA* 82 (1996) 65–82.

Johnson, W. Raymond, "Monuments and Monumental Art under Amenhotep III: Evolution and Meaning," *Amenhotep III: Perspectives on His Reign* (eds. D. O'Connor and E. Cline), Ann Arbor: University of Michigan Press, 1998, 63–94.

Kaufmann, Yehezkel, *The Religion of Isarel: From Its Beginnings to the Babylonian Exile*, trans. Moshe Greenburg, New York: Schocken Books, 1972.

Keel, Othmar, and Christoph Uehlinger, *Gods, Goddesses, and Images of God in Ancient Israel*, trans. Thomas H. Trapp, Minneapolis: Fortress Press, 1998.

Kees, Hermann, "Ein Onkel Amenophis' IV. Hohepriester von Heliopolis," *ZÄS* 53 1917, 81–83.

Kees, Hermann, *Der Gotterglaube im Alten Aegypter*, Berlin: Akademie-Verlag, 1956.

Kees, Hermann, "Die Weisse Kapelle Sesostris I. in Karnak und das *sed-fest*," *Mitteilungen des Deutschen Archäologischen Instituts* 16 (1958) 194–212.

Kees, Hermann, *Ancient Egypt: A Geographical History of the Nile*, Chicago: University of Chicago Press, 1961.

Keimer, Ludwig, "Die Pfanze des Gottes Min," *ZÄS* 59 (1924) 140–143.

Kemp, Barry, "Old Kingdom, Middle Kingdom and Second Intermediate Period, c. 2686–1552," *Ancient Egypt a Social History* (eds. B. Trigger, B. Kemp, D. O'Connor, and A. Lloyd), Cambridge: Cambridge University Press, 1983, 107–182.

Kemp, Barry, "The Kom el-Nana enclosure at Amarna," *Egyptian Archaeology* 6 (1995) 8–9.

Kemp, Barry, *The City of Akenaten and Nefertiti: Amarna and Its People*, London: Thames & Hudson, 2012.

Kemp, Barry, el al., "Tell el-Amarna, 2012–2013," *JEA* 99 (2013) 20–32.

Kendall, Timothy, "Napata," *The Oxford Encyclopedia of Ancient Egypt*, Vol. 2, Oxford: Oxford University Press, 2001, 492–493.

Kendall, Timothy, "Talatat Architecture at Jebel Barkal: Report of the NCAM Mission 2008–2009," *Nubia & Sudan* 13 (2009) 2–19.

Kitchen, Kenneth A., "Egypt, Ugarit, Qatna and Covenant," *Ugarit Forschungen* 11 (1979) 453–464.

Kitchen, Kenneth A., "Egypt, History of (Chronology), *ABD*, Vol. 2 (1992) 321–331.

Kitchen, Kenneth A., *Poetry of Ancient Egypt*, Jorsered, Sweden: Paul Åtröms Förlag, 1999.

Kitchen, Kenneth A., "Regnal and Genealogical Data of Ancient Egypt (Absolute Chronology I): The Historical Chronology of Ancient Egypt, A Current Assessment," *The Synchronisation of Civilisations in the Eastern Mediterranean in the Second Millennium B.C.* (ed. M. Bietak), Vienna: Österreichischen Akademie der Wissenschaften, 2000.

Kitchen, Kenneth A., *On the Reliability of the Old Testament*, Grand Rapids, MI/Cambridge, UK: Wm. B. Eerdmans Publishing Company, 2003.

Klemm, Rosemarie, and Dietrich Klemm, *Stones and Quarries in Ancient Egypt*, London: British Museum, 2008.

Kozloff, Arielle, *Amenhotep III: Egypt's Radiant Pharaoh*, Cambridge/New York: Cambridge University Press, 2012.

Kozloff, Arielle, "Chips off Old Statues: Carving the Amenhotep IV Colossi of Karnak," *KMT* 23, no. 3 (Fall 2012) 18–33.

Krauss, Rolf, *Das Ende der Amarnaziet: Beiträge zur Geschichte u. Chronologie d. Neuen Reiches*, Hildesheim: Gerstenberg, 1978.

Krejcí, Jaromír, "Appearance of the Abusir Pyramid Necropolis in the Old Kingdom," *Egyptology at the Dawn of the Twenty-first Century: Proceedings of the Eighth International Congress of Egyptlogist, Cairo 2000*, Vol. 1 (ed. Zahi Hawass), Cairo: American University Press, 2003, 280–288.

Krejcí, Jaromír, and Dušan Magdolen, "Research into Fifth Dynasty Sun Temples—Past, Present and Future," *The Old Kingdom Art and Archaeology: Proceedings of the Conference Held in Prague, May 31–June 4, 2004* (ed. M. Bárta), Prague: Academy of Sciences of the Czech Republic, 2006, 185–192.

Lacau, Pierre, and Henri Chevier, *Une Chapelle de Sésostris 1er à Karnak*, Cairo: IFAO, 1956.

Lacau, Pierre, and Henri Chevier, *Une Chapelle de Sésostris 1er à Karnak, Planches*, Cairo: IFAO, 1969.

Lang, Bernhard, *Monotheism and the Prophetic Minority*, Atlanta, GA: Almond Press, 1983.

Lauer, Jean-Philippe, *The Royal Cemetery of Memphis*, New York: Charles Scribner's Sons, 1976.

Lauffray, Jean, *Karnak d'Égypte domaine du divin*, Paris: Éditions du Centre Nationale de la Recherche Scientifique, 1979.

Lauffray, Jean, *Karnak VI*, Cairo: CFEETK, 1980.

Leahy, A., *Excavations at Malkata and the Birket Habu 1971–1974*, IV: *The Inscriptions*, Warminster, 1978.

Leeuw, Geradus Van Der, *Religion in Essence and Manifestation*, trans. J. E. Turner, Gloucester, MA: Peter Smith, 1967.

Legrain, Georges, "Notes Prieses a Karnak VI. Sur un Temple d'Aten a Hermonthis," *Recuil de Travaux Relatifs à la Philologie et à l'Archéolgie Égyptiennes et Assyriennes* 23 (1901) 62.

Legrain, Georges, "Les Stèles d'Aménôthès IV à Zernik et à Gebel Silseleh," *ASAE* 3 (1902) 259–266.

Legrain, Georges, "Fragments du Canopes," *ASAE* 4 (1903) 138–147.

Lehner, Mark, *The Complete Pyramids*, London: Thames & Hudson, 1997.

Lemaire, André, *The Birth of Monotheism: The Rise and Disappearance of Yahwism*, Washington, DC: Biblical Archaeology Society, 2007.

Leprohon, Ronald J., "The Reign of Akhenaten Seen Through the Late Royal Decrees," *Mélanges Gamal Eddin Mokhtar* (ed. Paule Posener-Kriéger), Cairo: Institut français d'archéologie orientale du Caire, 1985, 94–96.

Lesko, Leonard, ed., *A Dictionary of Late Egyptian*, Vol. 1, Berkley: B. C. Scribe Publications, 1982.

Lewis, C. S., *Reflections on the Psalms*, New York: reprint of 1958 edition, Harvest/Harcourt, 1986.

Lichtheim, Miriam, *Ancient Egyptian Literature* I, Berkeley: University of California Press, 1973.

Lichtheim, Miriam, *Ancient Egyptian Literature* II, Berkeley: University of California Press, 1976.

Lichtheim, Miriam, *Ancient Egyptian Literature* III, Berkeley: University of California Press, 1980.

Lichtheim, Miriam, "The Great Hymn to the Aten," *The Context of Scripture*, Vol. 1 (eds. W. W. Hallo and K. L. Younger), Leiden: Brill, 1997, 44–46.

Löhr, Beatrix, "Aḥanjati in Memphis," *SAK* 2 (1975) 139–173.

Lorand, David, *Arts et Politique sous Sesostris Ier: Littérature, sculpture et archi– tecture dan leur context historique*, Turnhour: Brepols, 2012.

Lorton, David, "God's Beneficent Creation: Coffin Texts Spell 1130, the Instructions for Merikare, and the Great Hymn to Aton," *SÄK* 20 (1993) 125–155.

Ludwig, Theodore, "Monotheism," *The Encyclopedia of Religion*, 2nd ed. (ed. L. Jones), Detroit: Macmillan, 2005, 6155.

Luiselli, Maria, *Der Amun-Re Hymnus des P. Boulaq 17* (P. Kairo CG 58038), Wiesbaden: Harrassowitz Verlag, 2004.

MacDonald, Nathan, *Deuteronomy and the Meaning of 'Monotheism'* (Forschungen zum Alten Testament, 2. Reihe, 1), Tübingen: Mohr Siebeck, 2003.

Mahoney, C. Patrick, "Adolescent Gynecomastia," *Current Issues in Pediatric and Adolescent Endocrinology* 37, no. 6 (1990) 1389–1404.

Málek, Jaromír, "The Old Kingdom (c. 2686–2160 B.C.)," *The Oxford History of Ancient Egypt* (ed. Ian Shaw), Oxford: Oxford University Press, 2003, 83–107.

Mallinson, Michael, "The Sacred Landscape," *The Pharaohs of the Sun, Akenaten, Nefertiti, Tutankhamun* (eds. Rita Free, Yvonne Markowitz, and Sue D'Auria), Boston: Museum of Fine Arts, 1999, 72–79.

Manniche, Lisa, *The Akhenaten Colossi of Karnak*, Cairo: American University Press, 2010.

Martin, Geoffrey T., *The Royal Tomb at El-Amarna*, I, *The Objects*, London: Egyptian Exploration Society, 1974.

Martin, Geoffrey T., *The Memphite Tomb of Ḥaremḥeb, Commander-in-Chief of Tutʿankhamûn* I, London: Egypt Exploration Society, 1989.

Martin, Geoffrey T., *The Royal Tomb at El-Amarna*, II, *The Reliefs, Inscriptions and Architecture*, London: Egyptian Exploration Society, 1989.

Meltzer, Edmund, "Glossary of Amenophis IV-Akhenaten's Karnak Talatat," *The Akhenaten Temple Project*, Vol. 2 (ed. Donald B. Redford), Warminster: Aris and Phillips, 1988, 81–118.

Meltzer, Edmund, "Horus," *The Oxford Encyclopedia of Ancient Egypt*, Vol. 2, Oxford: Oxford University Press, 2001, 119–122.

Millard, Alan, "Ramesses Was Here ... And Others, Too!" *Ramesside Studies in Honour of K. A. Kitchen* (eds. M. Collier and Steven Snape), Bolton: Rutherford Press, 2011, 305–312.

Miller, Patrick D., *The Religion of Ancient Israel*, Louisville, KY: Westminster John Knox Press, 2000.

Miosi, Frank T., *A Reading Book of the Second Intermediate Period Texts*, Toronto: Benben Publications, 1981.

Mircea, Eliade, *The Sacred and the Profane*, New York: Harcourt, Brace & World 1959.

Mircea, Eliade, *Patterns in Comparative Religion*, Clinton, MA: Meridian, 1963.

Molen, Rami van Der, *A Hieroglyphic Dictionary of Egyptian Coffin Texts*, Leiden: Brill, 2000.

Morenz, Siegfried, *Egyptian Religion*, trans. Ann Keep, Ithaca, NY: Cornell University Press, 1973.

Morris, Ellen, "The Pharaoh and Pharaonic Office," *A Companion to Ancient Egypt*, (ed. A. B. Lloyd) Oxford: Wiley-Backwell, 2010, 201–217.

Moshier, Stephen O., and Ali El-Kalani, "Late Bronze Age Paelogeography along the Ancient Ways of Horus in Northwest Sinai, Egypt," *Geoarchaeology* 23, no. 4 (2008) 450–473.

Moursi, M., *Die Hohenpriester des Sonnengottes von der Frühzeit Ägyptens bis zum Ende des Neuen Reiches*, Munich: Münchner Ägyptologische Studien 26, 1972.

Müller, Maya, "Re and Re-Harakhty," *The Oxford Encyclopedia of Ancient Egypt*, Vol. 3, Oxford: Oxford University Press, 2001, 123–126.

Mumford, Gregory, and Sarah Parack, "Pharaonic Ventures into South Sinai: El-Markha Plain Site 346," *JEA* 89 (2003) 83–116.

Murnane, William J., *Ancient Egyptian Coregencies, Studies in Ancient Oriental Civilization* 40, Chicago: Oriental Institute, 1977.

Murnane, William J., "On the Accession Date of Akhenaten," *Studies in Honor of GeorgeR. Hughes* (eds. J. Johnson and E. Wente), *Studies in Ancient Oriental Civilization* 39, Chicago: Oriental Institute, 1977, 163–167.

Murnane, William J., "A Rhetorical History? The Beginning of Thutmose III's First Campaign in Western Asia," *JARCE* 26 (1989) 183–189.

Murnane, William J., *Texts from the Amarna Period in Egypt*, Atlanta, GA: Scholars Press, 1995.

Murnane, William J., "Observations on Pre-Amarna Theology During the Earliest Reign of Amenhotep IV," *Gold of Praise: Studies on Ancient Egypt in Honor of Edward F. Wente* (eds.Emily Teeter and John A. Larson), Chicago: Oriental Institute, 1999, 303–316.

Murnane, William J., and Charles Van Siclen, *The Boundary Stelae of Akhenaten*, London/ New York: Kegan Paul International, 1993.

Myśliwiec, Karol, "Amon, Atum and Aton: The Evolution of Heliopolitan Influences in Thebes," *L'Égyptologie en 1979: Axes prioritiaires de recherches*, Vol. II (ed. J. Lelant), Paris: Editions du centre national de la recherché scientifique, 1982, 285–289.

Myśliwiec, Karol, "Atum," *The Oxford Encyclopedia of Ancient Egypt*, Vol. 1, Oxford: Oxford University Press, 2001, 158–160.

Nagel, George, "À propos des rapports du psaume 104 avec les textes égyptiens," *Festschrif für Alfred Bertholet zum 80* (eds. Otto Eisssfeld et al.), Tübigen: J. C. B. Mohr, 1950, 395–403.

Nakhai, Beth Alpert, *Archaeology and the Religions of Canaan and Israel*, Boston: ASOR Books, 2001.

Newberry, Percy, "Akhenten's Eldest Son-in-law ʿAnkheperurēʿ," *JEA* 14 (1928) 3–9.

Niditch, Susan, *Ancient Israelite Religion*, New York/Oxford: Oxford University Press, 1997.

Noth, Martin, *Überlieferungsgeschectliche Studien*, Tübingen: Max Niemeyer, 1943; English translation: *The Detueronomistic History*, Sheffield: JSOT Press, 1981.

O'Connor, D., and D. Silverman, eds., *Ancient Egyptian Kingship*, Leiden: Brill, 1995.

Ockinga, Boyo, "An Example of Egyptian Royal Phraseology in Psalm 132," *Biblische Notizen* 11 (1980) 38–42.

Olyan, Saul, *Asherah and the Cult of Yahweh in Israel*, Atlanta, GA: Scholars Press, 1988.

Otto, Eberhard, "Weltanschauliche und politische Tendenzscriften," *Handbuch der Orientalistik*, Bd. 1, Aegptologie. 2. Abschnitt Literatur, Leiden: Brill, 1952.

Otto, Eberhard, *Egyptian Art and the Cults of Osiris and Amon*, London: Thames and Hudson, 1968.

Otto, Rudolf, *The Idea of the Holy*, trans. J. W. Harvey, London: Oxford University Press, 1946.

Pak, William M., "Genesis 12–36: An Investigation of the Patriarchal Theophanies using a Phenomonological Approach," Ph.D. dissertation, Trinity International University, 2012.

Peet, T. Eric, and C. L. Woolley, *The City of Akhenaten* I, London: Egyptian Exploration Society, 1923.

Peet, T. Eric, et al., *The City of Akhenaten* III, London: Egyptian Explorations Society, 1951.

Petrie, W. M. F., *Six Temples at Thebes, 1896*, London: Bernard Quaritch, 1897.

Petrie, W. M. F., *Heliopolis, Kafr Ammar, and Shurafa*, London: Bernard Quaritch, 1915.

Pillet, M., "L'art d'Akhenaton," *Mélanges Mariette* (ed. J. Garnot), Cairo: IFAO, 1961, 81–95.

Posener, G., *Littérature et politique dans l'Égypte de la XIIe dynastie*, Paris: Champion, 1956.

Propp, William, "Monotheism and 'Moses': The Problem of Early Israelite Religion," *Ugarit-Forshungen* 31 (1999) 537–575.

Quibell, J. E., and W. M. F. Petrie, *Hierakonpolis* I, London: Bernard Quaritch, 1900.

Quibell, J. E., *Excavations at Saqqara (1908–9, 1909–10): The Monastery of Apa Jeremias*, Cairo: IFAO, 1912.

Quirke, Stephen, *The Cult of Ra: Sun-Worship in Ancient Egypt*, London: Thames & Hudson, 2001.

Ranke, Hermann, *Die ägptischen Personennamen*, Bd. I, Glückstad: J. J. Augustin, 1935.

Raven, M et al., "Preliminary Report of the Leiden Excavations at Saqqara, Season 2001: The Tomb of Meryneith," *JEOL* 37 (2001–2002) 71–89.

Redford, Donald B., "The Identity of the High-priest of Amun at the Beginning of Akhenaten's Reign," *JAOS* 83 (1963) 240–241.

Redford, Donald B., *History and Chronology of the Eighteenth Dynasty of Egypt: Seven Studies*, Toronto: Toronto University Press, 1967.

Redford, Donald B., "Studies of Akhenaten at Thebes 1: A Report of the Work of the Akhenaten Temple Project of the University Museum, The University of Pennsylvania," *JARCE* 10 (1973) 77–94.

Redford, Donald B., "Studies of Akhenaten at Thebes 2: A Report of the Work of the Akhenaten Temple Project of the University Museum, The University of Pennsylvania, for the Year 1973–4," *JARCE* 12 (1975) 9–14.

Redford, Donald B., "The Sun-Disc in Akhenaten's Program: Its Worship and Antecedents, I," *JARCE* 13 (1976) 47–61.

Redford, Donald B., "Preliminary Report of the First Season of Excavation in East Karnak 1975–76," *JARCE* 14 (1977) 9–32.

Redford, Donald B., "A Royal Speech from the Blocks of the 10th Pylon," *BES* 3 (1981) 87–102.

Redford, Donald B., "Interim Report on the Excavations at East Karnak (1981–1982 Seasons)," *JSSEA* 13, no. 4 (1983) 203–223.

Redford, Donald B., *Akhenaten: The Heretic King*, Princeton, NJ: Princeton University Press, 1984.

Redford, Donald B., *The Akhenaten Temple Project*, Vol. 2, Toronto: Akhenaten Temple Project/ University of Toronto Press, 1988.

Redford, Donald B., "East Karnak Excavations," *JARCE* 28 (1991) 75–106.

Redford, Donald B., *Egypt, Canaan, and Israel in Ancient Times*, Princeton, NJ: Princeton University Press, 1992.

Redford, Donald B., "East Karnak and the Sed-festival of Akhenaten," *Hommages Jean Leclant*, Vol. 1 (eds. C. Berger, G. Clerc, and N. Grimal), Cairo: IFAO, 1994, 485–492.

Redford, Donald B., *The Akhenaten Temple Project*, Vol. 3, Toronto: Akhenaten Temple Project/ University of Toronto Press, 1994.

Redford, Donald B., "Textual Sources for the Hyksos Period, *The Hyksos: New Historical and Archaeological Perspectives* (ed. Elizer D. Oren), Philadelphia: University Museum, University of Pennsylvania, 1997, 1–44.

Redford, Donald B., "Akhenaten: New Theories and Old Facts," *BASOR* 369 (2013) 9–34.

Redford, Susan, "Theban Tomb No. 188 (The Tomb of Parennefer): A Case Study of Reuse in the Theban Necropolis," 2 Vol. (Ph.D. diss., Pennsylvania State University, 2007).

Reeves, Nicholas, *The Complete Tutankhamun*, London: Thames & Hudson, 1995.

Reeves, Nicholas, *Akhenaten: Egypt's False Prophet*, London: Thames & Hudson, 2001.

Reisner, George, "The Barkal Temples in 1916," *JEA* 4 (1916) 213–227.

Reisner, George, "The Barkal Temples in 1916 (*continued from Vol. IV, p. 227*)," *JEA* 5 (1918) 99–112.

Rendsburg, Gary, "The Date of the Exodus and Conquest/Settlement: The Case for the 1100s," *VT* 42 (1992) 510–527.

Richter, Sandra, *The Deuteronomistic History and the Name Theology:* lešakkēn šemô šam *in the Bible and the Ancient Near East*, Berlin: deGuyter, 2002.

Richter, Sandra, "The Place of the Name in Deuteronomy," *VT* 57 (2007) 342–366.

Ricke, Herbert, "Der 'Hohe Sand' in Heliopolis," *ZÄS* 71 (1935) 107–111.

Ricke, Herbert, and Siegfried Schott, *Der Harmachistempel des Chefren in Giseh*, Viesbaden: Harrasowitz, 1970.

Ringgren, Helmer, *Israelite Religion*, trans. David E. Green, Philadelphia: Fortress Press, 1966.

Ringgren, Helmer, *Religions of the Ancient Near East*, London: SPCK, 1973.

Ritner, Robert K., *The Mechanics of Egyptian Magic*, Chicago: The Oriental Institute, 1993.

Robins, Gay, "The Representation of Sexual Characteristics in Amarna Art," *JSSEA* 23 (1993) 29–41.

Rochholz, Mathias, "Sedfest, Sonnenheiligum und Pyramidbezrk. Zur Deutung der Grabalagen der Könige der 5. und 6. Dynastie," *Ägyptsiche Tempel— Struktur, Funktion und Program* (eds. R. Gundlach and M. Rochholz), Mainz: Hamburg Ägyptishe Beitrage, 1994, 225–280.

Roeder, Günther, and Rainer Hanke, *Hermopolis 1929–1939: Ausgrabungen des Deutschen Hermopolis-Expedition in Hermopolis, Ober-Ägypten*, Hildesheim: Gerstenberg, 1959–1969.

Roeder, Günther, and Rainer Hanke, *Amarna-reliefs aus Hermopolis, Ausgrabungen des Deutschen Hermopolis– Expedition in Hermopolis, 1929–1939*, Vol. II & III, Hildesheim: Gerstenberg, 1969, 1978.

Romanosky, Eugene, "Min," *The Oxford Encyclopedia of Ancient Egypt*, Vol. 2, Oxford: Oxford University Press, 2001, 413–415.

Saad, Ramadan, "Les travaux d'Aménophis au IIIe pylône du temple d'Amon-Re à Karnak," *Kêmi* 20 (1970) 187–193.

Saad, Ramadan, and Lise Manniche, "A Unique List of Amenophis IV Recently Found at Karnak," *JEA* 57 (1971) 70–72.

Saleh, Abdel Aziz, *Excavations at Heliopolis: Ancient Egyptian Ounu*, Vol. II, Cairo: Cairo University, 1983.

Samson, Julia, "Nefertiti's Regality," *JEA* 63 (1977) 88–97.

Samson, Julia, "Akhenaten's Successor," *GM* 32 (1979) 53–58.

Samson, Julia, "Akhenaten's Coregent Ankhkheperure-Neferneferuaten," *GM* 53 (1982) 51–54.

Samson, Julia, "Neferneferuaten-Nefertiti 'Beloved of Akhenaten,' Ankhkheperure Neferneferuaten 'Beloved of Akhenateon,' Ankhkheperure Smenkhkare 'Beloved of Aten,'" *GM* 57 (1982) 61–67.

Sandman, Maj, *Texts from the Time of Akhenaten*, Brussels: Queen Elizabeth Foundation of Egyptology, 1938.

Sauneron, Serge, *The Priests of Ancient Egypt*, Ithaca, NY: Cornell University Press, 2000.

Schaden, Otto, "KV 63: An Update," *KMT* 18, no. 1 (2007) 16–25.

Schulman, Alan, "Some Remarks on the Alleged 'Fall' of Senmut," *JARCE* 8 (1970) 29–48.

Seidlmayer, Stephan, "The First Intermediate Period (c. 2160–2055)," *The Oxford History of Ancient Egypt* (ed. Ian Shaw), Oxford: Oxford University Press, 2000, 108–136,

Sethe, Kurt, *Die Altaegyptischen Pyramidentexte* (Spruch 1–468) Leipzig: J. C. Hinrichs, 1908.

Sethe, Kurt, *Aegyptische Lesetücke zum Gebrauch in akademischen Unterricht*, Leipzig: J. C. Hinriches'sche, 1928.

Sethe, Kurt, *Amun und die acht Ürgotten von Hermopolis*, Berlin: Abhandlungen der Preussischen Academie der Wissenschaften, 1929.

Sethe, Kurt, *Urkunden der 18. Dynastie*, 4 vols., Berlin: Akademie-Verlag, 1961.

Shafer, Byron (ed.), *Temples of Ancient Egypt*, Ithaca, NY: Cornell University Press, 1997.

Sharma, Arvind, *To the Things Themselves: Essays on the Discourse and Practice of the Phenomenology of Religion*, Berlin/New York: de Gruyter, 2001.

Shaw, Ian, "The Gurob Harem Palace Project, Spring 2012," *JEA* 98 (2012) 43–54.

Sherwin, Simon, "Did the Israelites Really Learn Their Monotheism in Babylon?" *Israel: Ancient Kingdom or Late Invention* (ed. D. I. Block), Nashville: B & H Academic Group, 2008.

Shupak, Nili, *Where Can Wisdom Be Found? The Sages Language in the Bible and in Ancient Egyptian Literature*, OBO 120, Fribourg: University of Fribourg Press, 1993.

Silverman, David, "The So-called Portal Temple of Ramesses II at Abydos," *Akten des vierten internationalen Ägyptologen-Kongresses, München*, Vol. 2, Hamburg: Helmut Buske Verlag, 1985, 269–277.

Silverman, David, "Divinity and Deities in Ancient Egypt", *Religion in Ancient Egypt* (ed. B. E. Shafer), Ithaca, NY: Cornell University Press, 1991, 4–75.

Silverman, David, Josef Wegner, and Jenifer Wegner, *Akhenaten and Tutankhamun: Revolution and Restoration*, Philadelphia: University of Pennyslvania Museum of Archaeology and Anthropology, 2006.

Simpson, William Kelley, "The Hymns to Aten," *The Literature of Ancient Egypt: An Anthology of Stories, Instructions, and Poetry* (eds. R. O. Faulkner et al.), New Haven, CT: Yale University Press, 1973, 289–295.

Simpson, William Kelley, *Inscribed Material from the Pennyslvanian-Yale Excavations at Abydos*, New Haven/Philadelphia: Peabody Museum/University of Pennsylvania Museum, 1995.

Simpson, William Kelley, R. O. Faulkner, and E. F. Wente, *The Literature of Ancient Egypt*, New Haven CT: Yale University Press, 1973.

Smith, Ray W., and Donald Redford, *The Akhenaten Temple Project*, Vol. 1, Warminster: Aris and Phillips, 1976.

Smith, W. Steveson, *The Art and Architecture of Ancient Egypt*, Baltimore: Penguin Books, 1965

Smith, W. Steveson, "The Old Kingdom in Egypt," *Cambridge Ancient History*, Vol. 1, part 2 (eds. I. E. S. Edwards, C. J. Gadd, and N. G. L. Hammond), Cambridge: The University Press, 1971, 145–207.

Smith, Mark S., *The Early History of God: Yahweh and the Other Deities in Ancient Israel*, San Francisco: Harper & Row Publishers, 1990.

Smith, Mark S., *The Origins of Biblical Monotheism: Israel's Polytheistic Background and the Ugaritic Texts*, New York: Oxford University Press, 2001.

Smith, Morton, "The Common Theology of the Ancient Near East," *JBL* 71 (1952) 135–147.

Smith, Sutart T., *Wretched Kush*, London/New York: Routledge, 2003.

Snaith, Norman, "The Advent of Monotheism in Israel," *Annual of the Leeds University Oriental Society* 5 (1963–1965) 100–113.

Sourouzian, Hourig, "Investigating the Mortuary Temple of Amenhotep III," *Egyptian Archaeology* 39 (2011) 29–32.

Sowada, Karin, "Evidence for Late Third Millennium Weather Events from a Sixth Dynasty Tomb at Saqqara," *Studia Quaternaria* 30, no. 2 (2013) 69–74.

Spalinger, Anthony, "A Hymn of Praise to Akhenaten," *The Akhenaten Temple Project*, Vol. 2 (ed. D. Redford), Toronto: Akhenaten Temple Project/University of Toronto Press, 1988, 29–30.

Spalinger, Anthony, "Festivals," *The Oxford Encyclopedia of Ancient Egypt*, Vol. 1, Oxford: Oxford University Press, 2001, 521–525.

Speiser, Cathie, *Offrandes et purification à l'époque amarnienne*, Turnhourt, Belgium: Brepols, 2010.

Spence, Kate, and Palema Rose, "New Fieldwork at Sesbi," *EA* 35 (2009) 31–34.

Spence, Kate, and Palema Rose, et al., "Fieldwork at Sesebi, 2009," *Sudan and Nubia* 13 (2009) 38–45.

Spence, Kate, and Palema Rose, et al., "Sesebi 2011," *Sudan and Nubia* 15 (2011) 34–38.

Spencer, Jeffrey, *Early Egypt: The Rise of Civilisation in the Nile Valley*, Norman: University of Oklahoma Press, 1993.

Spencer, Patricia, "Heliopolis (Matariya), *Egyptian Archaeology* 41 (2012) 31.

Stadelmann, Rainer, *Die ägptischen Pyramiden*, Mainz: Harrssowitz, 1991.

Stadelmann, Rainer, "The Development of the Pyramid Temple in the Fourth Dynasty," *The Temple in Ancient Egypt* (ed. S. Quirke), London: British Museum, 1997, 1–16.

Standelmann, Rainer, "Sphinx," *Oxford Encyclopedia of Egyptology*, Vol. 3, Oxford: Oxford University Press, 2001, 307–310.

Stanley, J. -D., et al., "Short Contribution: Nile Flow Failure at the End of the Old Kingdom, Egypt: Strontium Isopotic and Petrologic Evidence," *GeoArchaeology: An International Journal*, 18, no. 3 (2003) 395–402.

Steindorff, George, and Keith Seele, *When Egypt Ruled the East*, Chicago: University of Chicago, 1957.

Stewart, H. M., "Some Pre-'Amārnah Sun-Hymns," *JEA* 46 (1960) 83–90.

Stewart, H. M., "Traditional Egyptian Sun Hymns of the New Kingdom," *Bulletin of the Institute of Archaeology* 6 (1966) 29–74.

Stuart, Douglas, *Hosea-Jonah*, Waco, TX: Word Biblical Commentary, 1987.

Tanner, Henry, "Long-Sought Temple Is Uncovered in Egypt," *New York Times*, February 22, 1976.

Tawfik, Sayed, "Aten and the Names of His Temple(s) at Thebes," *The Akhenaten Temple Project*, Vol. 1, (eds. Ray W. Smith and Donald Redford), Warminster: Aris and Phillips, 1976, 61–63.

Taylor, Glen, *Yahweh and the Sun: Biblical and Archaeological Evidence for Sun Worship in Ancient Israel*, Sheffield: JSOT Press, 1993.

Thausing, Gertrud, "Amarna-Gedanken in Einem Sargtext," *Festschrift für Prof. Dr. Viktor Christian Gewidmet von Kollegen un Schülern zum 70. Geburtstag* (ed. Kurt Sherbert), Vienna: Norting der Wissenschaftlichen Verbände Österreichs, 1956, 108–110.

Tigay, Jeffrey, *You Shall Have No Other Gods: Israelite Religion in the Light of Hebrew Inscriptions*, Atlanta, GA: Scholars Press, 1985.

Tobin, Vincent Arieh, "Amarna and Biblical Religion," *Pharaonic Egypt, the Bible and Christianity* (ed. S. Israelit-Groll), Jerusalem: The Hebrew University, 1985, 231–277.

Tobin, Vincent Arieh, "Amun and Amun-Re," *The Oxford Encyclopedia of Ancient Egypt*, Vol. 1, Oxford: Oxford University Press, 2001, 82–85.

Tolmatcheva, Elena, "A Reconsideration of the Benu-bird in Egyptian Cosmology," *Egyptology at the Dawn of the Twenty-first Century: Proceedings of the Eighth International Congress of Egyptologist, Cairo 2000*, Vol. 2 (ed. Zahi Hawass), Cairo: American University Press, 2003, 522–526.

Traunecker, Claude, "Donnés nouvelle sur le début au regne d'Amenophis IV et son oeuvre à Karnak," *JSSEA* 14, no. 3 (1984) 60–69.

Uphill, Eric, "The Sed-Festivals of Akhenaton," *JNES* 22 (1963) 123–127.

Valbelle, Dominque, "Kerma—les inscriptions," *Kerma Soudan* XLIX (2001) 229–234.

Van Seters, John, "A Date for the 'Admonitions' in the Second Intermediate Period," *JEA* 50 (1964) 13–23.

Van Seters, John, *The Pentateuch: A Social-Science Commentary*, Sheffield: Sheffield Academic Press, 1999.

Vandier, Jacques, *Mo'alla: La tombe d'Ankifi et la tombe de Sebkhotep*, Cairo: Institut français d'archéologie orientale. Bibliothèque d'étude, t. 18.

Velde, Hermann Te, "Seth," *The Oxford Encyclopedia of Ancient Egypt*, Vol. 3, 2001, 269–271.

Vergnieux, Robert, and Michel Gondran, *Aménophis IV et les pierres du soleil: Akhénaten retrouvè*, Paris: Arthasud, 1997.

Verner, Miroslav, "Discovery of an Obelisk at Abusir," *Rd'E* 28 (1976) 111–118.

Verner, Miroslav, "Pyramid," *The Oxford Encyclopedia of Ancient Egypt*, Vol. 3, Oxford: Oxford University Press, 2001, 87–95.

Verner, Miroslav, *Abusir: Realm of Orsiris*, Cairo: American University Press, 2002.

Walle, Baudouin van de, "Survivances mythologiques dans les coiffers royales de l'epoque atonienne," *Cd'É* 55 (1980) 23–36.

Waller, James, and Mary Edwardsen, "Evolutionism," *The Encyclopedia of Religion*, Vol. 5 (ed. M. Eliade), New York: Macmillan, 1987, 214–218.

Wellhausen, Julius, *Prolegomena to the History of Ancient Israel*, Gloucester, MA: Peter Smith, [1883] reprint, 1983.

Wellhausen, Julius, *Israelitische und Jüdische Geschichte* (9th ed.), Berlin: de Gruyter, 1958.

Welsby, Derek, "Kawa," *The Oxford Encyclopedia of Ancient Egypt*, Vol. 2, Oxford: Oxford University Press, 2001, 226.

Wente, Edward, "The Quarrel of Apophis and Seknenre," *The Literature of Ancient Egypt* (eds. W. K. Simpson, et al.), New Haven, CT: Yale University Press, 1973, 77–80.

Werner, Edward K. "Montu," *The Oxford Encyclopedia of Ancient Egypt*, Vol. 2, Oxford: Oxford University Press, 2001, 435–436.

Werner, Edward K., "Armant," *The Oxford Encyclopedia of Ancient Egypt*, Vol. 1, Oxford: Oxford University Press, 2001, 126–127.

Wilkinson, Richard, *Symbol and Magic in Egyptian Art*, London: Thames & Hudson, 1994.

Wilkinson, Richard, *The Complete Temples of Ancient Egypt*, London: Thames & Hudson, 2000.

Wilkinson, Richard, *The Complete Gods and Goddesses of Ancient Egypt*, London: Thames & Hudson, 2005.

Wilkinson, Richard, "Controlled Damage: The Mechanic and Micro-History of the *Damnation Memoriae* Carried Out in KV–23, the Tomb of Ay," *Journal of Egyptian History* 4 (2011) 129–147.

Willems, Harco, "The First Intermediate Period and the Middle Kingdom," *A Companion of Ancient Egypt*, Vol. 1 (ed. A. B. Lloyd), Oxford: Wiley-Blackwell, 2010, 81–100.

Williams, Roland J., "A Hymn to Aten," *Documents from Old Testament Times* (ed. D. W. Thomas), New York: Harper & Row Publishers, 1958, 142–150.

Williams, Ronald J., "Literature as a Medium of Political Propaganda in Ancient Egypt," *Seed of Wisdom: Essays in Honour of T. J. Meek* (ed. S. McCullough), Toronto: University of Toronto Press, 1964.

Williamson, Jacquelyn, "The 'Sunshade' of Nefertiti," *Egyptian Archaeology* 33 (2008) 5–8.

Wilson, John, *The Culture of Ancient Egypt*, Chicago: University of Chicago Press, 1951.

Wilson, John, "The Hymn to Aton," *Ancient Near Eastern Literature Relating to the Old Testament*, 3rd ed. (ed. J. B. Prichard), Princeton, NJ: Princeton University Press, 1969, 369–371.

Wood, Bryant, "The Rise and Fall of the 13th Century Exodus-Conquest Theory," *JETS* 48 (2005) 479–489.

Woschitz, Karl, "Axial Age," *Religion Past and Present*, Vol. 1 (ed. H. D. Betz, et al.), Leiden: Brill, 2007, 531.

Yamauchi, Edwin, "Akhenaten, Moses, and Monotheism," *Near East Archaological Society Bulletin* 55 (2010) 1–15.

Yusa, Michiko, "Henotheism," *The Encyclopedia of Religion*, 2nd ed. (ed. L. Jones), Detroit: Macmillan, 2005, 3913.

Žabkar, Louis, "The Theocracy of Amarna and the Doctrine of the Ba," *JNES* 13 (1954) 87–101.

Žabkar, Louis, "Adaptation of Ancient Egyptian Texts to the Temple Ritual at Philae," *JEA* 66 (1980) 127–136.

Zandee, Jan, *Der Amunhymnus des Papyrus Leiden 344, verso*, 3 Vols., Leiden: Rijksmuseum van Oudhelden, 1992.

Zevit, Ziony, *The Religions of Ancient Israel: A Synthesis of Parallactic Approaches*, London/New York: Continuum, 2001.

Zivie, Alain, "Hataiay, Scribe du temple d'Aton à Memphis," *Egypt, Israel and the Ancient Mediterranean World: Studies in Honor of Donald B. Redford* (eds. G. N. Knoppers and A. Hirsch), Leiden: Brill, 2004, 224–231.

NAME INDEX

Egyptian Terms

ȝbb, 161, 163
ȝby, 154
ȝḫt, 16, 19, 28, 50, 75, 78, 149, 224, 234
ȝḫt n itn, 93, 104, 175, 203
ȝḫt-itn, 93, 149, 176
ꜥnḫ, 22, 23, 218, 220, 222, 229, 235

Bḫdt/y, 71, 99, 206, 215
Biȝ/t, 42, 54, 151
Bin, 36, 162, 168
Bnbn, 10, 12, 14, 15, 17, 18, 27, 31, 51, 73, 101, 102, 117, 214
Bnw, 17

Gm pȝ itn, 96, 98, 99, 101, 107, 110, 122
Gmi, gm, gmt, 98, 142, 146, 155, 156, 157
Gm(t) pȝ itn, 96, 98, 99, 101, 108, 110, 111, 113, 114, 115, 116, 117, 118, 122, 125, 126, 129, 130, 142, 149, 155, 156, 157, 159, 170, 193, 207
Gm itn, 144
Grg, 33

Ḥwt bnbn, 11, 75, 101, 102, 103, 109, 214, 215, 216, 218
ḥb sd, 64, 67, 117, 120, 123, 193
ḥr ȝḫty, 75
ḥḏ, 217, 219, 224, 233, 253
ḫꜥ/ḫꜥi, 10, 14, 16, 217, 220, 224, 225, 226, 233, 253
ḫꜥyw/hꜥw, 218, 232, 234
ḫꜥꜥ, 16, 217, 219, 234, 253
ḫpr(w), 10, 82, 160, 164
ḫpr/r, 10, 82, 206, 215, 230, 231
ḫpr ḏs.f, 10, 230, 231, 232

iȝt, 11
ii, 205, 253
imn, 39, 46, 50, 190
ipt swt, 203
iri, iry, ir, irr/irt, 82, 217, 218, 219, 220, 222, 223, 226, 228, 235
isft, 33, 34
itm, 20
itn, 1, 4, 16, 58, 59, 77, 81, 85, 93, 129, 171, 174, 209, 210, 219, 234, 253
itn ꜥnḫ, 217, 218
iwnw, 5, 16, 65, 176
iwn(w)-mntw, 37

kȝ/kȝ.ti, 218, 226, 228
ḳd, 164, 170, 223

ḳd sw d̲s.f, 217, 222, 230, 231
ḳm3, 220, 222, 223, 226

m3ʿt, 33, 34
mn(w), 46
ms/msi/msw/msy, 8, 218, 219, 230, 231
ms sw (d̲s.f), 8, 223, 231
mt̲r, 154, 155, 161

nb/t pt, 59
nemes (crown), 18, 85, 133
nt̲rw, 161, 193, 202, 203, 233

p3 nt̲r wʿ, 220
psd(w), 78, 219, 220, 226, 232, 233, 253
Pr itn, 98, 101, 108, 116, 120, 126, 135, 175, 190, 203
pt, 16

rʿ, 5, 11, 28, 30
Rwd mnw (n itn r nḥḥ), 105, 117, 122

s3 rʿ, 9
sʿnḫ, 217, 218, 220, 222
sb3yt, 213, 264
sd̲d, 155, 161
sḥwt, 77
Sḫ-n-itn m Gm(t) p3 itn, 105
sḥd̲, 79, 234
sḫpr, 220
snt̲, 148
st n(y)t sp tpy, 147
st d̲srt n(y)t sp tpy, 12
stwt, 78, 79, 80, 81, 217, 218, 219, 224, 225, 228, 253
šnnt itn, 78
šnwt itn, 79
šw, 75, 85, 86, 133, 171, 174, 193

Tni mnw (n itn r nḥḥ), 106, 107, 117, 122
tḥn, 80, 217, 218, 234

w3/w3t/*w3.ti*, 220, 226, 228
wʿ /wʿ.ti/wʿ.ti, 218, 220, 223, 226, 227, 232, 233, 236
wʿ ḥr ḥw.f, 233
wbn, 10, 16, 17, 50, 77, 78, 80, 81, 217, 218, 219, 220, 225, 226, 228, 231, 232, 233, 234, 235, 252
wpwt /wpw-ḥr.f, 227, 243
wd̲, 53, 54, 156

yhw3, 262, 263

Arabic Terms

Mastaba, 25, 26

Serdab, 18
Serekh, 7, 8, 9

GENERAL INDEX

Abu Ghurab, 28, 29, 30, 31
Abusir, 23, 27, 28, 29, 168
Abydos, 36, 92, 170
Admonitions of Ipuwer, 34
Akhenaten Temple Project (ATP), 3–4, 94, 97, 106, 107, 108, 109, 114, 117, 126, 244
Akhet-Aten, 1, 3, 92, 121, 125, 136, 142, 146, 147, 148, 149, 150, 151, 154, 156, 157, 162, 163, 167, 175, 176, 195, 204, 210, 214, 239, 243, 244, 249, 264
Amarna, el-Amarna, 1, 74, 90, 93, 103, 108, 119, 121, 136, 143, 146, 149, 150, 154, 159, 169, 172, 174, 194, 195, 196, 210, 215, 216, 229, 232, 243, 264
Amarna Period, 14, 71, 171, 179, 183, 185, 190, 243
Amarna religion/theology, 142, 209, 210, 216
Amarna style (early), 67, 69, 75, 121, 133
Amenemhet I, 34, 41, 42, 46, 47, 48, 78
Amenhotep II, 19, 20, 59, 64, 83, 89, 190, 192, 199, 201, 230, 262
Amenhotep III, 1, 52, 54, 59, 60, 62, 65, 66, 68, 69, 72, 79, 80, 81, 87, 88, 89, 90, 92, 118, 119, 120, 124, 125, 129, 131, 132, 158, 160, 169, 190, 194, 200, 202, 207, 230, 231, 242
Amenhotep IV, 4, 61, 62, 64, 65, 66, 67, 68, 70, 71, 72, 73, 75, 76, 84, 85, 86, 87, 89, 92, 98, 100, 101, 103, 105, 106, 107, 113, 119, 120, 121, 122, 123, 124, 125, 134, 135, 161, 165, 166, 167, 195, 203, 207, 210
Amun (Amon), 3, 34, 37, 39, 40, 41, 42, 43, 44, 46, 48, 49, 51, 57, 58, 60, 73, 81, 82, 91, 114, 140, 141, 147, 156, 165, 192, 194, 197, 198, 199, 201, 203, 208, 209, 210, 230, 236, 242, 244, 264
Amun Bull of his mother (or Ka-Mutef), 43, 202
Amun-Min, 43
Amun-Re, 39, 42, 43, 45, 48, 49, 50, 51, 53, 55, 56, 57, 58, 61, 72, 73, 91, 102, 115, 116, 123, 134, 161, 192, 198, 199, 200, 202, 227, 231, 233, 235, 241, 264
Ankhesenpaaten / Ankhesenamun, 118, 239, 241, 242
Ankhkheperure, 180, 182, 185, 189, 238, 239
Ankhtifi, 35
Armant (Hermonthis), 65
Aten-disc, 70, 182, 183
Aten hymns, 82, 210, 213, 214, 221, 229, 232, 235, 236, 237, 247, 247, 250, 252, 253, 255
Aten temple(s), 90, 93, 94, 96, 97, 108, 112, 113, 134, 183, 186, 194, 197, 198, 214, 241, 243
Atenism, 76, 85, 90, 137, 161, 193, 194, 198, 204, 206, 207, 210, 213, 221, 235, 236, 237, 238, 244, 245, 251, 257, 265, 266
Atum, 6, 7, 8, 12, 20, 21, 64, 65, 69, 71, 78, 206, 230, 235, 238

Atum/Khopri, 10
Axial Movement/Age, 259, 264
Ay, 92, 190, 212, 213, 214, 218, 227, 241, 242, 264

Benben, 27, 30, 64, 91, 200
Benben, Mansion of, House of, or Temple of, 73, 101, 214, 218
Book of the Dead, 253, 255
Boundary Stela (Amarna), 136, 146, 147, 154, 163, 173, 194

Coffin Texts (CTs), 4, 11, 40, 41, 77, 78, 230, 231, 233, 234, 235, 252, 253
Colossi (colossus) of Amenhotep IV/Akhenaten, 109, 112, 125, 133
Coptos, 35, 42, 151
Co-regency (Amenhotep III & IV), 88, 119, 124, 207

Dazzling Aten, 4, 5, 80, 81, 87, 125, 207
Didactic name (of Aten), 73, 82, 85, 86, 92, 99, 127, 128, 176, 204, 205, 216
Djoser, 13, 15, 18, 23, 26, 31, 107
5th Dynasty, 9, 24, 24, 26, 27, 29, 30, 31, 33, 113

East Karnak, 74, 85, 108, 109, 110, 125, 167
Edfu, 35
Eight Chaos gods, 40
Ennead, 7, 12
Eloquent Peasant, 35

Final didactic name, 204
Fragile X Syndrome, 130

Gebel es-Silsileh, 72, 73, 76, 91, 97, 101, 103, 200
Gem Aten, 145, 146
Giza, 15, 18, 19, 24, 25, 64, 83, 84, 201
Great Hymn (to Aten), 3, 190, 211, 216, 218, 221, 222, 224, 227, 228, 246, 247, 256

Harakhti, Harakhty, Horakhty, 54, 72, 81, 82, 83, 206, 227, 264
Hatshepsut, 15, 16, 17, 48, 54, 55, 56, 58, 71, 72, 124, 199, 200, 202
Heb Sed, 118, 119, 121, 124
Heliopolis, Heliopolitan, 5, 10, 11, 12, 14, 16, 17, 18, 27, 29, 30, 33, 37, 41, 46, 47, 48, 64, 65, 69, 71, 81, 83, 84, 100, 102, 103, 106, 145, 162, 176, 183, 206, 215, 229, 231, 232, 236, 244
Henotheism, 206, 257, 261
Herakleopolis, 35, 36
Horemheb, 74, 91, 92, 169, 179, 184, 188, 189, 195, 197, 198, 210, 241, 243, 264
Horemakhet /Harmachis, 19, 83, 89
Horizon of Aten, 149, 175
Horus, Horus-falcon, 6, 7, 8, 12, 19, 22, 23, 47, 82, 168, 177, 200, 201, 208, 264
Hyksos (period), 48, 49, 242, 243

Iconoclasm/ iconoclast, 191, 194, 196, 202, 203, 209
1st Intermediate Period, 4, 33, 36, 37, 40

Karnak (Temple), 15, 21, 22, 37, 39, 44, 45, 49, 50, 51, 52, 55, 56, 59, 61, 65, 66, 69, 73, 79, 88, 90, 91, 93, 97, 103, 105, 108, 114, 115, 116, 117, 118, 120, 122, 134, 140, 142, 156, 159, 167, 168, 193, 194, 196, 197, 200, 203, 206, 208, 214, 224, 240, 241
Khepri / Kheperer / Khoperer / Khopri, 6, 7, 10, 20, 54, 78, 82, 89, 230, 231, 253
Kheruef, 67, 68, 69, 70, 72, 74, 75, 100
Kiya (queen), 131, 132

Live/Living Re, the Ruler of the Horizon, rejoicing in the Horizon in his aspect of Re the Father who has come (returns or appears) as the sun-god [Aten], 204–205, 213, 237, 264
LORD (God of Israel), 142, 158, 159, 236, 238, 244, 250, 258, 260, 261, 263, 265
Luxor Temple, 60, 61, 91, 97, 126, 200, 203

Ma'at (Maat), 71, 166, 195
Marfan's Syndrome, 130, 131, 132
Medamud, 12, 97
Memphis, 19, 35, 47, 50, 62, 63, 64, 165, 173, 174, 175, 183, 196, 208, 239, 244
Meryibre Khety, 35, 36
Merikare (Instruction of), 35
Meritaten, 104, 131, 174, 239
Min, 42, 151, 168
Monotheism/ monotheist / monotheistic, 137, 193, 203, 206, 207, 210, 227, 232, 236, 244, 245, 246, 257, 261, 264, 265, 266
Montu, 37, 52, 79, 115, 199, 200, 201, 202
Moses, 236, 245, 246, 260, 262, 263, 265, 266
Mut, 201, 203, 208

Nefertiti, 1, 69, 70, 74, 98, 99, 103, 105, 106, 112, 124, 126, 128, 131, 133, 173, 185, 189, 208, 212, 222, 239, 240
Nefer-neferu-aten (Neferneferuaten), 104, 189, 190, 238
Neferkheperrure waen-Re, 62, 71, 74, 107, 123, 132, 166, 212, 218
Nekhbet, 21, 22, 23
Nubia/ Nubian, 58, 87, 144, 157, 169, 196, 199, 262
Numinous, 138, 139, 141

Obelisk, 15, 16, 17, 27, 29, 31, 46, 53, 54, 57, 91, 102, 103, 104, 116, 200, 264
On, 5, 10, 12, 26, 30, 31, 47, 64, 230
Osiris / Osiride, 43, 127, 168, 170, 176, 208, 252

Papyrus Westcar, 25, 26, 27
Phenomenology, phenomenological, phenomenologist, 138, 139, 140
Prophecy of Neferti, 33, 34
Psalm, 104, 246, 247, 249, 250, 255, 256
Ptah, 50, 62, 63, 175, 196, 230, 231, 238, 244, 253
Pyramid/s, 8, 13, 14, 24, 25, 27, 29
Pyramidion, 10, 15, 27, 55
Pyramid Texts (PTs), 7, 8, 9, 10, 11, 12, 13, 16, 18, 40, 41, 82, 224, 231, 232, 233, 235, 254

Ramose (Vizier), 66, 67, 108, 201
Ramesses II, 39, 51, 60, 91, 93, 102, 123, 172, 179, 182, 184, 188, 241, 252, 263
Re or Ra, 5, 7, 8, 9, 11, 13, 21, 26, 28, 30, 31, 33, 47, 48, 49, 50, 51, 77, 82, 83, 140, 174, 193, 198, 200, 206, 231, 233, 234, 238, 244, 252
Re, crown of, 34
Re-Atum, 8, 12, 47, 68, 89, 232, 236
Re-Harakhty, 6, 7, 68, 69, 72, 73, 74, 84, 92, 99, 116, 117, 134, 145, 161, 174, 197, 200, 206, 207, 215
Re-Harakhty who rejoices in his horizon in his name of light which is in the disc (Aten) – 72, 76, 79, 82, 86, 89, 91, 100, 101, 113, 122, 133, 135, 150, 156, 160, 161, 164, 165, 204, 237
Re-Khepri, 79

Sahure, 24, 26, 28
Saqqara, 13, 18, 23, 24, 26, 27, 29, 107, 176
Sed / Sed-festival, 13, 31, 87, 88, 92, 99, 108, 109, 112, 117, 118, 119, 120, 121, 122, 123, 124, 125, 127, 148, 167, 170, 193, 195, 207, 210
Senusert I, 42, 43, 44, 45, 46, 49, 51
Sesebi, 144, 145, 146, 169
Seti I, 21, 22, 92, 144, 158, 200, 242
Short(er) hymn, 211, 213, 214, 215, 222
Shu, 10, 12, 75, 85, 86, 133, 193, 207, 264
Sinai, 177, 196
Sinuhe, 4, 78
Smenekhkare, 131, 185, 238, 242
Solar theology/religion, 18, 23, 64, 106, 134, 254
Son on Re, 9, 37, 49, 122, 193
Southern Heliopolis/On, 54, 65, 92, 93, 104
Sphinx, 18, 19, 20, 21, 31, 89
Sphinx Stela, 38, 79, 83, 84
Sun-god, 5, 6, 47, 48, 162, 232
Sun-disc, 58, 69, 70, 76, 78, 85, 99, 129, 206, 237, 239, 251, 254
Sun temple, 24, 26, 27, 28, 29, 30, 113

Talatat (block), 74, 93, 97, 100, 105, 108, 143, 167, 170, 171, 172, 173, 178, 179, 180, 224, 240
Tefnut, 10, 12, 75, 133, 134
Tell el-Borg, 178, 179, 180, 182, 183, 184, 185, 186, 187, 188, 190, 192, 198, 199
Thebes, Theban, Thebaid, 3, 18, 37, 38, 42, 61, 72, 75, 80, 88, 91, 93, 126, 134, 140, 149, 157, 174, 202, 216, 229, 233, 240, 244
Theophany (divine revelation), 99, 140, 148, 245, 263
Thutmose II, 51, 52, 53, 55, 56
Thutmose III, 53, 57, 58, 72, 102, 103, 162, 199, 200, 233
Thutmose IV, 20, 21, 37, 38, 59, 64, 79, 83, 84, 89, 102, 103
Thutmose (prince), 62, 63
Tutankhamun, 92, 120, 130, 132, 185, 189, 190, 195, 196, 197, 198, 240, 241, 242, 243
Tiye (queen), 64, 131, 170, 185, 190
Tjaru/Sile, 52, 177, 178, 190

Upper Egyptian Heliopolis, 65, 93
Uraeus/Uraei, 13, 19, 31, 99, 129

Waset, 37
White Chapel (of Senusert I), 42, 43, 44, 45, 46, 48, 49

YHWH or Yahweh (God of Israel), Yahwism, 3, 236, 237, 244, 245, 250, 251, 257, 258, 259, 260, 261, 262, 263, 265